QUIET

TIME

D1435379

QUIET TIME

ONE YEAR DAILY DEVOTIONAL WITH COMMENTARY

Word of Life Local Church Ministries

A division of Word of Life Fellowship, Inc.

Joe Jordan – Executive Director
Don Lough – Director
Jack Wyrtzen & Harry Bollback – Founders
Ric Garland – VP of Local Church Ministries

USA
P.O. Box 600
Schroon Lake, NY 12870
talk@wol.org
1-888-932-5827

Canada
RR#8/Owen Sound
ON, Canada N4K 5W4
LCM@wol.ca
1-800-461-3503

Web Address: www.wol.org

Publisher s Acknowledgements

Writers and Contributors:

Bill Boulet	Philippians
Dr. Tom Davis	1 Peter, Ezekiel, Isaiah, James, Romans
Don Kelso	1 Samuel, 2 Samuel, Hosea, Psalms
Todd Kinzer	Proverbs
Dr. Chuck Scheide	2 Corinthians
Dr. Marshall Wicks	Luke

Editor: Dr. Tom Davis
Associate Editor: Gary Ingersoll
Curriculum Manager: Don Reichard
Cover and page design: Boire Design

ISBN - 978-1-935475-15-6
Printed in the United States of America

helpful hints for a daily QUIET TIME

The purpose of this Quiet Time is to meet the needs of spiritual growth in the life of the Christian in such a way that they learn the art of conducting their own personal investigation into the Bible.
Consider the following helpful hints:

1 Give priority in choosing your quiet time. This will vary with each individual in accordance with his own circumstances.
The time you choose must:
- have top priority over everything else
- be the quietest time possible.
- be a convenient time of the day or night.
- be consistently observed each day.

2 Give attention to the procedure suggested for you to follow.
Include the following items.
- Read God's Word.
- Mark your Bible as you read. Here are some suggestions that might be helpful:
    a. After you read the passage put an exclamation mark next to the verses you completely understand.
    b. Put a question mark next to verses you do not understand.
    c. Put an arrow pointing upward next to encouraging verses.
    d. Put an arrow pointing downward next to verses which weigh us down in our spiritual race.
    e. Put a star next to verses containing important truths or major points.
- Meditate on what you have read (In one sentence, write the main thought). Here are some suggestions as guidelines for meditating on God's Word:

a. Look at the selected passage from God's point of view.

b. Though we encourage quiet time in the morning, some people arrange to have their quiet time at the end of their day. God emphasizes that we need to go to sleep meditating on His Word. "My soul shall be satisfied and my mouth shall praise thee with joyful lips: when I remember thee upon my bed, and meditating on thee in the night watches" (Psalm 63:5,6).

c. Deuteronomy 6:7 lists routine things you do each day during which you should concentrate on the portion of Scripture for that day:

— when you sit in your house (meals and relaxation)
— when you walk in the way (to and from school or work)
— when you lie down (before going to sleep at night)
— when you rise up (getting ready for the day)

■ Apply some truth to your life. (Use first person pronouns I, me, my, mine). If you have difficulty in finding an application for your life, think of yourself as a Bible SPECTATOR and ask yourself the following questions:

S – Is there any SIN for me to forsake?
P – Is there any PROMISE for me to claim?
E – Is there any EXAMPLE for me to follow?
C – Is there any COMMAND for me to obey?
T – Is there a TRUTH for me to embrace?
A – Is there an ATTITUDE for me to adjust?
T – Can I give THANKS for something?
O – Is there an OUTLOOK for me to change?
R – Is there a RELATIONSHIP for me to develop?

■ Pray for specific things (Use the prayer sheets found in the My Prayer Journal section).

3 Be sure to fill out your quiet time sheets. This will really help you remember the things the Lord brings to your mind.

4 Purpose to share with someone else each day something you gained from your quiet time. This can be a real blessing for them as well as for you.

my personal
prayer journal

daily prayer list

date | request   **date | answer**

2/22/11 - Spencer + writing test
       Mission trip + finances

daily prayer list

date | request   **date | answer**

daily prayer list

date | request   **date | answer**

daily prayer list

date | request   **date | answer**

sunday

Family

date	request	date	answer

Christian Friends

date	request	date	answer

Unsaved Friends

date	request	date	answer

missionaries

date	request	date	answer

monday

Family

date	request	date	answer

Christian Friends

date	request	date	answer

monday

Unsaved Friends

date | request   date | answer

missionaries

date | request   date | answer

tuesday

date	request	date	answer

Christian Friends

date	request	date	answer

Unsaved Friends

date	request	date	answer

missionaries

date	request	date	answer

Wednesday

date	request	date	answer

date	request	date	answer

Unsaved Friends

date	request	date	answer

missionaries

date	request	date	answer

thursday

date	request	date	answer

date	request	date	answer

Unsaved Friends

date	request	date	answer

missionaries

date	request	date	answer

friday

Family

date	request	date	answer

Christian Friends

date	request	date	answer

Unsaved Friends

date	request	date	answer

missionaries

date	request	date	answer

saturday

date	request	date	answer

Christian Friends

date	request	date	answer

Unsaved Friends

date	request	date	answer

missionaries

date	request	date	answer

daily praise list

date | I'm praising God for...

daily praise list

date | I'm praising God for...

daily praise list

date | I'm praising God for...

something for everyone

Some people just can't get enough! That is why we have several dimensions in the Word of Life Quiet Time. Along with the daily reading, content and application questions for each day, two reading programs are given to help you understand the Bible better. Choose one or both.

Reading Through the New Testament Four Times In One Year

Turn the page and discover a schedule that takes you through the New Testament four times in one year. This is a great method to help you see the correlation of the Gospels and other New Testament books.

Reading Through the Whole Bible In One Year

Turn another page and find a program of several pages that will guide you through a chronological reading of the entire Bible. Follow this schedule and you will move from Genesis through Revelation in one year.

The Choice is Up to You

Whether you have a short quiet time, a quiet time with more scripture reading or one with a mini-Bible study each day, we trust your time with God will draw you closer to Him in every area of your life.

Read through the new testament four times in one year

Weeks 1-13

- ☐ Matthew 1-3
- ☐ Matthew 4-6
- ☐ Matthew 7-9
- ☐ Matt. 10-12
- ☐ Matt. 13-15
- ☐ Matt. 16-18
- ☐ Matt. 19-21
- ☐ Matt. 22-24
- ☐ Matt. 25-26
- ☐ Matt. 27-28
- ☐ Mark 1-3
- ☐ Mark 4-5
- ☐ Mark 6-8
- ☐ Mark 9-11
- ☐ Mark 12-14
- ☐ Mark 15-16
- ☐ Luke 1-2
- ☐ Luke 3-5
- ☐ Luke 6-7
- ☐ Luke 8-9
- ☐ Luke 10-11
- ☐ Luke 12-14
- ☐ Luke 15-17
- ☐ Luke 18-20
- ☐ Luke 21-22
- ☐ Luke 23-24
- ☐ John 1-3
- ☐ John 4-5
- ☐ John 6-7
- ☐ John 8-10
- ☐ John 11-12
- ☐ John 13-15
- ☐ John 16-18
- ☐ John 19-21
- ☐ Acts 1-3
- ☐ Acts 4-6
- ☐ Acts 7-8
- ☐ Acts 9-11
- ☐ Acts 12-15
- ☐ Acts 16-18
- ☐ Acts 19-21
- ☐ Acts 22-24
- ☐ Acts 25-26
- ☐ Acts 27-28
- ☐ Romans 1-3

- ☐ Romans 4-6
- ☐ Romans 7-9
- ☐ Romans 10-12
- ☐ Romans 13-16
- ☐ 1 Cor. 1-4
- ☐ 1 Cor. 5-9
- ☐ 1 Cor. 10-12
- ☐ 1 Cor. 13-16
- ☐ 2 Cor. 1-4
- ☐ 2 Cor. 5-8
- ☐ 2 Cor. 9-13
- ☐ Galatians 1-3
- ☐ Galatians 4-6
- ☐ Ephesians 1-3
- ☐ Ephesians 4-6
- ☐ Philippians 1-4
- ☐ Colossians 1-4
- ☐ 1 Thes. 1-3
- ☐ 1 Thes. 4-5
- ☐ 2 Thes. 1-3
- ☐ 1 Timothy 1-3
- ☐ 1 Timothy 4-6
- ☐ 2 Timothy 1-4
- ☐ Titus 1-3
- ☐ Philemon
- ☐ Hebrews 1
- ☐ Hebrews 2-4
- ☐ Hebrews 5-7
- ☐ Hebrews 8-10
- ☐ Hebrews 11-13
- ☐ James 1-3
- ☐ James 4-5
- ☐ 1 Peter 1-3
- ☐ 1 Peter 4-5
- ☐ 2 Peter 1-3
- ☐ 1 John 1-3
- ☐ 1 John 4-5
- ☐ 2 Jn, 3 Jn, Jude
- ☐ Revelation 1-3
- ☐ Revelation 4-6
- ☐ Revelation 7-9
- ☐ Rev. 10-12
- ☐ Rev. 13-15
- ☐ Rev. 16-18
- ☐ Rev. 19-22

Weeks 14-26

- ☐ Matthew 1-3
- ☐ Matthew 4-6
- ☐ Matthew 7-9
- ☐ Matt. 10-12
- ☐ Matt. 13-15
- ☐ Matt. 16-18
- ☐ Matt. 19-21
- ☐ Matt. 22-24
- ☐ Matt. 25-26
- ☐ Matt. 27-28
- ☐ Mark 1-3
- ☐ Mark 4-5
- ☐ Mark 6-8
- ☐ Mark 9-11
- ☐ Mark 12-14
- ☐ Mark 15-16
- ☐ Luke 1-2
- ☐ Luke 3-5
- ☐ Luke 6-7
- ☐ Luke 8-9
- ☐ Luke 10-11
- ☐ Luke 12-14
- ☐ Luke 15-17
- ☐ Luke 18-20
- ☐ Luke 21-22
- ☐ Luke 23-24
- ☐ John 1-3
- ☐ John 4-5
- ☐ John 6-7
- ☐ John 8-10
- ☐ John 11-12
- ☐ John 13-15
- ☐ John 16-18
- ☐ John 19-21
- ☐ Acts 1-3
- ☐ Acts 4-6
- ☐ Acts 7-8
- ☐ Acts 9-11
- ☐ Acts 12-15
- ☐ Acts 16-18
- ☐ Acts 19-21
- ☐ Acts 22-24
- ☐ Acts 25-26
- ☐ Acts 27-28
- ☐ Romans 1-3

- ☐ Romans 4-6
- ☐ Romans 7-9
- ☐ Romans 10-12
- ☐ Romans 13-16
- ☐ 1 Cor. 1-4
- ☐ 1 Cor. 5-9
- ☐ 1 Cor. 10-12
- ☐ 1 Cor. 13-16
- ☐ 2 Cor. 1-4
- ☐ 2 Cor. 5-8
- ☐ 2 Cor. 9-13
- ☐ Galatians 1-3
- ☐ Galatians 4-6
- ☐ Ephesians 1-3
- ☐ Ephesians 4-6
- ☐ Philippians 1-4
- ☐ Colossians 1-4
- ☐ 1 Thes. 1-3
- ☐ 1 Thes. 4-5
- ☐ 2 Thes. 1-3
- ☐ 1 Timothy 1-3
- ☐ 1 Timothy 4-6
- ☐ 2 Timothy 1-4
- ☐ Titus 1-3
- ☐ Philemon
- ☐ Hebrews 1
- ☐ Hebrews 2-4
- ☐ Hebrews 5-7
- ☐ Hebrews 8-10
- ☐ Hebrews 11-13
- ☐ James 1-3
- ☐ James 4-5
- ☐ 1 Peter 1-3
- ☐ 1 Peter 4-5
- ☐ 2 Peter 1-3
- ☐ 1 John 1-3
- ☐ 1 John 4-5
- ☐ 2 Jn, 3 Jn, Jude
- ☐ Revelation 1-3
- ☐ Revelation 4-6
- ☐ Revelation 7-9
- ☐ Rev. 10-12
- ☐ Rev. 13-15
- ☐ Rev. 16-18
- ☐ Rev. 19-22

Read through the new testament four times in one year

Weeks 27-39

- [ ] Matthew 1-3
- [ ] Matthew 4-6
- [ ] Matthew 7-9
- [ ] Matt. 10-12
- [ ] Matt. 13-15
- [ ] Matt. 16-18
- [ ] Matt. 19-21
- [ ] Matt. 22-24
- [ ] Matt. 25-26
- [ ] Matt. 27-28
- [ ] Mark 1-3
- [ ] Mark 4-5
- [ ] Mark 6-8
- [ ] Mark 9-11
- [ ] Mark 12-14
- [ ] Mark 15-16
- [ ] Luke 1-2
- [ ] Luke 3-5
- [ ] Luke 6-7
- [ ] Luke 8-9
- [ ] Luke 10-11
- [ ] Luke 12-14
- [ ] Luke 15-17
- [ ] Luke 18-20
- [ ] Luke 21-22
- [ ] Luke 23-24
- [ ] John 1-3
- [ ] John 4-5
- [ ] John 6-7
- [ ] John 8-10
- [ ] John 11-12
- [ ] John 13-15
- [ ] John 16-18
- [ ] John 19-21
- [ ] Acts 1-3
- [ ] Acts 4-6
- [ ] Acts 7-8
- [ ] Acts 9-11
- [ ] Acts 12-15
- [ ] Acts 16-18
- [ ] Acts 19-21
- [ ] Acts 22-24
- [ ] Acts 25-26
- [ ] Acts 27-28
- [ ] Romans 1-3

- [ ] Romans 4-6
- [ ] Romans 7-9
- [ ] Romans 10-12
- [ ] Romans 13-16
- [ ] 1 Cor. 1-4
- [ ] 1 Cor. 5-9
- [ ] 1 Cor. 10-12
- [ ] 1 Cor. 13-16
- [ ] 2 Cor. 1-4
- [ ] 2 Cor. 5-8
- [ ] 2 Cor. 9-13
- [ ] Galatians 1-3
- [ ] Galatians 4-6
- [ ] Ephesians 1-3
- [ ] Ephesians 4-6
- [ ] Phil. 1-4
- [ ] Colossians 1-4
- [ ] 1 Thes. 1-3
- [ ] 1 Thes. 4-5
- [ ] 2 Thes. 1-3
- [ ] 1 Timothy 1-3
- [ ] 1 Timothy 4-6
- [ ] 2 Timothy 1-4
- [ ] Titus 1-3
- [ ] Philemon
- [ ] Hebrews 1
- [ ] Hebrews 2-4
- [ ] Hebrews 5-7
- [ ] Hebrews 8-10
- [ ] Hebrews 11-13
- [ ] James 1-3
- [ ] James 4-5
- [ ] 1 Peter 1-3
- [ ] 1 Peter 4-5
- [ ] 2 Peter 1-3
- [ ] 1 John 1-3
- [ ] 1 John 4-5
- [ ] 2 Jn, 3 Jn, Jude
- [ ] Revelation 1-3
- [ ] Revelation 4-6
- [ ] Revelation 7-9
- [ ] Rev. 10-12
- [ ] Rev. 13-15
- [ ] Rev. 16-18
- [ ] Rev. 19-22

Weeks 40-52

- [ ] Matthew 1-3
- [ ] Matthew 4-6
- [ ] Matthew 7-9
- [ ] Matt. 10-12
- [ ] Matt. 13-15
- [ ] Matt. 16-18
- [ ] Matt. 19-21
- [ ] Matt. 22-24
- [ ] Matt. 25-26
- [ ] Matt. 27-28
- [ ] Mark 1-3
- [ ] Mark 4-5
- [ ] Mark 6-8
- [ ] Mark 9-11
- [ ] Mark 12-14
- [ ] Mark 15-16
- [ ] Luke 1-2
- [ ] Luke 3-5
- [ ] Luke 6-7
- [ ] Luke 8-9
- [ ] Luke 10-11
- [ ] Luke 12-14
- [ ] Luke 15-17
- [ ] Luke 18-20
- [ ] Luke 21-22
- [ ] Luke 23-24
- [ ] John 1-3
- [ ] John 4-5
- [ ] John 6-7
- [ ] John 8-10
- [ ] John 11-12
- [ ] John 13-15
- [ ] John 16-18
- [ ] John 19-21
- [ ] Acts 1-3
- [ ] Acts 4-6
- [ ] Acts 7-8
- [ ] Acts 9-11
- [ ] Acts 12-15
- [ ] Acts 16-18
- [ ] Acts 19-21
- [ ] Acts 22-24
- [ ] Acts 25-26
- [ ] Acts 27-28
- [ ] Romans 1-3

- [ ] Romans 4-6
- [ ] Romans 7-9
- [ ] Romans 10-12
- [ ] Romans 13-16
- [ ] 1 Cor. 1-4
- [ ] 1 Cor. 5-9
- [ ] 1 Cor. 10-12
- [ ] 1 Cor. 13-16
- [ ] 2 Cor. 1-4
- [ ] 2 Cor. 5-8
- [ ] 2 Cor. 9-13
- [ ] Galatians 1-3
- [ ] Galatians 4-6
- [ ] Ephesians 1-3
- [ ] Ephesians 4-6
- [ ] Phil. 1-4
- [ ] Colossians 1-4
- [ ] 1 Thes. 1-3
- [ ] 1 Thes. 4-5
- [ ] 2 Thes. 1-3
- [ ] 1 Timothy 1-3
- [ ] 1 Timothy 4-6
- [ ] 2 Timothy 1-4
- [ ] Titus 1-3
- [ ] Philemon
- [ ] Hebrews 1
- [ ] Hebrews 2-4
- [ ] Hebrews 5-7
- [ ] Hebrews 8-10
- [ ] Hebrews 11-13
- [ ] James 1-3
- [ ] James 4-5
- [ ] 1 Peter 1-3
- [ ] 1 Peter 4-5
- [ ] 2 Peter 1-3
- [ ] 1 John 1-3
- [ ] 1 John 4-5
- [ ] 2 Jn, 3 Jn, Jude
- [ ] Revelation 1-3
- [ ] Revelation 4-6
- [ ] Revelation 7-9
- [ ] Rev. 10-12
- [ ] Rev. 13-15
- [ ] Rev. 16-18
- [ ] Rev. 19-22

Bible reading schedule

Read through the Bible in one year! As you complete each daily reading, simply place a check in the appropriate box.

- ☐ 1 Genesis 1-3
- ☐ 2 Genesis 4:1-6:8
- ☐ 3 Genesis 6:9-9:29
- ☐ 4 Genesis 10-11
- ☐ 5 Genesis 12-14
- ☐ 6 Genesis 15-17
- ☐ 7 Genesis 18-19
- ☐ 8 Genesis 20-22
- ☐ 9 Genesis 23-24
- ☐ 10 Genesis 25-26
- ☐ 11 Genesis 27-28
- ☐ 12 Genesis 29-30
- ☐ 13 Genesis 31-32
- ☐ 14 Genesis 33-35
- ☐ 15 Genesis 36-37
- ☐ 16 Genesis 38-40
- ☐ 17 Genesis 41-42
- ☐ 18 Genesis 43-45
- ☐ 19 Genesis 46-47
- ☐ 20 Genesis 48-50
- ☐ 21 Job 1-3
- ☐ 22 Job 4-7
- ☐ 23 Job 8-11
- ☐ 24 Job 12-15
- ☐ 25 Job 16-19
- ☐ 26 Job 20-22
- ☐ 27 Job 23-28
- ☐ 28 Job 29-31
- ☐ 29 Job 32-34
- ☐ 30 Job 35-37
- ☐ 31 Job 38-42
- ☐ 32 Exodus 1-4
- ☐ 33 Exodus 5-8
- ☐ 34 Exodus 9-11
- ☐ 35 Exodus 12-13
- ☐ 36 Exodus 14-15
- ☐ 37 Exodus 16-18
- ☐ 38 Exodus 19-21
- ☐ 39 Exodus 22-24
- ☐ 40 Exodus 25-27
- ☐ 41 Exodus 28-29
- ☐ 42 Exodus 30-31
- ☐ 43 Exodus 32-34
- ☐ 44 Exodus 35-36
- ☐ 45 Exodus 37-38
- ☐ 46 Exodus 39-40
- ☐ 47 Leviticus 1:1-5:13
- ☐ 48 Leviticus 5:14-7:38
- ☐ 49 Leviticus 8-10
- ☐ 50 Leviticus 11-12
- ☐ 51 Leviticus 13-14
- ☐ 52 Leviticus 15-17
- ☐ 53 Leviticus 18-20
- ☐ 54 Leviticus 21-23
- ☐ 55 Leviticus 24-25
- ☐ 56 Leviticus 26-27
- ☐ 57 Numbers 1-2
- ☐ 58 Numbers 3-4
- ☐ 59 Numbers 5-6
- ☐ 60 Numbers 7
- ☐ 61 Numbers 8-10
- ☐ 62 Numbers 11-13
- ☐ 63 Numbers 14-15
- ☐ 64 Numbers 16-18
- ☐ 65 Numbers 19-21
- ☐ 66 Numbers 22-24
- ☐ 67 Numbers 25-26
- ☐ 68 Numbers 27-29
- ☐ 69 Numbers 30-31
- ☐ 70 Numbers 32-33
- ☐ 71 Numbers 34-36
- ☐ 72 Deuteronomy 1-2
- ☐ 73 Deuteronomy 3-4
- ☐ 74 Deuteronomy 5-7
- ☐ 75 Deuteronomy 8-10
- ☐ 76 Deuteronomy 11-13
- ☐ 77 Deuteronomy 14-17
- ☐ 78 Deuteronomy 18-21
- ☐ 79 Deuteronomy 22-25
- ☐ 80 Deuteronomy 26-28
- ☐ 81 Deuteronomy 29:1-31:29
- ☐ 82 Deuteronomy 31:30-34:12
- ☐ 83 Joshua 1-4
- ☐ 84 Joshua 5-8
- ☐ 85 Joshua 9-11
- ☐ 86 Joshua 12-14
- ☐ 87 Joshua 15-17
- ☐ 88 Joshua 18-19
- ☐ 89 Joshua 20-22
- ☐ 90 Joshua 23 - Judges 1
- ☐ 91 Judges 2-5
- ☐ 92 Judges 6-8
- ☐ 93 Judges 9
- ☐ 94 Judges 10-12
- ☐ 95 Judges 13-16
- ☐ 96 Judges 17-19
- ☐ 97 Judges 20-21
- ☐ 98 Ruth
- ☐ 99 1 Samuel 1-3
- ☐ 100 1 Samuel 4-7
- ☐ 101 1 Samuel 8-10
- ☐ 102 1 Samuel 11-13
- ☐ 103 1 Samuel 14-15
- ☐ 104 1 Samuel 16-17

Bible reading schedule

- ☐ 105 1 Samuel 18-19; Psalm 59
- ☐ 106 1 Samuel 20-21; Psalm 56; 34
- ☐ 107 1 Samuel 22-23; 1 Chronicles 12:8-18; Psalm 52; 54; 63; 142
- ☐ 108 1 Samuel 24; Psalm 57; 1 Samuel 25
- ☐ 109 1 Samuel 26-29; 1 Chronicles 12:1-7, 19-22
- ☐ 110 1 Samuel 30-31; 1 Chronicles 10; 2 Samuel 1
- ☐ 111 2 Samuel 2-4
- ☐ 112 2 Samuel 5:1-6:11; 1 Chronicles 11:1-9; 2:23-40; 13:1-14:17
- ☐ 113 2 Samuel 22; Psalm 18
- ☐ 114 1 Chronicles 15-16; 2 Samuel 6:12-23; Psalm 96
- ☐ 115 Psalm 105; 2 Samuel 7; 1 Chronicles 17
- ☐ 116 2 Samuel 8-10; 1 Chronicles 18-19; Psalm 60
- ☐ 117 2 Samuel 11-12; 1 Chronicles 20:1-3; Psalm 51
- ☐ 118 2 Samuel 13-14
- ☐ 119 2 Samuel 15-17
- ☐ 120 Psalm 3; 2 Samuel 18-19
- ☐ 121 2 Samuel 20-21; 23:8-23; 1 Chronicles 20:4-8; 11:10-25
- ☐ 122 2 Samuel 23:24-24:25;
- ☐ 123 1 Chronicles 11:26-47; 21:1-30, 1 Chronicles 22-24
- ☐ 124 Psalm 30; 1 Chronicles 25-26
- ☐ 125 1 Chronicles 27-29
- ☐ 126 Psalms 5-7; 10; 11; 13; 17
- ☐ 127 Psalms 23; 26; 28; 31; 35
- ☐ 128 Psalms 41; 43; 46; 55; 61; 62; 64
- ☐ 129 Psalms 69-71; 77
- ☐ 130 Psalms 83; 86; 88; 91; 95
- ☐ 131 Psalms 108-9; 120-21; 140; 143-44
- ☐ 132 Psalms 1; 14-15; 36-37; 39
- ☐ 133 Psalms 40; 49-50; 73
- ☐ 134 Psalms 76; 82; 84; 90; 92; 112; 115
- ☐ 135 Psalms 8-9; 16; 19; 21; 24; 29
- ☐ 136 Psalms 33; 65-68
- ☐ 137 Psalms 75; 93-94; 97-100
- ☐ 138 Psalms 103-4; 113-14; 117
- ☐ 139 Psalm 119:1-88
- ☐ 140 Psalm 119:89-176
- ☐ 141 Psalms 122; 124; 133-36
- ☐ 142 Psalms 138-39; 145; 148; 150
- ☐ 143 Psalms 4; 12; 20; 25; 32; 38
- ☐ 144 Psalms 42; 53; 58; 81; 101; 111; 130-31;141;146
- ☐ 145 Psalms 2; 22; 27
- ☐ 146 Psalms 45; 47-48; 87; 110
- ☐ 147 1 Kings 1:1-2:12; 2 Samuel 23:1-7
- ☐ 148 1 Kings 2:13-3:28; 2 Chronicles 1:1-13
- ☐ 149 1 Kings 5-6; 2 Chronicles 2-3
- ☐ 150 1 Kings 7; 2 Chronicles 4
- ☐ 151 1 Kings 8; 2 Chronicles 5:1-7:10
- ☐ 152 1 Kings 9:1-10:13; 2 Chronicles 7:11-9:12
- ☐ 153 1 Kings 4; 10:14-29; 2 Chronicles 1:14-17; 9:13-28; Psalm 72
- ☐ 154 Proverbs 1-3
- ☐ 155 Proverbs 4-6
- ☐ 156 Proverbs 7-9
- ☐ 157 Proverbs 10-12
- ☐ 158 Proverbs 13-15
- ☐ 159 Proverbs 16-18
- ☐ 160 Proverbs 19-21
- ☐ 161 Proverbs 22-24
- ☐ 162 Proverbs 25-27
- ☐ 163 Proverbs 28-29
- ☐ 164 Proverbs 30-31; Psalm 127
- ☐ 165 Song of Solomon
- ☐ 166 1 Kings 11:1-40; Ecclesiastes 1-2
- ☐ 167 Ecclesiastes 3-7
- ☐ 168 Ecclesiastes 8-12; 1 Kings 11:41-43; 2 Chronicles 9:29-31
- ☐ 169 1 Kings 12; 2 Chronicles 10:1-11:17
- ☐ 170 1 Kings 13-14; 2 Chronicles 11:18-12:16
- ☐ 171 1 Kings 15:1-24; 2 Chronicles 13-16
- ☐ 172 1 Kings 15:25-16:34; 2 Chronicles 17; 1 Kings 17
- ☐ 173 1 Kings 18-19
- ☐ 174 1 Kings 20-21
- ☐ 175 1 Kings 22:1-40; 2 Chronicles 18
- ☐ 176 1 Kings 22:41-53; 2 Kings 1; 2 Chronicles 19:1-21:3
- ☐ 177 2 Kings 2-4
- ☐ 178 2 Kings 5-7
- ☐ 179 2 Kings 8-9; 2 Chronicles 21:4-22:9
- ☐ 180 2 Kings 10-11; 2 Chronicles 22:10-23:21
- ☐ 181 Joel
- ☐ 182 2 Kings 12-13; 2 Chronicles 24
- ☐ 183 2 Kings 14; 2 Chronicles 25; Jonah
- ☐ 184 Hosea 1-7
- ☐ 185 Hosea 8-14
- ☐ 186 2 Kings 15:1-7; 2 Chronicles 26; Amos 1-4
- ☐ 187 Amos 5-9; 2 Kings 15:8-18
- ☐ 188 Isaiah 1-4
- ☐ 189 2 Kings 15:19-38; 2 Chronicles 27; Isaiah 5-6
- ☐ 190 Micah
- ☐ 191 2 Kings 16; 2 Chronicles 28; Isaiah 7-8
- ☐ 192 Isaiah 9-12
- ☐ 193 Isaiah 13-16
- ☐ 194 Isaiah 17-22
- ☐ 195 Isaiah 23-27
- ☐ 196 Isaiah 28-30
- ☐ 197 Isaiah 31-35
- ☐ 198 2 Kings 18:1-8; 2 Chronicles 29-31
- ☐ 199 2 Kings 17; 18:9-37; 2 Chronicles 32:1-19; Isaiah 36

Bible reading schedule

- [ ] 200 2 Kings 19; 2 Chronicles 32:20-23; Isaiah 37
- [ ] 201 2 Kings 20; 2 Chronicles 32:24-33; Isaiah 38-39
- [ ] 202 2 Kings 21:1-18; 2 Chronicles 33:1-20; Isaiah 40
- [ ] 203 Isaiah 41-43
- [ ] 204 Isaiah 44-47
- [ ] 205 Isaiah 48-51
- [ ] 206 Isaiah 52-57
- [ ] 207 Isaiah 58-62
- [ ] 208 Isaiah 63-66
- [ ] 209 2 Kings 21:19-26; 2 Chronicles 33:21-34:7; Zephaniah
- [ ] 210 Jeremiah 1-3
- [ ] 211 Jeremiah 4-6
- [ ] 212 Jeremiah 7-9
- [ ] 213 Jeremiah 10-13
- [ ] 214 Jeremiah 14-16
- [ ] 215 Jeremiah 17-20
- [ ] 216 2 Kings 22:1-23:28; 2 Chronicles 34:8-35:19
- [ ] 217 Nahum; 2 Kings 23:29-37;
- [ ] 2 Chronicles 35:20-36:5; Jeremiah 22:10-17
- [ ] 218 Jeremiah 26; Habakkuk
- [ ] 219 Jeremiah 46-47; 2 Kings 24:1-4, 7; 2 Chronicles 36:6-7; Jeremiah 25, 35
- [ ] 220 Jeremiah 36, 45, 48
- [ ] 221 Jeremiah 49:1-33; Daniel 1-2
- [ ] 222 Jeremiah 22:18-30; 2 Kings 24:5-20; 2 Chronicles 36:8-12; Jeremiah 37:1-2; 52:1-3; 24; 29
- [ ] 223 Jeremiah 27-28, 23
- [ ] 224 Jeremiah 50-51
- [ ] 225 Jeremiah 49:34-39; 34:1-22; Ezekiel 1-3
- [ ] 226 Ezekiel 4-7
- [ ] 227 Ezekiel 8-11
- [ ] 228 Ezekiel 12-14
- [ ] 229 Ezekiel 15-17
- [ ] 230 Ezekiel 18-20
- [ ] 231 Ezekiel 21-23
- [ ] 232 2 Kings 25:1; 2 Chronicles 36:13-16; Jeremiah 39:1; 52:4; Ezekiel 24; Jeremiah 21:1-22:9; 32:1-44
- [ ] 233 Jeremiah 30-31, 33
- [ ] 234 Ezekiel 25; 29:1-16; 30; 31
- [ ] 235 Ezekiel 26-28
- [ ] 236 Jeremiah 37:3-39:10; 52:5-30; 2 Kings 25:2-21; 2 Chronicles 36:17-21
- [ ] 237 2 Kings 25:22; Jeremiah 39:11-40:6; Lamentations 1-3
- [ ] 238 Lamentations 4-5; Obadiah
- [ ] 239 Jeremiah 40:7-44:30; 2 Kings 25:23-26
- [ ] 240 Ezekiel 33:21-36:38
- [ ] 241 Ezekiel 37-39
- [ ] 242 Ezekiel 32:1-33:20; Daniel 3
- [ ] 243 Ezekiel 40-42
- [ ] 244 Ezekiel 43-45
- [ ] 245 Ezekiel 46-48
- [ ] 246 Ezekiel 29:17-21; Daniel 4; Jeremiah 52:31-34; 2 Kings 25:27-30; Psalm 44
- [ ] 247 Psalms 74; 79-80; 89
- [ ] 248 Psalms 85; 102; 106; 123; 137
- [ ] 249 Daniel 7-8; 5
- [ ] 250 Daniel 9; 6
- [ ] 251 2 Chronicles 36:22-23; Ezra 1:1-4:5
- [ ] 252 Daniel 10-12
- [ ] 253 Ezra 4:6-6:13; Haggai
- [ ] 254 Zechariah 1-6
- [ ] 255 Zechariah 7-8; Ezra 6:14-22; Psalm 78
- [ ] 256 Psalms 107; 116; 118
- [ ] 257 Psalms 125-26; 128-29; 132; 147; 149
- [ ] 258 Zechariah 9-14
- [ ] 259 Esther 1-4
- [ ] 260 Esther 5-10
- [ ] 261 Ezra 7-8
- [ ] 262 Ezra 9-10
- [ ] 263 Nehemiah 1-5
- [ ] 264 Nehemiah 6-7
- [ ] 265 Nehemiah 8-10
- [ ] 266 Nehemiah 11-13
- [ ] 267 Malachi
- [ ] 268 1 Chronicles 1-2
- [ ] 269 1 Chronicles 3-5
- [ ] 270 1 Chronicles 6
- [ ] 271 1 Chronicles 7:1-8:27
- [ ] 272 1 Chronicles 8:28-9:44
- [ ] 273 John 1:1-18; Mark 1:1; Luke 1:1-4; 3:23-38; Matthew 1:1-17
- [ ] 274 Luke 1:5-80
- [ ] 275 Matthew 1:18-2:23; Luke 2
- [ ] 276 Matthew 3:1-4:11; Mark 1:2-13; Luke 3:1-23; 4:1-13; John 1:19-34
- [ ] 277 John 1:35-3:36
- [ ] 278 John 4; Matthew 4:12-17; Mark 1:14-15; Luke 4:14-30
- [ ] 279 Mark 1:16-45; Matthew 4:18-25; 8:2-4, 14-17; Luke 4:31-5:16
- [ ] 280 Matthew 9:1-17; Mark 2:1-22; Luke 5:17-39
- [ ] 281 John 5; Matthew 12:1-21; Mark 2:23-3:12; Luke 6:1-11
- [ ] 282 Matthew 5; Mark 3:13-19; Luke 6:12-36
- [ ] 283 Matthew 6-7; Luke 6:37-49
- [ ] 284 Luke 7; Matthew 8:1, 5-13; 11:2-30
- [ ] 285 Matthew 12:22-50; Mark 3:20-35; Luke 8:1-21
- [ ] 286 Mark 4:1-34; Matthew 13:1-53
- [ ] 287 Mark 4:35-5:43; Matthew 8:18, 23-34; 9:18-34; Luke 8:22-56
- [ ] 288 Mark 6:1-30; Matthew 13:54-58; 9:35-11:1; 14:1-12; Luke 9:1-10

Bible reading schedule

☐ 289 Matthew 14:13-36; Mark 6:31-56; Luke 9:11-17; John 6:1-21

☐ 290 John 6:22-7:1; Matthew 15:1-20; Mark 7:1-23

☐ 291 Matthew 15:21-16:20; Mark 7:24-8:30; Luke 9:18-21

☐ 292 Matthew 16:21-17:27; Mark 8:31-9:32; Luke 9:22-45

☐ 293 Matthew 18; 8:19-22; Mark 9:33-50; Luke 9:46-62; John 7:2-10

☐ 294 John 7:11-8:59

☐ 295 Luke 10:1-11:36

☐ 296 Luke 11:37-13:21

☐ 297 John 9-10

☐ 298 Luke 13:22-15:32

☐ 299 Luke 16:1-17:10; John 11:1-54

☐ 300 Luke 17:11-18:17; Matthew 19:1-15; Mark 10:1-16

☐ 301 Matthew 19:16-20:28; Mark 10:17-45; Luke 18:18-34

☐ 302 Matthew 20:29-34; 26:6-13; Mark 10:46-52; 14:3-9; Luke 18:35-19:28; John 11:55-12:11

☐ 303 Matthew 21:1-22; Mark 11:1-26; Luke 19:29-48; John 12:12-50

☐ 304 Matthew 21:23-22:14; Mark 11:27-12:12; Luke 20:1-19

☐ 305 Matthew 22:15-46; Mark 12:13-37; Luke 20:20-44

☐ 306 Matthew 23; Mark 12:38-44; Luke 20:45-21:4

☐ 307 Matthew 24:1-31; Mark 13:1-27; Luke 21:5-27

☐ 308 Matthew 24:32-26:5, 14-16; Mark 13:28-14:2, 10-11; Luke 21:28-22:6

☐ 309 Matthew 26:17-29; Mark 14:12-25; Luke 22:7-38; John 13

☐ 310 John 14-16

☐ 311 John 17:1-18:1; Matthew 26:30-46; Mark 14:26-42; Luke 22:39-46

☐ 312 Matthew 26:47-75; Mark 14:43-72; Luke 22:47-65; John 18:2-27

☐ 313 Matthew 27:1-26; Mark 15:1-15; Luke 22:66-23:25; John 18:28-19:16

☐ 314 Matthew 27:27-56; Mark 15:16-41; Luke 23:26-49; John 19:17-30

☐ 315 Matthew 27:57-28:8; Mark 15:42-16:8; Luke 23:50-24:12; John 19:31-20:10

☐ 316 Matthew 28:9-20; Mark 16:9-20; Luke 24:13-53; John 20:11-21:25

☐ 317 Acts 1-2

☐ 318 Acts 3-5

☐ 319 Acts 6:1-8:1

☐ 320 Acts 8:2-9:43

☐ 321 Acts 10-11

☐ 322 Acts 12-13

☐ 323 Acts 14-15

☐ 324 Galatians 1-3

☐ 325 Galatians 4-6

☐ 326 James

☐ 327 Acts 16:1-18:11

☐ 328 1 Thessalonians

☐ 329 2 Thessalonians; Acts 18:12-19:22

☐ 330 1 Corinthians 1-4

☐ 331 1 Corinthians 5-8

☐ 332 1 Corinthians 9-11

☐ 333 1 Corinthians 12-14

☐ 334 1 Corinthians 15-16

☐ 335 Acts 19:23-20:1; 2 Corinthians 1-4

☐ 336 2 Corinthians 5-9

☐ 337 2 Corinthians 10-13

☐ 338 Romans 1-3

☐ 339 Romans 4-6

☐ 340 Romans 7-8

☐ 341 Romans 9-11

☐ 342 Romans 12-15

☐ 343 Romans 16; Acts 20:2-21:16

☐ 344 Acts 21:17-23:35

☐ 345 Acts 24-26

☐ 346 Acts 27-28

☐ 347 Ephesians 1-3

☐ 348 Ephesians 4-6

☐ 349 Colossians

☐ 350 Philippians

☐ 351 Philemon; 1 Timothy 1-3

☐ 352 1 Timothy 4-6; Titus

☐ 353 2 Timothy

☐ 354 1 Peter

☐ 355 Jude; 2 Peter

☐ 356 Hebrews 1:1-5:10

☐ 357 Hebrews 5:11-9:28

☐ 358 Hebrews 10-11

☐ 359 Hebrews 12-13; 2 John; 3 John

☐ 360 1 John

☐ 361 Revelation 1-3

☐ 362 Revelation 4-9

☐ 363 Revelation 10-14

☐ 364 Revelation 15-18

☐ 365 Revelation 19-22

Psalms

Our English word "Psalms" is derived from a Greek word denoting *poems sung to the accompaniment of string instruments.* The English translation of the Hebrew title is "Book of Praises." The book of the Psalms is actually an artistic arrangement of five collections of psalms – each collection ending with a *doxology* Psalm (or, a Psalm of Praise). The superscriptions in the Hebrew text ascribe authorship of seventy-three Psalms to David and twenty-seven to various other writers. Fifty Psalms are anonymous. However, New Testament references and textual content indicate that some of the fifty were authored by David. Truly, David was "raised up on high, the anointed of the God of Jacob" not only to be king, but also as "the sweet psalmist of Israel" (2 Samuel 23:1).

The Psalms contain praise, petition, prophecy, and perspective on the past history of God's people. A number of them are songs about Creation, glorifying the Creator. Others extol the veracity and power of God's Word. The prophetic Psalms are especially intriguing. Sixteen of these are designated *Messianic* because, in whole or in part, they foretell events concerning either the first or the second coming of the Messiah (Greek for "the Christ"). The words of the risen Christ Himself in Luke 24:27 and Luke 24:44 should alert us to search for our Lord in many of the Psalms.

Several Scriptures let us know that the human authors of the Psalms, as well as other Old Testament books, were aware that they were writing under the power and in the wisdom of a Divine Author. See 2 Samuel 23:2, Psalm 102:18, and 1 Peter 1:10-12.

If you'll find time to meditate on the words of the Psalms, here are some promises for you. You will be fruitful and prosperous in all that you do (1:2-3). You will sleep well (4:4, 8). Your soul will be satisfied (63:5-6). You will be glad in the Lord (104:34). You will not sin against your God (119:11) but will have respect unto His ways (119:15). You will be wiser than your enemies and understand more than your teachers and elders (119:97-100).

Please note that each year, in the Word of Life Quiet Time, we cover a different portion of the Psalms. In six years you will work your way through all 150 Psalms!

Psalm 104:1-13

What is the writer saying?

How can I apply this to my life?

pray India – Effective ministry to nearly 400 million youth, many of who are in crisis.

Psalm 104 is a sequel to Psalm 103. Both praise God for His blessings to His people. This hymn focuses on the Lord's greatness and power as manifested in His creation. The entire psalm presents us with a poet's meditative thoughts, which loosely follow the creation story of Genesis: verses 1-5 compare with Genesis 1:1-5, the first day of Creation; verses 6-9 compare with Genesis 1:6-8, the second day of Creation; and verses 10-18 compare with Genesis 1:9-13, the third day of Creation.

In verse 1, "clothed" is a metaphor intended to picture God's character and commitment to His people (such as a favorite jacket identifying a coach). "Honor" refers to God's awe-inspiring authority, glory, and vigor (that is, His active involvement). "Majesty" is a related word that reflects on the splendor of God's actions, which display His goodness, holiness, and worthiness of praise.

In verse 2, to declare that God's garment is light reminds us that God is light (1 John 1:5); God is the giver of light—both physical and spiritual (Genesis 1:3; 2 Corinthians 4:6)—and that God dwells in light (1 Timothy 6:16). To be clothed in light pictures God's character as holy and good. Notice that Jesus, when He was transfigured, was covered in raiment "white as the light" (Matthew 17:2).

The verse's second half ("Who stretches out the heavens like a curtain") is intended to reinforce the first half. God stretches out His tent-curtains of the heavens, which became His dwelling place; God lives in light, therefore He has no darkness.

The metaphor is extended in verses 3-6, causing us to marvel about God, the great builder, Who used these materials to construct the Earth as His exclusive, inner chamber where He may personally dwell.

Life **stEp** Despite God's dwelling in the vast heavens, we are blessed by His personal interest in our little world.

Psalm 104:14-23

What is the writer saying?

How can I apply this to my life?

pray Austria – For cults and the New Age activists to be thwarted in their efforts to ensnare young adults.

In this second section of the psalm, the writer shifts his view from grand things of God's creation to the smaller and more delicate created things that are all around us. These too are under God's care.

The verbs in yesterday's passage were in the past tense as the psalmist retold what God did in Creation. Today the verbs are in the present tense because the psalmist is adding an emphasis on the Lord's continuing care for people as He watches over His created wonders.

The psalmist recalls God's work from the third and fourth days of Creation as God oversees plant growth, which both fills the dry land and meets our daily needs (vv. 14-18). It is God Who "causes" these things to "bring forth food" (v. 14)!

In verses 16-18 the psalmist takes us for a nature walk through the forests and hills, which are filled with birds, goats, and other wild animals to remind us that these were "planted" by God and are now watched by Him. The trees are "full of sap," the birds raise their young in their nests, and the lions find meat and lay down in their dens. All are cared for by God's bountiful *providence* (timely care that shows foresight).

Finally, we are to consider God's work of "appointing" the sun, moon, and seasons to guide our days and labors (vv. 19-23).

According to Psalm 19:1-4 and Romans 1:19-20, God's actions through His creation speak to every human being. The observable creation declares, *There is a God who made you and all that surrounds you. Consider His providence. Seek His face.*

Life stEP Take time to pause and look closely at the created world around You, and thank God for it. Reflect on God's *providence* (timely care that shows foresight). If God takes care of all these little things, surely He will take care of you.

tuesday 1

Psalm 104:24-35

What is the writer saying?

How can I apply this to my life?

pray   Mexico – For Bible schools to be characterized by doctrinal accuracy, depth, and personal integrity.

This last half of the psalm loosely continues the psalmist's thoughts on the fifth and sixth days of the creation story (Genesis 1:20-31). The writer marvels at God's "manifold works" ("many colored," or diverse) both in His original Creation and His ongoing care of the world:

In verse 24, the earth's "riches" allude to God displaying His skill, insight, and craftsmanship in all He created. Verses 33-35 show that not only the godly will see His wisdom; the "sinners" and "wicked" will, too. Their failure to recognize and submit to God will become, in part, the basis for their being "consumed" by God's judgment.

Verses 25-27 say that all living things, from the small to the great, depend on their Maker for food.

Both God's attitude and His thoroughness in providing for His creatures are being pictured in verse 28. Since most wild animals can do nothing to prepare their daily food, it is a marvel that year by year their food is prepared for them to eat. God is pictured as a farmer who takes an extra handful of grain from His storage silo so that He can enjoy spreading it on the ground and then standing aside to watch the wild birds eat from His bounty.

In verse 28, the word "renew" means either renovating or rebuilding something, such as a building, which has been damaged or restoring or revitalizing a thing that has been disrupted, such as a relationship or condition. Think of a forest fire that has swept over a mountain; before long, through the scarred landscape, new green life is emerging. This too is a part of the ongoing care of God!

Life stEP   God doesn't just care for His creatures. What are some of the "manifold" ways He cares for you?

Wednesday 1

Psalm 105:1-12

What is the writer saying?

How can I apply this to my life?

pray Netherlands Antilles – For the Papiamento Bible that was published in 1997 to be an impact on those who use it.

Psalm 105 is a tribute to the Lord for His faithfulness in keeping His "everlasting covenant" (v. 10) to the descendants of Abraham, Isaac, and Jacob. It looks back to Genesis 12:2-3, where the Lord made a seven-fold promise to Abraham (v. 9a). In Genesis 15 the Lord put the promise in the form of a unilateral, unconditional, permanent covenant, which was later confirmed to Isaac (v. 9b; Gen. 26:3-4) and then to Jacob and his descendants (v 10; Genesis 28:13-14).

Although the Lord's covenant was unconditional and forever, there were requirements for each generation if the people were to enjoy its blessings (Leviticus 26:3, 14). The first five verses of Psalm 105 list twelve stipulations, or conditions, required in order to assure the blessings: give thanks unto the Lord (v. 1); call upon the name of the Lord, make His deeds known to other nations, sing unto the Lord (v. 2); talk about His wondrous works (miracles), glory in His holy name (v. 3); seek the Lord with a rejoicing heart, seek the Lord's strength (v. 4); seek His face continually, remember His works (v. 5); remember His wonders, and remember His words. In verses 7-12, the psalmist praises the Lord for remembering His covenant with the nation of Israel. While Israel began as just "a few men in number" (v. 12), God made it into a nation.

Life stEP Review the list from verses 1-5. These are actions God still wants to see from us today. How can you give thanks (Ephesians 5:20)? How are you seeking the Lord (Hebrews 11:6)? How can you "remember" His working in your life (Ephesians 2:11-13)?

thursday 1

Psalm 105:13-25

What is the writer saying?

How can I apply this to my life?

pray El Salvador – For sound, Bible-believing churches to be planted among the Amerindian people.

Soon after King David established his new capital at Jerusalem, he brought the Ark of the Covenant there with great ceremony (1 Chronicles 16:1-7). He delivered a medley of psalms to his chief musician, Asaph, for use in the celebration. The medley in 1 Chronicles 16:8-36 is a partial recording of three Psalms: 105:1-15, all of 96, and 106:1, 47-48.

Today's portion of Psalm 105 was intended to be a reminder of God's continued blessings, which had resulted in Israel becoming a strong country with a powerful king. David reminds Israel of God's personal care for Israel when the nation was just a single family and "strangers" (v. 12, or "foreigners") in the land God had promised the Israelites (see Hebrews 11:9-16). Through their journeys, they were still under God's special directing of events.

Verses 16-22 continue with a summary of Joseph (Genesis 37-50). The many events that took place in Joseph's life—being sold into slavery (v. 17), cast into prison (v. 18), and then promoted to the Pharaoh's personal administrator of Egypt (vv. 20-21)—were seen as steps in God's directing events to fulfill His plan.

Next we have a summary of the history of Israel in Egypt (vv. 23-25; Exodus 1). At first, the family of Israel had been welcomed guests in Egypt, which allowed for Israel's growth. Eventually, Egypt brought sorrow, slavery, and despair upon their Hebrew guests.

While most Christians are not in this Hebrew family, we have all been adopted into God's eternal family! Since God has not changed His character, how can you expect His faithful care in your life today? How can you express faith in God when you are faced with hard situations, such as those endured by Joseph?

friday 1

Psalm 105:26-36

What is the writer saying?

How can I apply this to my life?

pray Nigeria – For the HIV/AIDS epidemic in Nigeria. If the epidemic continues, by the year 2020, 60% of Nigerians will have HIV/AIDS.

Let's begin by noting that today's passage is bracketed by Israel *entering* (v. 23) and *leaving* (v. 38) Egypt. This continues the narrative of God's ongoing care and direction in history, which resulted in His transforming Israel into a great nation. Israel had entered Egypt by God's command, and with God's promise that He would "surely bring you up again" (Genesis 46:3-4).

Today's passage looks at how God raised up Moses and Aaron (v. 26) to do God's "signs…and wonders" (v. 27) in Egypt so Israel could go to the land God had promised it (v. 42).

The ordering of eight of the ten plagues presented here is interesting: We begin with the ninth (v. 28a) and an observation concerning the whole process; that is, Egypt's continuing defiance of God's command to let His people go (verse 28b in context probably means "they did not respond to His word"). Since all ten plagues can be symbolized as a "dark" time of God's wrath upon the Egyptians, the ninth plague of "darkness" is artfully presented first. Our text then backtracks through the plagues to recount the steps that lead to this observation: the first (v. 29), second (v. 30), fourth and third (v. 31), seventh (vv. 32-33), eighth (vv. 34-35), and then the grim climax of the tenth (v. 36) (see Exodus 7-12).

The purpose of this passage was to remind the reader that God had repeatedly shown His loving care for His people. These events were evidences of God's power over the events of history as He brought about His will in the world. They were to cause believers to thank God and look on Him with admiration and reverence as they realized how God brought His blessings.

Think back through the various stages of God's powerful workings in your own life. What has God done that should cause you to thank and praise Him for His timely care for you?

saturday 1

Psalm 105:37-45

What is the writer saying?

How can I apply this to my life?

pray Angola – For committed translators to bring the scriptures to the 20 language groups that have none.

Today's passage is a summary of the fifth stage of God's continued blessings upon Israel. In these verses the psalmist recounts seven ways that the Lord provided for the new nation of Israel:

- God provided the people, who were slaves, with "silver and gold," as prophesied to Moses (v. 37a; Exodus 3:21-22). This was their wages for the years of slavery (Exodus 12:35-36).
- He gave them the physical strength needed for their journey (v. 37b).
- He gave them the cloud by day for a covering from the heat of the desert sun (v. 39a—apparently like an umbrella!) and for assurance of His presence. He gave them fire by night as a source of light, guidance, and protection (v 39b; Exodus 14:20-21; 40:34-38).
- He provided quail for meat (v. 40a; Exodus 16:13).
- He also provided manna for bread (v. 40b; Exodus 16:15).
- He provided water from a rock in the desert (v. 41; Exodus 17:6).
- He fulfilled His promise to bring Israel from Egypt to the land promised to Abraham (vv. 42, 44).

The reasons for God's miraculous provision of blessing include: first, that God Himself would keep the promises in His word (vv. 8, 42), and second, that God would become the ruler of this new kingdom, where they would seek Him (v. 4) and keep His commandments (v. 45).

- The psalm climaxes with the observation that Israel was filled with joy and gladness (v. 43) because of God's great faithfulness. It concludes with a call for all readers to respond with their own praise to the Lord (v. 45b) for His continuing goodness to them.

Life stEP God still wants a people on earth today who will carefully study the history of His working in the world and then who will make it their purpose to live in a manner that pleases Him. How can you, by your conduct today, bring praise to the Lord?

Psalm 106:1-15

What is the writer saying?

How can I apply this to my life?

pray Bolivia – For the Holy Spirit to bring about maturity in the lives of those studying for the ministry.

This psalm begins with a praise (v. 1a), a proclamation (vv. 1b-3), and a prayer (vv. 4-5). It ends with a prayer (v. 47), a proclamation (v. 48a), and a praise (v. 48b). Between the psalm's introduction (vv. 1-5) and conclusion (vv. 47-48) there is a three-part review of Israel's history:

- Israel's sinful failure to consider God *in Egypt* (vv. 7-12).
- Israel's sinful failure to consider God *in the wilderness* (vv. 13-33).
- Israel's sinful failure to consider God *in the land* (vv. 34-46).

The psalmist, as the nation's representative, is offering a prayer of confession and repentance (vv. 6-7—notice the use of "we"). "We have sinned" points to the failure of meeting God's standard of righteousness. "We have committed iniquity" is saying they did what was inherently wrong. "We have done wickedly" means their deeds were the opposite of godliness.

The psalmist points out the source of Israel's past sinful conduct: their "fathers" (v. 7), who had failed to consider God's wondrous works (seen in vv. 8-10, 14-15).

When the psalmist says "our fathers *understood* not" (v. 7), he is saying:

- They failed to *look carefully* at the implications of God's wonderful deeds. Thus they did not *gain insight* into God's character.
- They failed to *wisely consider* the lessons to be learned. Thus they did not gain a right *perspective*.
- They failed to *prudently act* upon the foundational truths presented. Thus they did not prosper in their future endeavors.

Life stEP

How do you respond to God's care for you? Are you learning from your own spiritual failures and sin? What would God want you to "understand"? What has God done for you that needs your careful look? What lessons have been presented for your own wise consideration? How can you act prudently the next time around?

Psalm 106:16-31

What is the writer saying?

How can I apply this to my life?

Today we look at the second of three divisions in this psalm: The people of Israel's sinful failure to consider God *in the wilderness.*

- In verses 13-14, their sin of lust refers to a desire or craving for things they had in Egypt that were no longer available, particularly tasty fruits and vegetables (see Numbers 11:4-5).
- They envied Moses and Aaron (v. 16). Numbers 16:1-3 points specifically to Korah, a Levite, who with 250 princes of Israel accused Moses and Aaron of taking the leadership they wanted for themselves.
- The people exchanged their knowledge of the true God so they could worship a grass-eating ox-god (vv. 19-22; Exodus 32:4)!
- They refused to believe God would care for them if they took the land God had promised them (vv. 24-25; Numbers 13:27-14:4).

- They even worshipped the god of the Moabites, Baalpeor (vv. 28-29; Numbers 25:1-3).

In all these ways Israel was not believing God's word (v. 24), which led to their murmuring against God (grumbling and complaining, v. 25).

Life **stEP** "Now all these things happened unto them for examples: and they are written for our admonition" (1 Corinthians 10:11). With these examples, we have to ask ourselves: How should I act if I believe God will care for me as I seek to live for Him? How can I faithfully follow His Word as a guide for my actions?

tuesday 2

Psalm 106:32-48

What is the writer saying?

How can I apply this to my life?

pray Argentina – For the salvation of the president and the stabilization of this country's economic and judicial systems.

Today we look at the final part of the psalm's history of Israel: *Israel's history in the land* (vv. 34-46). Here Israel is committing the sin of disobedience with regard to "not destroying the Canaanites (v. 34; per Deuteronomy 7:1-2), whose land the Israelites had conquered. Instead, Israel "mingled among" the Canaanites (v. 35; Judges 3:5-6). Sadly, Israel's sin became a "snare" that drew them into greater sins. Soon Israel was learning about the Canaanites' gods (vv. 35-36), worshipping their idols (v. 36; Judges 2:11-12), and even sacrificing their children to the demons associated with these idols (vv. 37-38). They became spiritual adulterers (v. 39) who incurred the "wrath of the LORD" (v. 40).

Verses 35-45 summarize the repeating history ("many times," v. 43) of Israel during the time of the Judges; that is, a continuing cycle of rebellion, retribution, repentance, restoration, and then rest (see Judges 2:10-19).

Despite Israel's continual unfaithfulness and sin, the psalm says the Lord saved His people again and again (v. 43), showing His heart of mercy and commitment to His own faithfulness (vv. 44-46) as well as His worthiness of our praise (v. 48).

The petition in verse 47 brings this history lesson to a climax: show Your mercy again and save us. The words "gather us from among the heathen" suggest that the psalm is from a time after Israel had been dispersed from the Promised Land. As a result, it also looks forward to that final re-gathering when Israel will receive her Messiah, saying "Blessed is he that comes in the name of the Lord" (Luke 13:35).

Life stEP

Has your life been a continuing cycle of sin, suffering, and repentance, followed by God's deliverance? The psalmist wants you to remember that God will be faithful and willing to show mercy. Of what sin do you need to repent so that God might demonstrate His mercy to you?

Psalm 107:1-16

What is the writer saying?

How can I apply this to my life?

Psalms 105, 106, and 107 form a trilogy. Each begins with a *call to thanksgiving* and then an exhortation to make known the wondrous works of the Lord. All three look at Israel's history from different perspectives: Israel being given a land (Psalm 105), Israel being exiled from their land (Psalm 106), and re-gathering Israel from exile (Psalm 107). Although there have been limited re-gatherings, verse 3 looks to the ultimate re-gathering, when all the people of Israel will return to the land (Isaiah 43:5-6; Jeremiah 31:8-10).

The introduction (vv. 1-3) calls us to give thanks to God (v. 1). The same Hebrew word for mercy (v. 1) is used in the conclusion, where we are to observe (v. 43) the loving-kindness of the Lord. In the first stanza of the psalm (vv. 4-9), Israel is likened to a **wanderer** in a spiritual wilderness—alone, with no place of its own. The second stanza (vv. 10-16) likens Israel to a **prisoner** in a dungeon being punished for its rebellion against God. No one is concerned about its sad state.

The same pattern is found in both: a **plight** (vv. 5, 12), a **plea** (vv. 6, 13), a **provision** (vv. 7, 14), and a **praise** (vv. 8-9, 15-16).

The words *mercy* (v. 1), *goodness*, and *loving-kindness* all come from the Hebrew word *hesed,* which is widely used in the Old Testament to declare an important aspect of God's love: His persistent desire to show abundant kindness and be bountifully good to His people (see Exodus 20:6).

In your trials and troubles, do you take the time to see that God has also shown you His goodness and lovingkindness? Since the Lord also desires for you to reflect His "goodness" and "lovingkindness" to others (Hosea 6:6), how can you act towards someone else in a good and kind way today?

thursday 2

Psalm 107:17-32

What is the writer saying?

How can I apply this to my life?

pray Bermuda – Pray for unity among believers so that God's agenda can remain the focus of their hearts.

Psalm 107:17-18 gives the third poetic picture (already seen: the wilderness wanderer and the prisoner)—a **foolish person** who has become so sick that he cannot eat and is near death. A *fool* is one who attempts to run his life without regard for God's Word. They live on transgression (v. 17, conduct against the law) and iniquities (actions that are inherently wrong, such as cruelty and arrogance).

The fourth picture (vv. 23-27) is that of **seamen** doing regular, honest business (v. 23) when a storm suddenly comes and threatens to destroy all with its powerful winds and waves.

These mariners have learned to see (v. 24, to look at so as to gain or perceive an insight) that it is the Lord Who allows such storms—and it is He Who, in due course, will make the storm calm (v. 29). Thus, such great storms are a summons to trust God! The men in this psalm respond to the storms of life by crying out to God (v. 28), then rejoicing because they know God will guide them (v. 30).

How do you respond to unexpected and overwhelming storms in your life? Will you **see** that such events are a summons to prayer? How can you trust and wait for the Lord to guide you to peaceful havens? Have you taken the time to praise God for His goodness to you?

f**r**id**a**y 2

Psalm 107:33-43

What is the writer saying?

How can I apply this to my life?

pray   Australia – For the 630,000 university students who need a gospel witness.

The psalm so far has illustrated God's goodness in response to various cries of distress from His people. Verse 43 says a wise person will note these situations and know that God is always working changes in the world, whether for blessing or judgment. God works in the natural world (vv. 33-38), with the contrast of barrenness and fruitfulness, as well as the inner spiritual world (vv. 39-42), with the contrast of chastisement and prosperity.

When the psalmist tells those who want to be wise to observe the workings of God, he is implying that many people never see God's work in their own lives. A righteous and wise person will understand that God has considered everything beforehand so He may provide for our needs (or if our situation calls for it, our chastisement!).

Righteous (v. 42) refers to one who is straight or level in his ethical and emotional choices. As applied here, the righteous person chooses to do what is right and pleasing before God's eyes, knowing that God Himself sees and responds! Such a straight life is foundational to becoming a wise person.

Life stEP

The psalmist has reminded us that the Lord has complete control of our lives. But the writer has also shown us that our conduct influences how He chooses to *work* in our lives. What choices are before you today, and what will be your straight and level response? Take a few minutes and look closely at how God has been working in your own inner spiritual world.

saturday 2

Psalm 108:1-13

What is the writer saying?

How can I apply this to my life?

pray North Korea – For the abandoned children on the streets to find a place of refuge.

Psalm 108 is a composite psalm. It begins with praises from Psalm 57:7-11, which was recording a personal plea to God from David while he fled from King Saul. His plea turns to praise when faith overcomes fear. Psalm 108:6-13 repeats Psalm 60:5-12, from when David was king. His armies had suffered an earlier defeat by Edom, and so Psalm 60 was a national plea for God's help as Israel prepared to attack Edom again. David says he is trusting in God to grant him victory.

The three stanzas of Psalm 108 are thus a refashioning of earlier materials to form a liturgical psalm used in public worship. Each stanza of Psalm 108 contains a prayer: that God would be lifted up in glory above all else (vv. 1-5), that God's people would be delivered, as God promised (vv. 6-9), and that God would help those in crisis (vv. 10-13).

Each stanza also brings a truth about God into view: God's unfailing love is the highest thing (vv. 1-5); God has spoken, thus committing Himself to give help (vv. 6-9); and God's power alone is sufficient to meet the crisis (vv. 10-13). The three stanzas teach us how to praise, pray, and plan: Our hearts must be fixed, like an arrow focused on a target, on praise (vv. 1-5); our prayers must be declarations of faith in the promises of God (vv. 6-9); and our plans depend on God for success, since only through Him can we act valiantly—that is, with His strength to be righteous in behavior, strong in influence, and known by virtue (vv. 10-13).

 Like the Israelites, who refashioned these verses into a psalm of reflection, we should also reflect upon these verses! How has God shown his unfailing love to you? What promises has He made that apply to a current trouble in your life? How can you, with God's help, plan to act valiantly in response to your troubling situations?

Psalm 109:1-10

What is the writer saying?

How can I apply this to my life?

---

pray Pray for the elderly in your church and those who are shut-ins.

Psalm 109 is David's prayer for help against his enemies, as it calls on God to avenge him. David had learned not to take action himself, but that vengeance belongs to God (Deuteronomy 32:35). For instance, he did not avenge himself against Saul or Nabal (1 Samuel 24:4-7, 25:32-34, 26:8-10).

David's prayer is based on a retribution principle, that is, punishment proportional to the sin is just. What David calls for in verses 6-15 must be balanced against the continuous malicious conduct by sinful men against David. In verses 1-5, David presented his case of how the "wicked" are against him before asking God to repay those wicked men (v. 6).

David had shown that he was honorable:

He had kept his focus on praise (v. 1) and prayer (v. 4).

He had acted with love towards these sinful men (vv. 4-5; this is an act of kindness or goodwill), the same love as in the Law of God in Leviticus 19:18, 34 that says to "love thy neighbor as thyself."

His conduct was blameless (v. 3, "without cause"). His speech was full of prayer (v. 4), not lies and deceit (v. 2).

He had done good only to receive a reward of evil (v. 5). Yet he chose to do what was kind, proper, and benevolent.

As in David's day, we sometimes face wicked and malicious men who war against our good. When facing such hateful attacks, how can you stay focused on praise and prayer? How can you still act with kindness and goodwill? How can you keep from fighting back with the same wicked words? How can you do what is kind and proper?

monday 3

Psalm 109:11-20

What is the writer saying?

How can I apply this to my life?

pray — Austria – For cults and the New Age activists to be thwarted in their efforts to ensnare young adults.

David calls for judgment on wicked men, but rather than focusing on this, let's look at his reasons for believing thinking the wicked man deserves a reciprocal judgment from God:

Verse 16a: He never shows kindness or love. He is without compassion.

Verse 16b: He takes advantage of the poor and needy, even killing them if it serves his purposes.

Verse 17: He did not delight in seeing others do well.

Verse 20: He speaks evil against others.

David sums up his list by asking God to "reward" these men with the judgment He described in verses 6-15. In contrast to the way wicked men act, let's make up our own list of traits that would be worthy of the Lord's official praise:

Let's show kindness and love. May others see our compassion!

Let's look to minister and serve the poor and needy. Also, we should refuse to be self-serving in our actions.

Let's not seek retaliation. And when we need to speak up for ourselves, let us be careful to not twist the truth!

Let's delight in seeing others doing well, and rejoice with them when they receive public praise for their accomplishments.

Let's be known as people who wear a cloak of humility.

Life stEP — Which of these character traits needs your prayer to become a reality today? What can you do so others will see actions that will convince them of the true qualities of your heart?

tuesday 3

Psalm 109:21-31

What is the writer saying?

How can I apply this to my life?

pray Netherlands Antilles – Praise God for faithful radio staff that keep the gospel accessible to many.

There is now a marked change in David's prayer. He turns away from fretting about his adversaries to focusing on God. Instead of continuing to ask for specific judgments, he simply places his trust in God. He is at rest knowing God will do what is right ("do thou for me," v. 21).

David begins by emphatically calling out to God using an unusual combination of God's names, which denote God as both Savior and Judge. First, David looks to God to save (v. 26) him from his "poor and needy" condition (v. 22). But David is also asking God to be a righteous judge Who restrains the adversaries of the poor and weak.

David asks God to act for "Your name's sake," which is saying that God's reputation was at stake—that is, God will always act to affirm the character represented by His name. Thus David is sure that God would act with mercy (kindness, steadfast love) and goodness (v. 21b).

A little later in his prayer, David again calls out to God (v. 26). This time David uses the most common name of God, His personal name, Jehovah (or Yahweh, commonly translated "LORD"). This name points out God's work as Redeemer (Psalm 19:14). He bases his plea on God's reputation before men (v. 27) and His mercy to His servants (v. 28).

In verse 30, David knows he has the victory! He resolves to spend his time publicly praising the Lord instead of fretting about his enemies. David closes with words of confidence, knowing God will not let His people stand in the harsh court rooms of life without being at their side ("right hand," v. 31) as their Advocate. In contrast, Satan is at the right hand of David's adversaries (v. 6). So, who is better off?

Life stEP Are there troubles and adversaries afflicting your life? Take some time in prayer, as did David, to settle your heart so that you too can say to God, *Lord, do as you want in my life so long as I and others can see that Your hand of steadfast love and goodness is on me.*

Wednesday 3

Psalm 110:1-7

What is the writer saying?

How can I apply this to my life?

pray   Indonesia -- For the Muslims to be exposed to the Gospel by the few missionaries remaining.

This psalm has more quotes and references appearing in the New Testament than from any other psalm does—there are more than twenty–five references from verse 1 alone. Jesus quoted from verse 1 (Matthew 22:42-45) to prove that the Messiah must be both David's son and Lord—both man and God. Peter quoted verse 1 on the day of Pentecost (Acts 2:34-35) to prove that the resurrection was "according to the Scriptures" (1 Corinthians 15:4).

David is speaking as one of the prophets when he reveals the heavenly conversation between God the Father and the Messiah in this verse. This was fulfilled when Jesus ascended into Heaven (Luke 24:51; Hebrews 1:3, 10:12). Verse 2 speaks of a coming day when the God of Heaven will send the Messiah to be God on Earth (Joel 3:16; Revelation 19:11-16). This coming Lord will make all his enemies subject to Him (v. 1b, "footstool"; Hebrews 10:13), and

He will rule as king (v. 2: "rod" = scepter) over Israel and Israel's enemies. The nation of Israel will also receive Jesus as its Messiah (v. 3; Zechariah 12:10), and the people of Israel will *willingly* offer themselves as *free-will offerings* to God.

Verse 4 adds another important prophetic detail: this Lord will also be a "priest for ever after the order of Melchizedek" (the king-priest who Abraham went to in Genesis 14:18). The book of Hebrews reveals this "priest" to be Jesus Christ (Hebrews 5:10, 6:20), Who is a greater priest than Aaron and the Levitical priests (Hebrews 7:11-19).

Verses 5-6 prophesy of Armageddon, when Jesus will manifest Himself as the Messiah by destroying this world's system and establishing His kingdom on Earth (Daniel 2:44). Verse 7 sees the kingdom as the time of refreshing and restitution (Acts 3:19-21).

Life **stEP**   Just as Israel will one day be willing to serve its Lord, we must not forget that we are called to serve our Lord as *living sacrifices* (Romans 12:1-2). How can you serve your Savior today?

thursday 3

Psalm 111:1-10

What is the writer saying?

How can I apply this to my life?

pray Hungary – For summer outreach and camping ministries as they evangelize and disciple youth.

Psalm 111 is a twenty-two-line acrostic poem (vv. 1-8 are two-line couplets; vv. 9-10 are three-line triplets). After an introductory "praise the Lord" (hallelujah!), each of the twenty-two lines begins with one of the twenty-two letters of the Hebrew alphabet.

The "works of the Lord" are the occasion for the psalmist's call to praise God. Five times His works are applauded (vv. 2-4, 6-7).

Because of the magnitude of His works, those who take pleasure in them seek them out (v. 2), or ponder or inquire about them. They want to examine His works so that they can gain insight into the Lord's character, because what He does comes from what He is: righteous (v. 3b) and "gracious and full of compassion" (v. 4b).

Likewise, God's words and commandments, which express what He is, are "sure" (v. 7b; providing stability and confidence), continue to "stand fast forever" (v. 8a; sustaining by providing support), "true" (v. 8b; providing holy standards for one's conduct) and "upright" (v. 8b; literally a straight path, thus ethically pleasing in God's eyes).

The greatest manifestation of the Lord's character is the redemption (v. 9) that He, by His own efforts, provides for His people by paying the price necessary for their release from their enslavement to sin. He redeemed not with silver and gold but "with the precious blood of Christ, as of a lamb without blemish and without spot" (1 Peter. 1:19). As a result, His name is regarded with holy awe and reverence (v. 9b; to show an attitude towards God of a respectful fear).

Such reverence towards God is the starting point for a life of "wisdom" (v. 10; the ethical skill of choosing a path of conduct that is prudent and virtuous.

How can you make this "wisdom" apply to your life? Where do you need to see God's guidance for true and right choices?

fRiday 3

Psalm 112:1-10

What is the writer saying?

How can I apply this to my life?

pray Italy – For more believers to attend Bible schools and seminaries before entering the ministry.

This psalm is a sequel to Psalm 111, which was about the awesome Lord God, Who is to be feared. Psalm 112 builds upon 111 as it presents the blessings for the one who does fear God.

Psalm 112 moves through five areas of God's blessings:

In verses 1-2, God blesses this person's family, who will inwardly delight in obeying God's ways and outwardly delight in doing right.

In verses 3-4, prosperity will come to this person's house as prudent and virtuous choices will tend to bring moral wealth and spiritual worth to his home. When dark days come, the godly man will be able to see his path lit by God's truth so that his conduct will reflect God's own character of graciousness, compassion, and righteousness.

The "good" man, who reflects God's own character, will maintain a generous attitude towards others (vv. 5-6). He will always want to show true compassion.

He carefully weighs how he will be able to best help others.

He is not easily shaken by hostility or threats from "evil" men (vv. 7-8) because his heart is "fixed" (standing firm on ground prepared by God) and "established" (leaning on the supports provided by God) from trusting God.

The accolades in vv. 9-10 are usually said in our praises to God, but here they are applied to the man who fears the Lord! He has enduring righteousness because he consistently chooses right actions and attitudes. He is a person of "honor"—having a reputation that is heavy—that is, a consistent and glorious lifestyle worthy of respect.

 Wow, what a list of worthy achievements for a godly person's life! Which of these qualities need to be developed in your life? Which of these do you need to spend time talking over with God?

Psalm 113:1-9

What is the writer saying?

How can I apply this to my life?

---

pray New Zealand – To see many won to Christ through church–run food banks and counseling ministries.

For centuries Psalms 113 through 118 have formed a family of hymns that are recited during the Jewish Passover, or Seder (Matthew 26:30).

The *first stanza* of this psalm (vv. 1-3) is a call to worship the "name of the LORD." "Name" and "praise" are both repeated three times in this stanza. Since God Himself revealed His names to Israel as a means of illuminating His character, our psalm is calling upon all to praise Him for Who He is. The invitation to "praise" is wide-ranging, calling all types of people.

The *second stanza* (vv. 4-6) gives us what is arguably the greatest reason for our praise as it declares two great truths about God:

God is "high above" (v. 4) and "dwells on high" (v. 5). God exists apart from the entire universe He created, and He surpasses all things in quality.

This High One, however, has crouched down (v. 6, "humbles Himself"), or lowered Himself, so He can see what is in Heaven and on earth. That is, He has condescended (to voluntarily descend to the level of persons that God wishes to assist) to intervene in the affairs of people.

The *third stanza* (vv. 7-9) gives two examples of this condescending:

God has a special interest in the poor and needy, and He will exalt them to high places.

The childless women who will be given homes and children that will bring "joy" to their lives are also considered. Some Biblical examples are Sarah, Rachel, and Hannah.

Life stEP The point of this psalm is that the great High One has chosen to look down and graciously deal with our needs and distresses. Consider how God has looked down and blessed your life. Then follow the psalmist's call by spending some time personally praising the Lord!

This second letter by the Apostle Paul to the church at Corinth was written within one year of his first letter. That earlier letter had dealt with numerous problems the church was facing (i.e., divisions, immorality, lawsuits among believers, abuses of the Lord's Supper, confusion over the role of women, heresies about the afterlife, etc.).

Many of these problems were caused by, or at least exacerbated by, carnal, immature behavior (see 1 Corinthians 3). After writing the first letter, Paul found it necessary to make a hurried, painful visit to Corinth since the problems had not yet been resolved (2 Corinthians 2:1; 12:14; 13:1-2).

He followed that visit up with a severe and sorrowful letter (he refers to it in 2:4), which has been lost to us. Some scholars believe the closing chapters (10-13) of 2 Corinthians embody portions of this severe letter, but there is no good manuscript evidence to support this theory. Titus delivered that letter. Unable to meet Titus on his return to Troas, Paul went on to Macedonia, where Titus caught up with him and passed on the good news that a revival had broken out in Corinth.

The Corinthians had repented of their rebelliousness and unrespectful treatment of the apostle. In part, this letter was written as preparation for Paul's third visit to the city. It gives us a more intimate look at Paul's attitude toward his ministry than we find in any other epistle. He wrote the letter to defend himself against the slanderous attacks his enemies raised against him wherever he preached. The accusations were numerous and varied, saying he was carnal, cowardly, undignified, not an original apostle, boastful, deceitful, untrustworthy, and not qualified to teach. Even his sincerity was questioned.

Paul defends himself and his apostolic authority by placing before the church overwhelming evidence of his sincerity in serving God. The result is that this letter is very personal and deeply autobiographical. It has numerous words that express very vividly the pain he faced in endeavoring to minister to these Corinthian believers, such as: affliction, anguish, beating, distress, fasting, fighting, labors, perils, persecutions, sorrow, stripes, sufferings, tears, and weakness. At the same time, because Titus had made Paul aware of the Corinthians' repentance, a tone of joy also prevails throughout the letter.

The word *comfort*, in one form or another, is found more frequently in this letter than in any other of Paul's epistles. Also, such words as *joy, rejoicing*, and *triumph* are also prominent. No other servant of Christ could match the sufferings and achievements recorded in chapters 10, 11, and 12. One writer calls this epistle "one of the most valuable in the New Testament," in part, because of its picture of the Christian ministry, its information on life after death, and its teaching on financial stewardship.

2 Corinthians 1:1-11

What is the writer saying?

How can I apply this to my life?

Paul begins this letter by identifying himself. He is an apostle of Christ Jesus, a position that some had challenged, but he meets the challenge head-on at the outset and will vigorously defend his position in chapters 10-12. He then goes on to open his heart to his readers in this strongly autobiographical epistle. Following some brief salutatory remarks (vv. 1-2), he admits some of his own fears and failings as he tells of sufferings he had endured. Yet in those sufferings, he makes it clear he was not alone, for "the God of all comfort" (v. 3) was there to undergird, support, and deliver him (vv. 8-10). God being the God of all comfort makes it clear that all comfort comes from Him, even if it may come indirectly. In fact, that is part of Paul's emphasis here in these opening verses (vv. 3-4). We (Paul, the Corinthians, and we ourselves) are comforted by God as we go through difficulties and are in need of comfort. This is not simply so we can be made comfortable, but so that we in turn may pass that comfort on to others. In verses 3-7, the word *comfort* is used ten times, sometimes translated *consolation*. It is the same word Jesus used in John 14:16 ("paraclete") of the Holy Spirit, Who stands ever ready at our side to provide comfort when troubles arise. Paul uses the word *tribulation* (v. 4) early and often (used in this letter twelve times) to let readers know troubles will definitely arise. When those times come, Paul's advice is that one's trust is to be placed in God and God alone (vv. 8-11). His advice is not theoretical, but has been nurtured in the crucible of experience (see 11:16-33).

God is the God of all comfort, which means we will be comforted in our struggles. We should also look to comfort to others when they struggle. Remember the ministry of Barnabas to Paul in Acts. His name means "Son of Comfort!"

2 Corinthians 1:12-24

What is the writer saying?

How can I apply this to my life?

Paul now turns his attention to one of the book's key purposes: defending himself against a series of false charges. The first charge he addresses is that of being undependable. It was a charge based on his promise to visit the Corinthians twice (1 Corinthians 16:5; 2 Corinthians 1:15-16), on his way to Macedonia and on his return. The latter had not taken place. His plans, with validity, had changed. He defends his actions, for not only was his personal reputation at stake, but so was the integrity of his message. In his defense, he affirms a clear conscience (v. 12; compare with Acts 23:1) and assures them that his letters were honest and trustworthy, something they will discover when the Lord returns to judge (vv.12-14). In these verses, he makes it clear that his actions and his words were in complete agreement, something these Corinthian believers should be able to acknowledge after having profited earlier from his eighteen-month ministry (Acts 18:11). Having defended his integrity and the integrity of his message, Paul explains why his visit had been delayed (vv. 23-24): "To spare you I came not as yet unto Corinth." It was out of love and concern that he had stayed away. Had he come as originally planned, he would have had to come "with a rod" of correction (1 Corinthians 4:21). Instead, his delay gave the Corinthians time to deal with a matter of discipline, which at that point was still pending, perhaps the immorality issue of 1 Corinthians 5. (Chapter 2 makes it clear that the visit's delay did, in fact, accomplish its purpose. The church had carried out discipline in a biblical manner with positive results.)

Life stEP

Remember that there are two sides to every story. Fellow Christians might have very good reasons for doing what they do. We shouldn't be quick to condemn. On the flip side, we should make sure that our actions are not open to misinterpretation, in order to minimize conflict.

2 Corinthians 2:1-13

What is the writer saying?

How can I apply this to my life?

In these verses Paul further explains the reasoning behind his changed plans. After putting off an earlier visit to spare the Corinthians sorrow, he now wants to visit when his presence will bring them joy. That would be impossible, however, if they had not yet dealt with the discipline problem as instructed by Paul in 1 Corinthians.

But Titus (who had delivered Paul's earlier letter) has returned from Corinth with a positive report (v. 13; 7:6-14): the pending discipline had been dealt with, and the one guilty of sin had been repentant and was now restored to fellowship (vv. 6-8; 7:11-12). With the disciplinary action an accomplished fact, Paul expresses another concern. Just as he did not want them to be lax on discipline, he does not want them to be lax on forgiveness. Although they had been wronged, Paul encourages them to demonstrate genuine love and sincere forgiveness (vv. 8, 10). If they didn't do this, Satan may have been able to generate a spirit of bitterness that would thwart their ministry (v. 11). On the other hand, properly restored fellowship would deal a heavy blow to Satan's schemes and prohibit this incident from driving a wedge between the church and Paul.

In summary, Paul's plans had changed, but he was still thinking of the Corinthian church's well-being. Rather than a stern, distasteful visit, he had sent a letter, which accomplished its purpose. While waiting, Paul did not "rest" easy (v. 13) but was still thinking of the Corinthians.

Life stEP Open sin must be confronted openly. The repenting sinner should be forgiven unconditionally, as Christ also forgives us.

wednesday 4

2 Corinthians 2:14-3:5

What is the writer saying?

How can I apply this to my life?

In these verses, Paul stresses the importance of the ministry of the Word (v. 17) after noting that he had been called to preach the Gospel (v. 12). Chapter 2 concludes with a song of triumph (based on Roman triumphal parades) and contains an important and encouraging truth: the faithful messenger of God's Word is "unto God a sweet savor" (v. 15), not only to them who are saved through that ministry, but also to them that are lost. The thought here is centered on a concept familiar to first-century believers, with the picture of a returning victorious Roman general. Captives in chains both preceded and followed him into the city. Both groups arrived carrying censers with the fragrant odor of incense rising above them. To those in front who were to be set free, it was an aroma of life (similar to the sinner who responds to the fragrance of the Gospel). To those who followed, condemned to die, it was like the stench of death, for they (like the Gospel rejecter) were continuing on the road to destruction. This two-fold consequence of Paul's ministry boggled his mind. He asks, "Who is sufficient for these things" (v. 16)? His answer is found in 2 Corinthians 3:5: God, for no personal sufficiency exists.

Paul notes that some people had corrupted (made merchandise of) the Word of God, but not Paul (v. 17). His ministry was sincere. These corrupters often carried with them epistles of commendation (3:1), or letters of dubious credibility that were unavailable for scrutiny (4:2). Paul came with no paper evidence; his credibility was his Corinthian converts, who were visible for all to see and read about the work of Christ. They were *authored* by Christ, *penned* by Paul using the spiritual *ink* of the Holy Spirit—not on "tables of stone" but on "fleshy tables of the heart" (v. 3).

Life stEP When we share the Gospel, we are inviting people to leave Satan's kingdom and to join the victorious parade of Christ's kingdom.

thursday 4

2 Corinthians 3:6-18

What is the writer saying?

How can I apply this to my life?

pray Honduras – For godly moral leaders to be elected to positions within the government.

Paul's reference to Moses's "tables of stone" (v. 3) was prompted by the opposition of the Judaizers. These people argued that faith in Christ alone was not sufficient for salvation but that the potential believer must also obey the Law of Moses.

Paul counters by explaining the superiority of the new over the old. The old was never given to impart life (or bring salvation); it was a legal document to condemn criminals to death (v. 7). While the Old Testament ministry certainly had its share of God's glory (over Israel in the wilderness and later in the temple), this glory was fading. Paul alludes to this glory being "done away" when he points to Moses's veil experience in Exodus 34. These false teachers were telling people to reject Paul's Gospel of grace (the new glory) and obey the law (which was fading in purpose). In verse 9, Paul says, "If the ministration of condemnation be glory, much more doth the ministration of righteousness exceed in glory." Paul provides a spiritual application for the fading glory of the Law, noting that there is still a veil over the hearts of many Jewish people when they read the Old Testament (vv. 14-15), and this veil keeps them from seeing Christ. When their hearts turn to Christ, the veil is taken away (v. 16). When Moses entered the Lord's presence (Exodus 34:34), his veil was removed. In the new covenant, it is the Spirit who removes the Christians' veils, bringing freedom (v. 17). Under the old covenant there was slavery to the Mosaic system. Now, redeemed from the penalty of the law by believing in Christ alone, people can become children of God (Galatians 4:5-7). This freedom is confirmed by the Spirit, Who enables the believer to call God "Father" (Romans 8:15; Galatians 4:6).

 Life stEP Thank God for lifting the veil of spiritual darkness from your eyes and making you part of His family. Be a light and "sight-giver" to the watching world.

fRiday 4

2 Corinthians 4:1-7

What is the writer saying?

How can I apply this to my life?

pray El Salvador – For those taking Bible correspondence courses to gain a passion for studying the Word.

In verse 18 of yesterday's passage, Paul said the new covenant was glorious because of Christ's certain victory and the Spirit's transforming work. Today, he starts talking about the ministry of this new covenant. While the ministry has great effects (2:15), it also brings difficulties. Paul was physically challenged (4:10), deeply distressed (1:8), and under heavy spiritual demands (7:5), some brought on by those he served (2:4) and some by those he opposed (7:5). But God's mercy and power (vv. 1, 7) kept him going. Once again in this chapter, we find Paul defending himself to a congregation that should have known better as he did before in 2 Corinthians 1:7, 2:17, and 3:1 and will do in 2 Corinthians 6, 7, and 10-13. He makes it clear that as a messenger of truth, he was obliged to conduct himself in truth, perhaps implying that his opponents had no such scruples. Because eternal issues were at stake, only the truth would be acceptable (v. 2).

Paul speaks of the Gospel as being hidden (v. 3), or *veiled* (literally), not only to Israel, but also to all men. It is a veil of unbelief that has been placed there by Satan (the god of this age) (v. 4), and only God can remove it. This veil that covers all people (Isaiah 25:7) and can be penetrated only by the light of God's Word (v. 6). The way that this light is spread, though, is through other people. Like Gideon of old, whose torch was in a pitcher (Judges 7:16-25), "We have this treasure in earthen vessels, that the excellency of the power may be of God, and not of us" (v. 7). In one further rebuke of the false teachers, Paul writes, "For we preach not ourselves, but Christ Jesus the Lord; and ourselves your servants for Jesus' sake" (v. 5).

Life stEP We are the earthen vessels that God uses to carry His light to a world veiled by Satan's lies. How can you be a light today and spread God's truth?

2 Corinthians 4:8-18

What is the writer saying?

How can I apply this to my life?

pray Netherlands Antilles – For a well-staffed body of believers on each of the five islands.

One writer has called these verses "Paul's Hymn of Tribulation." In them he contrasts physical suffering with the glory of the new covenant. Only the Bible can explain how an apparent defeat can become a glorious victory. In these verses, Paul expands what he said in chapter 1. He parallels comments made in 1 Corinthians, when he compared himself and his fellow apostles to men "appointed to death" (1 Corinthians 4:9). In verses 8-9, in describing the demands of the ministry, Paul contrasts human helplessness with divine enablement. The contrasts include both physical (1:8-9; 6:5, 9) and psychological affliction (6:4, 8; 7:5-6), which apart from God's intervention, would have broken Paul (1:8-10). The apostle's response under the pressures he was facing is certainly a strong rebuttal to the charge of his enemies that he was out for personal gain. In spite of all he suffered, he never compromised his message—clear proof of his sincerity as a servant of Jesus Christ and of his unselfish concern for the churches.

Paul and his co-workers were often in imminent danger of being slain by their foes (even as Jesus was), yet on many occasions, they were wonderfully delivered by the Lord (see Acts 23:11). And so he writes, "Death works in us, so that life may work in you" (v. 12). He was willing to go anywhere and endure anything if it brought glory to God and good to the churches. Paul's unswerving commitment was the result of his living in the light of eternity (vv. 16-18), evaluating everything by eternity's yardstick. Note the contrasts in verses 16-18: outward/inward, light/weight, moment/eternal. Verse 18 is a paradox to the unbeliever but a wonderful truth to the believer who "walks by faith, not by sight" (5:7).

Paul lived with eternity's values in view making God's way his lifestyle. How can you live with your eyes on eternity today?

sunday 5

2 Corinthians 5:1-10

What is the writer saying?

How can I apply this to my life?

pray France – For godly elected officials who will provide leadership to a government and a country at an important crossroads.

To the one who walks *by sight,* there is much in this passage that is less than clear. To the one who walks *by faith* (v. 7), one thing becomes crystal clear: the believer does not have to fear death, for death can only touch the body since it has been abolished by the Savior (2 Timothy 1:10). Paul develops the assurance of immortality as he contrasts a tent or tabernacle, which is temporary, with a temple, which is solid and permanent. Remember what Paul said in chapter 4. He referred to his outward man (his body) as perishing (v. 16). Now he compares his body to an earthly house in the process of being dissolved (v. 1). But when that happens, the replacement is far better—"a house not made with hands [like the tent was], eternal in the heavens" (v. 1). Groaning (vv. 2, 4) will come to an end; being "burdened" (v. 4) will be replaced by joy (Luke 6:21; 1 Corinthians 15:51-55); and that which is mortal will be swallowed up by life (v. 4). Paul considered his present life to be like nakedness (v. 3): a life marked by humiliation and frustration. Instead he focused on eternal things. For the believer, death is simply a doorway into a more abundant life. So, if in our bodies we are crushed by persecution (4:8-9), who cares? All that does is send us home to Heaven sooner (v. 8). When Paul says "wherefore we labor" in verse 9, he is then saying that since we are living to one day be with Christ, our aim now is to please Him, whether here or there. The "judgment seat of Christ" (v. 10) is where we will be judged for whether we have done "good" (worthwhile) or "bad" (worthless) things on earth (v. 10). The judgment for our sin has already been taken care of, but God looks to reward us for serving Him.

 Life stEP Missionary C. T. Studd said, "Only one life, 'twill soon be past; only what's done for Christ will last." We must live *with eternity's values in view* if we desire a good evaluation at the judgment seat of Christ.

monday 5

2 Corinthians 5:11-21

What is the writer saying?

How can I apply this to my life?

pray Panama – For youth ministry workers to commit their time, creativity, and love to Christ's use.

This fifth chapter describes the seriousness of the ministry in terms of its motivation and responsibilities. The prospect of appearing at the judgment seat (v. 10), and the grave responsibility of carrying the message of reconciliation to men (v. 18), should drive us to a life of unceasing service. That was true with Paul. His commitment to his calling was so intense that he was looked at as crazy. (Compare verse 13 with his actions: facing a riotous mob (Acts 19:30); returning to the scene of a stoning (Acts 14); his words (2 Corinthians 11:23); the reactions of others (Acts 26:24).) What motivated Paul? At the top of the list would be "the love of Christ" (v. 14). That love *constrained* him (constricted or controlled him, like a mountain stream squeezed into a narrow gorge— such streams have great power). It was not his love for Christ, but Christ's love through him (as a channel) that drove Paul on. Christ's love was a love for dead sinners that took Him to Calvary. Those who were given life by His act could then live for Him (vv. 14-15). The way we live for Him is to carry out "the ministry of reconciliation" (vv. 18-19) in a selfless manner. From Paul's conversion on, he no longer evaluated people on the basis of externals, something his opponents did (v. 12). From the time of his wonderful conversion experience on (Acts 9:1-20), he looked at every man as either saved or lost, headed either to Heaven or Hell, as part of the new creation or old (v. 17). That perspective caused Paul to accept his new role as an "ambassador for Christ" with great passion, begging the lost to be reconciled to God (v. 20). He summarized his message in verse 21: Christ was made sin for us that we might become the righteousness of God in Him.

Life stEP After looking at Christ's intense love for him, all Paul wanted to do was share with others how they could become right with God, just as he had. How can you share this with those around you today?

2 Corinthians 6:1-10

What is the writer saying?

How can I apply this to my life?

 pray Canada – Pray for Bible institute ministry teams to have a lasting impact in local churches.

In verses 1-2, Paul addresses the urgency of the need to tell others about Christ (compare John 4:24-38). Here, the "day of salvation" refers to this present age of opportunity (the Church Age). If those who have come to know the grace of God through salvation do not *seize the day*, then in effect, God's grace, which has already been bestowed upon us and is waiting for our acceptance, will have been in vain (v. 1; compare 1 Corinthians 15:10-11).

In verses 3-10, Paul defends his ministry (not himself). He knew, of course, that the message of the cross would offend many (2:16; 1 Corinthians 1:18), and he knew that many considered him a fool (11:16). But he worked to live in such a way that his conduct wouldn't dishonor God or cause a fellow believer to stumble (compare 1 Corinthians 8:9). In verses 4-5, he notes that as servants and ministers of God, he and his co-workers had demonstrated much patience or endurance, something that should have commended them to their Corinthian brothers (3:1; 5:12). Here he lists nine testings: three beyond the control of the servant of Christ; three brought on by Satan; and three which the servant willingly takes on himself in order to further the work of Christ. He follows those nine testings with inner qualities or characteristics of a true servant. Then he outlines nine paradoxes, the positive side of which he claims for himself as a minister of the Gospel. Not every servant of Christ has to go through all these things, but all who want to be used by God and found faithful must be willing to encounter these things if needed. Chapter 11 shows that Paul knew what he was talking about because he had experienced many of these testings.

Life **stEP** Faithfulness in spite of obstacles is what the Lord is looking for in His servants. He found faithfulness in Paul; what will He find in you?

wednesday 5

2 Corinthians 6:11-7:1

What is the writer saying?

How can I apply this to my life?

pray Japan – For this country's youth to turn from drugs and materialistic pleasures to the living God.

Paul deals here with the critical issue of separation between Christians and the rest of the world. His appeal begins, "Be ye not unequally yoked together with unbelievers" (v. 14). This is Scripture's strongest appeal to the separated life. It reminds us of the prohibition in Deuteronomy 22:10, "Thou shalt not plow with an ox and an ass together." While today's believer is not under the Law, the application is clear. There is to be no yoking—the joining of people together for any intense or prolonged activity—of the believer with an unbeliever. The applications of this command are manifold. Certainly it applies to marriage. Other areas would be business relations, and even close friendships. All have the potential of dwarfing one's spiritual life and damaging or watering down one's testimony. Paul then asks five questions, all of which demonstrate the foolishness of the unequal yoke (vv. 14-16). The contrasts in the questions should be carefully noted. They are opposites and will never result in harmony. These verses emphasize the main reason a Christian must be separate: if that Christian is truly aiming to believe in and follow Christ, someone not pursuing Christ will not help the Christian's quest (and may harm it). Furthermore, since the believer is the temple of God (v. 16) and the object of numerous promises from God (vv. 16, 18), he must take care to keep his temple clean. Because some of the Corinthian believers were apparently caught up in this unacceptable practice, Paul adds to his earlier command by saying, "Come out from among them, and be ye separate" (v. 17). The seventh chapter begins with the same theme. He challenges them with holiness, the positive side of separation.

Life stEP Do you have any relationships that violate the "unequally yoked" warning? Ask God to show you how to change those dangerous relationships to honor Him or, if possible, graciously break from them.

2 Corinthians 7:2-16

What is the writer saying?

How can I apply this to my life?

pray   Bolivia – That redeeming love will break the long-held bondage to idolatry and superstition.

Paul had given the Corinthians excellent spiritual guidance in 1 Corinthians. Prior to visiting them again, he sent Titus ahead to see if his advice had been taken. Titus returned with good news: the Corinthians had received and acted on the advice. This brought Paul much comfort (v. 4), and he once again opens his heart to the Corinthians and repeats his request of 2 Corinthians 6:13 for a similar response. He denies the charges brought against him (v. 2) and assures them that because of his love for them, he does not condemn them for believing these charges (v. 3). Instead, he writes, "I am exceeding joyful" (v. 4, 7). Prior to the comfort brought by the report of Titus, Paul wondered if his earlier rebuke had been too severe. But their repentance made him glad he had written. Even though it caused temporary sorrow, it was a "godly sorrow," the kind that produces a repentance that seeks to make things right, as opposed to a "sorrow of the world" that is simply a feeling of shame in being found out (v. 10). The repentance had brought a restoration of fellowship, which was Paul's real reason for lovingly rebuking them. Failure to deal with the matter could have been devastating, for a "little leaven leaveneth the whole lump" (1 Corinthians 5:6). How grateful Paul was for their positive response! He closes the chapter by stating his confidence in their complete loyalty.

Life stEP   Although the rebuke of a Christian brother, and the repentance involved in returning to Christ, may be difficult, it is much worse to not deal with sin. Is there sin in your life—or that of a struggling brother—that needs to be addressed today?

fRiday 5

2 Corinthians 8:1-15

What is the writer saying?

How can I apply this to my life?

pray   Dominican Republic – To escape occultism's bondage by responding to the call of the Holy Spirit.

In chapters 8 and 9, with an assist from 1 Corinthians 16, Paul develops the biblical doctrine of Christian stewardship. Putting it in context, he directs the attention of the Corinthians to a collection for the poor in Jerusalem, which he had been organizing for several years (see Galatians 2:10; Romans 15:25-28). The Corinthians heard of his efforts and asked how to be involved (1 Corinthians 16:1). His answer produced good intentions but no action, so Paul sent Titus to check things out (v. 6). These two chapters develop Paul's encouragement to follow through. He uses the churches of Macedonia to illustrate sacrificial, biblical giving. His instruction was heeded, and the financial needs were met (compare Romans 15:26; Acts 24:17). In this passage, Paul develops the principle that giving is a grace-gift of God (vv. 4, 6-7, 19)—because man is basically selfish, he doesn't give unless God gives him the grace to do so.

The Macedonians demonstrated liberality of the most sacrificial type, giving out of deep poverty, not because they were commanded to do so, but out of their own free will. Paul encourages a similar response from the Corinthians, as a demonstration of their sincere love (vv. 7-8). Paul then gives a second illustration: Christ, although rich, became poor for the Corinthians' sake (v. 9). He urges a faithful follow-through of their earlier promise (vv. 10-11). God does not expect us to give what we don't have (v. 12), but He does expect us to give in proportion to how He has allowed us to prosper. Paul explains that at this time, out of "abundance," the Corinthians could help meet the needs of the Jerusalem saints. The day may come when their roles may be reversed (v. 14).

Life stEP   Many of God's struggling servants could be blessed if we give as sacrificially with our money as they sacrificially give themselves.

2 Corinthians 8:16-24

What is the writer saying?

How can I apply this to my life?

Ethical handling of donated money is very important. Rightly or wrongly, it is easy to be accused of mishandling funds. Paul wanted to be blameless in this matter (v. 20), so he writes: "Providing for honest things, not only in the sight of the Lord, but also in the sight of men" (v. 21). Taking his own advice, he assigned the task of handling the funds to three men: Titus, a man gifted with administrative skills (check out his assignment in Crete, Titus 1:5-16), and two others, one possibly being Luke. Whether Luke or not, the phrase "in the Gospel" (v. 18) probably means he was a well-known preacher and worker in the church. Along with a third individual (v. 22), these three acted as *trustees* of the money to ensure complete propriety in its handling. Paul believed they could be counted on to follow through (v. 22c). He gives a written credential for Titus and his fellow trustees: Titus was Paul's "partner and fellow-helper," but even more than that, with the other two individuals, a messenger of the church (v. 23). Paul closes with an appeal to the Corinthians for "proof of your love," which, of course, would be the church wholeheartedly supporting of the offering, something Paul had boasted about earlier. Now was the time to deliver (v. 24).

Life stEP Something as simple as keeping the books was a big testimony to the character of Titus and the two trustees, who Paul stood behind because he knew they had character—that they would do the right thing when no one was looking. How does your character stack up against these guys—are you faithful to do right when you're not being watched?

2 Corinthians 9:1-15

What is the writer saying?

How can I apply this to my life?

pray Bermuda – For teens to mature and develop godly leadership skills through Bible clubs.

In chapter 8, Paul developed some Christian-giving principles. Now he notes three promises that are there to be claimed by faithful stewards. Note that nearly one-sixth of this book (two of thirteen chapters) is given over to stewardship in general and the care of those in need in particular. In challenging the Corinthians to be faithful in following through on their earlier commitment, Paul lets them know that their giving should be cheerful and purposeful, not entered into "grudgingly, or of necessity" (v. 7). **Promise One** (vv. 1-5): the giving of the Corinthians would be an encouragement to the churches of Macedonia, whose giving had earlier encouraged them (8:1-5). Hebrews 10:24 urges believers to provoke one another to good works; Paul notes that a faithful follow-through by the Corinthians in this special offering would do exactly that. But failure to do so would bring shame to both him (for boasting of their faithfulness) and them (for failing to follow through on their pledge). **Promise Two** (vv. 6-11): faithfulness in stewardship will bring a bountiful harvest (v. 6). This harvest can be summed up in the comprehensiveness of the *alls* of verse 8: "all grace…all sufficiency… all things…every good work." Such "bountifulness" results in thanksgiving to God through the giver (v. 11). **Promise Three** (vv. 12-15): proper giving not only "supplieth the want of the saints," but brings glory to God (vv. 12-13). Paul then closes this chapter with a doxology: "Thanks be unto God for his unspeakable [indescribable] gift" (v. 15). While not specifying what that gift is, it is most likely a reference to the person and work of Christ, and the salvation (and much more) that He provided for those who receive Him.

These two chapters teach us that giving—systematic, generous, proportionate, and cheerful giving motivated by a heart of gratitude—is to be a positive habit in the life of the believer. Is that a habit you have?

ɱoɴday 6

2 Corinthians 10:1-18

What is the writer saying?

How can I apply this to my life?

pray Pray for the President of the United States to submit to the wisdom and guidance of the Holy Spirit.

The final section of 2 Corinthians begins here. These chapters (10-13) are intensely personal, for in them Paul vigorously defends his apostolic authority, which has been challenged by those who both slandered his ministry and misrepresented his character. His attitude in doing so, however, was not one of retaliation, but rather of "meekness and gentleness" (v. 1). His defense here in chapter 10 revolves around the charge that his presence was weak while his letters were powerful—a cowardly charge that was only "bold" from a distance. Paul's response is that he is far more interested in winning the hearts of his hearers than simply vanquishing his opponents, although that was also necessary. He answers that his meekness (not weakness, but power under control) is one that follows the example of Christ (v. 1). His critics, apparently Hebrew people (11:22),

behaved just the opposite, adopting haughty attitudes and claiming a higher authority than Paul (v. 7). Furthermore, Paul used spiritual weapons (vv. 2-6) to accomplish God's work, not the carnal methods employed by his opponents. He did walk "in the flesh" (the human body with its limitations), but he did not *war* in the flesh (see Ephesians 6:10-12), something his critics were doing. Paul continues by challenging his readers not to judge by outward appearance (vv. 7-11), for that is superficial. *Look at the facts*, Paul says, *and especially, at me. I've got nothing to hide. I belong to Christ, and I've been called by Him to preach the Gospel* (Galatians 1:1, 12; Ephesians 4:11-12). Finally, let God, not self, be the commender (vv. 12-18).

The battle between those living for God's purposes and those living for themselves (spiritual warfare) is not always "fair," by human standards, in this life. Those following God will often seem to get the "short end." What God is concerned with, though, is that we meet these attacks as Christ and Paul did—with *meekness* and *gentleness*.

tuesday 6

2 Corinthians 11:1-15

What is the writer saying?

How can I apply this to my life?

pray Cuba – For more Bibles, books, and teachers to train the leaders and pastors.

Paul's defense of his person and ministry continues. False teachers had looked to undermine him in an effort to lead the Corinthians away from the simple Gospel message. To combat their efforts, he had to assert his apostolic authority in a manner personally uncomfortable—that of boasting. He calls his procedure "folly" and asks his readers to bear with him (v. 1). His opponents had bragged so forcefully about their supposed attainments that a counter-attack was necessary because, if his credibility could be damaged, his message would be rejected in favor of that of his enemies' message. Paul sarcastically calls these false teachers *super-apostles* (v. 5), for they claimed to be superior to all others. Their error is threefold: (1) preaching a Jesus not identical to the historical Jesus Paul preached; (2) insisting on the reception of a spirit other than the Holy Spirit; and (3) proclaiming a different Gospel (v. 4). (Compare these false teachers

with the Judaizers of Galatians 1:6-9.) Paul's defense was that his abilities were not inferior to his rivals (v. 5), and while his speech may not have been eloquent, he had earned the right to deliver his message because of his life and ministry (v. 6). His motives, unlike theirs, were not suspect. Paul then notes the personal sacrifice he had made to minister to the Corinthians, even *robbing* other churches to do so (v. 8). By not accepting a salary, he removed one of the charges his enemies could have used—that he was in it for the money (v. 12), something they were, in fact, guilty of. Paul then identified his opponents for who they really were: false prophets, deceitful wolves in sheep's clothing (see Acts 20:29-30), under Satan's control, seeking to devour the flock they pretended to care for.

The Gospel message must be protected at all costs. For Paul, it included going against his natural inclinations and boasting. Can you convincingly explain why you do the ministry-related things that you do?

2 Corinthians 11:16-33

What is the writer saying?

How can I apply this to my life?

Paul's defense continues. He once again apologizes for his "foolishness" in bragging (v. 16). He did not want to appear immodest and notes that Christ had never indulged Himself in such a practice (v. 17). But the nature of the charges and the damage they could cause forced him to respond. His manner, however, was quite different than that of his critics. They boasted of their supposed *qualifications*; he talked about his apparent failures, weaknesses, frustrations, and sufferings (v. 21). These verses hint at the origin and claims of his rivals. They were of Jewish blood and claimed to be loyal to the Law. They spoke as "Hebrews"; uncontaminated by Gentile culture, they were "Israelites" (implying spiritual-mindedness), and were of the "seed of Abraham" (v. 22). Paul makes it clear that he takes a back seat in none of these areas. By birth and by training, he was as fully a Jew as any of his opponents, or even more

so. In verses 23-33, he catalogues the hardships and sufferings he experienced in carrying out his ministry. He had earned his title to apostleship. Through his sufferings, which had elevated him above the class of his critics, who had never suffered for Christ like he had. The list of dangers he endured makes it clear that there was no end to the lengths to which he would go to deliver the Gospel message. On top of all that, there was the added daily burden of the churches he ministered to (v. 28), which had problems such as heresy (Galatia), dissension and immorality (Corinth), and confusion (Thessalonica). Paul closes this section by calling God as his witness. The Lord Himself would affirm that the record just noted was the truth. Paul said so earlier (1:23) and will again (1 Timothy 2:7).

Ministry often carries a heavy price tag. People often shoot the messenger when they dislike the message. Brace yourself, but make sure it is the message, and not the messenger, who is offensive!

thursday 6

2 Corinthians 12:1-10

What is the writer saying?

How can I apply this to my life?

pray   Canada – For youth living in a country with the third highest youth suicide rate in the world to find hope in Christ.

Paul's uncomfortable but necessary boasting continues. In verses 1-6, he speaks of a personal experience of being caught up into Heaven and given unspeakable revelations. He had experienced visions and revelations on various occasions, often for encouragement and guidance in his ministry (compare Acts 16:9; 18:9-10; 22:17-18). Some writers think this experience took place at Lystra when Paul was stoned and left for dead (Acts 14:19-20), suggesting that "whether in the body, or out of the body, I cannot tell" (v. 3) means Paul didn't know whether or not he actually died at Lystra. The important truth is this: there is a Heaven, and it is a place of conscious, rational existence. Paul does not "glory," or capitalize, on this great experience. Instead, in humility, he glories in his infirmities (v. 5) and identifies one of them as his "thorn in the flesh" (v. 7). While many suggestions have been made for what this "thorn" could be, the most probable candidate is an eye ailment. Supernaturally blinded at conversion (Acts 9:9), it is possible there were lingering after-effects (see Galatians 4:15; 6:11). Regardless of what it was, this thorn's presence was proof of Paul's revelational experience, noted earlier in the chapter. This teaches us that the Christian life is not promised to be thornless, but that when the thorns come, God has a purpose in them and power over them. No matter how difficult they may be, God's grace is always sufficient (vv. 9-10).

Life stEP   In 1 Corinthians 11:1, Paul encouraged his readers to imitate him. When the *thorns* come, anticipate and thank the Lord for His sufficiency, and "count it all joy" (James 1:2).

friday 6

2 Corinthians 12:11-21

What is the writer saying?

How can I apply this to my life?

pray Ecuador – For those in authority to deal honestly, to resist social bribery, and to receive Christ.

Paul's *boasting* now comes to an end. He acknowledges once again that he had "become a fool" in doing so, but he had no choice. Since the Corinthians had not defended him, he was "compelled" to act so. They saw in his ministry "the signs of an apostle" (vv. 11-12) and should have immediately provided defensive support. His claim was legitimate—in no way was he *inferior to* the self-styled *super-apostles* or false teachers. All were forced to acknowledge that he had performed miracles—"signs, and wonders, and mighty deeds," all of which are evidences of divine power, and demonstrate apostolic authority (compare Acts 2:22; Hebrews 2:4). Paul did not claim to have done these works in his own strength, but indicated they were God's endorsement of his ministry. No such claim could be made by the false teachers.

Paul's defense concludes with another shot, somewhat left-handed and sarcastic, at his critics. He begs the pardon of his readers for not having been a "burden" to them (vv. 13-14, 16). Although he certainly exercised his apostolic gifts among them in an unusual way, he refrained from exercising the apostolic right of demanding support. His rivals apparently had no such scruples and were commending themselves in order to extract funds. Paul's selfless ministry to the Corinthians was a demonstration of his love. He closes this section (vv. 19-21) by making it plain that he is not writing in this manner simply to defend himself but rather for their help and edification (v. 19). When he visits, he doesn't want to find a situation rife with discord and dissension. His encouragement is meant for them to deal with sin. If they didn't, he would be forced to do so (vv. 20-21).

 Life stEP Paul's ministry demonstrated the seal of God's approval. While signs, wonders, and mighty deeds are not promised today, the evidence of God's hand on one's ministry should be obvious to all.

2 Corinthians 13:1-14

What is the writer saying?

How can I apply this to my life?

The letter closes with Paul warning that when he comes, he will, if necessary, exert apostolic authority, and those who have sinned will be judged. His critics had charged him with weakness; he was ready to disprove that charge. They questioned his apostleship, wanting proof he was Christ's spokesman (v. 3). Instead, they should have examined themselves, checking the authenticity of their own salvation. They seemed to have forgotten that if they were true believers, Christ would dwell in them (v. 5). If they weren't, they were "reprobates" —discredited, having failed the test—and were counterfeit Christians. Paul makes it clear (v. 6) that he does not fit in that category, for he has *passed the test*. In verses 7-10, Paul's heart concern for the Corinthians comes to the surface. He wants them to understand him and know that the only motive behind his behavior was his love for them. He wants his visit to be one of edification (building up); not one of "sharpness," leading to "destruction," or tearing down (v. 10). The book closes with some brief exhortational words of cheer. "Farewell" calls the Corinthians to rejoice. "Be perfect" means fully equipped, complete. "Be of good comfort" reflects his opening words in 2 Corinthians 1:3-7. "Live in peace" is an all-inclusive word for peace; it presupposes purity, an indispensable condition of power. Paul declares that the result of such behavior will be that "the God of love and peace shall be with you" (v. 11). In the conclusion, Paul takes us from Bethlehem ("grace"—He became poor for us); to Calvary ("the love of God"); to Pentecost ("the communion of the Holy Spirit"—baptizing all believers into the body of Christ).

Life stEP Despite the Corinthian church being divisive, immature, and unspiritual, Paul was always looking to encourage its members and point them back to truth and repentance. How can you point struggling Christians you know toward the truth? Are you showing an attitude of love?

First and Second Samuel are important Old Testament books. The two books were originally one but were divided when they were translated from Hebrew into Greek, simply because the Greek words take more space. Although not attributed to a specific author, tradition says they are the work of, first, Samuel, and then of the prophets, Nathan and Gad (1 Chronicles 29:29).

The book of Judges ends about 1100 B.C., after some 300 years in Israel's Promised Land. The final four chapters of Judges tell of the sad spiritual and moral state of Israel, which had cut loose and drifted far from its ancient moorings. 1 Samuel begins there and carries Israel's history forward another ninety years (to the death of Saul, 1010 B.C.) with the key purpose of telling the story of how Samuel and David, with help from the Lord, piloted Israel back to its anchorage in God.

The book divides into three parts according to its leading characters:

Part 1 (chaps. 1-8) centers on Samuel, the last of the judges and the first of the prophets. Although Abraham (Genesis 20:7), Moses (Deuteronomy 34:10), and others were called prophets, the Lord chose Samuel to institute the office of prophets (Acts 3:24; Hebrews 11:32).

This part includes Samuel's family background, beginning with his mother Hannah's remarkable prayer of praise and prophecy. It tells of his training under the high priest, Eli, who apparently was also a judge of Israel (1 Samuel 4:18). It tells of the capture of the Ark of the Covenant by the Philistines and its return to Israel and ends with the people's demand for a king.

Part 2 (chaps. 9-15) presents Saul, *Israel's first king*. The story tells of Saul's successes and failures in a time of constant warfare.

Samuel, *the last judge*, continues as an important part of the story, as the first of a *new type of prophet* that would function as a divine messenger and counselor to the kings of Israel (and later Judah).

Part 3 (chaps. 16-31) spotlights the history of David, *Israel's most famous king*, before he received the kingdom. It tells of his family, his anointing as king, his valor in battle, his life in the royal court of Saul, his marriage, and his years as a fugitive. The familiar stories of his triumph over Goliath and his friendship with Jonathan are included in this part. Also recorded here are the deaths of Samuel, Saul, and Jonathan.

Time Period Covered by 1 Samuel:

A. 1 Samuel begins with the birth of Samuel, about 1100 B.C.

B. 1 Samuel (25:1) notes Samuel's death, about 1020 B.C.

C. 1 Samuel tells of David's anointing and early trials, about 1028 B.C.

D. 1 Samuel ends with the death of Saul, in 1010 B.C.

1 Samuel 1:1-18

What is the writer saying?

How can I apply this to my life?

pray Bulgaria – Outreach to Turk and Gypsy men who are largely unemployed and enslaved by alcohol.

Samuel's father, Elkanah, was a Levite who served the tribe of Ephraim (v. 1). Our text points out that Elkanah had "two wives" (v. 2). While in the ancient world most men had only one wife, the likely reason Elkanah acquired his second wife was that Hannah was barren (v. 2). Note that after Elkanah finally had children, the fulfilled life and happiness he sought still evaded him. Instead of satisfaction, he was vexed with a divided home and a sense of guilt, which he sought to overcome by giving Hannah "double" gifts. Yet this favoritism caused Peninnah to become an "adversary" or rival who "provoked" Hannah to tears (vv. 6-7). Look at the way Hannah responded (vv. 6-7, 10-11, 15-16).

When Elkanah noticed that Hannah was not eating at the family's sacrificial feast in Shiloh near the tabernacle (v. 7), he gently rebukes her (v. 8) for her lack of thankfulness to the Lord. This appears to cause Hannah to consider her own self-absorbed conduct. She leaves the family's feast (v. 9) and goes back to the tabernacle, Israel's house of prayer, to redirect her grief in prayer to God (v. 10). Here she has an encounter with Eli, the priest (vv. 12-17). The encounter ends with Eli's assurance that the Lord would answer prayer (v. 17).

In her prayer, Hannah displays a modest and humble spirit. We see that she prays in hope of mercy with a quiet voice in a public place; she is praying only to God. She also makes a solemn vow to the Lord, that if He would give her a son, she would give up that son in service to God (v. 11). She includes in her vow that the child would be raised as a Nazarite.

Life **stEP** Hannah suffered grief because God had a special purpose for her and her son Samuel. How can you redirect grief in your life by prayer? Can you say with the Psalmist, "It is good for me that I have been afflicted," and "thou in faithfulness hast afflicted me" (119:71, 75)?

1 Samuel 1:19-2:11

What is the writer saying?

How can I apply this to my life?

pray Columbia – Pray for the safety and accuracy of those participating in Bible translation projects.

Samuel means "asked of the Lord." When Samuel is three years old, Hannah and Elkanah bring a special offering for their son's dedication as a Nazarite.

We note that Elkanah responds to his wife's request in verse 22 with the words, "only the Lord establishes *His word*" (v. 23b). This is a statement of hope that the words of Eli, "God grant you your petition" (v. 17), be not just partially fulfilled (by their child's birth) but that God would completely fulfill Hannah's prayer—that Samuel would serve the Lord "all the days of his life" as a faithful and godly Nazarite, fully dedicated to God. This, of course, was in contrast with the "very great" sin (2:17) of the morally worthless (2:12) sons of Eli—Hophni and Phinehas (v. 3)—who were priests at the Tabernacle.

Chapter 2 begins with Hannah's *prayer of rejoicing*, which is both her personal testimony and a song of thanksgiving to the Lord. Hannah's testimony is, "mine horn is exalted in the Lord" (2:1). She is remembering her defenseless condition before Peninnah, Elkanah's second wife (1:6-7), when Hannah was like a *hornless* and thus like a *threatened* cow. Since God has answered her prayers, she is now like a cow with *horns*; able to defend herself against her "adversary." It is important to note here that Jesus, our Messiah, is given the name, *horn of our salvation* (2 Samuel 22:3; Luke 1:69) because of the strength and defense He provides for those that seek Him!

While Hannah was praying, the Lord empowered her to prophesy about the coming Messiah (2:10; Matthew 25:31-32). She becomes the first to refer to him as the "anointed" one, which is the same as the New Testament "Christ" (John 1:41; see also Psalm 18:2, 75:10)!

When you are troubled by the hard things of life, do you find strength through prayer to the *Horn of your Salvation*, the Lord Jesus? How can He give you strength and defense against your adversaries?

1 Samuel 3:1-21

What is the writer saying?

How can I apply this to my life?

pray Brazil – For many to accept Christ through the ministry of Christian concerts and musical dramas.

Time has passed (see 2:26; compare to 3:19; Luke 2:52), and Samuel is about twelve when he receives his first assignment as a prophet of the Lord.

The assigned task was not a pleasant one (v. 15). The Lord was not speaking directly to Eli because Eli had been derelict in his duties as priest and the father of priests. He had been confronted earlier by a prophet (2:27), who had warned him of coming judgment upon his household (see 2:31-34 and 3:11-14). Now the Lord (v. 18), through Samuel, tells Eli that God's judgment had come.

"And the word of the LORD was precious in those days" (v. 1). "Precious" is used elsewhere to refer to *precious gems* and *costly* building materials. Here it is means "valued," yet sadly "rare."

"The LORD was with him (Samuel), and did let none of his words fall to the ground" (v. 19). A key insight from this passage is our seeing what character traits made up Samuel's "Here am I" (vv. 4-6, and 8) attitude:

Even as a young child, Samuel *ministered* (2:11, 18—to *serve* as a domestic servant). Note the contrast to Eli's own sons (2:12, 17) who only *served* their own greed and lust.

Notice Samuel's eagerness to serve, even when called in the middle of the night (v. 5).

Even though Samuel lay awake the rest of the night (v. 15), in the morning he was still faithful to his daily chores!

Notice that the whole country knew that Samuel was "established" as a "prophet of the LORD" (v. 20) in part because the Lord continued to minister to Samuel (v. 21).

Life stEP Perhaps we should ask ourselves: (1) Is the Word of God evident in our lives as it was in Samuel's? (2) Do we have Samuel's "here am I" attitude when God wants to direct us into His service?

1 Samuel 6:1-15

What is the writer saying?

How can I apply this to my life?

Since today's passage jumps ahead in the story, let's begin with an overview. Chapter four tells of a great defeat of Israel—the capture of the ark of God and the death of Eli and his two wicked sons (see 2:12-18). Chapter five tells of the Philistines bringing the ark of God to the temple of their god, Dagon. While the Philistines intended to display of ark as a trophy of Dagon's victory, the true God of Heaven instead showed them (5:1-6) that He was not a defeated god hiding in the ark!

And so today's passage begins with the Philistines asking their priests and diviners (6:2) how they should deal with the ark, which they now feared as the cause of their problems.

The diviners first advised that, in order to avert further judgments by this angry God, they were to give a "trespass offering" of gold to the God in the box (vv. 3-4). Second, they were, in effect, to ask God a yes-or-no question: Should we send You home to Israel? This was done by setting up a situation where the Lord would have to direct the mother cows carrying the ark back to Israel. Untrained cows would have been frightened by the "yoke"; would not leave their suckling calves; and would wander about, not go directly back to Israel (vv. 7-8). Notice the definite results observed by the Philistine to this diviner's test; the cows took the "straight way" (v. 12) back to Israel!

While Scripture teaches that we are not to use such methods as used by these "diviners," God will continue to deal with people who do not know Him to convince them that their sins have angered Him. How can you be God's ambassador to such people, who are fearful of God's judgment? God has provided a way, through the Lord Jesus, so that you can tell them how to receive God's forgiveness and salvation!

1 Samuel 7:1-17

What is the writer saying?

How can I apply this to my life?

pray Chile – For the perseverance of Chilean saints as only 38% attend church regularly.

Our chapter begins with the moving of the ark to Kirjath-Jearim (a town in the tribal area of Benjamin, eight miles northwest of Jerusalem). It will remain here for some seventy-five years, until King David moves it to Jerusalem (2 Samuel 6). Apparently, the Philistines had also taken and destroyed Shiloh, forcing Israel to relocate the tabernacle after the death of Eli to the town of Nob (1 Samuel 21—located four miles northeast of Jerusalem).

In verse 2, Israel is lamenting (to weep and mourn) for twenty years while the ark was being kept in the house of Abinadab. During this time Samuel grows from a boy to young man and enters into his ministry as Israel's last judge. At this time, we could say that Samuel was preaching his first sermon (v. 3).

The people lived in fear of another attack by the Philistines (v. 7). Samuel promised the people that the Lord would protect them, if they turned from their idols to Him with all their hearts.

To prepare their hearts, Samuel called a prayer meeting where the people poured out water before the Lord and fasted (v. 6). This symbolized the pouring out of their sorrow over their sin. The result was the Lord gave them a great victory over the Philistines (vv. 10-11).

Next, Samuel, wanting to teach the people the Word of God, starts a teaching/preaching circuit (v. 16), going from city to city to administer governmentally and minister spiritually to the needs of the people.

If Samuel was with you today, would he have to address things from which you need to turn away so that you can, with all your heart, serve the Lord only? You may not keep a golden statuette of Ashtoreth (v. 4) in your room, but what interests in your life have become idols that turn your attention away from God?

friday 7

1 Samuel 8:1-22

What is the writer saying?

How can I apply this to my life?

pray   Finland – For the hopelessness that pervades society to be replaced by the joy of salvation.

The elders of Israel present three reasons to Samuel for wanting a king (v. 5):

Samuel was "old," and the elders were worried about the nation's future (under Samuel they had enjoyed "peace"— see 7:13-14).

Samuel (not the Lord) had appointed his own sons to be "judges over Israel" (v. 1), even though they "did not walk in his ways" (v. 2).

The elders wanted a government with a king, like other countries.

Samuel was displeased with the request of the elders. So he prayed to the Lord (v. 6). The Lord told him their demand for a king was a rejection of the Lord's reign over them (v. 7) and His ability to raise up righteous leaders to guide them. Samuel was to give in to their demands after warning how life would be under the rule of a king (vv. 11-18).

Refusing to heed Samuel's warnings, the people still wanted a king (vv. 19-20). As with their fathers before them, God "gave them their request, but sent leanness into their soul" (Psalm 106:15).

In Deuteronomy 17:14 the Lord told Moses the time would come when Israel would want a king so they could be "like all the nations." So the Lord gave instructions for such a king. In particular, the Lord would do the choosing of their king (Deuteronomy 17:15). Importantly, the king was to obtain a copy of God's Word. He was to "read therein all the days of his life: that he may learn to fear the LORD his God, to keep all the words…to do them" (17:19). The point was this: regardless of who is ruling, God wants a leader to be a godly person who ruled His way.

Life stEP

The real issue here is whether God's people choose to walk by faith or by sight (2 Corinthians 5:7; Colossians 2:6). People want a visible leader. It is more desirable to follow a person they can idolize, with all of his human errors, than an all-powerful but invisible God. "But without faith it is impossible to please Him" (Hebrews 11:6).

saturday 7

1 Samuel 9:1-3, 15-27

What is the writer saying?

How can I apply this to my life?

pray Costa Rica – For the growth and strengthening of Bible schools that train leadership.

Our passage introduces us to **Saul**. Handsome and tall, he was from an eminent family of the tribe of Benjamin, yet he was unknown in Israel.

Verses 3-14 tell us of events that God used to raise up Saul to be His "captain" (v. 16). The story begins with Saul's unassuming origins—he is out in the hills looking for his father's lost donkeys! The intent is to give insights into his character. Saul was diligent in his assigned business. He was undemanding in spirit and direct in his methods but also thorough, honest, dutiful, and considerate of his parent's concerns.

Next in our introduction to Saul (vv. 15-27), we see God's directing in the calling Saul into God's special service. God uses the "man of God", Samuel, who was recognized in Israel as God's "prophet" and "seer" (vv. 9-10) to announce God's choice for their king. God had chosen

Saul to "save My people" (v. 16; a calling like that of Moses or Joshua!).

In the Old Testament, priests, prophets, and kings were also anointed into office (Exodus 40:15; Leviticus 4:3, 5, 1 Kings 19:16). Oil is a symbol of the empowering of the Holy Spirit. This anointing was a symbolic declaration that the authority came from the Lord. Ultimately, the "Anointed One" would be the Messiah, who is our Lord Jesus Christ.

Samuel's message to Saul (v. 20) about the donkeys authenticated to Saul that Samuel was the Lord's true prophet. Saul's answer (v. 21) shows Saul's attitudes of honesty, modesty, and meekness.

In verses 22-27 are the actions used to show Israel that Saul was God's choice for king.

Life stEP The elders asked for a king "like all the nations" (8:5, 20) but they did not have the king's spirituality in mind as a desired factor. Yet the Lord gave them a man with excellent spiritual qualifications. How can you work at putting into practice the same qualities that were evident in Saul's life: duty, consideration, honesty, and meekness?

1 Samuel 10:1-10, 17-19

What is the writer saying?

How can I apply this to my life?

In verse 1, Samuel privately anoints Saul as king of Israel. This act symbolized God's setting Saul apart for His special service over God's "inheritance." By using "inheritance" we see that God retained His ownership of Israel as Israel remained subordinate to God, and not their king.

Next we see God giving Saul three "signs" (v. 7) to confirm God's approval of Saul's appointment. First, Saul would meet two men who would tell about the lost donkeys (v. 2). Next, Saul would meet three men who would give him bread (vv. 3-4). Third, Saul would meet a "company of prophets" with whom Saul, by the Spirit, would "prophesy" (vv. 5-6).

This act of the Spirit coming upon Saul was just as God had done with the judges of Israel, (Othniel, Gideon, and Jephthah—see Judges 3:10, 6:34, and 11:29). God had given each His Spirit as a divine source of power to equip the leader in his assignment. By this, Saul's personality is changed "into another man" (v. 6)—from an inexperienced and timid man to a bold and confident leader of God's people.

We pick up the story in verse 17 as Samuel calls the people together for the public inauguration of Saul. Samuel first reminded them of the Lord's faithfulness in delivering them from enemies through the years and of their insistence on having a king (vv. 18-19). Follow the next few verses to see how people react to this kingly figure.

Life stEP

In a similar way, the Lord provides each Christian with the indwelling Holy Spirit (John 14:17). The Spirit is with us to *teach* (John 14:26), to *comfort* (John 16:7), and to *guide* (John 16:13). He does this through the *written word* (John 17:8, 17). By the Holy Spirit, God intends to equip you for His special service. How can you live by faith today?

1 Samuel 12:1-5, 13-25

What is the writer saying?

How can I apply this to my life?

pray China – For the 44,000,000 members of unregistered house churches, persecuted by officials.

After being presented as God's chosen king (10:24), Saul hesitated in assuming his office and went home. There he received a message that the Ammonites were besieging the border city of Jabesh. The Spirit of God came upon Saul (11:6), and he led the armies of Israel to a great victory. Afterwards, Israel reaffirmed Saul as their king (11:14-15).

Now, in today's passage, Samuel—in an act of self-denial, courtesy, and generosity towards Saul—publicly relinquishes his judgeship over Israel. He receives the acknowledgement of the people that his rule had been one of integrity, honesty, and justice (v. 5).

In verses 6-12, Samuel rehearses the Lord's faithfulness to Israel. His point was that the Lord's *kingship* had not been a failure.

In verses 13-25, Samuel instructs the people about the conditions that will bring God's blessings upon them and their king:

"Fear the LORD" (v. 14): To reverence, honor, and keep His laws.

"Serve Him" (v. 14): A joyful, obedient work as a worship of God.

"Obey His voice" (v. 14): To listen with attention so one can obey by doing what the Lord has instructed.

"Continue following the LORD" (v. 14): To still look to God even though an earthly king had been appointed (vv.17-18—God shows His sovereignty by sending a thunderstorm during harvest, when it *never* rains).

"Turn ye not aside" (v. 21): While the verb means "to turn away" here, it is picturing a departing from an established path to follow another one that the people thought would be more profitable or beneficial.

Life **stEP** What path are you following? Are you seeking to honor, serve, and obey the Lord? Or have you foolishly *turned away* to follow a path that you think will bring you greater profit? Such paths are "vain"!

tuesday 8

1 Samuel 13:1-14

What is the writer saying?

How can I apply this to my life?

Chapter 13 introduces us to Jonathan (v. 2), Saul's oldest son (14:49). We also see Saul sending home the majority of the army that was called up to battle the Ammonites in chapter 11, keeping just 3,000 thousand trained soldiers in two brigades lead by Saul and Jonathan.

The first deed of Saul's standing army was the destruction of a Philistine "garrison" (v. 3) at Geba (located between his two brigades at Michmash and Gibeah). Apparently this garrison was a *monument* (a different word is used than in 13:23 and 14:1) that declared Philistine control over the area. The Philistines came against Israel with great force armed with chariots and horsemen. The Israeli army panicked, with many fleeing. Note that Saul's brigade of 2,000 shrinks to just 600 (v. 15)!

And so Saul withdraws with his army to Gilgal. Evidently he had received instructions that Samuel would meet him here in seven days. When Samuel did not arrive, Saul decided that he must do something to revive the courage of his army. He violated Samuel's instructions by offering sacrifices to God, hoping to gain God's blessing and guidance. To emphasize that Samuel's delay had been a test from God, as soon as Saul had offered his presumptuous sacrifice, Samuel appears (v. 10)!

Immediately Samuel asks, "What have you done?" (v. 11). When faced with his sin, Saul responded with *excuses* rather than *repentance*. Saul says that he had "forced" himself (v. 12) to do what he knew was wrong. His failure was that he thought himself so important that he was justified in exercising priestly duties.

 Life stEP We often act like Saul, thinking of ourselves as so important that we are above blame for doing what we know to be wrong. What actions do you allow into your life for which you make excuses to God rather than kneeling before God in repentance for your sin?

wednesday 8

1 Samuel 14:47-15:11

What is the writer saying?

How can I apply this to my life?

pray   India – Protection and boldness for believers facing persecution by Hindu extremists.

The portion of Chapter 14 before today's passage tells of a great victory of Saul, Jonathan, and the Israelites over the Philistines. This victory brings to Saul the allegiance of all the Hebrews (see 14:21, 47a). However, we also see Saul's pride, rashness, and stubbornness (vv. 24, 39, 44) mixed in with Saul's desire to serve the Lord.

Under Saul's leadership, Israel goes on to win battles against other enemies around them. A summary is given of victories against five neighboring countries that had been occupying portions of Israel's territory (vv. 47-48).

The Amalekites, the sixth nation listed (v. 48), were a nomadic people located primarily in the Sinai Desert to Israel's south. Now, after centuries of them harassing and raiding, Saul was given the task of annihilating this people (15:3). The episode cited in 15:2 happened 400 years previously, under Moses (Exodus 17:8-16; Deuteronomy 25:17-19).

Saul begins his assignment from the Lord by vigorously carrying out his task. In his first invasion of foreign territory, he fights a series of running battles across the Sinai until he had captured Agag, the Amalekite king. Sadly, Saul and his army did not obey God's clear instructions to "utterly destroy all" (15:3). Instead, Saul spares the king (for pride and glory) and keeps the "best" sheep and oxen (for profit and reward). The rest are destroyed in partial obedience to God's order.

The Lord soon sends His "word" to Samuel (vv. 10-11) about Saul's selfishness and disregard for God's clear commands.

As a Christian, God has also given you clear commands of what He wants you to do with your life. Are you obeying His directions? Or are you putting pride, selfishness, and profit ahead of God's plan for you? Take a few minutes and consider your reasons for recent choices.

thursday 8

1 Samuel 15:12-29

What is the writer saying?

How can I apply this to my life?

pray Czech Republic – For continued and increased growth and depth within Bible-believing churches.

Our passage begins with Saul setting up a monument for himself (v. 12b) to celebrate his victory over the Amalekites. Sadly, Saul was seeking fame before he finished his assignment!

The purpose of the detail in the text is to confirm Saul's failure as king. In the previous passage we saw Saul's **willful disobedience** (v. 9); now we see Saul's **repeated dishonesty** as he seeks to hide his sin:

On Samuel's arrival, Saul quickly declares "I have performed the commandment of the LORD" (v. 13)! Saul knew he was being *deceitful* and was *lying by exaggeration.*

When Samuel exposes Saul's sin by asking why he was hearing sheep and oxen (v. 14), Saul responds with excuses! Saul's words, "The people spared the best," imply he had no part in their greed (see v. 9). Then he says, "The rest we have utterly destroyed" (see v. 8),

knowing he had stopped pursuing the Amalekites! Saul was portraying **partial obedience** as completed performance. Saul's defense was to blame his people (vv. 20-21). He seeks to **deflect his guilt** upon them. But as king, he was responsible for allowing them to act against God's will!

Verses 20-21 show additional fabrication intended to give a good twist to the original sin of disobedience.

Three times Saul is accused of not obeying God's commands (vv. 19, 23, and 26). Finally, Saul confessed his sin (v. 24). Yet, even this includes excuses. Saul also failed to identify the sources his sin: selfishness, pride, and disobedience.

 Life stEP Verse 22 contains the key lesson for us. Often we, like Saul, think we can satisfy God's instructions for our lives by **partially doing His will** and partially satisfying our own selfishness, pride, and desires. How have you, in your conduct, been **dishonest** towards God?

friday 8

I Samuel 16:1, 6-23

What is the writer saying?

How can I apply this to my life?

pray Bolivia – For the continued spiritual hunger and turning to Christ taking place within the Bolivian army.

Chapter 16 opens with two declarations, that God had rejected Saul yet provided another king, David. God had decreed (Genesis 49:10) that Israel's kings come from the tribe of Judah, but the people had insisted upon a king (8:5) before the Lord's choice was available. In King Saul, of the tribe of Benjamin, the Lord "gave them their request; but sent leanness into their soul" (Psalm 106:15). The time had come for the Lord to choose a king with the right "heart" (v. 7—referring to *inner character*).

The use of "provided" in verse 1 indicates a process; first to "look at carefully" so as to *observe* and *inspect*, then to *consider*, and finally to *select*. In fact, this Hebrew word is used later in our text when Samuel "*looked* on Eliab" (v. 6, David's oldest brother).

When verse 7 says God *looks* at the heart rather than outward appearances, the passage is declaring that God already knew David thoroughly. Before He directed Samuel to go and anoint David as Israel's next king, God had already *observed*, *considered* and *selected* David based upon David's inner spiritual character (i.e., his "heart").

Since David was not yet of age, apparently Jesse chose not to include his youngest son for consideration (v. 11b)! Yet we see that the Lord's choice for Israel's next leader had already been observed by God as a good and faithful shepherd—so much so that David was willing to give his life for his sheep (17:34-36)! God had chosen a king who already had the right kind of heart to lead God's people.

Life **stEP** What is God looking for in your inner character as He prepares you for His special assignment? God is not impressed with your reputation in the world or your appearance. Rather, He is concerned with the care and dedication you give to your responsibilities. David faithfully kept his sheep; what can you be doing faithfully today?

saturday 8

1 Samuel 17:1-16

What is the writer saying?

How can I apply this to my life?

pray Joe Jordan, Executive Director of Word of Life, for a consistent pursuit of holiness and God's direction for the ministry.

Today's passage tells of another invasion by the Philistines, who wanted to reassert their dominance over Israel. Saul had countered this invasion by blocking the approach into Israel. The armies faced off at Shochoh, a town near the Philistine border, for forty days across a mile-wide valley. Each army was staying on the stony hills on its side of the valley. While the Philistines were stronger, apparently they were not willing to attack the Israelites who, no doubt, were improving their defenses on their side of the valley. Thus the Philistine offer of single combat between each army's champion makes good sense, especially since their champion was a nine-foot giant, Goliath!

Such giants, while not common, are reported in ancient documents. Some, the "sons of Anak", had lived amongst the Canaanites when Israel had invaded under Joshua. These were wiped out in the land of Israel, but others had survived with the Philistines (Joshua 11:22; Numbers 13:33; 2 Samuel 21:22).

As Israel's champion, and as a king who was taller than all others in Israel (9:2, 10:23), Saul was expected to represent Israel in such single-combat situations. Yet as we have seen, the God-given spirit of courage and valor had departed from Saul (16:14). Instead, he and all Israel "were dismayed, and greatly afraid" (v. 11) of Goliath's challenge.

Note that Eliab, Abinadab, and Shammah (David's oldest brothers) were warriors with Saul (v. 13). Samuel had considered these three (16:6-9) as replacements for King Saul. Now we can see what the Lord had observed when He had declared that their hearts were not right; they had hearts full of fear rather than hearts of faith in the God's power!

When you are faced with a powerful spiritual enemy, do not make the mistake of Saul and Eliab, who looked only at Goliath's size and armor! Remember to look at the *size* of the Lord.

1 Samuel 17:17-30

What is the writer saying?

How can I apply this to my life?

pray Canada – For "fruit that remains" within the local churches where Bible institute ministry teams serve.

Our story reminds us that armies from ancient times were manned by militia who heeded a call to arms and came with their own provisions for the few days of a battle. Since this battle was an apparent stalemate, the militiamen needed provisions. David was able to fulfill this need, showing his character as an obedient son.

- David had been passed over for the original call to arms (v. 14).
- David was obedient and submissive to his father's command (v. 17).
- David was eager to begin his extra responsibilities (v. 20a).
- David carefully maintained expected responsibilities (v. 20b).
- David saw beyond the size of Goliath to spiritual battle (v. 26).
- David had to face the contempt of his oldest brother, ("left" = to leave uncared for)!
- David faced accusations concerning his motives (v. 28).

David controlled his temper and did not respond in kind.

It is important to note a contrast. In verse 25 King Saul had offered a reward to the man who would take up Goliath's challenge and kill Goliath. The **king's motive** was clearly to entice one of Israel's great warriors to risk all to win fortune, position, and fame. But **David's motive** was a desire to remove the **disgrace** that had come upon Israel (v. 26). More importantly, he desired to eliminate the **dishonor** and **disrepute** that had come upon the God of Israel.

Life stEP As children of our Heavenly Father, we must not forget our "cause" of service (v.29). First, how can you be faithful to your *expected* spiritual responsibilities (your own "few sheep") that have become your daily chores? Also, how can you live today so that others will honor the Lord?

1 Samuel 17:31-47

What is the writer saying?

How can I apply this to my life?

pray Pray for those who teach in your church to be faithful to the word, enthusiastic in their presentation, and compassionate toward the lost.

Israel had refused to enter the Promised Land years before because they saw giants there (Numbers 13:33). Here, they are "sore afraid" of another giant, Goliath (v. 24).

In the past, David had relied upon God's faithfulness (vv. 34-36). Now David was trusting the Lord for a similar victory over Goliath (v. 36b).

Saul missed the spiritual element here by looking at the size of the boy instead of the power of God. Saul did not understand such faith in God's protection, and so he wanted to give David his own armor to protect the boy from the giant. David knew the armor was useless since he had not "proved" it (v. 39—had not tested it). Instead, David took his *proven* shepherd's instruments (v. 40) to do battle in "the name of the LORD" (v. 45). He wanted both armies to know "that the LORD saves not with the sword: for the battle is the LORD's; He will deliver [Goliath] into our hands" (v. 47).

Remember the lesson here: the most memorable one-on-one battle in the entire Bible is told in two verses (vv. 48-49), yet it took the previous 47 verses to tell us why David was Israel's true champion! David, while small, had total confidence in the LORD to be his armor, his strength, and his enabler, giving him victory over great adversaries!

God delights in using weak instruments to do great things though their faith. We must gain experience in the use of our faith as our shield and God's Word as our sword (Ephesians 6:11-17). Such faith is the source of our victory.

Life stEP Today, God still wants to use little people (or *little-known people*) with *proven* instruments to do His work. What spiritual equipment has He given to you to enable you, by faith, to have great success over "giant" spiritual adversaries? How can you be like David, a true champion for God, by faith in God?

1 Samuel 17:48-58

What is the writer saying?

How can I apply this to my life?

The descriptive words in these verses show the extraordinary victory won by David. Neither army expected to see a victory by a seemingly inexperienced, unarmored, and unarmed young man against a great "champion".

The Philistines, seeing their champion defeated and beheaded, lost all courage and fled. In contrast, the army of Israel, which had been afraid, took on the courage of their new champion, David, and "pursued the Philistines" (v. 52). The Philistines were expelled from Israel and were forced to retreat to their walled cities of Ekron and Gath.

Just as David moved forward quickly with assurance of victory, in the on-going conflict between the people of God and the followers of evil, we as Christians should do the same in our spiritual battles. To the world we may also seem weak, unready, and defenseless, but we can prevail in our spiritual battles as we claim by faith verses such as 2 Corinthians 2:14, "Now thanks be unto God, who always causeth us to triumph in Christ."

Although David had previously been called to serve as Saul's musician and armor bearer (16:19-23), Saul still asked, "whose son is this youth" (17:55)? Previously it may not have been important to Saul from what family the young musician had come. Also, several years had passed and David had grown from a boy to a young man. But now that Saul had made a public commitment to give his daughter to the slayer of Goliath and to provide for his father's house (17:25), it seems Saul had good reason to inquire about David's family.

Life stEP How can you proceed in your own spiritual battles, prudently preparing while trusting in the Lord's enablement? How do you pray and seek His guidance? When the opportunity for action presents itself, will you move forward trusting the Lord for victory?

wednesday 9

1 Samuel 18:1-16

What is the writer saying?

How can I apply this to my life?

pray Fiji – For the success of church planting ministries, as Mormons and Jehovah's Witnesses grow in numbers.

Today's passage develops a strange situation: David had been anointed to be the next king of Israel, but Jonathan, son of king Saul, is human heir to the same throne—and Saul is seemingly secure in his possession of this throne. The description in the text shows the character qualities of these individuals in this difficult situation.

Presented to us first is **Jonathan** and his unwavering friendship with David. He makes a covenant with David (v. 3), binding each to always promote the welfare of the other. In the ensuing years, Jonathan proved himself faithful to his friend. He was also unselfish in that he shared his *princely* possessions with the *shepherd boy*, David (v. 4).

Saul is confident in his reign, taking David into his court (v. 2), setting him over the men of war (v. 5b), and sending him out on various affairs of government (v. 5a). Soon, though, David's wise conduct (v. 5) was bringing greater praise than the king was receiving (v. 7). And so begins Saul's opposition to David. Saul reacted with anger, jealousy, and fear as he suspected that David had some treasonable motive to steal his kingdom (v. 8, 11-12, 15).

Yet our text repeatedly notes that **David**, in all of this, "behaved himself wisely" (vv. 5, 14, 15). His character impressed those who came into contact with him (v. 5, 16). In an evidence of God's Spirit being upon David, David did not become prideful.

The remainder of Chapter 18 tells of David's marriage to Saul's daughter, Michal, and of Saul's plans to use her to have David killed. The scheme failed, and David became Saul's son-in-law.

It was said of David that he "behaved himself wisely" (to act with consideration, insight, and prudence). What situations will you face today that need you to respond wisely in all your ways? Take a few minutes and ask our Lord to guide you in making wise choices.

1 Samuel 19:1-18

What is the writer saying?

How can I apply this to my life?

 pray Korea – For youth ministries working among South Koreans, as they disciple believers to maturity.

Saul now makes known to his court his desire to kill David. He orders Jonathan and his staff to slay David. Again Jonathan chooses to defy his father's orders, as he had done before (14:28-30). Jonathan chose to be a true friend towards David by seeking to protect him (v. 2). The next morning, he sends David to wait in a secret hiding place while Jonathan pleads David's case before Saul. He used Scriptures to warn his father that shedding innocent blood violated God's Law (Deuteronomy 19:10-13, 21:8-9). In verse 6, Saul responds to his son's rebuke with a pledge to protect David's life. However, as soon as David achieves another great victory over the Philistines (v. 8), Saul again enters into an uncontrolled frenzy and attempts to murder David (vv. 9-10).

David escaped to his home, where his wife, Michal, tells him that her father's soldiers were guarding the house with orders to slay him (v. 11). She devised a plan for his escape (v. 12), deceives her father's soldiers to assist in his escape (v. 13), and lies to her father to save herself from his wrath (v. 17).

David flees to Samuel at Ramah (six miles north of Jerusalem), showing that he understood that his only defense was to seek God's protection (with Samuel being the Lord's agent). David's only and true hope was to trust in God as his deliverer (Psalm 59:1-2) and his shield (Psalm 59:11)!

The remainder of chapter 19 tells how the Lord thwarted all attempts by Saul to capture David.

Life **stEP** Both Jonathan and Michal accepted the risks and costs of doing right. Are you facing harsh demands to take part in some wrong action? In the midst of such hard steps towards doing right, how can you trust in the Lord to be your deliverer, guide, and shield?

1 Samuel 20:1-23

What is the writer saying?

How can I apply this to my life?

With King Saul occupied with Samuel at Ramah, David takes the opportunity to consult with his friend, Jonathan, the son of Saul, who is a few miles away at Gibeah, Saul's capital.

David immediately brings his case before Jonathan: "What have I done" (v. 1b)? Jonathan assures David that he would be faithful to David (v. 4) rather than his own father, King Saul. Apparently, David was certain that he was in imminent danger of being killed by Saul (v.3b). His friend, Jonathan, was not yet convinced of King Saul's "evil" and lethal intent towards David (v. 9). Thus Jonathan devises a plan to "sound out" his father then to reveal the results to David (v. 12).

While our passage deals with Jonathan's aid towards David, much is revealed about Jonathan's personal character. It is important for us to see that Jonathan believed God had called David to be Israel's next king, which would bring a reversal of their roles; that is, while David was now at the mercy of Jonathan, the Lord would bring about the situation where Jonathan would be at the mercy of David (v. 16).! Thus, Jonathan asks David to "show the kindness of the LORD" (v. 14) towards himself and his family when David's time to be in power comes.

Most importantly, Jonathan would not allow his own political ambitions (or suspicions of any political ambitions on David's part) interfere with his good and honorable conduct. Certainly, Jonathan understood that his right conduct would keep him from becoming Israel's next king, but he refused to pursue position, pride, and power.

Are you like Jonathan, a true person of faith? Jonathan knew what God had declared concerning who would be the next king. He chose to act in accord with God's will. In those tough situations you are facing, what is the right and good thing for you to do? How can you please the Lord and do right? How about asking the Lord to help?

1 Samuel 20:24-42

What is the writer saying?

How can I apply this to my life?

In verses 24-28, David and Jonathan follow their plan to find out whether Saul still wanted to kill David. As David had surmised (v. 6), his absence from the king's feast would result in Saul asking questions (v. 27). When Jonathan offered the deception that David had to go home to his family (vv. 6, 28-29), he only made Saul angry (v. 30). Seeing through his son's dishonesty, Saul cursed him for siding with David (v. 30). Saul then ordered Jonathan to deliver up David to be executed. In verse 31, the reason for Saul's malice is revealed: he knows that David being alive will keep his descendants from taking the throne.

This time Jonathan responds by speaking truthfully to his father. He asks questions that point out Saul's unjust and selfish attitude (v. 32). In rage, Saul tried to kill the very heir whose throne he claimed to be protecting (v. 33)! By this Jonathan "knew" (v. 33b; compare with v. 9: "if I knew") that his father's actions had not just been erratic behavior but were the determined reasoning of an insecure king seeking to establish his own dynasty.

For the next ten years David was a fugitive. Chapters 21-31 present a number of episodes that occurred during these years. During this period, Samuel dies, and the sad time ends with Saul and his sons dying in a battle that is lost to the Philistines.

Many of David's psalms were derived from his experiences during this time period (see Psalms 34, 52, 54, and 57).

During his fugitive years, David learned many lessons he needed in order to become an effective king, such as patience and relying on the Lord alone rather than on falsehoods, schemes, and men. What is your reaction when God permits trials, adversity, and waiting in order to make you fit for service? How can you learn David's patience?

2 Samuel begins after Israel's crushing defeat by the Philistines in 1011 B.C. In this defeat, Israel's leader, King Saul, and three of his four sons are killed, and the central area of Israel (Ephraim and Manasseh) is occupied by the Philistines. Thus, 2 Samuel is the remarkable story of Israel's transition from a nearly destroyed and subjugated people to a great regional empire with significant political, military, and economic power.

It is also the story of David's rise to become Israel's greatest king. For his first seven years as king, he rules over just the tribe of Judah from its capital, Hebron, and then for another thirty-three years he rules over the reunited kingdom of Israel from its new capital, Jerusalem (5:5). During his reign, David subjugates all the enemies that surrounded Israel, brings prosperity to the nation, and prepares for the building of the temple.

As David's story is being told, we see much about his godly character:

- His seeking of God's direction (2:1).
- His meekness (submission to God's authority) as he recognizes that his promotion to king was the work of God (5:1-12).
- His humility in attributing his military victories to God (5:20).
- His great joy at seeing the Ark of the Covenant come to Jerusalem (6:1-5).
- His desire to exalt the Lord by building a temple for Him at Jerusalem as a place of worship (chaps. 7-8).

- His kindness to Mephibosheth, the son of Jonathan and David's last potential political rival (chap. 9).
- His broken-hearted repentance from his sin of adultery with Bathsheba, and then his submission to God's appointed judgment upon his sin (chap. 12).

Since the book's purpose is to tell David's story, we can properly outline it from the perspective of David's reign as king:

1. 2 Samuel 1-10   David's Triumphs as King:
   a. 1-4   His rule over just Judah.
   b. 5-7   His rule, from Jerusalem, over a reunited Israel.
   c. 8-10   His conquests and political wisdom.

2. 2 Samuel 11-24 David's Troubles as King:
   a. 11-12   His troubles with his sin
      - Bathsheba, Uriah, Nathan, the infant
   b. 13-18   His troubles with his family
      - Amnon, Tamar, Absalom
   c. 19-20   His troubles with his nation
   d. 21-24   His later years: an appendix of five incidents

sunday 10

2 Samuel 5:1-10

What is the writer saying?

How can I apply this to my life?

Upon the death of Saul, the Lord directed David to establish his reign over just the tribe of Judah. During this time, Ish-bosheth, the surviving son of Saul, had been crowned king over the remainder of the nation (2:8-9). When Ish-bosheth died, the line of King Saul ended. As a result, the government of Saul collapsed, weakening the nation of Israel and leaving it open to further attacks by the Philistines.

And so we pick up the story in today's passage with the elders of Israel humbly coming to David to ask him to be king over the entire nation. They give David three reasons for why they were seeking him to be their king: they were all of the same "flesh" and "bone" (v. 1); David, while serving Saul, had led Israel in military campaigns (v. 2a); they knew of the Lord's calling of David to lead them as king (v. 2b).

In response, David made a contract (v. 3) with all Israel. It obliged David, as their *ruler* (v. 2), to give his attention to being their *judge* in peace and *captain* in war. The contract obliged the people to obey David. It is important to note that we Christians have entered into a similar contract with our spiritual King, the Lord Jesus (1 Corinthians 15:25; Hebrews 2:8); that is, Jesus gives His attention to our care, and we are to obey Him!

After being anointed king, David moved his government to Jerusalem. Its location, on the border between Judah and the northern tribes, would emphasize the national character of his government. Since Jerusalem had been a neutral, Jebusite city (from Canaanite people), David was also wisely declaring that he would serve all Israel by making it his capital.

Life stEP Two aspects of David's character come into view: First, he humbly accepts his new service for God. Second, he conducts his first acts as king in a manner that would not offend those he was to serve. How can you humbly accept God's "service assignments"? How can you serve God and at the same time not offend God's people?

2 Samuel 9:1-13

What is the writer saying?

How can I apply this to my life?

With David's kingdom now well-established by warfare against external enemies, the book of 2 Samuel turns its attention to problems (chaps. 9-20) from within the kingdom with which David must deal. This portion of the book begins with David's steps to establish his dynasty within Israel by endearing himself to the various Israelite tribes.

We see David's renewed interest in the surviving members of Saul's family. Upon inquiry, he learned about Jonathan's surviving son, Mephibosheth (2 Samuel 4:4), a cripple who had been living a quiet and obscure life on the far side of the Jordan River. In the ancient world, such an "under-the-radar" existence would be necessary for a former king's heir. But David was not seeking to eliminate potential rivals of his rule; rather, he remembered his pledge to show **kindness** to Jonathan's progeny (1 Samuel 20:14-17)

We are not surprised to see Mephibosheth "fall on his face" before David, for Mephibosheth would have thought he was a condemned man (v. 8, 19:28) being summoned to the king so that the king could have him quietly put to death.

Out of respect for Mephibosheth's father, Jonathan, David restored to Mephibosheth the lands and servants of his grandfather, King Saul, along with the profits from their enterprises. David also gave to him the privilege of eating at the king's table as if he was "one of the king's sons" (v. 11).

It is important for Christians to realize that we have a similar obligation to fellow believers. 1 Pet 3:8-9 says "Finally, all of you, be ... **tenderhearted** ... not returning evil for evil or reviling for reviling, but on the contrary, blessing ..." We too are to do unexpected *kindnesses*!

Life stEP Who is a *rival* in your life — at work or school, amongst your family and relatives, in your close group of friends? Ask the Lord Jesus to place on your heart an appropriate, howbeit unexpected, **kindness**. Perhaps try a helpful action or a thoughtful note!

2 Samuel 11:1-13

What is the writer saying?

How can I apply this to my life?

pray For teens to be saved at evangelistic events being held around the country.

The episode recorded in 2 Samuel 11 occurred when David was about fifty years old, approximately halfway through his forty-year reign. He was a victorious, prosperous, and highly esteemed king. For thirteen years he commanded his army and his nation, subduing and ruling. Now he may have thought it was time to let his faithful army complete the "mopping up" operations while he relaxed at his palace enjoying the fruits of his long and faithful service. Whatever he desired was at his beck and call, including a harem of wives and concubines (5:13), which sadly were forbidden by the Law of God he professed to love (Deuteronomy 17:17). Let's review for a minute: Eve "saw" and "took" (Genesis 3:6). Lot "lifted up his **eyes**" and "chose" (Genesis 13:10-11). Achan "saw" and "took" (Joshua 7:21). Samson "saw" and demanded (Judges 14:1-2). Now it was David's turn; he also "saw" (v. 2) and "took" (v. 4). In each case, the door to lust and sin was the **eye-gate**. In each case the end result was someone's death. In each case, the "lust of the flesh" was awakened by the "**lust of the eyes**" (1 John 2:16). "Then when lust hath conceived, it bringeth forth sin: and sin, when it is finished, bringeth forth death" (James 1:15). According to Proverbs 6:27-29, when David took Bathsheba into his bed, he was pressing his body against fiery coals which would leave a nasty, lifelong scar.

In attempting to cover up his shameful deed, David failed to consider the faithfulness of his devoted servant, Uriah (23:39). David only valued his own desires and did not consider the costs of fulfilling his lusts.

1 Corinthians 10:11-12 indicates that God gave us all these **eye** stories as a warning to us to guard what we allow ourselves to **see**!

Life stEP How can you stay away from becoming the next in a long list of believers who fell into sin because of the **lust of their eyes**?

2 Samuel 11:14-27

What is the writer saying?

How can I apply this to my life?

pray Cuba – Increased freedom in the areas of Bible printing, importation and distribution.

We now find David sinking deeper into sin. His desperate attempts to cover his sin of adultery have failed. His stratagems to cajole Uriah to set aside his gallant behavior and go sleep with his wife only displayed David's loss of standing as the nation's champion. And so David writes to the army's commander, Joab, to set in motion battle orders that would bring Uriah's death, and then gives a follow-up order to press the attack on the city (v. 25), causing even more deaths in order to mask the intentional murder of Uriah.

The man whom God anointed to dispense justice exemplified the very epitome of injustice and deceit! After hearing Uriah express his heart (v. 11), David conceives the dastardly deed of making Uriah the loyal messenger who unwittingly transports his own death warrant (v. 14).

What about Joab? How could he agree to such orders? Was he blindly loyal to the king, or did he have his own motive? The letter certainly gave him a power over the king that could be used to his advantage later.

We can see hints about Bathsheba's heart in this affair. First, she does not protest David's initial advances (and perhaps she allowed herself to bathe on her rooftop to give David something to see!). She does not reveal the truth to her husband. She must have been aware of the real cause of Uriah's death after he returned to the army (at the least she would have been suspicious). To assist in the covering of sin, Bathsheba allowed only the shortest time for mourning Uriah's death. She submitted to David's call to go into his house as his wife.

The passage concludes with God's opinion concerning the whole matter of Uriah (1 Kings 15:5): "the thing ... displeased the Lord" (v.27).

Sin causes us to lose all sense of justice. It also causes us to hide our sin (Genesis 3:8). The only solution is to confess sin to God and by this, gain His forgiveness. Honestly consider your own life. Is there a secret sin which you need to confess?

2 Samuel 12:1-14

What is the writer saying?

How can I apply this to my life?

"He that covereth his sins shall not prosper: but whoso confesseth and forsaketh them shall have mercy" (Proverbs 28:13). David covered his sins of murder, adultery and coveting, violating the sixth, seventh, and tenth commandments (Exodus 20:13, 14, 17). In Psalm 32:3-4 he reflected upon the misery he endured during these months of hiding his sin.

The Lord gave His prophet, Nathan, a story to tell David that would cause David to pronounce his own condemnation (v. 5). Nathan made certain David understood that he was the villain in the story (v.7). David was judged with a sentencing of the same kind; he would suffer the sword as had Uriah, and David's wives would be taken from him as Bathsheba had been stolen from Uriah.

The prophecy of verse 10 was fulfilled as the sword devoured David's sons, Amnon (13:28-29), Absalom (18:15), and Adonijah (1 Kings 2:24-25). Fulfillment of verse 11 is seen in the rape of David's daughter, Tamar, by her half-brother, Amnon (13:14), and in the shameful treatment of David's concubines (16:22) by his own son, Absalom.

While the sentencing against David was harsh, we are led to wonder why he was not punished with death, as his crimes would require by Old Testament Law (Exodus 21:12; Leviticus 20:10). The answer must surely be that David's repentance — "I have sinned against the LORD" (v. 13) — was the genuine contrition of a remorseful heart, (see Psalm 51). Yet while David was restored to fellowship with God, the consequences would affect his life and Israel.

Life **stEP** The lesson before us is this: if we try to *cover up* our sins, God will surely uncover them. But if we confess our sins, He will cover them with the blood of our Savior Jesus Christ. "Blessed are they whose iniquities are forgiven, and whose sins are covered," says Romans 4:7, quoting Psalm 32:1, which was written by David! Is there sin in your life for which you need to express your own genuine contrition of a remorseful heart?

2 Samuel 12:15-31

What is the writer saying?

How can I apply this to my life?

God's grace is extended to those who respond to His chastening with repentance (v. 13: "I have sinned!"). But God's justice in government requires Him to demonstrate that He does not overlook sin (v. 15). David's anguish (verses 16-18) was only the beginning of his suffering; for the rest of his life, he would be troubled by repercussions from his sin.

During the months following David's sin with Bathsheba, he wrote four psalms that reflect the process of his restoration (in historical order, Psalms 38, 6, 51, and 32). He progressed from being overwhelmed with remorse for his sin (Psalm 38) to the joyous realization of his sin being forgiven (Psalm 32). When these psalms are read in order, they can be of great help to those in the throes of despair because of their past sins.

Two often-confusing theological issues find practical illustration here in the sad events that troubled David's life:

We see that David, who prayed and fasted while his newborn child was "very sick" (v. 15), believed that his earnest prayer (v. 22) would perhaps change the expected outcome of the child's illness. Obviously, David hoped that God, in His grace and in response to David's intense prayer, might spare the child in spite of the fact that Nathan had clearly announced God's will in judgment upon David (v. 14b). Thus, David believed that ardent prayer does change what God allows to happen!

We see that David, in his comments after his child's death, believed that he, when he died, would join his son who was already in Heaven with God in that eternal realm of redeemed believers (v. 23, "I shall go to him").

Consider David's confidence in his prayer influencing God's actions! When you pray, do you earnestly keep at it, as did David, until the *prayer need* happens? What is a current *prayer need* in your life, and how might God "be gracious to" you (v. 22) in regards to it?

2 Samuel 23:1-7

What is the writer saying?

How can I apply this to my life?

Today's passage jumps to the last section of 2 Samuel (chaps. 21-24), which is a collection of information and events from David's later years as king of Israel. David voices a *victory song* as he reviews God's many works in his life. Part of this *victory song* is *in retrospect* and part is *in prospect* as David, one last time, considers his life. He presents four prominent truths:

It was God's choice to raise "up on high" David, a lowly shepherd-boy, to become the "anointed" king of Israel (v. 1b) who sought to rule Israel justly (righteously) and "in the fear of God" (v. 3).

David recalls the fellowship he had enjoyed with the "Spirit of the LORD" (v. 2), Who spoke through David. David uses a passive tense here as he expresses the Spirit's *work of inspiration* and David's *work as receiver* of the many psalms that David then wrote out.

More importantly — and speaking prophetically — David looks to the future, when a son, the promised Messiah (Jesus the Christ) would arise (the "seed" of David, according to 2 Samuel 22:51). This "seed," Who will come according to God's everlasting covenant with David (see 2 Samuel 7) would be the true "light of the morning" (v. 4).

Sadly, David was also reminded that his "house" (v. 5, that is, David's family history) had not always lived up to God's standard for Israel's kings — ruling with righteousness and living in the fear of God. Nor did David have the prospect that all of his successors would live as righteous "seed." And so David ends with a warning that ungodly rulers would be like "thorns" that are dug up and "burned" (vv. 6-7).

While very few Christians will ever be "raised up" by God to be kings, all Christians are called to be God's "ambassadors" (2 Corinthians 5:20). How can you today live your life in a *just*, *righteous*, and *in-the-fear-of-God* (v. 3) manner so that you admirably represent your heavenly King?

James is the Greek/English rendition of the Hebrew name Jacob, which means "heel-catcher" or "supplanter" (a reference to Jacob's competition with his older twin Esau). There are three other men named James in the New Testament. James, the son of Zebedee, was a Galilean fisherman and the brother of John, both of whom were apostles (Matthew 4:21). James, the son of Alphaeus, was another of the Twelve Apostles (Matthew 10:3; Acts 1:13), also called "James the less," the son of Mary (Mark 15:40). James is also the name of the father of the Apostle Judas (not Iscariot) or Thaddaeus.

The final James, of the Book of James, is the brother of Jesus who, along with his brothers Joses, Simon, and Judas (Jude) (Matthew 13:55), did not accept the messianic claims of Jesus until after His resurrection (Mark 3:21; John 7:5). After the risen Jesus had appeared to him (1 Corinthians 15:7), he became the head of the church at Jerusalem (Galatians 1:19; 2:9; Acts 12:17). His brother Jude was also an early church leader and author of a New Testament epistle. James presided at the first Council of Jerusalem, which discussed the inclusion of Gentiles in the church. He wrote the proclamation that was sent to the churches of Antioch, Syria, and Cilicia (Acts 15:19-23). James was still in Jerusalem for Paul's last visit (Acts 21:18). According to the Jewish historian Josephus, James was stoned to death around A.D. 61 at the instigation of the high priest Ananus. Legend names him "James the Just" for his piety. James received the nickname "Old Camel Knees," apparently as a result of the long conversations he had with his brother, Jesus, in Heaven on his knees in prayer.

James, written in A.D. 49, is the earliest book written in the New Testament. The theme is *practical Christianity*. The five chapters can be organized around the topic of our *faith walk*: chapter one, faith tested by trials; chapter two, faith proven through works; chapters three and four, faith evidenced by conduct; and chapter five, faith: experienced through persecution.

James says less about the Master than any other writer in the New Testament, but in his speech, he is the most like the Master! In the108 verses of this small book, he makes references to twenty-two Old Testament books and has fifteen parallels to the Sermon on the Mount. In his emphasis on the practical application of Christianity to our daily lives, James is basically a commentary of Leviticus 19:10-18, which discusses some of the Ten Commandments.

sunday 11

James 1:1-8

What is the writer saying?

How can I apply this to my life?

pray   Kenya – Pray that Christians within the government would provide wisdom to avert political collapse.

Although a half-brother of Jesus and leader of the church in Jerusalem, James humbly identifies himself as a servant. He writes specifically to Hebrew Christians, the same type of people who would have made up his congregation in Jerusalem. His comments must be understood in light of the fact that his listeners were expected to know the Old Testament and what God required of His chosen people.

Martin Luther was disappointed with James because he felt that James put too much emphasis on man's righteousness, and modern critical theologians have attempted to pit Paul's *gracious* gospel against James's *works* salvation. This is not valid, as Paul wrote to Gentiles who had no knowledge of God. James, on the other hand wrote to those who should have known that salvation comes through believing God. They should have understood that sanctification involves a demonstration of the saved condition with the fruits of a righteous lifestyle.

"Divers"(v. 2) is an Old English word for *various*. "Temptations" refer to the tug of the world to cave into sinful desires, the persecutions foisted on the believer by Satan, and the normal struggles of life. "Patience"(v. 3) comes from a Greek word that means "to abide under," implying that the individual is not struggling to escape. Verse 4 is reminiscent of Psalm 23:1: "The Lord is my shepherd; I shall not want." "Perfect" means *complete*, not sinless. "Upbraideth not" means *does not scorn the request*. "Wisdom" is the proper application of facts and understanding in everyday life. It is living life from God's point of view, as also described in the Book of Proverbs. If we fall short, God makes up the difference if we ask. Solomon asked for wisdom and was greatly rewarded for that selfless request.

One foot in the world and one foot with God will not produce spiritual stability (v. 6). Once we are single-minded, then God's integrity results in God providing the wisdom that we seek.

monday 11

James 1:9-18

What is the writer saying?

How can I apply this to my life?

pray Angola – Pray for churches to develop a unity in Christ that transcends tribal loyalty and politics.

The church at Jerusalem must have had people from every social stratum, as James is very concerned with the way the rich regard and treat the poor. Persecution in Jerusalem certainly would have compounded the problem. During another trying period in Israel's history, in Nehemiah, the greed and heartlessness of the rich had to be rebuked for the benefit of the whole body of believers. In Acts 2, the immediate result of the first response to the post-resurrection preaching of the Gospel of the kingdom was for the believers to share their worldly goods with those in need. This was no doubt in light of the kingdom blessings that could be anticipated once the Messiah returned. While the riches of this world are fleeting, James argues that true riches are the rewards of faithful living.

"Endureth" (v. 12) comes from two words, *under* and to *remain*. It conjures the image of a man placed under a heavy load but nevertheless standing strong. When we bear up under struggles we prove our *mettle* (Old English for "what we're really made of"—related to "metal") and are rewarded by God with the "crown of life."

James equates *loving God* with *standing for God*. James then addresses the moral aspect of trials, which we normally call temptation. While God can bring trials into our lives to strengthen us, He does not tempt us to sin. That moral struggle is totally a result of Satan's work, the world system in which we live, and our own fallen flesh ("the world, the flesh, and the devil").

 Notice the progression: first, we have an impulse; then we dwell on that desire; then the thought leads to the act; and finally, the act kills even while pretending to satisfy the impulse. Satan provides the evil gift, but God's gifts are life-giving, not destructive.

tuesday 11

James 1:19-27

What is the writer saying?

How can I apply this to my life?

pray El Salvador – Praise the Lord for the establishment of a democracy and for religious freedom.

When Paul says "wherefore" in verse 19, he is saying that, based on the gigantic struggle for our loyalty and the good provisions God makes for us (described in verses 1-18), we must respond to life in a righteous manner. For instance, God gave us two ears but only one mouth. We should devote twice the effort to listening rather than "speaking our minds" and "giving our two cents." Heated emotions (v. 20) steam the brain. One of the Greek words for pride means *smoke-brain*! "Superfluity" (v. 21) comes from a word that is similar to *perimeter* and speaks of excessive liquid flowing over the edge of a cup. The natural state of man is to wallow in the muck and mire of this world and overflow with evil (Old English *naughty*—"that which is naught [nothing] of good"). "Meekness" (v. 21) is not weakness but rather a selfless attitude that puts God's will and other's good ahead of our desires. The Greek word translated "engrafted" means "implanted," like a seedling that will take root and grow. Enmeshed with our souls, the alien seed kills the virus of sin and imparts eternal life. If this growth process has begun, it will evidence itself with fruit (v. 22—"doers of the word"). The guidance of the New Testament ("law") is complete ("perfect") for all of our needs, and it liberates ("liberty"). This seems contradictory because we usually associate law with oppression. We must remember, however, that a river overflowing its banks is a mess while channeled water is a beneficial power source. The Word of God channels the power and lets us be productive.

 Life stEP What are the marks of a true Christian? James suggests: (a) continual mindfulness of the Bible, (b) obeying the Bible, (c) controlling the tongue, (d) having compassion on widows and orphans, and (e) being pure.

James 2:1-9

What is the writer saying?

How can I apply this to my life?

pray Pray for the salvation and protection of those serving in the military around the world.

Chapter one talked of our *faith, tested by trials*. Chapter two discusses our *faith, proven through works*. Notice how often James refers to the recipients as "my brethren." That was true racially, religiously, and spiritually (racially and religiously they were Jewish; spiritually they were believers in *Yeshua haMashiach*—Jesus the Messiah).

Verse one is saying, do not claim to be a follower of Jesus while at the same time disdaining certain classes of human beings. He is the "Lord of glory" ("manifested excellence"). We worship Him by declaring His *worthship* or *worthiness* to receive attention.

Showing partiality is identified as "evil thoughts" because our real motivation is to get something for ourselves by befriending the wealthy. The poor have nothing to offer us, and therefore we economize our efforts on their behalf because there seems to be no profit. In God's economy, however, he who has much does not see himself as needy and thus bypasses God, to his eternal hurt. The poor, on the other hand, are aware of their need and are more likely to reach out to God, to their eternal benefit.

Once again, loving God is equated with participation in His kingdom (v. 5). "Despised (v. 6) means "no honor." Ironically, the rich despise us through oppression, lawsuits, and character assassinations. James identifies the noblest portion of the Law (how we treat others) as the "royal law" (v. 8). The "law of liberty" and "royal law" are not mandates to follow in order to merit salvation. Instead, they are principles to follow to demonstrate the saved condition, to grow in grace, and to show our love and respect to the One Who saved us.

Life stEP Love for God is demonstrated by love for others and treating them at least as well as we treat ourselves.

James 2:10-18

What is the writer saying?

How can I apply this to my life?

---

pray Pray for your pastor and the leadership of your local church.

James bears down on those professing but not possessing faith. His test: show me the fruit of your faith. Despite the strong emphasis on works, at no point does James imply that salvation is earned by works. Even under the Old Testament Law, with its 613 positive and negative commands, the issue of obtaining salvation was not law-obedience but rather faith. Abraham "believed in the LORD; and he counted it to him for righteousness" (Genesis 15:6). In fact, even under the law, God was gracious in His dealings with mankind. He did not kill David for his double sin of adultery and homicide. He told Moses that salvation is not "far off" (Deuteronomy 30:10-14). In James 2:10, James points out the inflexible and fragile nature of the law. If you offend just one of the 613 rules, you are guilty of breaking them all. Therefore, we have no hope of meriting salvation by law-observance. We have to cast ourselves on the mercy of God. Once saved, however, the same principle applies, in that just obeying a select few of the laws does not please God. He wants us to perform in all areas to demonstrate our saved condition, aid our spiritual growth, and show our appreciation to Him. If we treat others in a merciless manner, we demonstrate a lack of salvation and are heading toward our own merciless eternity. On the other hand, we must resist the implication that unless we have shown mercy to every human on the planet, we have not had our faith verified. Notice that James says, "If a brother or sister" be in need. The implication is that we are responsible for a limited range of humans, not the entire human population. That James is not promoting works-righteousness is seen in the final phrase, "I will show thee my faith by my works."

Faith without works is dead. Not dying...dead. Not half-dead. Dead dead.

James 2:19-26

What is the writer saying?

How can I apply this to my life?

pray   Ecuador – Development of close relationships between existing churches and new missionaries.

James continues his discussion about true faith. Here he compares head knowledge (knowing facts about God) with heart knowledge (knowing God in a personal relationship that constitutes true faith). James would have had extensive contact with moral individuals who professed belief in God but whose motivation was personal glory. Witness Christ's condemnation of the Pharisees (Matthew 23:13-39). There is nothing wrong with starting with head knowledge, but it must work down to the heart (will-center of the individual) to effect eternal life.

The self-righteous man (v. 20) is "vain" or *empty*. Abraham, already proclaimed to be saved by faith (Genesis 15:6), goes on to demonstrate the nature of his saving faith by obeying God and offering up Isaac on the altar. In that story, Isaac asks where the sacrifice is, and Abraham, still operating in faith, says, "God will provide himself a lamb" (Genesis 22:8). Hebrews gives further detail: "Accounting that God was able to raise him up, even from the dead; from whence also he received him in a figure" (Hebrews 11:19). Abraham's action did not merit salvation (produce saving faith) but rather perfected (made complete) his faith in that it verified it as genuine. James then quotes Genesis 15:6.

"Imputed" (v. 23) is an accounting term that is also translated "reckoned" and means "considered to be so or placed on the account." "The Friend of God" (v. 23) comes from the story of Genesis 18 and statements found in 2 Chronicles 20:7 and Isaiah 41:8. James then uses another story, this time of a non-Jew, the prostitute Rahab. She believed that God would destroy Jericho and in faith took care of the Israelite spies in return for protection.

Life stEP Repentance (a change of mind about God's claim on my life) speaks to the works side of faith but really is just the flip side of faith. One cannot exist without the other.

James 3:1-10

What is the writer saying?

How can I apply this to my life?

pray   Bolivia – For youth outreach activities to the 53% of the population that is 19 or under.

The five chapters of James can be organized around the topic of our *faith walk*: chapter one, *faith tested by trials*; chapter two, *faith proven through works*; and now chapters three and four, *faith evidenced by conduct*.

"Be not many masters" means that not many should strive to be leaders. James is very practical and points out that being a leader involves more public activity and therefore more opportunity to mess up, plus greater scrutiny. The word for "masters" is actually the word *teacher,* since in the first century, teachers were accorded great respect. The context in this passage is that of controlling the tongue, which is particularly appropriate for a profession or activity that involves extensive use of the tongue. James says that it is easy to say something that offends someone, and that if a man has not offended anyone, then he is a master of his own person—great self-control. He illustrates the power of the tongue with other small objects that have great control over larger objects. "Listeth (v. 4) is Old English for "desires." Fire is a great example because it looks like a tongue (for example, the flame of a candle), but it can start a huge forest fire.

"World" (v. 6) is *cosmos,* which speaks of an orderly system. Satan is the "god of this world" (2 Corinthians 4:4), and we are warned not to be conformed to the world (the system of thought and action designed by Satan) in Romans 12:1-2. This organized galaxy of iniquity has its origin in hell (*gehenna*). Hell (v. 6) is not yet inhabited and is certainly not the kingdom of Satan, but it is the place prepared for Satan and hence an apt analogy for his type of behavior. Remember, he was a murderer and a liar from the beginning (John 8:44).

Life **stEP**   In James's words: "My brethren, these things ought not so to be" (James 3:10).

James 3:11-18

What is the writer saying?

How can I apply this to my life?

pray Costa Rica – For a new generation of godly, effective leaders for the churches that will commend the Gospel.

James continues his discussion concerning the amazing power and danger of the tongue. In verse 10 he pointed out the irony of using the same instrument to both praise God and curse men. In verses 11-12 he illustrates the unnatural nature of this situation. We would not expect one faucet to give both salty and fresh water. We go to cherry trees expecting cherries, not bananas. Therefore, what comes out of the mouth of man is a pretty solid indicator of what is truly rolling around inside.

"Endued" (v. 13) means "skilled." The one who knows how to live life skillfully knows how to control the tongue. "Conversation" here (v. 13) starts with the idea of *speaking*, which is the context of the statement. However, the word "conversation" is also used in the New Testament to refer to our whole manner of life—everything that is *hearable* to the listening and watching world. This quality of life should not be boastful. It

should not be self-righteous or smug. It behaves this way, not to gain attention, but because it is the right way to live. *Envy* (v. 16) is that green-eyed monster that resents the success of others and operates under the controlling principle of self-advancement. James concludes the section by comparing the fruit of one controlled by hellish principles versus those controlled by heavenly wisdom. "Pure" (v. 17) is the Greek word for fire (*puros*) and speaks of the effect that fire has on precious metal. It refines the metal, burning off the dross and impurities. "Entreated" (v. 17) means "good to obey" and conveys the idea of being agreeable. The wise Christian is not a hypocrite, a word which speaks of an actor hiding behind a mask.

When people look at us to see if we are like Christ, how will our fruit pass the test?

monday 12

James 4:1-5

What is the writer saying?

How can I apply this to my life?

pray Dominican Republic – Pray for the more than 3,500 villages that have no evangelical witness.

To better understand the progression James envisions in this passage, let's work backward from verse 5 to verse 1. In verse 5 he *does theology* by pointing out that the Old Testament Scriptures teach that man's immaterial part (soul or spirit) has been tainted by the sin of our ancestors, Adam and Eve (this is the concept of the depravity of man). Isaiah 57:15 says, "For thus saith the high and lofty One that inhabiteth eternity, whose name is Holy; I dwell in the high and holy place, with him also that is of a contrite and humble spirit, to revive the spirit of the humble, and to revive the heart of the contrite ones." You'll notice that in Isaiah, the word *spirit* is used both of us and the Holy Spirit. Likewise in James 4:5, spirit could be referring to our sinful spirit. An equally valid translation is that the Spirit of God longs (*lusteth*) to dwell in us, to control us for good, and is envious if we play the harlot and flirt with the world (notice the reference to adultery in verse 4). To finish James's progression: When we cheat on God and flirt with Satan, Satan's world system becomes our philosophy of life and pattern of living. We then pray for things but don't get them because we are only trying to satisfy our carnal longings. We then steal from others, even killing if need be, to satisfy our cravings. These activities are motivated by our carnal desires—the desires of Adam's flesh, not yet totally controlled by the salvation God offers and the power His indwelling Spirit provides.

Believers are engaged to be married to Jesus Christ. Are we faithful to Him? Does He provide our motivation in life, or are we driven by the desires of the flesh?

James 4:6-10

What is the writer saying?

How can I apply this to my life?

pray Guatemala – For more willing hearts to join the 100 missionaries sent from Guatemala in the last 15 years.

James's words seem harsh. Do believers really murder and steal to satisfy their frustrated desires? Normally, no. But the path is slippery, and the logical conclusion of hating a person is to eventually act on that hatred and kill. "But for the grace of God, there go I" is James's idea in verse 6. This verse is quoting Proverbs 3:34 (which Peter also uses in 1 Peter 5:5), reflecting the principle that God wants to pour out mercy and grace on the humble (Isaiah 54:7-10; Zechariah 12:10).

In verses 7-10, James gives terse commands that need immediate attention from his audience if they expect to overcome this world's system. "Submit" is a military term referring to soldiers in their proper ranks. "Resist" means "to take a stand against." Unfortunately, many times we *flee* Satan and try to instead *resist* youthful lusts, which we are told to *flee* in 2 Timothy 2:22.

When we draw near to God in faith, He reciprocates the favor and draws near to us in friendship and empowerment (v. 8). "Cleanse" is the Greek word *cauterize*, which we apply to the burning of the flesh by heat or chemicals to kill infection. Hands are the instruments of obvious sin.

In the next phrase, hidden sins of the mind are also addressed. In chapter 1, James tells us that a double-minded man (one foot in the world and one foot with God) is unstable in all of his ways. Sober thinking (not continuous depression) is the mark of a true believer who has humbled (emptied) himself, casting himself on God's provision for sin (vv. 9-10).

Life stEP

We must take the red-hot poker of the Word of God and use it to burn out the sin that poisons our soul. Does it hurt? Yes, but it is better than the alternative.

James 4:11-17

What is the writer saying?

How can I apply this to my life?

pray Cuba – For the persecuted Christians to be encouraged and continue their service for the Lord.

What are the signs of a false religionist (such as the Pharisees in Matthew 23)? They are not satisfied to study the Word of God to construct their own lifestyle preferences, yet they also condemn others who don't live up to their preferences. After reading these verses, too many people conclude that we can never evaluate another person's behavior, but that is an improper conclusion to this passage (and the equally famous "beam in your own eye" passage in Matthew 7). The correct approach is, when the Bible speaks clearly on a subject, the group of believers (the church) is to insist that the members obey, even to the point of church discipline (compare 1 Corinthians 5, 2 Thessalonians 3, and Matthew 18).

James here is talking about two perversions of this process. First, the critic has by-passed the Matthew 18 formula and has become judge, jury, and executioner. Second, there was an issue of preferences versus clear teachings.

For instance, it is one thing to say that I prefer not to shop on Sunday, but it's another to say that your neighbor sins by shopping on Sunday, since the Bible does not directly address the issue. (Sunday is the first day of the week; it cannot and should not be called the "Christian Sabbath" since the Sabbath always has been and always will be the seventh day of the week.) James argues that to evaluate a person on such preferences puts us in the role of lawmaker. We don't have that authority; only God does. That these self-righteous individuals have an ego problem is further illustrated by their lack of respect for the frailty of their existence. Their success—their very breath—is in the hands of God. They should therefore give Him more recognition in their daily life.

Pride goeth before a fall, and humility is a great cushion when you do mess up.

James 5:1-6

What is the writer saying?

How can I apply this to my life?

Social justice is one of the obvious themes of the later prophets (see Malachi and Nehemiah 5). The Hebrew Christian, James, seems to have great concerns in this area as well. It must be remembered that the Bible does not say, "Money is the root of all evil," but rather, "The *love* of money is the root of all evil" (1 Timothy 6:10). Abraham, Joseph, David, Job, and many other saints were financially rich. They knew how to use their wealth for God's glory. Here James condemns those consumed with the love for money to the point that they have cheated others to get more for themselves. "Fraud (v. 4) refers to *holding back what is owed.* This is not a criticism of poor pay, but rather a failure to pay the price agreed. "Sabaoth (v. 4) is the word for armies, referring to the angelic hosts; it is sometimes translated "Lord of Hosts" or "Almighty God" since the power to judge is the emphasis.

Two different words for pleasure are used in verse 5. Both have root meanings of *self-indulgence.* These rich men's self-indulgence is like the sword that is never satisfied—it always wants more blood. Another way to understand the passage is that these men have reveled in fleshly pleasures even though it was the last days (v. 3), and they had only succeeded in fattening themselves for the judgment and slaughter. Just as they showed no mercy to the poor, and the poor were unable to stop the rich, likewise the Heavenly Judge will show them no mercy, and the rich will not be able to stop His just judgment.

Life **stEP** — We might not have much in this life, but if we live wisely with what we do have, God will give great reward in the next life where "neither moth nor rust doth corrupt, and where thieves do not break through nor steal: For where your treasure is, there will your heart be also" (Matthew 6:19-21).

friday 12

James 5:7-12

What is the writer saying?

How can I apply this to my life?

 Australia – Sensitivity and skilled communication for those sharing the gospel in Aboriginal areas.

Having alluded to the last days and the final judgment, James now encourages the faithful believers with a reference to the return of Jesus Christ. Imagine James's thoughts on this topic. He would have longed for the return of Christ, both as his heavenly Savior and as his earthly brother! There are some who want to downplay the importance of expecting Christ's return. While there are good cautions against sensationalism and excessive speculation, the fact is that the imminent (any moment) return of the Lord was on the minds of all eight of the New Testament authors (Matthew, Mark, Luke, John, Paul, Peter, James, and Jude). Imminence does not demand immediacy. In fact, all eight New Testament writers indicate that while we wait, we are to be busy, making the most of every opportunity to further the cause of Christ. Just as the farmer waits patiently for the crop to finish growing and ripening, likewise we must not lose heart but rather wait patiently for the Lord's return. Elsewhere we are told that the Lord's patience in this matter is for the express purpose of bringing more people to the point of salvation.

"Patience (v. 7) comes from a Greek word that means "to go a long time before boiling over." The early rain (v. 7) is the fall rainy season, and the latter rain is the spring rainy season in Israel. "Grudge (v. 9) refers to low-frequency annoyance signals (muttering and grumbling). "Stablish (v. 8) is Old English for *establish,* which implies a thorough grounding in foundational issues. Under divine inspiration, James says that the judge is already at the door, ready to return and evaluate the behavior of all for the sake of eternal reward.

Life stEP

Nothing focuses the mind like imminent death, or in this case, an imminent audience with the master of the universe.

James 5:13-20

What is the writer saying?

How can I apply this to my life?

pray Czech Republic – For godly public school teachers who will use their religious freedom to evangelize.

"Afflicted" (to suffer badly) refers to persecution or troubles. James says, "Take it to the Lord in prayer." Those who are happy, though, should sing the Psalms of David (v. 13).

In verse 14, James says those who are sick should seek the help of the church. This starts a potentially confusing discussion of healing the sick. James is clearly not talking about the gift of healing that Christ and the apostles possessed. They could touch someone and immediately cause physical healing, and even resurrection from the dead. Some churches acknowledge that God no longer guarantees healing, but they would say that James 5 is a proper procedure for asking God for physical healing. We would not criticize those who practice this process as long as they explain that any resulting healing would be an answer to prayer, and like all prayers, they are only answered in the positive if it is God's will at that time.

Actually, James is probably not referring merely to a physical illness, but rather one caused by sinful behavior. There are two terms for "sick" in these verses, and both are used of spiritual weakness in the New Testament epistles. The healing must be understood in the light of repentance and restoration of the sinning believer. Notice the emphasis on repentance in verses 15-16. Also, the illustration of Elijah has a spiritual emphasis (the power of his prayer life in combating the false god Baal), as opposed to a physical healing, such as the resurrection that Elijah performed. Finally, while oil is a symbol of the Holy Spirit, it was also used for refreshment. As the elders prayed for and exhorted the individual, they would also refresh him with the perfumed anointing oil.

Life stEP Sin has deep results, even affecting us emotionally and physically. With reason, the old timers said, "If you slept well last night, you must have a clear conscience!"

In the Bible, the word "proverb" denotes a concise saying of practical wisdom and often conveys moral direction. A proverb is a kind of truth that is most commonly true but is not what is certainly true. A proverb was designed to be a teaching tool in which a pointed, compact saying would give an insight into the governing of one's conduct in life.

Proverbs, as used in several ancient cultures, were designed for oral transmission [While they did have books, most people could not afford their own copy. Rather they would memorize large portions of Scripture!]. They were artfully structured in several ways to impact the hearer so he could *see* the teaching and also for ease of memory.

1. Frequently a contrasting couplet was used: "a fool *uttereth all* his mind; but a wise man *keepeth it in* till afterwards" (Proverbs 29:11).
2. "Commit thy works unto the LORD, and thy thoughts shall be established" (16:3) is an example of a completive couplet.
3. Whereas, "Better is *a little* with righteousness than *great revenues* without right" (16:8) is a comparative couplet.

Proverbs 1:1, 10:1, 25:1 and Ecclesiastes 12:9 tell us that King Solomon both *authored* proverbs and *collected and edited* other wise sayings already in existence. The exceptions are the last two chapters where Proverbs tells us that Agur and Lemuel authored those portions.

According to 1 Kings 4:32, Solomon "spoke three thousand proverbs" [thus, our book of Proverbs holds only some of his proverbs].

1 Kings 4:31 says "he was wiser than all men." That statement, of course, was no longer true when Christ became a man, for in Him "are hidden all the treasures of wisdom and knowledge" (Colossians 2:3). The story of how Solomon acquired such wisdom is found in 1 Kings 3:5-13.

Some of the virtues commended in Proverbs are the pursuit of wisdom, respect for parents, liberality, marital fidelity, honesty, humility and piety. Vices condemned include lust, drunkenness, lying, cheating, laziness, strife, greed, pride, folly, gluttony and vengeance.

The principle theme of the book is wisdom. Thus words wise and wisdom occur more than one hundred times in the text. Similarly, Solomon's use of contrasting words, fool, foolish, etc., are also used over one hundred times! The intent was for this book to be a source of instruction for Solomon's *own son*, Rehoboam (1:8; 2:1; etc.). But Solomon also intended for these proverbs to guide all *youth* (4:1) and ultimately for *all men* (8:1-5).

Just a word about why we are starting and ending in the middle of Proverbs: We note that most subjects in Proverbs are presented a *"little at a time"* but *"again and again"*. This was an ancient teaching style that reinforced the teachings on a subject over time.

Proverbs 21:1-12

What is the writer saying?

How can I apply this to my life?

pray   Cuba – Protection for those making undeclared mission trips into this country.

Three times in the first four verses, Solomon addresses the human heart. In verse 1 he says that man's heart is subject to the sovereign will of God, meaning God can turn man's heart wherever He pleases. God's sovereignty is emphasized here by referring to the heart of the king, who holds the highest position of human authority. If God is able to move the heart of the king, he is able to move each man's heart. Second, in verse 2, the Lord *weighs* the heart, referring to God's ability to discern the motives of man's actions (see also 16:2 and 24:12). This is set in contrast to man's own ability to understand himself (v. 2). Man may think that his ways are right, but God is able to discern his true motives. Finally, verse 4 refers to the proud heart as wicked and associates this sinful condition of man's heart with an external haughty look and wicked actions. Beginning in verse 4, Solomon alludes to six different kinds of people addressed throughout the book: the wicked (v. 4), the diligent (v. 5), the guilty (v. 8), the scoffer (v. 11), the simple (v. 11) and the wise (v. 11). The book of Proverbs looks at the wicked man not only here (vv. 7, 10 and 12) but also eighty-five times throughout the book (see 2:22, 3:33). In this section Solomon describes the wicked man with the following characteristics: he is violent (v. 7); he refuses to live his life justly (v. 7); he desires evil (v. 10); he is impossible to please, looking critically at those around him (v. 10); and his end is destruction at the hand of a righteous God (v. 12).

Life **stEP**   God sees my heart and discerns the motives behind my actions. Do my motives reflect a life that is yielded to God, or does my heart portray one of the other types of people mentioned in this section?

Proverbs 21:13-22

What is the writer saying?

How can I apply this to my life?

Verse 13 condemns one who ignores poor people in their time of distress and promises a similar fate to the person who had the means to meet that need but didn't. James addresses this same mentality (James 2:15-16), claiming that one who shuns his brother or sister in need has a disconnect between what he claims to believe and how he lives his life (see also 1 John 3:17).

Next, Solomon pointedly addresses the affections of the fool, saying one specific way some become poor is through the pursuit of pleasure. If one always strives after the things in life that lead to supposed pleasure (here "wine and oil"), lack of wealth will soon follow. The source of perceived pleasure is vanity, and it will be fleeting. But being wise is not necessarily equated with being poor. Verse 20 notes that the wise man may have precious treasure in his home. However, he understands what brings true value in life — wisdom! Solomon contrasts the wise and the foolish man and their varied responses to possessions of wealth. The foolish man squanders those items of value. The term translated "spendeth" in verse 20 refers to the foolish man's greed and extravagant use of money. Shown jn contrast is the wise man, who understands how to live within his means and handle his possessions wisely; as a result, he still has his possessions. By displaying this contrast between the wise man and foolish man, Solomon emphasizes that wealth has no lasting value without the wisdom to know how to live within those means. Verse 21 explains what has true value: life, righteousness, and honor.

Proverbs 21:23-31

What is the writer saying?

How can I apply this to my life?

pray Guatemala – Reconciliation between the Mayan and Spanish – speaking believers divided by past war.

Solomon addresses five kinds of people in verses 23-31 who show up throughout the book of Proverbs: the controlled man, the proud man, the lazy man, the wicked man, and the lying man.

The *controlled man* (v. 23) is recognized by his sound speech (v. 23). He knows the power of his tongue and is self-controlled in what he says to others. As a result, he keeps his soul from trouble. The tongue is a theme Solomon sporadically addresses throughout the book. He talks about the gentle tongue (25:15), the backbiting tongue (25:23), the lying tongue (6:17, 26:28), the flattering tongue (6:24, 26:28), the righteous tongue (10:20), the perverse tongue (10:31), and the kind tongue (31:26). The tongue has the power to bring destruction or to bring life and healing (12:18, 15:4, 18:21). Ultimately, the tongue acts as an indicator of one's inner spiritual state and character (15:2). Solomon exhorted his son to guard his tongue in order to keep his soul from trouble in life.

The *proud man* (v. 24) is in contrast to the controlled man. Instead of being careful to guard his speech, the "scoffer" conducts himself with pride. He hates rebuke (9:8, 13:1), and judgment is prepared for him (19:29). In the punishment of the scoffer, the simple are made wise (21:11). Psalm 1:1 says the spiritually blessed man is the one who does not listen to the counsel of the scoffer — while the scoffer delights in his scoffing (Proverbs 1:22), the blessed man "delights" in the law of the Lord and meditates on it day and night.

What kind of speech best characterizes your life? Do you flatter, backbite, and lie, or do you speak with kind and gentle words? Do you seek God's grace to control your tongue, or is your speech like that of the scoffer?

Proverbs 22:1-16

What is the writer saying?

How can I apply this to my life?

This section alludes to a variety of people addressed throughout the Book of Proverbs. Solomon contrasts the rich and the poor (vv. 2, 7, 9, 16) and the prudent and the simple (v. 3). He also continues to develop our understanding of the scoffer (v. 10), the lazy man (v. 13), and the immoral woman (v. 14). In addressing these kinds of people, the writer presents instruction relating to wise or skillful living. Within these various statements of wisdom, Solomon broaches the topic of finances five times, specifically addressing one's attitude toward the poor (vv. 2, 7, 9, 16, 22). Verse 7 gives the principle that one who borrows is automatically subject to the one from whom he borrows. In verse 9 Solomon says that the one who is generous with his wealth toward the poor is blessed. This person is characterized by generosity as he gives from his own resources to the one in need.

In sharp contrast to the generous man in verse 9 is the man in verse 16, who oppresses the poor in order to increase his own personal wealth. Solomon says this man will come to poverty himself. In Old Testament times, special provision was made for the poor so that there was no partiality shown to them in issues relating to justice (Leviticus 19:15) and so they were taken care of in social and cultural issues because of their poverty (Exodus 23:11; Leviticus 19:10). The poor were also taken into consideration in the sacrificial system in the Mosaic Law so the cost to them was proportionate to their income (Leviticus 14:21).

God has a tender heart for the poor (Psalm 113:7) and calls for His people to accurately reflect Him in this area. Proverbs 14:31 says, "He who oppresses the poor reproaches his Maker, but he who honors Him has mercy on the needy." How do I show a generous spirit to those in need?

Proverbs 22:17-29

What is the writer saying?

How can I apply this to my life?

Verse 17 opens with two commands: first, a command for the reader to listen to the words of the wise; second, a command to apply that knowledge to the reader's heart. The term "bow down thine ear" means *incline*. *Incline* has the idea of listening closely with the intent of responding. David cries out to God in Psalm 31:2, "Bow down Your ear to me; deliver me speedily; be my rock of refuge, a fortress of defense to save me."

So Solomon exhorts his son to listen closely to the "words of the wise," or to "knowledge," with the intent of applying that instruction to his life practically. Why does Solomon stress the importance of these words of wisdom? Verse 21 explains that he instructs his son in an attempt to make him understand "words of truth," and that by knowing this truth, he might come to "trust" (literally *confidence*) in the Lord (v.19). The term *confidence* has in view the object of one's trust. Solomon wanted his son to find his confidence and certainty in life in the Lord, which comes only by embracing God's truth. Proverbs 14:26 echoes this thought when Solomon writes, "In the fear of the LORD there is strong confidence, and His children will have a place of refuge." The result of a life grounded in truth is a "pleasant" life (v. 18). This pleasant life is conditioned on keeping these words of wisdom as the foundation of life ("fixed upon your lips," v. 18). A life that embraces these words of wisdom not only has a personal benefit of being grounded in truth but also brings a benefit to those around the person who pursues wisdom ("those who send to you," v. 21).

We have an abundance of "truth" in Proverbs. Are we listening closely with the intent of applying it? As we apply that "truth," our lives will be grounded in wisdom, and God Himself will be our confidence — a "pleasant" life indeed.

Proverbs 23:1-14

What is the writer saying?

How can I apply this to my life?

pray Chile – For future church leaders to be called from among those saved at evangelistic activities.

Verses 4 and 5 touch on a wise perspective on work and wealth. Solomon commands the reader not to slave away for the purpose of getting rich (v. 4). The term "labor" means "to toil or grow weary." Solomon is not condemning hard work, rather, he cautions against becoming weary for the sole purpose of getting rich. Why this caution? Verse 5 says that wealth, by nature, is fleeting; it is transient and elusive. The basis for this admonition is "understanding" (v. 4b). "Understanding" is a theme predominant throughout Proverbs; it was the stated purpose for the writing of the book (1:2). Solomon put such a stress on obtaining understanding that he wrote, "Wisdom is the principal thing; therefore get wisdom. And in all your getting, get understanding" (4:7). So Solomon concludes that when a person gains understanding, he will understand the fleeting nature of wealth and will not wear himself out striving for it. In verse 5, when he speaks of "setting your eyes" on riches, he is referring to one's priorities in life. In this case of wealth, the priority being addressed is one that the person does not possess but is still striving to obtain. This priority becomes the focus of his or her life. Solomon is instructing the reader to reassess his or her priorities and not to set their sights on something that will disappear, but on something that is stable and dependable, namely "understanding" (v. 4).

Life stEP Wealth is not wrong, nor is laboring to be wealthy wrong, as long as that wealth has proper priority in life. One must have the understanding or wisdom to have the right priorities, to know how much to work in obtaining wealth, and to understand how to handle the wealth that may come.

Proverbs 23:15-25

What is the writer saying?

How can I apply this to my life?

pray Praise the Lord for His sovereignty over details of your life.

Verses 15-16 and 24-25 form bookends to our passage. They address the joy that wise children bring to parents. Solomon shows the connection between the state of the human heart (internal spiritual reality — v. 15) and the speech (external action — v. 16) that comes out naturally in a person's life. If wisdom is found in the heart of the son, then "right things" will come from his lips; the converse would also be true. A wise heart and wise choices are the prerequisites for joy in the life of the parents.

What would it look like for a child to be wise? First of all, verse 17 says that he or she would not envy sinners. A similar thought echoes in 24:1, with the word "envy" being the Hebrew word meaning "to be jealous or zealous for." (Genesis 30:1 says that Rachel envied her sister Leah because she was able to have children.) In contrast to the envy of sinners, the wise child will have a life characterized by a consistent ("all the day," v. 17) "fear of the Lord", a theme developed extensively throughout Proverbs (1:7, 29; 2:5; 8:13; 9:10; 10:27; 14:26; 15:16, 33; 16:6; 19:23; 22:4).

A second characteristic of a wise child is the kind of friends he or she makes (v. 20). Solomon admonishes his son not to mix with those given to excess in wine (drunkards) and in food (gluttons). Both of these types of people are characterized by poverty and laziness (v. 21). In contrast, the wise son will devote himself to truth, wisdom, instruction, and understanding, priorities that bring delight to the heart of the parents (v. 24).

Does my mindset about sinners, and my choices in friendship, reflect a wise heart that fears God? My choices have a direct influence on others around me. Are my choices bringing joy or grief to those who care about me?

Proverbs 23:26-35

What is the writer saying?

How can I apply this to my life?

pray — Dominican Republic – For believers to be godly, impartial witnesses to the oppressed Haitians.

Solomon gives two warnings in this section, against the immoral woman and against abusing alcohol. In addressing both of these issues, he understood that his example as a father played an important role in the choices that his own son would make. The term "observe" in verse 26 actually means "to be pleased with" or "to accept favorably." Solomon was encouraging his son to delight in the example that he saw in his father.

The specific term "harlot" surfaces in chapters 6 and 7, where Solomon warns his son about the harlot's dress and speech and the destructive repercussions of associating with her. In verse 26 Solomon uses two metaphors to describe the harlot: a deep pit and a narrow well. The terms describe a perilous or destructive situation for the young man who gets involved with this woman. The term "lies in wait" (v. 28) is also found in 7:12, of the harlot who lurks at the corner for the unsuspecting young man in order to entrap him.

The second potential pitfall Solomon addresses is drinking wine. He admonishes his son not to look after the wine because his senses would be dulled, his speech would be disgraceful, and he would begin the cycle of domination that alcohol can bring (v. 35). In a broader Old Testament context, an Israelite who took the Nazarite vow, consecrating himself to the Lord, had to abstain from drinking wine (Numbers 6:3, 20). In addition, both the priest (Leviticus 10:9; Ezekiel. 44:21), the king (Proverbs 31:4), and the prophet (Isaiah 28:7) were not allowed to drink wine because they were in positions of spiritual leadership.

Life stEP — Wine and ungodly women were two things that Solomon knew could sidetrack his son from living a wise life. Am I open to words of caution from wise people around me, or do I think I know better?

monday 14

Proverbs 24:1-12

What is the writer saying?

How can I apply this to my life?

pray   Chile – Pray for a reverence and obedience to the Word and a rejection of sensationalized faith.

In verses 1-2 Solomon addresses the two potentially unwise heart responses toward "evil men" — being envious of them or desiring to be with them. Verse 2 develops two personal characteristics of these evil men, and in doing so, Solomon lays out the specific reasons why he doesn't want his son to associate with them. First, he describes the nature of their hearts (or the aim of their *minds*). By saying that an evil man's heart "devises violence," Solomon gives us a window into this person's thought process. Psalm 2:1 uses the same word *devise* to describe the plotting or scheming of the nations against God, leading to their destruction (2:5). So the term *devise* not only implies the content of the thoughts that the evil man thinks but also demonstrates the spiritual condition of the heart from which these thoughts stem — a heart that rebels against God.

But how does Solomon know what is going on inside the mind of the evil man? Verse 2 continues by giving a second characteristic of this violent man — his lips "talk of troublemaking." The evil man's speech flows naturally from his heart and mind, demonstrating outwardly the condition of his heart. Verse 8 builds on verses 1-2 by saying that the person who plots to do evil (that is, *the evil man*) will be called a schemer. "Wisdom" is contrasted with the potentially foolish attitudes of this evil man. Verses 3-7 emphasize the priority of being established in wisdom in order to be strong (v. 5), successful (v. 6), and safe (v. 6b) in life.

What is my attitude toward the foolish and "evil" people around me today? As we make choices about relationships, we need to be sensitive to others' speech and what it indicates about their heart. How does my speech reflect my heart? Is my heart a heart of wisdom?

tuesday 14

Proverbs 24:13-22

What is the writer saying?

How can I apply this to my life?

pray Philippines – For seminary graduates willing to work among the rural poor.

This section contrasts the righteous and the wicked (see also Proverbs 10:3, 6-7; 12:26; 13:25; 15:28; 24:1). Solomon uses nine admonitions to teach his son how to live wisely as he observes the wicked around him. In verses 13-14 Solomon compares the sweetness of honey to the "knowledge of wisdom" and its effects on the soul. The result of having wisdom in one's life is hope (v. 14), a blessing that eludes the wicked man (10:28). Solomon addresses the hope-deprived wicked man again in this chapter in verse 15, when he highlights the malicious actions of this man toward the righteous. He exhorts him not to "spoil" (assault) the dwelling place of the righteous; the hostile intent of the wicked man toward the righteous is evident in Solomon's phrase "lie in wait" (v. 15), which is repeated in Proverbs 1:11, 18 and 12:6, where Solomon graphically fleshes out their destructive intent by using the phrase "lie in wait" for blood. Verses 16 and 22 demonstrate the demise of the wicked when he speaks of the "fall by calamity" brought about by God's wrath (v. 18). The terms "stumbles" (v. 17) and "will be put out" (v. 20) underscore this future calamity. In contrast, the righteous man is characterized by resilience. Even though he may fall seven times, he will get up (v. 16). Verses 17-20 detail attitudes the righteous should have toward the wicked. The two extremes of fretting and being envious are both condemned. Equally shunned is the response of joy at the destruction of the wicked (v. 17).

Do you find yourself fretting or being envious of the wicked? We need to have a wise, long-term perspective, understanding both the hope of the righteous and the certain calamity of the wicked at the hands of a righteous God.

Proverbs 24:23-34

What is the writer saying?

How can I apply this to my life?

pray Finland – For believers to abandon church hopping and become committed church members.

Two main themes comprise these eleven verses: my words (vv. 23-29) and my work (vv. 30-34). Four times in verses 23-29 Solomon refers to the "lips" or to a specific conversation. Verses 23-25 give a straightforward condemnation of speech that is partial in judgment (literally "to pay regard to face"). Partiality is also frequently condemned by the Mosaic Law. Justice is the very nature of God (Genesis 18:25), and as a result, God demanded justice of His people (see Deuteronomy 1:17 and Leviticus 19:15). Verses 24-25 give two examples to show the contrast in speech between one who is partial and the one whose judgment is just. The one who shows partiality perverts justice, calling evil good. This person is cursed by the nation because he is unfair. In contrast, the one who is just in his judgment rebukes the wicked with his speech. Because of his fairness, he is a "delight" to others, and his life is characterized by blessing (v. 25).

Verses 30-34 address the work ethic and highlight the life of the lazy man. The word *lazy* is found fifteen times in the Old Testament (often translated "sluggard"), fourteen of which appear in Proverbs (see 6:6, 9; 10:26; 13:4; 15:19; 19:24; 20:4; 21:25; 22:13; 24:30; 26:13-15). Solomon says that the lazy man is characterized by being "devoid of understanding." He or she has failed to understand the benefit of hard work. The lazy man's field shows evidence of lack of care; it is overgrown with weeds and useless. The lesson: laziness leads to poverty (v. 34)! Solomon alludes to the subtle nature of the poverty of the lazy man — he doesn't fall into poverty; it sneaks up on him.

Life stEP Do my speech and work ethic as a Christian reflect accurately the nature of God to those who watch my life? In what areas can I improve my speech or work ethic?

Proverbs 25:1-10

What is the writer saying?

How can I apply this to my life?

Verses 2-7, which address the king's life, could be summarized this way: verse 2, the glory of the king; verse 3, the heart of the king; verses 4-5, the reign of the king; verses 6-7, one's mentality before the king.

Verse 2 compares the glory of God and the glory of the king. The word "glory" is used 200 times in the Old Testament; it means "abundance" or "honor" and refers to the weightiness or fame of a person. When Joseph finally told his brothers in Egypt who he was, he said to them, "And you shall tell my father of all my glory in Egypt" (Genesis 45:13). In a national context, the glory of the LORD abided in the tabernacle during Israel's wilderness wanderings (Exodus 29:43) and often took on visible form (Exodus 24:16). 1 Kings 8 describes the awesome scene of the glory of God coming to dwell among men as it filled the temple at Solomon's dedication. In contrast, Ezekiel 11 describes the departure of the glory of God from the temple because of the nation's rebellion against God. In Proverbs 25:2, Solomon says that it is the "glory of God" to conceal a matter. God's glory is demonstrated as He understands a matter that is unknown to men, and as He uses all His resources and power to keep a matter concealed until He wants to make it known.

Verses 6-7 describe the humble approach that one should take before a king. Rather than assuming a place of exaltation, called here the "place of the great," one should take a humble approach. Solomon says that it is better to be asked to move up to a place of honor than to be asked to move down and be humbled.

Do I understand that the "glory of God" should be the focus of my life (1 Corinthians 10:31)? What would that look like practically? A life focused on the glory of God leads naturally to exalting God rather than to exalting self.

Proverbs 25:11-20

What is the writer saying?

How can I apply this to my life?

pray   Mexico – That the Mexicans find their identity in a personal faith in Christ.

These ten verses are filled with analogies, metaphors, and word pictures. Solomon speaks of apples of gold (v. 11), an earring of gold (v. 12), an ornament of gold (v. 12), the cold of snow (v. 13), clouds without rain (v. 14), a club (v. 18), a sword (v. 18), a sharp arrow (v. 18), a bad tooth (v. 19), a foot out of joint (v. 19), taking away a garment in cold weather (v. 20), and vinegar mixed with soda (v. 20). Six times within these illustrative word pictures, he addresses the topic of wise speech.

The word pictures and comparisons illustrate the power and influence of one's speech for either the positive or the negative in life situations. In verses 11-12 Solomon speaks of the *timely* tongue. He compares a word fitly spoken (its circumstance — the right words spoken at the right time) to a thing of beauty, such as apples of gold. In verse 12, Solomon speaks of the *rebuking* tongue. He says that when a wise rebuker confronts someone who listens, it is like an earring or an ornament of gold. Proverbs 9:8 echoes this truth by saying that if a person rebukes a wise man, he will love you; the outcome of a confrontation between two wise people (one confronting and one listening) is a thing of beauty. Verse 15 addresses the *gentle* tongue. Solomon writes that the gentle tongue breaks a bone, saying that even a gentle and sensitive tongue can be a powerful force. "Gentle" means *delicate, soft,* or *tender* and is used elsewhere in Proverbs of a "soft answer turning away wrath" (15:1). Contrasted against the positive metaphors of the tongue in this section is the "false witness" (v. 18). Both verses 14 and 18 describe the destructive and misleading speech of the fool.

Are my words timely, wise, and gentle, or have they been misleading and destructive? Either wisdom or foolishness is always reflected in my speech!

Proverbs 25:21-28

What is the writer saying?

How can I apply this to my life?

pray That the leadershipof your church will live justly, love mercy, and walk humbly with God (Micah 6:8).

This eight-verse section is comprised of seven statements that address the response to one's enemies, a caution about a contentious woman, the peril of seeking one's own glory, and the tragedy of a lack of self-control. In verses 21-22 Solomon instructs his son about what his mentality should be toward his enemies. The noun "enemy" is actually a strong participle in Hebrew and could be translated "one who hates you." In contrast to the natural response of reciprocating hate or vengeance on one's enemy, Solomon sharply commands his son to provide for his or her needs (such as providing food or water). The Mosaic Law presents the same guidelines to govern the nation of Israel (Leviticus 19:17-18). The approach of loving one's enemies can also be seen in the teachings of Christ in the Sermon on the Mount (Matthew 5:43-48) and in Romans 12:14, 17-21 where Paul actually quotes this section of Proverbs as he instructs the Roman believers not to take revenge on their enemies. They were to instead entrust the situation to God, allowing Him to take vengeance sovereignly and justly on those who mistreated others. Verse 22 gives the two-fold result of taking this loving approach with one's enemy: (1) "you will heap coals of fire on his head" and (2) "the Lord will reward you." The phrase "heaping coals of fire on his head" has been much debated, as it seems to go against the loving approach spelled out in verse 21. Some have held that the phrase is a metaphor for the contrition and repentance that comes from giving food and water. Others have suggested that coals of fire are literal live coals given to restart the enemy's fire that had gone out, another kind gesture for one's enemy similar to giving food or drink.

Has my response to those who mistreat me been consistent with this section? Practically, what would it look like for me to love those who do not treat me well?

The Apostle Peter writes to Christians in Asia Minor (modern Turkey) toward the end of his earthly life (A.D. 64) from "Babylon" (1 Peter 5:13).

Impetuous Peter is a beloved character because we can identify with his shortcomings and admire his zeal for the Lord. After his dismal denial of the Lord at His initial interrogations by the high priest, Christ graciously gave Peter three opportunities to publicly proclaim his love for the Lord (John 21). Peter was the key leader in the early chapters of Acts, but as the Jews continued to reject the preaching of the kingdom, the Book of Acts transitions to the ministry of Paul among the receptive Gentiles. Peter and Paul agree that Peter would concentrate on the Jews, and Paul the Gentiles (Galatians 2:7-9).

The last time Peter is mentioned by name in the Book of Acts is in his miraculous release from prison (chapter 12). He is rebuked by Paul in an undated encounter at Antioch (Galatians 2), which must have transpired before the issue (Mosaic Law observance) was settled by the Council of Jerusalem in Acts 15 (about A.D. 50).

The believers Peters writes to are a mixture of Jewish and Gentile converts. Peter draws heavily on Old Testament Scripture and analogies. Asia Minor was Paul's territory, so it very well could be that Peter is writing to people influenced by Paul. Peter also demonstrates knowledge of Paul's writings, including Ephesians (compare to 1:1-3 and 3:1-6 with Ephesians 1:1-3 and 5:22-24). "Babylon" (1 Peter 5:13) could refer to the actual city in Mesopotamia, where a large Jewish population would benefit from Peter's ministry. It could also be a cryptic reference to Rome as the current enemy of God. Trustworthy tradition places Peter's death in Rome during the persecutions of Nero (who reigned from A.D. 54-68). Peter supposedly was crucified (as a non-Roman) but requested to be hung upside down, feeling unworthy to die in the exact manner as his Lord.

1 Peter 5:12 ("I have written briefly, exhorting, and testifying that this is the true grace of God wherein ye stand") states the purpose for the book; namely, a reminder of the grace of God. Peter develops the concepts of the believer's salvation (1:1-22), sanctification (1:23-2:12), submission (2:18-3:7), servitude (3:13-4:11), and suffering (4:12-5:14). The style is similar to Peter's sermons in the Book of Acts. The Greek grammar is much better than that in 2 Peter, indicating that his associate Silvanus edited the letter for him as he wrote it (see 5:12). Peter levels thirty-four commands in the five chapters and mentions suffering sixteen times. By way of comparison with 2 Peter, 1 Peter concerns itself with the external pressures of suffering, whereas 2 Peter is concerned with the internal pressures of false teachers.

1 Peter 1:1-8

What is the writer saying?

How can I apply this to my life?

"Strangers" (v. 1) does not mean that the believers were unknown to Peter; it is the Jewish way of referring to people living in a land other than where they belong. The names of geographic places represent Asia Minor (modern Turkey). People from these areas were present at Pentecost (Acts 2). Paul ministered there, and the Book of Revelation contains messages to seven key cities of western Asia Minor.

Salvation is based on the cleansing blood of Jesus (pictured in terms of the temple ceremony of "sprinkling" water or blood for cleansing). This salvation is applied by the Holy Spirit, Who *sets us apart* ("sanctification") to God according to the plan that God has established ("elect," "foreknowledge"). Only by following God's plan can humans hope to have "grace" and "peace" (the typical Greek and Hebrew greetings of the day, respectively). Notice that all three members of the Godhead are mentioned. Peter will elaborate on their ministries in verses 3-12 (vv. 3-5, the Father; vv. 6-9, the Son; vv. 10-12, the Holy Spirit).

Gold has always been the most precious commodity known to man. Valued for its beauty and malleability, it still represents ultimate material wealth. Our faith is worth more than gold, and like gold ore, our faith needs to be refined. Today, tons of rock are crushed, bathed in chemicals, and then subjected to great heat to separate the pure gold from the dross. The Greek word for "fire" is the word *puros,* from which we get the English word *pure.* In the fires of purification, our faith and character are tried, and they come out improved.

Life stEP

Diamonds are the product of intense pressure, and these valuable rocks are crafted into gemstones with the violence of a hammer and cleaver. The pearl likewise is the product of an irritating grain of sand in the oyster's soft lining. As William Penn said, "No pain, no palm; no thorns, no throne; no gall, no glory; no cross, no crown."

1 Peter 1:19-16

What is the writer saying?

How can I apply this to my life?

The Resurrection took a band of defeated, discouraged disciples and changed them into the dynamic apostles that turned Jerusalem *right side up* with their message of hope. Peter concludes that the person of Christ is a reliable (*living*) source of salvation, and although these readers have not laid eyes on Him, their faith will not go unrewarded. The Old Testament prophets were aware that their messages transcended their own time and ability to comprehend. Daniel had to be told to relax, for his message was for "the time of the end" (Daniel 8:17), and he would be long in the dust of the earth by the time it was fulfilled. The prophets were interested in both the plan's details and timing (vv. 10-11).

Peter has a recurring theme of suffering *followed by* glory. Having dramatically described the splendors of our salvation and the blessings we have in Christ, Peter then applies theology to practical living. In verse 13, Peter refers to the practice of the ancients wearing special girdles to hold in place their long, flowing robes, which would impede progress in warfare, running, or work. As with modern weight-lifters, the tight girdle around the middle was thought to add strength to the body for exertion.

Notice that the command center of the Christian is *not* the emotions or feelings, but rather *the mind* (v. 13).

Hope" in old English meant *calm assurance*. In Christ, we are adult sons (v. 14) in the family of God by adoption (*son-placing*). This means we have all the rights *and* responsibilities of members of the family of God. We can call God "Abba," which is not just Father, but the Aramaic word for "Daddy."

Life stEP Good theology leads to good practice. (And conversely, all atheists are not born atheists. There came a point in time when they wanted to do something they knew God did not want them to do, so they changed their theology to allow their desired practice.)

1 Peter 1:17-25

What is the writer saying?

How can I apply this to my life?

pray   Cayman Islands – For the wealth of the island to be used to extend God's kingdom.

"Fear" does not refer to terror or dread of damnation, but rather to *respect*. Our eternal destiny is not in question, but rather our reward at the judgment seat of Christ since our sin was dealt with permanently at the cross. When we sin as believers, however, our fellowship and power source is severed. During this interval of *power interruption*, any efforts are fleshly efforts not worthy of reward, and in that sense, we will suffer loss at the judgment seat of Christ.

Peter mentions the transient nature of our stay in this world system. The things of this world are "corruptible" (subject to termination) with the exception of the blood of Christ and the human soul.

Despite their persecutions, these believers were living out an ancient plan. For the New Testament writers, the "last days" (v. 20) started with the cross of Christ.

Verses 23-25 honor the power of the Word of God. The breath of God is a creative force. With it, He spoke the universe into existence. He breathed into man the breath of life. He breathed out the written Word of God. Jesus is also referred to as the "Word of God" in John 1. The Greek word for "word" (*logos*) was used by Greek philosophers to refer to ultimate truth, as indicated by its occurrence in the word "logic." We are privileged to have both the "written word" and the "living word" from God.

The quote in verse 24 is from Isaiah 40:6-8. The nations of the world who have dared to touch the apple of God's eye will wilt and disintegrate like grass in the hot sun.

Life stEP

If we want to know where we came from and why we are here, then we have to talk to someone who was there when it happened. If we want to know where we are going, then we have to talk to someone who holds the future.

1 Peter 2:1-10

What is the writer saying?

How can I apply this to my life?

pray Brazil – Pray for a stable financial climate so that inflation will not diminish missionary support.

"Wherefore" draws a logical conclusion based on previous material. Verse 1 is saying that in light of what God has done for them, those who possess the truth, and the benefits it bestows, are expected to live differently than they once did. Verse 2 does not necessarily mean the readers were new or young Christians. Regardless of their maturity in Christ, Christians should still long for the Word as a baby desires his milk. In 1:23, Peter called salvation being "born again." Now in verse 2, he refers again to a born one.

"Laying aside" (v. 2) can be used of taking off clothes, a word picture Paul uses in the parallel of *putting off* evil deeds and *putting on* good deeds. Malice is the broadest of the sins mentioned, so we could call the rest of these deeds illustrations of malicious behavior. They all deal with interpersonal relationships. In verse 5, believers become stones in a building—apparently a temple, for we are also priests in this building, offering up sacrifices. Verse 4 introduces the new analogy by calling Christ a "living stone." In verse 6, this is specified as a "corner stone," which is the perfectly laid starting stone from which the whole building develops in all three dimensions. "Precious" (v. 7) has a root idea of honor, whereas "offense" (applied in v. 8 to those who don't believe) is the Greek word *scandalize*. The spiritual sacrifices we offer as "a royal priesthood" (v. 9) would include our own bodies (Romans 12:1-2), plus prayer, praise, and good works. One day, Israel will finally be the missionary force God intended. This will happen when the light of the church is removed at the Rapture. The tribulation period will witness an explosion of Jewish evangelists bringing multitudes to the Savior even in the world's darkest hour.

Life stEP Chosen people are not chosen because there is something special about them, but because the Chooser has a job for them to do.

1 Peter 2:11-17

What is the writer saying?

How can I apply this to my life?

In the Old Testament, Gentiles were outside of the *chosen people*, which did not mean there was no opportunity for salvation, but rather as saved individuals, they would need to follow the Jewish rituals. Circumcision would be a major inhibitor for the average Gentile. The cross of Christ, however, made a theological transition possible (this is first explained in Ephesians). The ground is level at the cross. Now every man can walk with God through His sacrifice, not the Mosaic ritual, because of His grace and mercy. (Grace is *God giving us something we don't deserve* while mercy is *God withholding what we do deserve— punishment.*) While the ceremonial law has been superseded, there is still a principle to follow. Christians are still called to separation in the moral realm in the same way as the Jews were in the ceremonial realm. "Conversation" (v. 12) refers to the whole manner of living, not just our words. Both Peter and Paul (Romans 13) emphasize the importance of good citizenship (God has decreed several human institutions: the family, the church, and the state). Peter warns against premature triumphalism over the wicked Gentile rulers. In due time, God will crush all evildoers under the feet of His Messiah. In the meantime, rulers have been ordained by God as part of His plan for efficiently controlling mankind. The exhortation to obey the king presupposes that the king is not asking for something forbidden by the higher authority, God. Peter and Paul both eventually lost their lives for obeying God rather than the king. Notice that Peter and Paul did not waste time attacking social ills (such as slavery and infanticide), as they realized these were the symptoms of sin-sickness, not the root cause.

1 Peter 2:18-25

What is the writer saying?

How can I apply this to my life?

pray New Zealand – For support to be raised to send pastors and missionaries to Bible schools.

Peter has discussed the blessings of our salvation, the requirements of our sanctification, and now the believer's need for submission. "I know my rights!" is a common exclamation in our day and age. Biblically, we have no rights (we are not our own—we've been bought with a price). Therefore the epistles call for the Christian to give up his rights and let God take care of revenge and fairness. In this passage, the response of a Christian slave to an unethical master is discussed. Peter implies that this situation will build the character of the believer, allow him to be a testimony to the watching world, and eventually be rewarded by God. Christ is to be our example in this matter. The word *example* here means *under write* and refers to a teacher's copy of the alphabet that a student would trace as he learned to write. As we pattern our life after Christ's, we are to *stay within the lines*. His example of patient suffering is without parallel in human history. If we follow in His steps, we can expect vindication in the next world.

"His own self" (v. 24) teaches the substitutionary aspect of the atonement. (As the hymn says, "In my place condemned He stood, sealed my pardon with His blood.") "Bare our sins" speaks of the spiritual death He experienced (separation from His Father) during the last three hours on the cross (when darkness covered the land and He cried out, "My God, My God, Why hast thou forsaken me?"). "Stripes" (scars) speak powerfully in the context, as slaves were subject to lashings.

Psalm 22 speaks of the death of Christ (a *past* ministry). In John 10, we are told that the Good Shepherd gives His life for the sheep. Psalm 23 talks of the *present* ministry of the Lord as our Great Shepherd (Hebrews 13:20). Psalm 24 talks of that *future* day when the King comes to establish His kingdom. 1 Peter 5:4 looks forward to the return of the Chief Shepherd, Who will reward all the *under-shepherds* (pastors).

1 Peter 3:1-7

What is the writer saying?

How can I apply this to my life?

pray Ecuador – For an end to anti – missionary propaganda from anthropologists, traders, jungle exploiters, and those with a political agenda.

The discussion of submission started with government in 2:13 and moved to masters in 2:18. Now husbands are in view. "Subjection" is not domination or an implication of intrinsic inferiority. It speaks of a chain of command established for ease of accomplishing complicated tasks—in this case, raising the next generation. It is a military term that envisions soldiers marching orderly in proper rank and file. Lest a woman feel that such a role is unfair, notice the parallel in the Godhead. Each member of the Trinity is equally Jehovah, but in the chain of command, God the Father tells God the Son what to do, and the Son sends the Holy Spirit.

Verses 1-2 in today's passage speak of *missionary submission*. In a situation where the husband is unsaved, the submissive wife can, by her godly example, lead her husband to salvation. A factor in submission is the modesty of the dress and behavior of the wife, especially to avoid undue attention from other men. The word for "adorning" is *cosmos,* which is the opposite of *chaos* and the root of the word *cosmetology*. Submission can be a terrifying concept. For the believer in a difficult situation, the key is trusting God. In our prayer life we can discuss the problem with God and then trust that He is bigger than our government, boss, or husband. Saints of old are examples for us to follow. Sarah comes to Peter's mind. Even Gentile Christians are "daughters of Sarah" if they live as she did. Women and children are the future of the race. The role of women in forming the "next generation" is a vital and noble task.

Life stEP Meek is not *weak*. The Christian woman must find the balance between total independence and total dependence—neither dominating her man nor manipulating him with pseudo-submission.

1 Peter 3:8-12

What is the writer saying?

How can I apply this to my life?

Having addressed some particular groups (slaves, wives, husbands), Peter now broadens out to his whole audience. "Finally" is used to draw his discussion of submission, not the entire book, to a close. Once again, our patience in the face of interpersonal conflict is attributed to the divine plan of God. We are called to endure conflict and retaliate with love. In these situations, as we give a blessing, we are also blessing ourselves, as that will be the reward we receive from the Good-Great-Chief Shepherd.

"One mind" (v. 8) is *mono-minded*. This is reminiscent of Christ's plea for His disciples to be of the same mind as He and His Father were. "Compassion" is the word *sympathy,* which means "to feel the same thing." Empathy would be another good synonym. "Pitiful" loses something in the translation because it literally means *good innards,* the equivalent of our *love from the heart.* "Courteous" comes from the word for *lowly* or *humble-minded.* "Railing" is cursing or abusive speech. "Blessing" is the word *eulogy*—saying good words about someone—which does not need to wait until a funeral. "Life" (v. 10) is the normal word for earthly life, but in the larger context looks beyond this life to eternal life (v. 7: "heirs...of life"; v. 9: "inherit a blessing"). "Tongue" is the word for *language* in Greek, and "lips" is the word for *language* in Hebrew. "Guile" involves anything from outright deception to exaggeration (see Proverbs 6:16—three of the seven things the Lord hates involve the tongue). Verse 11 says as citizens of the *city of peace* (Jerusalem), we are to seek peace (Hebrew *shalom*). Not casually, but as a hunter tracks his quarry ("ensue" is Old English for "pursue").

Life **stEP** What does a child want? The eyes of his father. ("Watch this, Daddy.") The ears of his father. ("Daaadddyyy!") But not always his father's full attention ("Face me, son.").

1 Peter 3:13-22

What is the writer saying?

How can I apply this to my life?

pray France – Passionate outreach to the nearly 50,000,000 people who have no real link with a Bible – believing church.

Peter implies that we have better odds of avoiding a fight if we control our mouths. In verse 13, what is translated as "followers of what is good" is a bland way of saying zealots for good. Verse 15 tells us what to do in order to not "be troubled" (v.14). We must first enshrine God in our lives. "Sanctify" means *to set apart* and shares its root with a variety of terms: holy, saint, sanctification, and sanctuary. God used to "dwell" (Hebrew *shakan,* from which comes Shekinah glory) in the temple. Since Pentecost (Acts 2), He has been dwelling in the bodies of believers. Because of this, verse 15 says instead of fighting with our mouths, we should be ready to rationally (that is, calmly) explain to our antagonists why we believe what we believe. It is the word *apologian* ("a word back") from which we get "apologetics," not a debate or argument.

The point of 1 Peter 3:19-20 is this: *Don't be surprised that some will mock you and make life difficult for you. Why,* *you should have been there in Noah's day! His neighbors laughed themselves silly, while really Christ was preaching through Noah that they should repent and join Noah's eight family members in the ark of safety. Well, they didn't, and who's sorry now?* Verse 19 says that in spirit form, Christ communicated with "spirits" of Noah's day. No time is specified, so this could have taken place through Noah *in* Noah's day. The rejection of the message by those around Noah led to their subsequent incarceration (in Hades).

Verse 20 emphasizes God's patience even in the face of sinful behavior. "Longsuffering" means "to go a long time before boiling over."

Peter is not saying that baptism saves. The waters of baptism *symbolize* the death, burial, and resurrection of Christ.

Life stEP Mean-spirited people abound. A soft answer turns away wrath. Believers should purpose to be peacemakers in their communication.

1 Peter 4:1-6

What is the writer saying?

How can I apply this to my life?

pray Dominican Republic – Praise – For a major increase in the planting of evangelical churches.

Just as Christ's reaction to physical suffering led to total victory over the physical, we should accept our sufferings as steps to domination of the sin nature and ultimate glorification in sinless perfection in Heaven.

Misery loves company. The unsaved are not satisfied to live in sin themselves but want to drag everyone down to their level. Peer pressure, pressure from the sin nature, pressure from Satan—all are avenues of temptation to sin even after experiencing the liberating power of God in salvation. But evildoers will not continue on forever. A day is coming when God will judge both those who have already died and those still actively harassing believers. Verse 3 would indicate that at least some of the recipients were Gentiles (although Jews certainly could mimic the excesses of the Gentiles). Peter has great disdain for pagan idolatries. Many ancient religions involved riotous feasting and sexual immorality.

"Lasciviousness" (v. 3) refers to uncontrolled behavior and is applied to Sodom and Gomorrah. "Lust" speaks of strong desire and comes from a root word for *burning incense*. "Excess of riot" pictures a river overflowing its banks and is probably chosen by Peter because of his recent mention of the flood. "Speaking evil" is the Greek word *blaspheme*. Verse 6 mentions the preaching of the Gospel to those now dead. This is not a second chance after death, but rather a statement that they had heard the Gospel before they died.

Those who want you to join them in their sinful ways have no concern for you personally. They will gloat just as heartily at your struggle with sin as they mocked your attempts at righteousness. The pleasures of the world seem so glamorous, but what will years of parties, wine, women, and song mean to a man five seconds into eternity? In the final analysis, who will have had a more pleasurable life?

1 Peter 4:7-11

What is the writer saying?

How can I apply this to my life?

pray   Finland – For God's Word to ignite a passion in Finnish hearts to overcome apathy and nominalism.

Peter encourages the readers with the thought *hang on, the cavalry is coming.* The return of Christ is a motivator for evangelism, holy living, and endurance. Peter says not to worry about missing a party because it's not party time; it's time to get serious and pray about the eternal destinies of eternal souls. This also is part of the Noah story, as repeated by Christ in Matthew, where He mentions the people of Noah's day eating, drinking, marrying, and giving in marriage until the rain fell and their day of salvation was gone. "Sober" comes from "to save the mind" and speaks of sound thinking. "Watch" speaks of self-control that enables times of prayer, whether it is by staying awake or using meal time (fasting) to pray. "Charity" is commanded—the fervent kind ("stretched out," as in, "he really outdid himself"). Peter suggests that hospitality fits the bill nicely. The church is a mutual aid society, both for physical needs (hospitality) and for spiritual

(the gifts mentioned here). The various passages that mention the spiritual gifts indicate that every Christian has at least one gift for the edification of the body of Christ. As the Word of God is ministered, previously blind eyes are opened, deaf ears hear, the shackles of sin fall off the stiffened limbs, and the sinner walks forth from the tomb in newness of life, metamorphosed.

In verse 10, "gift" is *charisma*, or a *grace gift.* "Minister" comes from the word for servant—*diakonos*. It literally means "through the dust" (a general is *adiakonos*—"one who does not go through the dust"). "Steward" implies a household activity. Verse 11 seems to divide the gifts into the simplest categories: speaking and working gifts (see Acts 6).

Life **stEP**   When you do something nice for someone else, past offenses are forgotten, and a new chemistry develops that leads to more harmony in the family of God. Christ came not to be ministered unto but to minister. Likewise, we are saved to serve.

thursday 16

1 Peter 4:12-19

What is the writer saying?

How can I apply this to my life?

pray El Salvador – For their Christian Institutes and Media to continue the impact they have already brought to El Salvador.

"Fiery trial" refers to fires of refining and purification (see 1:7). Church history shows that during times of persecution, the church grows stronger. This is partly because the dead wood is pruned and partly because each believer is drawn closer to God. "Partakers" (v. 13) comes from the root for *fellowship* (see Philippians 3:10). "The spirit of glory" is a euphemism for God in rabbinic writings (as they avoided using *God* out of respect). "Busybody" is a large Greek word meaning *one who is an overseer (episkopos) of another man's affairs.* It was a legal term formally charged against Christians. They were accused of being hostile to civilized society, trying to conform Gentiles to Christian standards, and thereby meddling in others' affairs. "Not ashamed" (v. 16) is a recurring theme in the New Testament. Verse 17 implies that suffering was allowed by God for the purpose of purifying His church. If He deals so harshly with His

own children, then imagine what He'll do to His enemies. The concept of judgment beginning at the "house of God" is drawn from Ezekiel 7:7 and 9:6, where the time had come for the judgment of sinful Jerusalem, beginning with the elders in the temple itself. Verse 18 is a quote from Proverbs 11:31. The author of the proverb probably had Moses and David in mind, two children of God who nevertheless were severely chastised for their failures. The proverb is preceded by, "The fruit of the righteous is a tree of life; and he that winneth souls is wise." Verse 19 introduces a new title for God in 1 Peter: Creator. "Commit" (*to place near*) is the word for entrust, a display of trust such as depositing money in the bank. It is the word used when Christ released His spirit to the Father at His death (Luke 23:46).

Life stEP The great hymnist, Isaac Watts, once wrote, "Must I be carried through the clouds on flowery beds of ease while others fought to win the prize and sailed through bloody seas?"

1 Peter 5:1-7

What is the writer saying?

How can I apply this to my life?

Peter uses three synonyms for church leaders in this section: "elders" (*presbyters*), "overseers" (also "bishops," from *episkopos*), and "shepherds" (as in *pastor*). "Feed the flock" contains special memories for Peter, as that was Christ's final exhortation to him personally (John 21). Pastors are to lead by example (Greek *tupos,* from which we get "type") from the front of the flock, not driving the sheep from behind as practiced today with the use of dogs, horses, and even aircraft. Faithful service results in the shepherd's crown, which, unlike the wicked of chapter 1, will never wither and fade. Since "the clothes make the man," the concept of clothing is a powerful analogy (like politicians who wrap themselves in the flag for political purposes). Here in chapter 5, Peter offers designer humility as the clothing of choice for Sunday services (and throughout the week as well). Pride was the very first sin in the entire universe (see Isaiah 14:12-14 for the five "I wills" of Lucifer).

The word *resist* is a military term from the same root as submit. It means "to be arrayed against." The word *proud* means "above to appear" indicating they have a superiority complex. "Humble" comes from a word that means *low*. Metaphorically, it is always used in a good sense. Humility is *lowliness of mind.* "Mighty hand" is an Old Testament figure of speech for God's miraculous deliverance of Israel, such as in the Exodus or in the future ingathering (Ezekiel 20:33). "Care" comes from a word that means *pulled in different directions* and can be translated "anxious." Even our petty cares are important to God.

There are people who make things happen, people who let things happen, and people to whom things happen. We need to be part of the cure and not part of the problem. In order to humble yourself under the mighty hand of God, you have to know God and know where His hand is.

1 Peter 5:8-14

What is the writer saying?

How can I apply this to my life?

"Sober" means "free from intoxication" and is used metaphorically of being clear-headed. Coupled with "vigilant" (awake), the phrase indicates total military alert. This type of alert was enjoined in the parable of the householder and thief (Matthew 24:42). "Adversary" comes from the court of law. "Devil" means *accuser*. "Roaring lion" is used in Psalm 22:13 to describe Christ's enemies; Job 1 shows Satan walking about the earth and accusing Job. "Devour" means "drink down," like Proverbs 1:12, which speaks of the violent swallowing up of the righteous like *sheol* (the grave) does the dead. "Resist steadfast in the faith" speaks of a refusal to do what is known to be wrong and to actively do what is right even when tempted not to. It does not envision verbal arguments with Satan or esoteric knowledge of the demonic world. In fact, 2 Peter 2 and Jude imply that arrogant verbal attacks upon Satan are a sign of a false teacher, not a child of God who allows the Lord to take care of Satan.

"Perfect" is a word used of mending nets. "Stablish" is the same word Christ gave to Peter before his denial (Luke 22:32: once converted, to "*strengthen* the brethren"). Verse 12 is our theme verse, stating the purpose for the writing. Marcus is none other than Mark, the cousin of Barnabas who so greatly disappointed Paul by turning back from the first missionary journey. He later rebounded to the point that not only was he Peter's associate and writer of the Gospel of Mark, but Paul also speaks of him fondly at the end of his life (2 Timothy 4). In verse 14, brotherly love would be demonstrated by the kiss on the cheek practiced by the ancients between members of the same gender. Today a firm handshake and pleasant words are an appropriate substitute.

Life stEP

What we need to know about Satan's powers is that a pure life, vibrant prayer life, and faithful preaching of God's Word will defeat Satan in our lives and in the lives of those we minister to.

As the early church moved from Judea to Samaria and then to the uttermost parts of the earth, it encountered a number of different obstacles. The timing of the gospels reflects the changing landscape within that church. Matthew, which was written very early, focuses on Christ's legitimate claim to the throne of David. John was written much later and focuses on the deity of Jesus Christ and His relationship to the revelation that had come through the apostles. Mark and Luke were written in the middle era. By this time, the church has shifted from a primarily Jewish phenomenon to a mostly Gentile event. Mark focuses on a Roman audience and emphasizes Jesus as the busy servant. Luke writes to the Greek culture and emphasizes the humanity of Jesus.

This is not to say that the gospels were merely a reaction to the community within which the apostles ministered, for there are always two authors to consider when one approaches a book of the Bible. The first is God, the Divine Author. God chose to produce this book in this particular historical setting because it was the best setting for understanding the absolute truth that was about to be revealed. This does not affect the meaning of the book, only its application. The reader knows that whatever is communicated is inspired of God and profitable for doctrine, reproof, correction, and instruction in righteousness (2 Timothy 3:16).

The second author is equally important but in a different way. Revelation, for example, cannot be accurately interpreted without context. The human author's historical situation becomes the standard measurement by which meaning is defined. Just as a measuring device is often placed by a piece of evidence to give it context, so the human author provides context for the divine message.

Christ's humanity, the focus of the book, is important for the same reason. Salvation is a divine provision that becomes meaningful for and available to man because Jesus became human. (His atonement was not meaningful for angels.) His message is also available to man because men wrote it. To correctly understand that message, one must turn back the pages of time and understand the message in the same way the original audience would have. At that one place, the reader, the writer, and the Holy Spirit unite in such a way that transcendent yet accessible truth is created.

This kind of truth is not convenient today. The postmodern church wants a super book that renews itself for every generation. They want a book that belongs to the people, not to the authors. They want application without meaning. Men have become the masters of the text and not its servants.

Yet those who serve truth see it as an absolute and shining beacon in a world filled with darkness. Luke writes his gospel so the reader can fully appreciate the humanity of Jesus Christ and better understand how we as humans can walk in His footsteps.

That is the real issue here. Is Jesus Christ truly our example? How can we see in Him a kindred spirit if He did not experience life the same way that we do?

This question has been part of theological struggles throughout the years. All battles, whether literal or theological, have unintended consequences. From the earliest times humanity struggled to accept the deity of Jesus Christ. That struggle has played out across the entire Church Age. In fact, the deity of Christ is the most important of all the issues involved—to deny His deity is to deny His salvation. (Denying the humanity of Jesus Christ is also prevalent.) The danger lies in the process. Defending Christ's deity is of utmost importance, but it must not be pursued at the expense of His humanity. If the life of Christ is going to have exemplary value to us as humans, it is vital that we understand what it means when we say that He was like us in every way except with regard to sin.

In Jesus' life, we see the difficulties the society He entered had with reconciling His purposes as a man, and as God. Men respect power and despise weakness. The nation of Israel was looking for a King, a strong leader who would lead them in military victory and conquest. Jesus offered to lead them into servitude. He told them that he who would be greatest of all must be servant of all. He not only spoke these words but also lived them. He did not come to help mankind defeat these enemies but to love and serve its enemies. This was unacceptable to the Jewish leadership of that day and ultimately led to Christ's crucifixion.

To Jesus, this service was more than a motto or a credo; it was His life. He demonstrated that heart change was sufficient to overcome the capriciousness of life. He showed that weakness can indeed conquer strength. He became like us to show us that our circumstances were not the real enemy. The real enemy is the one who lives within. It is a heart that chooses life over death, that chooses first over last, that chooses being served over serving.

So, we are left to ask, who was this Jesus of Nazareth? Does He really know how we feel? Did He really live His life with same kind of limitations that we have? Did He not always have an escape clause that would allow Him to unleash His divine power to rectify any injustice He might encounter? Or, did He live His life with the same restrictions and seeming futility that we do? Was His weakness a true weakness, or was it merely for show?

The theological truth is clear: Jesus was 100% God and 100% man. Luke is not questioning that. What is not clear is what it means that Jesus was 100% man. What does that look like on a day-to-day basis? That is Luke's special place among the gospels. It is his mission to help us understand what the humanity of Christ looked like.

sunday 17

Luke 1:1-12

What is the writer saying?

How can I apply this to my life?

pray Pray for many salvation decisions to result from the Christmas presentations being presented in many churches.

Luke writes this material for Theophilus who was probably a man of some rank and may have been Luke's supporter. Luke appears to be the only gospel writer who had no firsthand knowledge of the earthly life of the Savior. Rather than a weakness, though, this turns out to be a strength. It becomes a perfect example of how the divine and the human constantly intersect and coexist in our everyday experience. Luke studied and researched his topic in the same way any scholar of that day would have.

The result of his labor was still the Word of God, because the Holy Spirit moved him. The relationship between the two was seamless and can be seen in the text being both understandable and authoritative. Its human qualities give us the ability to know what it means, and its divine qualities guarantee that what it means is without error.

Luke's research into the life of Jesus Christ begins with the extended family, Zacharias and Elisabeth. They were an elderly couple and without children when the angel appeared to Zacharias as he performed his duties in the Holy Place. God spoke to Zacharias while he served in the Temple. Apparently God had not spoken to mankind since the last prophet of the Old Testament, Malachi. The last words of Malachi predicted the coming of a forerunner of the Messiah and now Zacharias is told that his son would be that man.

Life stEP God's Word is truly an amazing book. It flowed from the hearts and minds of men, but when written, it contained only the clear and compelling words of Almighty God.

155

Luke 1:13-25

What is the writer saying?

How can I apply this to my life?

The interaction between Zacharias and the angel, who identifies himself as Gabriel, is very instructive. One would think that the mere presence of an angel in the Holy Place would be sufficient "evidence" that the message was accurate, but Zacharias appears unwilling or unable to accept that message, even when the angel demonstrates from Scripture that these things were prophesied. But the promise of God had been dormant for many years, and this childless couple had no doubt experienced disappointments before. Zacharias felt that he needed more to go on than the word of an angel, so he asked for a sign. The response to this request is enlightening: it did demonstrate God's power, but it severely limited Zacharias' lifestyle and ministry. The lesson is that when men fail to believe God's initial offering, any additional help often comes at a price. Consider King Ahaz in Isaiah 7. He lost the chance to be a physical ancestor of the Messiah.

Verse 22 is almost humorous. Here is a man of God who has just been given the most incredible news both personally and for all mankind, but he cannot speak. God's plan marches forward. Elisabeth conceives and remains in seclusion for five months. There is no question that this family felt blessed—blessed to be with child and blessed to be a part of God's plan. But this is true of all of us. Each one experiences and appreciates God's blessing to the degree that his faith allows.

This passage clearly shows that God wants to use us. His blessing does not depend on our initial response, but it is certainly more pleasurable if we believe Him immediately and implicitly. Don't wait for signs, because signs come at a price if they ever come at all.

Luke 1:26-38

What is the writer saying?

How can I apply this to my life?

pray Fiji – For ministries to the University of the Pacific in Fiji, which impacts students from each island.

What unfolds in these few verses is the greatest mystery that man has ever faced. The almighty God, the Creator of the universe, the Holy One of Israel, stooped to earth and became a man. The Hebrew word used in Isaiah 7:14 would indicate that Mary was a young girl who had just come of age to marry. Unlike Zacharias, she does not question the facts, only the method. She did not ask *if* this could happen but rather *how* this could happen. The simple faith found in Mary is the most elevated trait in Scripture. While Mary is not to be worshiped, she is still to be respected and admired.

Luke's choice of the word *charis* (translated "favor" here but usually "grace") is clearly to be understood in the way that Paul uses the word. Correctly understood, the grace of God, acknowledged by faith, will produce peace in the most unusual of circumstances. Mary had to know that few, if any, were going to believe her story. Not even Joseph believed her at first. Her purity would be questioned. Her life was about to change forever. Her childhood was past. But she has the peace to say, "Be it unto me according to thy word." Wow!

One other point to note is that the child in her womb was Jesus from day one. It was not an extension of her body that would eventually become Jesus. Children are persons from the moment of conception. The life that quivered in her womb was cleary Who He was from the moment she was overshadowed by the Highest.

This is truly a precious and well-known Christmas story, but it is more than that. It is the account of a person just like us, a young girl who was willing to put her whole future in the hands of the God she trusted. Would we have such faith!

Luke 1:39-56

What is the writer saying?

How can I apply this to my life?

Elisabeth was perhaps the only person who could understand how Mary felt. Both had come face to face with the true grace of God and recognized it for what it was, and both were about to be the mother of a fulfillment of God's promise. Both were relentless in their acceptance and appreciation of God's will for their lives. The whole passage exudes an atmosphere of joy.

The words of Elisabeth to Mary are accurate but often misinterpreted. Blessing is something that God entrusts to mankind. It is never earned and never owned, always available but seldom seen. Blessing is the world we live in and the air we breathe. By faith we participate in this blessing, but when our faith fades, the blessing *appears* distant. Mary was not blessed because she was a woman of faith; she was blessed because she understood and accepted God's will for her life.

Mary's song is a simple psalm of praise. Its wording and structure are similar to the Psalms we find in the Old Testament. Mary truly understands her humble estate. She knows that the path before her is one of incredible blessing, and that the hardships are but a pittance in comparison to the opportunity she has been given. The song has no self-pity, no hint of complaint, and no suggestion of an alternate future. The words reflect just a simple peace that only faith in God can bring.

The generation of people that left Egypt with Moses did not enter the Promised Land. They looked at things through the eyes of facts, and figures, and grim reality. They should have looked through the eyes of faith like Mary's and Elisabeth's. What kind of eyes do you have today? Do you see opportunity or opposition?

thursday 17

Luke 1:57-66

What is the writer saying?

How can I apply this to my life?

pray Indonesia – For missionaries to reach every inhabited island to share the Gospel.

For nine months Zacharias has been silent, unable to speak. Imagine his frustration. For years he had heard his friends talk of their children. For years he had carried the desire to be a father and to hold his own child. And now, throughout the whole process, he is not much more than a silent bystander. But there is no resentment building in this man, as can be seen by his reaction to the birth.

The custom in those days was to name a child after the father or an honored relative. The officials at the circumcision, where this was usually done, assume that the child will be named after his father and announce it as so. Elisabeth stops the proceedings and declares that the child is to be named John. When Elisabeth announces this, the officials turn to the Zacharias, who then writes on a tablet that he is to be called John. Suddenly, his mouth is opened, and the first words out of his mouth are words of praise. He did not say, "Whew, glad that's over!" He has grown a bit since he first spoke with Gabriel.

Interestingly, a name is really a sign used to identify a person. In the recent past, signs had been important to Zacharias, but not now. He knew his son would never follow in the family tradition; he was a special child with a special name because he had a special future. With joy, Zacharias recognized this and, as Abraham with Isaac, he put his son's future totally in the hands of the Holy One of Israel. As word of all this began to spread, many began to ask, "What manner of child shall this be?" (v. 66).

Children are a gift from the Lord. They are blessings on loan from their Maker. We love them and cherish them, but we never own them. Their road of blessing may lead into the wilderness, and as parents we need to be careful we do not stand in the way.

Luke 1:67-80

What is the writer saying?

How can I apply this to my life?

pray
Pray for an unsaved friend or family member.

Zacharias' benediction has probably been in process through the nine months of silence. Like Mary's song, this doxology is patterned after the poetry that we find in the Old Testament. It is a Psalm of praise. The most common type of psalm we find in the Old Testament is the lament. Those poems start out with a call for help and end up with a faith resolution. But with both Mary and Zacharias, there is no call for help, just the simple recognition that the hope that was sought throughout the whole of the Old Testament has arrived.

Zacharias ties the birth of John to two key promises. In fact, these two promises are the central promises made to Israel: the Davidic covenant and the Abrahamic covenant. Both are unconditional covenants. We should never forget that the initial emphasis of God's salvation was directed toward Israel. God has not changed His mind about the elements within these covenants. Blessing is presently offered apart from the nation of Israel, but the restoration of the nation is indispensable to God in completing His salvation.

Verse 80 requires a special comment. By itself it would raise little interest. However, when similar statements are made about Jesus a little later in the text, we are left to wonder how a divine child and a human child can have this kind of growth in common. How is it possible for deity to mature in the same way that a human child matures? Luke's comparison of the two children is designed to emphasize similarities as well as distinctions.

Life stEP

What makes us human? Why are we different from the rest of the creation around us? How could God himself become one of us? More importantly, why did God choose to do such a thing? What an awesome God we serve!

Luke 2:1-14

What is the writer saying?

How can I apply this to my life?

The narrative now returns to the central figure in this gospel. Mary is great with child, and the wheel of Providence begins to turn. Cyrenius, the governor of Syria, had no idea that he was a part of the unfolding drama. His decree was purely to collect more taxes, but it started Mary and Joseph on a journey that would connect the prophetic dots laid out in the Old Testament. Micah 5:2 was clear about the fact that the Messiah would be born in Bethlehem, and it was to that city that Joseph returned with his young wife. The "swaddling clothes" and the "manger" are mentioned only by Luke. They have become a constant element within the Christmas story partly because they are uncommon items in our culture. Swaddling an infant (wrapping tightly) with strips of cloth was thought to produce good posture and to keep the child from accidentally scratching himself. A manger was a wooden or stone bin designed to hold hay for animals. Both of these elements suggest a sense of normalcy. Nothing about this child was out of the ordinary for human eyes. He required the same kind of motherly care of any infant born in that era.

What was not visible to the eye was announced by the heavenly host of angels. This very ordinary appearing child was in fact the promised Son of David, the Savior, the Messiah, and the Lord. Peace was now available. The favor (grace) of God to Mary had opened the door so that all mankind could now experience real peace.

Life stEP Familiarity often breeds apathy. We too often read Luke's retelling of the Christmas story and miss the major emphasis. This was a very routine birth but a very special person.

sunday 18

Luke 2:15-24

What is the writer saying?

How can I apply this to my life?

pray Pray for unity among the staff and the membership of your local church.

Luke has obviously chosen to recount different events from the nativity than Matthew. Matthew was focused on the child as the true heir of David, but Luke takes a different approach with his specific and unique purpose for writing. As the shepherds approach the stable, the spectacular is replaced by the common: no angels, no choirs, just a baby lying in a manger, bundled up like any other baby of that day. The shepherds' story was not based on what they saw in the stable; it was founded on the message they had heard in the field where they tended their sheep.

Eight days pass and, as was required, the child was circumcised. When cut, he no doubt bled and cried like any of us would. Thirty-three days after that, the child was brought to the temple so his parents could offer a sacrifice of dedication. Generally a lamb was offered, but if people were poor they could offer a pair of turtledoves or two young pigeons. Remember that, while a part of the royal line, Jesus' family was not wealthy. Jesus was not treated any differently than any child from his social level since, from all outward appearances, this child was no different than His contemporaries. All of this was done to emphasize His identification with us, with common everyday people. He grew up from his earliest days with the same kinds of physical limitations you and I face. There were probably nights that he went to bed hungry.

The transition from the transcendent glory of Heaven to the cold reality of life on planet earth was, for Jesus Christ, a decision. He was not there because He had to be, He was there because He wanted to be. He chose to be there because He loved you and me.

Luke 2:25-38

What is the writer saying?

How can I apply this to my life?

Just as the birth of Christ was followed by a divine announcement (the angelic host), so is the sacrifice of dedication. Mary hid these things in her heart and perhaps rightly so. People would be tempted to dismiss her as an over-zealous mother. But it was not Mary who spoke; God sent messengers. An angelic chorus appeared at Jesus' birth, and now God sends Simeon and Anna. Later He sends John the Baptist.

Simeon is an older saint who has been waiting for the Savior. He got to see what every generation of faithful Israelites had longed for. He saw the Lord, not "high and lifted up with his train filling the temple" as Isaiah had, but low and carried by a young girl out of a very different sanctuary. His message was one of exaltation and warning: he exalted in what was about to be accomplished yet warned about the road that must be traversed.

Anna's exact words are not recorded in the text. We only know that she recognized the child for Who He was and gave thanks to God for Jesus' appearing. She spread the word throughout Jerusalem that the Messiah had come.

Anna and Simeon were the exceptions. The message they proclaimed appears to have fallen on deaf ears. A short time after this, according to Matthew, wise men would come from the east, asking about this child, but nobody seemed to remember. How could such a thing happen? God was walking among His people, and only a few old people noticed. How easily the divine is overlooked in the day-to-day, hectic pace of our busy lives.

Life stEP God was walking among His people. The vast majority just yawned and went on about their daily lives. Will we do the same?

Luke 2:39-52

What is the writer saying?

How can I apply this to my life?

We must constantly remember that each gospel shows a different (but not contradictory) view of Christ. Matthew shows Him as king, Mark as a servant, and John as the Son of God. Luke presents the humanity of Christ. With today's passage we wrap up the materials that Luke has chosen to share with us about Jesus' early years. (Let there be no doubt that Luke has chosen this material. He is aware of what Matthew had written and most likely what Mark had written.) In this last passage, he draws his argument to a close, making what may be the most puzzling statements found anywhere in Scripture: Jesus "increased in wisdom and stature and in favor with God and with man."

The confusion is not with the words but with the theology that accompanies them. How can an unchanging God grow or increase in any way? The very concept seems incompatible with the God we see described throughout Scriptures. Other passages also confirm this mystery. Christ was tested in every way that we are, yet He did not sin (Hebrews 4:15). He emptied himself and was made in the image of man (Philippians 2:5-9). Though He was rich, for our sakes He became poor (2 Corinthians 8:9). All of these verses describe but never define the relationship between the human and the divine in Jesus. Maybe it cannot be defined in a way that we can understand. But we must not miss the point—Jesus was truly man. Each incident Luke recounts, including His conversation in the temple with the law experts, says as much about His likeness to us as it does His uniqueness.

Life stEP   What Jesus did, He did with the same limitations that we face. He became like us so we could walk in His footsteps.

Luke 3:1-14

What is the writer saying?

How can I apply this to my life?

pray France – Outreach among the growing Muslim population. Islam is now the second religion of France.

At least eighteen years pass between the close of chapter two and the opening of chapter three. We know next to nothing about those years. Now the voice of John is heard, the forerunner of the Lord. His initial message is simple: repent for the remission of sins. It is not clear, given today's use of these words, what exactly John was asking them to do. The word used here to refer to repentance is *metanoieo*. It literally means to change one's mind. Based on a correct understanding of Matthew's gospel and of Paul's teaching (Luke was an associate of Paul), it seems clear that John is asking them to change how they deal with sin. The nation of Israel had fallen under the tyrannical hand of a law-based self-righteousness that made salvation impossible and caused men to hate one another. John is preaching a new way: a way that depends upon being buried and resurrected in newness of life. This is the same message Paul described in his preaching about being crucified with Christ and yet being alive (Galatians 2:20). The content was different, but the message was the same.

Luke is building to a very special climax in his gospel. His idea was not new; it is the same message that has constantly been preached throughout Scripture. Jesus became like us so that we could become like Him. We must reckon ourselves to be dead to sin (here, buried with Him by baptism) in order to live (be resurrected) in newness of life. This is an act of faith, not an act of the flesh. Jesus died in the flesh so that we could participate in His death and no longer be a slave to the flesh.

Life stEP

John does not ask for a change in the degree that men keep the law; he asks for them to abandon works in pursuit of fruit. The nation of Israel needed to change their whole approach to righteousness. They needed fruit, not works. Do we not need the same?

Luke 3:15-22

What is the writer saying?

How can I apply this to my life?

While John's message was not new to Scripture, it was new to the people of Israel. They had not heard these words from their religious leaders. The message was so unique and powerful that some began to suggest that John was the Messiah. John's answer is profound on a number of levels. First, it was a clear assertion that he was not the Messiah. Second, he communicated that his baptism was only a picture of spiritual realities, and not a spiritual reality in and of itself. It was only water! The only meaningful baptism was the death, burial, and resurrection of Jesus Christ. Anyone who by faith participates in that baptism will receive the Holy Spirit (and produce the fruit of the Spirit). The fires of judgment will consume anyone who rejects that baptism, for "by the deeds of the law there shall no flesh be justified" Romans 3:20.. We need to be very careful that we do not confuse the symbolic with reality. Water baptism cannot save us or make us holy; it is a simple recognition that our life in now totally identified with the death and resurrection of Jesus Christ.

No doubt John knows his cousin by sight. He may have been fully aware of Who his cousin was, and so Jesus coming to be baptized is a shock to him—why would Jesus need to be baptized? He was sinless. This tells us a lot about baptism, showing it was not an efficacious act but rather a symbolic one. It did not deal with a person's sin but shows a person how to deal with sin. This also marks the beginning of Jesus' public ministry. His was a Spirit-enabled life.

The voice from Heaven quotes Psalm 2:7, a psalm that celebrates the beginning of a King's reign.

Life stEP If Jesus waited on God's timing to begin His ministry, how much more do we need to allow the Spirit time to prepare us?

Luke 3:23-38

What is the writer saying?

How can I apply this to my life?

pray Czech Republic – For Czech citizens to turn to Christ to fill the void left by years of Communism.

Modern readers do not enjoy genealogies. In fact, because the names are so obscure and hard to pronounce, we often just skip over them. But we do need to ask ourselves why they take up so much precious space. God clearly thinks they are important. Genealogies are not included in Scripture because the nation of Israel thought them important; Israel esteemed them highly because God constantly included them in Scripture. They go back to the very beginning, when God promised that the seed of the woman would crush the head of the serpent (Genesis 3:15). From the time of that promise until the birth of Jesus Christ, men like Simeon waited and longed to see that deliverer. Luke's genealogy is different from Matthew's in several ways. Luke would be aware of Matthew's, so these differences were by design. Luke traces the family tree from Jesus back to Adam. Matthew, however, starts at Abraham. Luke records the families in a traditional way, while Matthew arranges his genealogy in three groups of fourteen. The names in the two lists are different from David to Jesus. These differences are accounted for by the different purposes in writing. Matthew is proclaiming Jesus to be the true king of Israel and therefore traces Joseph's family, only going back to Abraham. Luke is interested in His humanity and, therefore, gives us Mary's family and goes back to Adam. Luke shows that Jesus is related to us all, for we have all descended from that one original couple. The Greek grammar indicates that Luke knew that Heli was Joseph's father-in-law, not father (23).

There is much to learn from genealogies if we are willing to put in the effort. Luke is convinced that it is a big deal that Jesus Christ is a direct descendent of Adam and therefore one of us. We are all like Adam.

Luke 4:1-15

What is the writer saying?

How can I apply this to my life?

pray Pray for those in your church who have lost a loved one this year.

The Greek word here translated *tempted* is in other places translated *tested*. Greek does not have different words for *tempt* and *test* as there are in English. This has created some confusion. We are left to decide with each occurrence of the word whether it should be translated *tempt* or *test*. Because it has been so often translated "tempt" in this passage, many have come to believe that Jesus could be tempted to sin. This is a wrong conclusion. God cannot be tempted (James 1:13) and, when we see Him and are like Him (1 John 3:2), we will not be able to be tempted either.

Try to keep thinking in terms of a substitutionary salvation, or trading places. Jesus is taking our death place so that we can have His life place. In the Garden the original couple failed the test. They were in a perfect place, with perfect food, perfect weather, and a perfect spouse, but they failed the test. Jesus was forty days in the wilderness without food, without company, and without any of the nice things of physical life, but He passed the test we could not. The tests were the same: the lust of the flesh (feed yourself), the lust of the eyes (look at the kingdoms), and the pride of life (cast Yourself down so the world can see the angels and know Who You are). It was the same tester: Satan. The outcome was what changed.

We should also note that Jesus did not use any resource except what man has: He quoted Scripture. He did not invoke his personal status as the Son of God but dealt with the tests of life using only those resources that any human could use. He fought his battles by faith, using the tools that we can also use, prayer and the word of God.

Life st**EP** Jesus willingly chose to be a little lower that the angels in order to accomplish His mission, which is not only to save us but also to make us like Him.

Luke 4:16-30

What is the writer saying?

How can I apply this to my life?

This encounter in Nazareth is only recorded in Luke; therefore, like the childhood incidents, it must have a special relationship to Luke's primary message. The correct focus of this passage is upon the reaction of the people of Jesus' hometown. These are people who would have known Him from a child. Do they appear convinced that He is a special person? Have they been overwhelmed by His mere presence? Apparently not! In fact, it appears that He is held in disdain. When the crowd asks, "Is not this Joseph's son?", they are clearly referring to the uncertainty associated with His conception. It appears that no one accepted Mary's accounting of what happened, and they considered Joseph a fool for believing her. They thought it was a cover-up of some kind. Jesus had been saddled with this stigma His whole life, and nothing about His appearance or abilities seemed able to convince the townsfolk otherwise. To them He was but a cruel joke played by Mary on Joseph. Because of this, they were offended that He would even suggest that He could be the Messiah, even though "they wondered at the gracious words which proceeded out of His mouth."

Some of the false gospels record amazing miracles performed by Jesus in His childhood, but it would appear from this passage that there was nothing about Him that impressed His community. He was just Jesus, the kid next door, no different from all of the other kids running around the streets of Nazareth. This was so engrained in the town that when He tried to convince them otherwise, they quickly took up stones to kill Him.

Life stEP The prophet Zechariah wrote about those that despise small things (Zechariah 4:10). Would we see Jesus for Who He truly was if He lived in our town? Do we see the invisible people in our world: the orphans and the widows in their distress (James 1:27)?

Luke 4:31-44

What is the writer saying?

How can I apply this to my life?

Having been rejected in Nazareth, Jesus sets up His headquarters in Capernaum. This was a much larger town about 25 miles northeast of Nazareth. Here, His ministry begins to flourish.

This is the first time that Luke describes specific miracles for the reader. Jesus casts out a demon and heals Peter's mother-in-law. These were not the only miracles He performed (see verses 40-41), but they are the ones Luke chooses to emphasize.

One important detail is that the demons knew Who Jesus was (v. 41). It seems rather ironic that the demons were doing what the people of Nazareth refused to do. Interestingly, Jesus forbids the demons from proclaiming this message. There can be no alliance between good and evil, even if the particular evil seems to promote the same agenda that Jesus does.

This day in the life of the Lord was like many of His days. He traveled about doing good and meeting the needs of people. But He did not have limitless physical resources. Verse 42 says the next day "He went into a desert place." Jesus' body was tired. He needed sleep and food. He carried on His shoulders the weight of the world, but those shoulders were like our shoulders, and there were days that He needed to rest. This again fits with Luke's purpose for writing this gospel. Jesus labored with the same physical limitations that are common to all men.

Life stEP Physical limitations are not service limitations. Jesus accomplished His mission while living with our weaknesses. Weakness is not an excuse; in fact, it is a strength. Only when we are weak can God truly be strong through us.

Luke 5:1-11

What is the writer saying?

How can I apply this to my life?

Lake Gennesaret is another name for the Sea of Tiberius or the Sea of Galilee. About thirteen miles long and eight miles wide, it is 680 feet below sea level and empties into the Dead Sea via the Jordan River.

Today's passage suggests that Christ preached using one of the boats as a pulpit and/or platform (v. 3). After the message he tells Simon Peter, who owned the boat, to launch out into the deep. Peter, who considered himself to be somewhat of an expert, said they had "toiled all night" and caught nothing. Peter knew that night was the time to fish in the area, for fish usually came into the shallow waters during that time. Peter must have thought that the Lord needed some advice on the art of fishing. Peter finally obeys, and the result is so "great a multitude of fish" that their net broke! Others were called to help, but the boat began to sink. What a catch!

We need to remember that these men had been with Jesus prior to this. They were not new to His ministry or His miracles. After all, Peter's mother-in-law had been healed recently. But the text says they were astonished at this particular miracle.

This point appears to be when it all became very personal for Peter. The encounter was no longer about a great prophet and the nation of Israel; it was about Jesus the Son of God and Peter a son of man, just the two of them. Peter fully grasped the significance of the situation and fell to his knees. Like Isaiah (chap. 6) he understood the precariousness of the moment: a sinful man in the presence of a holy God.

Life stEP

There is a gap between the objective and the personal. Many of us have a clear and clinical understanding of the Gospel and of the Savior, but it has never become personal. A miracle is as meaningless as a magician's illusion if we do not come face to face with the God behind the miracles.

Luke 5:12-26

What is the writer saying?

How can I apply this to my life?

In the previous miracles described by Luke, Jesus has shown mastery over physical weakness (fever), spiritual wickedness (demons), and natural laws (fish). The next two miracles shift the emphasis away from persons and onto their sin. In the Old Testament, leprosy was an affliction designed by God to punish specific sins—a spiritual problem, not a physical one. When the leper approached Jesus and said Jesus could heal him if He wanted to, he was in effect equating Jesus with God since leprosy was given by God and could only be removed by God. Jesus was doing far more than any prophet could do. He said simply, "I am willing," and thereby accepted the position of God with respect to the leper.

The next miracle is even clearer. Before Jesus heals the invalid, He says, "Thy sins are forgiven thee." This statement was as much for the crowd as it was for the paralytic. They rightly thought in their hearts, "Who can forgive sins but God alone?" Jesus then heals the man as proof that His statements concerning forgiveness were true. This is the proper role of miracles in the New Testament. They are not designed to thrill the crowd; Christ and the apostles use them judiciously to verify their claims. Doing a miracle did not make Jesus God, but claiming to be God and then doing a miracle was a totally different matter. If Jesus wanted the miracles to simply attract a crowd, why would He command the leper to not tell anyone?

Life **stEP**   Some people look for miracle workers today, but there can be no supernatural activities without supernatural authority. We have the writings of men who proved themselves to be truth-tellers by their Holy Spirit-enabled powers. The only truth we have is the text. Where there are no authorized messengers, there are no authorizing activities.

thursday 19

Luke 5:27-39

What is the writer saying?

How can I apply this to my life?

Levi was a tax collector or publican (a public contractor who worked for the Roman government). As such, he was one of the most unpopular kinds of men in the land. Jesus did not despise him, however. In fact, Levi was another name for Matthew, who later wrote the gospel that is named after him.

The feast and the resulting questions reintroduce John the Baptist into the discussion and mark this as a summary point in the Gospel. It allows Luke to reassert the message that had opened the section: repent for the remission of sins. Remission can never be accomplished by putting new wine in old skins. To save one's life, one must lose it. There is no salvation in our old skin; we need a new skin to hold the new life. The old man must be buried, as pictured in John's baptism, and resurrected in newness of life.

Levi gave up the old and embraced the new. Most of the religious crowd understood *he* had to change, but they did not think that they themselves had to. After all, they were the spiritual ones and not publicans.

Jesus' last words are ominous. As long as a person is satisfied with the old, they are never going to accept the new. Jesus was offering a new life, not an improved old life. The religious leadership enjoyed their elite status. They did not want to give up all that they had worked for and start anew with the likes of Levi. Their self-righteous, spiritual pride locked them in the darkness, and they refused to even taste the new wine.

Life stEP Luke's message, simply put, is that the only genuine Christian is a dead Christian. Paul beseeches us to be living sacrifices, to die daily, and to be crucified with Christ. As long as we worship at the faucet of old wine, we will never truly live the new life.

Luke 6:1-12

What is the writer saying?

How can I apply this to my life?

pray Finland – For more Finns to respond to the call to full – time Christian service and missions.

This chapter marks a new emphasis in Luke's gospel. We now begin to see the opposition of those who are content with the "old wine."

The Sabbath was established in the very beginning and instituted as a part of the Mosaic Law as the fourth of the Ten Commandments. But it is also the only commandment that is not reaffirmed by the New Testament. This is certainly by divine design. This is a perfect test case because it involves no evil desires of the heart, as is the basis for the other nine. Keeping the Sabbath is merely outward conformity to God's command.

Luke did leave us in somewhat of a logical quandary as he closed the last section. If those who have lived and loved the old are doomed to stick with the old, how will anyone be made new? We need to be convinced that the old is not as good as we thought it was. That is where Luke's emphasis is now headed. The religious crowd wants to talk about the Sabbath. They want to fight the battle on their own terms. Jesus makes it a war of the heart and of human nature. The example of David is perfect. Man by nature is a lawbreaker. Therefore, he was not made for the law. The law was made for him. But why was it made? A study of all related passages indicate that it was not designed to frustrate man, but so we could have life and have it more abundantly.

That Jesus went into the mountain to pray about His choice of disciples (v. 13) is another look into the genuine humanity of Jesus. His praying would be a meaningless exercise if He already knew who to pick.

Life stEP There are only two kinds of righteousness that a man may possess. One is a self-righteousness that comes from human effort and never reaches the glory of God's righteousness. The other is the righteousness graciously offered to us by God Himself.

Luke 6:13-26

What is the writer saying?

How can I apply this to my life?

There are nine incidents (some have multiple mentions) of the Lord praying in Scripture. Seven of the nine are unique to Luke. He alone emphasizes this aspect of Jesus' life, such as in this passage, where He takes the important decision of choosing His disciples to His Father in prayer.

The names of the twelve are not always listed in the same order, but it appears that Peter, Matthew, Phillip, and James had leadership roles within the administrative setup of the group.

The message recorded in verses 20-49 is another sample of what we generally refer to as the Sermon on the Mount. Jesus would have preached this sermon on numerous occasions. According to Matthew, it was "the gospel (good news) of the kingdom." The good news was that the kingdom was not for the so-called spiritual elite. It was for everyone and anyone who wanted to participate. That is why Jesus opens with a very profound statement: "Blessed be ye poor."

Matthew is a little less cryptic, saying, "Blessed are the poor in spirit." Both versions communicate the exact same information. In order to participate in the new, one must break fellowship with the old. Those who seek righteousness find it, but those who think they have found righteousness never look for it. Therein is the enigma. In order for one to embrace the provided righteousness, he must let go of all earned righteousness. He must die to the old in order to benefit from the new.

Life stEP Blessing comes in the strangest of routes. It requires that we let go of what was counted as blessing and embrace a new life. Jesus' message was good news for the desperate soul but a warning to the rich.

Luke 6:27-38

What is the writer saying?

How can I apply this to my life?

pray Honduras – For God to provide the teaching staff and funding needed to keep Bible schools operating.

The reporting of this sermon is much shorter and more cryptic in Luke than it was in Matthew. This was probably a different occasion, but there is no reason to believe that both Matthew and Luke did not condense the message for their gospels. Luke's research would have brought him into contact with Matthew's account, so we may assume that he had a purpose for including this sermon in his gospel as well. Matthew used the sermon to emphasize the difference between the true intent of the law and the Pharisees' use of the law. Luke is more focused on the broader community. This message was not just for the Jews; it was for all mankind. Just as the Pharisees had used the law to promote their own status and agenda, men from all tribes and people used various laws in general as a means to righteousness. Jesus was offering a righteousness that came from outside of the universe—righteousness from God Himself. This is an infinite righteousness that can only be meaningful when put to use, a righteousness that enables us to love our enemies, a righteousness that enables us to sacrifice for those who do not deserve it, and a righteousness that allows us to be gracious to all and never resent it. It is a simple fact of spiritual life—the kind of righteousness we embrace is the kind of righteousness we will respect.

One may be tempted to ask, as Paul did in 2 Corinthians 2:16, "Who is sufficient for these things?" The answer is simple, no one but the Lord Jesus Christ. If we are to walk the walk and talk the talk, we must decrease so He can increase (John 3:30).

Life stEP Trees grow fruit so that fruit can grow trees. We need the lasting fruit of the Spirit, not the works of the improved flesh.

Luke 6:39-49

What is the writer saying?

How can I apply this to my life?

pray For Christian writers as they develop curriculum for churches with biblical content, clarity, and creativity.

The lesson that began two days ago concludes in today's passage. If we look back to verse 20, we discover that Jesus was speaking these words to his disciples. He was asking them to live as He, their "teacher," lived. The nature of fruit trees is to produce fruit, He teaches, and it is not enough to accept salvation; they too must become the same kind of people. Jesus took care of their sin and lived sinlessly in reality so that they could partake of this lifestyle by faith.

Ground zero for this new life is inside of each one of us: our hearts. The way this message of a transformed life is proclaimed is from a transformed heart. Men who set aside the old and embraced the new, such as Matthew the tax collector and Simon the zealot, proclaimed it.

Jesus' disciples were a band of fishermen and common laborers brought together by a carpenter from Nazareth. None of them were religious leaders. Jesus was relentless in communicating to them the simple but profound message of new life in new skins, and they appreciated the good news because they knew they needed it.

Jesus is equally clear about the nature of this information; it is the foundation upon which all other teaching must be built. This is a place to begin, not a place to finish.

We often postpone opportunities needlessly and think that being spiritual is a distant target. Jesus saw it differently. He called the disciples to immediate change. The same is true for each of us—today is the day of salvation.

Luke 7:1-10

What is the writer saying?

How can I apply this to my life?

After recounting this wonderful sermon, Luke follows up with a number of incidents that flesh out the principles he has been focusing on.

Looking at the broader picture for a moment will be helpful. The word "faith" is used four times in the next two chapters. It has only been used once so far by Luke (5:20) and will not be used again until 12:28. In these two chapters Luke points to three incidents of exceptional faith and one incident of questionable faith. What is interesting is that the great faith comes from the least expected sources: a centurion in 7:9; a sinful woman (perhaps a prostitute) in 7:50; and another woman considered unclean by the law because of a bleeding issue in 8:48. While these three show faith, the faith of the disciples is questioned.

Jesus' "blessed are the poor" principle is clearly exhibited. Those with nothing to lose embrace what is a challenge to those who perceive themselves to be blessed already.

The centurion was a friend of the Jewish population and perhaps already a "God-fearer," but he would still be considered a Gentile and outside of the chosen. He was permitted to watch from the perimeter but never really allowed into the congregation. For the Jews, he was spiritually invisible. Yet Jesus commends him as having greater faith than anyone in Israel. His faith was so great that the text says that Jesus marveled at him. (An aside: Jesus' humanity is again evidenced in that He is genuinely surprised by this man's faith—the Holy Spirit withheld information from Him until He needed it for ministry.)

Sometimes we equate influence and faith. We expect great faith to come from strength. But truly great faith can only come from weakness since it is a dependence on God, not a dependence on faith. We need to be strong, but it needs to be Christ's strength in us.

Luke 7:11-23

What is the writer saying?

How can I apply this to my life?

Today's passage contains two incidents: the raising of the widow's son and the question sent by John the Baptist via his disciples. Widows in that ancient world were generally objects of pity. They would be seen as non-contributing members of the community, and like the centurion, they were spiritually invisible. Widows were most often viewed as an opportunity for the more affluent members of the community to publicly demonstrate their righteousness with alms. (James remarked, however, in his epistle that true and undefiled religion was "to visit the fatherless and widows in their affliction" (1:27).)

In verses 16-17, the crowds are calling Jesus a great prophet. When John is told of these things, he sends an emissary to Jesus to ask Him if he is indeed the Messiah or is he just another prophet. This is another case of the weak and the strong. More than anyone, John should have been convinced that Jesus was indeed the Messiah, but even he had moments of doubt. John himself did have much to lose since he had preached about the coming Savior. He had baptized Jesus and declared him to be the Messiah. But now John wondered about his position in the program.

Jesus' only response was to offer John what was available to anyone who lived in that region. Now it was John's choice to respond in faith.

Faith is not the doorway to a new life; it is the new life. Whether one is a widow who just lost her only son, or the greatest prophet born of a woman, we are all equally in need and can only please God by our faith.

Life stEP   The eye of the flesh cannot see blessing. We must first believe and then experience. Experience cannot precede blessing, or the faith dynamic is jeopardized.

Luke 7:24-35

What is the writer saying?

How can I apply this to my life?

pray For our country and its leaders to see their need for the freedom that only Christ can provide.

Jesus uses John's question as an opportunity to ask the crowd about John. He uses the same question ("What went ye out in the wilderness to see?") three times, showing the importance of the issue. The people did not go out to see healings and miracles. They did not go out to see a well-dressed man. They did not go out to see an important official. They went out to hear a very special message, a message of hope, a message of change, and a message of salvation. And yet this simple man, with a simple lifestyle and a non-miraculous ministry, drew great crowds. He was as great as any prophet that ever lived. What John said defined his ministry.

But the crowds following John, then Jesus, missed the message. People were attracted to Jesus' miracles rather than His point: repent and change your mind about what it means to be blessed. Those who rejected John said he was a weirdo who lived in the wilderness.

The same leaders said that Jesus was a party animal who didn't understand true spirituality. Their objections were about the outward things, but it was always the message they couldn't handle. They would not admit to being poor. They would not repent. The truly wise man is the one who is able to see through the spectacle and discern the message behind the miracle—and then follow it.

Life **stEP** Reducing our accomplishments to nothing, or disowning our hopes and dreams, is not easy. But it is essential. We need to accept Jesus' accomplishment and believe in His hopes and dreams for us.

Luke 7:36-50

What is the writer saying?

How can I apply this to my life?

Today we are introduced to the second of the three people commended for their faith: a woman who was known to be a sinner. The episode starts with a prominent Pharisee who invites Jesus to dine with him. During the meal a woman approaches Jesus and begins to wash Jesus feet with her tears and wipe them with her hair. Notice that the crowd makes two observations. They still suggest that Jesus is only a prophet, and they know who this woman is and what she does. Despite all these people knowing her past, however, this woman is the only one who recognizes Who Jesus is. She comes not to be healed, but to have her sins forgiven. The rest of the crowd did not realize they were just as needy as she.

Notice Jesus' words to Simon. He is not complaining about how He was treated. He is telling Simon that there is only one thing that really matters in life, and that is what one does with Jesus Christ.

We can write Christ off as a great teacher, a good example, or even a great prophet, but if we do that, we will never understand His mission or His provision. Jesus came to save sinners; He alone occupies the seat of the righteous. Simon felt he could deal with Jesus as an equal, but he, and the whole crowd, should have been on their knees begging for forgiveness. Only the woman got it. She understood the grace of God was walking in their midst.

Life stEP Repentance is not a selective activity; it is lifestyle. We must live our lives at Jesus' feet. We need to rejoice not in ourselves but in Who Christ is and what He has done. Never take salvation for granted.

Luke 8:1-15

What is the writer saying?

How can I apply this to my life?

As with many of the sermons and illustrations used by Christ, there is no reason to think they were only spoken on one occasion or that they were always used for the same purpose. The parable of the sower is also recounted in Matthew in a somewhat different context but with a very similar application. The point emphasized in Luke is that the impact of the seed is determined by the nature of the soil. Not every person will respond to the Gospel in the same way. In this case the good ground was a centurion and a woman involved in a public sin. The unproductive soils were the religious leaders and the population who followed them.

The seed is eternally the same, though— an absolute in a constantly changing world. That seed can only germinate and produce fruit when it falls on the right kind of ground, however.

Parables are a unique kind of communication. Jesus uses them intentionally so those who reject His primary message would be blinded by it: "That seeing they might not see, and hearing they might not understand" (v. 10).This dual purpose of parables is explained more extensively in Matthew 13:11-17. Parables are illustrations of the truth and not purveyors of truth. Unless one grasps the truth that is being illustrated, the parable may be used in different ways. For the one willing to accept the truth, a parable makes the truth clearer. For the one unwilling to accept the truth, it provides an occasion to suggest an alternate truth.

Life stEP The sower sowed the seed indiscriminately. He didn't just choose the best soil. So it is with the Gospel; we sow, and it produces results. We should never try to sow just on good ground.

sunday 21

Luke 8:16-25

What is the writer saying?

How can I apply this to my life?

Too often we fall prey to the same kind of warped thinking that afflicted the disciples in today's passage. The wrong thinking, shown here, is that once we humble ourselves, God is obligated to enrich us with the very things that are destroying those who have rejected the truth. The lesson is: If weakness produces reliance and faith, shouldn't we then be looking for more weakness? And if self-righteousness produces God-rejecting pride and arrogance, should we then not strive to be less self-righteous? That is exactly what Jesus is teaching in the parable in verses 16-18. The same power that produces this high-quality justification is the controlling power for all our dealings with God. As we mature in Him, we should expect to become more dependent on Him.

The disciples have spent time with the Lord and have seen Him heal the centurion's servant, raise the widow's son, and forgive the sinful woman. They have listened to the parable of the seed and the sower. And yet, as the capriciousness of life presses on them, they revert to their old ways, overvaluing the old life and undervaluing the new. They forget Who it is sleeping aboard the boat and begin to fear the storm instead of fearing the God who is Master of the storm. One would think that the disciples would be the most likely to pass the faith test. But they failed where a centurion and a sinful woman had succeeded. Especially meaningful is how they are still asking what manner of *man* is this.

Faith does not come to us naturally, and it never emerges from strength. Faith can only flourish in weakness since it is accepting our failure and celebrating in Christ's success. This is perhaps the reason that Jesus had to become weak (100% man) in order for us to become strong.

Luke 8:26-40

What is the writer saying?

How can I apply this to my life?

pray Italy – For perseverance among missionaries, as an average of only 10% return for a second term.

Two to three people groups emerge for consideration in this passage. The demoniac generally receives most of the attention. But his response is clarified by the reaction of the general population. The people in the region not only dismissed a miracle of this magnitude but also resented it. They may have reacted this way because of the loss of livestock when the pigs ran into the lake and were drowned. If that was the case, then they put their financial security ahead of a human life.

The demons reacted in a similar way. They wanted to get away from Jesus as fast as possible. Only the demoniac wanted to associate himself with Jesus. As terrible as it seems that these people lost their personal property, remember that it was unlawful for Jews to eat pork or any part of the pig. These farmers were promoting and enabling the people of the area to break the law. Even if they were selling the product to Gentiles, they were still compromising their status as law-abiding members of the Jewish community.

The demoniac cannot be put in the same category as the centurion and the sinful woman because he was not healed in response to his faith. As a demoniac, those evil creatures bound his will. Still, he clearly responded properly to Jesus' intervention. The more important theme, life through death, is advanced. He was a man who had nothing, and yet he was the only person that Jesus was able to help.

Life stEP Do you see a pattern here? The religious crowds, with all their supposed righteousness, were fighting Jesus at every turn. Only the helpless and the hopeless clung to Him.

Luke 8:41-56

What is the writer saying?

How can I apply this to my life?

Many have discussed why the primary miracle in this passage (raising the dead) is interrupted by a lesser miracle, the issue of blood. As well as these events happening this way, Luke also looks to highlight the differences. Jairus was a part of the religious crowd, the ruler of the synagogue. We cannot discern what he believed about Jesus, but he did recognize His ability to perform miracles.

This woman, on the other hand, was afflicted with an issue of blood that made her legally unclean. She wouldn't have been able to participate in most social gatherings, such as attending synagogue.

The woman becomes the third person commended for their faith in this particular section of Luke, and Jesus tells her to "go in peace."

In contrast to this woman's faith is the situation with Jairus' daughter. The girl has now died. Jesus still wants to see her, but Luke tells us that "all" laughed when Jesus said that she was not dead. How the parents responded is not clear, but Jairus did not rebuke the crowd. After Jesus raised the daughter from the dead, He told Jairus and his wife that they should tell no one. The fact that they were astonished by what was done seems to put them in the same category as the disciples, who marveled when Jesus calmed the sea. Because there was no demonstration of faith by these people, Jesus did not give them an admonition to serve.

Again, the weak understand, and the strong miss the true meaning of what is happening.

Life **stEP** Faith can only be exercised from a position of weakness, and the weakest position that we can place ourselves in is to be crucified with Christ. We must die daily if we want to be able to live daily.

Luke 9:1-11

What is the writer saying?

How can I apply this to my life?

pray Pray that God will give your church a greater burden to reach the lost in your community.

If at all possible, ignore the chapter breaks. Luke did not put them in the text, and sometimes they create a sense of separation that should not be there. Jesus has just told Jairus and his wife to "tell no man what was done." Now He sends out His disciples, not only to tell the story, but also to perform similar miracles. Their faith is growing, and they can now be entrusted with greater tasks.

The principle of "To whom much is given, much is required" (Luke 12:48) is true on two counts in today's passage. First, the disciples were given a great privilege when they were chosen to walk with the Lord. That privilege was quickly converted to responsibility. They were sent out as authorized representatives to share the same message Jesus has been proclaiming. This was showing that, by its very nature, spiritual growth cannot be contained. It always overflows into ministry. Second, the villages where the disciples ministered were also given a special privilege. Very few humans have been so privileged as to see the kinds of miracles that were being performed by Jesus and His disciples. Therefore, their rejection was dealt with harshly.

Another small point seems important. Judas was one of those who was sent out. Every gospel writer, upon the first mention of his name, proclaims him as the traitor. It would appear that he too was able to do these miraculous works. This empowerment does not appear to be limited by salvation or related to spirituality. It is an administrative capability.

We must not miss the true nature of our salvation. We were born to reproduce, and all our fruit is to point toward leading others to Christ. That is what fruit is for. Jesus reproduced His ministry through the lives of the disciples. But He still reached out to the unsaved. We need to keep a big focus and feed the hungry, not the full.

Luke 9:12-22

What is the writer saying?

How can I apply this to my life?

 pray Harry Bollback, Co-founder of Word of Life, as he and his wife Millie travel and minister.

The feeding of the 5,000 is the only miracle mentioned in all four Gospels. Although it may not be the most dramatic miracle (Jesus once fed 7,000), it is still very pivotal. The disciples have returned from an awesome ministry experience. They have had a great time of testimony and fellowship. Now they are faced with a somewhat common problem: a shortage of food. Immediately, they suggest a common solution: "Send the multitude away." Perhaps their focus is still on their own comfort. They could be fellowshipping, they could be testifying, but instead Jesus suggests that they should serve a mass of unruly people? Casting out demons is pretty cool, but serving tables is for, well, servants—not heroes.

Therein is the message: Living like Christ is never about what we want to do; it is always about what Jesus asks us to do. Faith cannot act independently; it can only exist in conjunction with an instruction from on high. Our will must be disabled so His will can flourish. At this point, Jesus asks a ministry-defining question of the disciples, "Who say ye that I am?" Back in 8:25 they had asked, "What manner of man is this?", but now they were ready to draw a better conclusion. Now they understood that this was God incarnate Who stood before them.

Verse 21 is a little perplexing. These words are not a response to the disciples' personal commitment but rather an assessment of the national condition. Teaching and preaching all this publicly was no longer safe.

Life stEP Often, a time of ministry can move our focus away from simple faith in God and toward looking at results or the impact of certain types of ministry instead. Whatever God has us do, we need to constantly be focused on a better understanding of Who He is, and what that makes us as we serve Him.

Luke 9:23-36

What is the writer saying?

How can I apply this to my life?

pray El Salvador – For believers willing to commit to the discipleship of new converts.

Luke chooses a much different passage after Peter's profession than Matthew does because of his different purpose in writing. What has been stated with regard to new birth (justification) is now stated with regard to new life (sanctification). If the foundational element within justification is an exchange of places (Christ takes our judgment, and we inherit His blessing), then the same ought to be true for spiritual growth. Too many have taken this passage and offered it out of context as some new dynamic that only applies to disciples and not converts. Paul, Luke's mentor, clearly defines this principle in the book he wrote to the Galatians.

To "deny" one's self means exactly that. It does not mean to deny ourselves some pleasure in life; it means to deny that we as people have any power or ability at all to live righteously. This empowers Christ, Who lives in us. To deny ourselves is to be crucified with Christ. Only then can the life that we live be Christ living in us.

To "carry our cross" does not mean that we have to suck it up and endure pain; it means that we have to leave behind the flesh-approved way of life and choose the Spirit-approved way. The cross that the disciples were forced to bear was that they were willing to forego justice and accept grace. After all, in a just world all mankind ends up in Hell since none are righteous. The solution is not to carry a bigger load or do a better job. The answer is to find a world, a grace world, where we do not need to carry that load, a world where the burden is easy and the yoke is light (Matthew 11:30) because Christ carries the weight.

Life stEP To live big, we need to become small. We need to be like the sinful woman who wept at Jesus feet, like the woman who reached out to touch His garment. Even if we do all that can be done in the flesh, we will still fail. Jesus calls us to give up our work and accept His grace.

Luke 9:37-50

What is the writer saying?

How can I apply this to my life?

Men can only see what the heart allows them to see. As the disciples' hearts began to change, they were now ready to see an even clearer picture of who Jesus was. They believed He was the Christ, and now they saw that He certainly was.

In his second epistle, Peter holds the event in today's passage forward as the best "eyewitness" event people had experienced. Yet today we have something better. Peter says we have a more sure word, a word written by holy men of God moved by the Holy Spirit (2 Peter 1:21).

The disciples clearly understood what the Transfiguration—Christ standing between Moses and Elijah—meant, but they still did not understand a greater moment—Christ hanging between two thieves at His death. Jesus suggested that these things needed to "sink down into their ears" because they would not see the Lord in His glory again in their lifetimes.

Rather than deal with the harsh reality of Jesus' words, though, the disciples chose to squabble about their positions in the kingdom. At this point Jesus brings them back to the same message He has been constantly preaching: he who is least will be greatest in the kingdom of God. The greater the man is, the smaller the Christ living in the man. Only when the man is buried with Christ can Christ's life be evident in the man.

Life **stEP** Paul says, "Let this mind be in you which was also in Christ Jesus..." (Philippians 2:5). We need a new mind to understand this new life. The human heart cannot explain a life lived solely by faith.

Luke 9:51-62

What is the writer saying?

How can I apply this to my life?

As we read through today's passage, a shift in the tone of the gospel becomes clear. The specter of the cross now looms large over Jesus and the shrinking crowd following Him. When the passage tells us that Jesus set His face to go to Jerusalem, it is speaking primarily of the cross. Rejection is rising, and a positive outcome of Christ's work on earth is not in plain sight for those following. In verses 57-62, those who once jumped at the chance to follow are now offering excuses to pack up and go home.

As the crowds gathered early in Christ's ministry, they cheered the miracles and also the message. But they were now beginning to fully understand the implications of what Jesus was teaching, that following Him (and ultimately saving their lives) meant losing their lives. They were not up to the commitment. Luke is not trying to tell us that it is wrong to own a house, or bury one's father, or bid farewell to one's loved ones. What He is saying is that these kinds of "present life" responsibilities must be considered as nothing in comparison to the responsibility to follow Christ. In another place (Luke 14:26), Jesus says, "If any man come to me, and hate not his father, and mother, and wife, and children, and brethren, and sisters, yea, and his own life also, he cannot be my disciple." All earthly relationships, even good ones, must pale in comparison to our commitment to Christ.

The meaning here is not to despise or reject important family responsibilities; rather, they must be secondary to our relationship with Jesus Christ. The word translated "hate" in the Greek language is a comparative term that means to consider less important.

Luke 10:1-12

What is the writer saying?

How can I apply this to my life?

This is the second time Jesus sends out the disciples to proclaim the Gospel. In Chapter 9 He sent out the twelve disciples, and now He sends out seventy. This second witnessing trip probably takes place in a different geographical region than the first.

Luke alone records this event and spends more time on it than he does the first. The content is very similar, but this commissioning is much more detailed. In this episode, with Jesus gives the seventy power to heal the sick. This would be very much in keeping with the biblical tradition. In the Old Testament prophets generally had a group of associates (sons of the prophets) who would be sent throughout the countryside to proclaim any revelation that the primary prophet would receive. These associates would also be given the ability to prophesy, but not in the same sense as the primary prophet. This ability to "send" disciples out with power was the sign of a primary "truth-giver." When such a person spoke or wrote, there could be no questioning his words. Jesus would later give this ability (to transfer sign gifts) to the apostles so that their writings would be confirmed as Scripture.

The negative consequences of rejection are emphasized more in this passage. The early ministry of Christ focused on "blessed are those who." Here, there is a significant addition with the statement, "It shall be more tolerable in that day for Sodom."

Life stEP   The primary emphasis of the Gospel is life. Jesus came that we would have life and have it more abundantly (John 10:10). But we must never forget that the alternative is not neutral; it is an eternal existence in the lake of fire.

Luke 10:13-24

What is the writer saying?

How can I apply this to my life?

pray Guatemala – For the rapid and accurate completion of the 17 Bible translation projects in progress.

The life of Christ is generally broken down into three distinct phases. Phase one is the period of obscurity, which covers the time from His birth to His baptism. Phase two is the period of popularity, from His baptism until His transfiguration. Phase three is the period of rejection, covering His transfiguration until His crucifixion. Luke spends much less time on the second phase than Matthew does. He moves through it quickly because his primary concern is the humanity, or the self-imposed weakness, of Christ. The rest of the book of Luke is dominated by conflict and how Jesus taught the disciple to handle it.

Luke now recounts one of the many "woes" that Jesus pronounced on the cities of that day. This is a common prophetic device going all the way back to the blessings and the curses contained in the Law (Deuteronomy 29). These pronouncements sometimes seem harsh to our postmodern ears, but the curses described in Scripture are always made with the intent to move people back toward blessing, not to exclude them from it. That element can be seen in this passage when the seventy return. There was opposition to the ministry, but there were also victories.

Jesus says He beheld Satan falling from Heaven. Revelation 12:7 says that Satan is cast out of heaven shortly before the Messianic Kingdom comes to earth. Here in Luke 10, Jesus is telling the disciples that their successful ministry is an indication that the Kingdom could come soon.

God has graciously allowed His servants to have a glimpse of the eternal with His life and His love, which are in each believer's heart. Look at the simple faith exhibited by the disciples. Childlike faith can see what the most educated miss.

Luke 10:25-37

What is the writer saying?

How can I apply this to my life?

The kingdom did not come. It was close, but it did not happen. In today's passage we get a glimpse why. The lawyer who asks the question is not trying to gain information but rather to test Jesus. He has no desire to learn, only a desire to dismiss. Jesus immediately turns the tables and asks the lawyer what the Law says one must do to inherit eternal life. The lawyer clearly thinks that what Jesus is teaching is opposed to the Law of Moses. When Jesus agrees with the lawyer's answer, the lawyer is left in an awkward situation and tries to reverse the tables once again.

Jesus answers with a parable that creates a clear contrast between Jesus' understanding of the Law and the lawyer's. The priest and the Levite were following the letter of the Law, but the Samaritan followed the intent of the Law. If a priest or a Levite touched a dead body, they would be made unclean and could not carry out their religious responsibilities until they offered a sacrifice and were made clean. The traveler was left for dead, and they could not be sure that he was alive or would survive. Therefore, they used an individual law to defy the purpose of the Law just as they would use the letter of the Law to crucify the Lord of the Law. The lawyer would have understood this perfectly. It would have been his responsibility as a lawyer to defend the behavior of the priest and the Levite. But in this context, he was forced to concede to Christ and recognize his own faulty reasoning.

Life stEP As we study scripture we should determine the intent of God's teachings and seek to satisfy His desires for our spiritual development, not just seek to obey the letter of the law.

thursday 22

Luke 10:38-42

What is the writer saying?

How can I apply this to my life?

pray Japan – Praise the Lord for the new openness caused by economic, social, and natural disasters.

The following account of Christ's visit with Mary and Martha reinforces what Christ taught the lawyer who questioned Him Martha was trying to impress Christ with her efforts, and by human standards, she should have been commended for her effort. In the grace world, though, one is not rewarded for works but rather for faith.

Jesus has just demonstrated that the Mosaic Law can be used to frustrate the truth of God's Word. In this case He is demonstrating that the very concept of choosing behavior (works) over grace is equally futile. Martha did not cite any law. She simply invoked what she felt was common to the human experience, that is, that certain behaviors ought to be rewarded, and other behaviors ought to be judged. This is a law that is written on the human conscience. But it too fails the test. We ought not live right because we want to be rewarded, but rather because we love God and our neighbor. Martha's attempt to be a servant was commendable until she started to judge her sister and to judge Christ. When she called Jesus out for letting Mary be lazy, she revealed the motives in her heart. If her motives were pure, she would have rejoiced that her efforts were providing opportunity for Mary to spend quality time with Jesus. Instead she complained. This is a hard lesson but one we must learn. We cannot compare amongst ourselves; we must always look to Christ.

Life stEP

Fairness is the Devil's greatest weapon. Once we become convinced that our ideas of justice must rule, we forfeit grace. What would be most fair would be if everyone paid for his own sins. Jesus offers an alternative: grace. We cannot accept grace but then expect others to live by any law other than the obedience of faith.

Luke 11:1-13

What is the writer saying?

How can I apply this to my life?

Many portions of Christ's teaching were given in more than one context. The Lord's Prayer was first recorded as a part of the gospel of the kingdom in the Sermon on the Mount. Here Jesus teaches it in a different context—in response to the disciples' request. Jesus is not offering this as a prayer to be repeated verbatim (that is established in Matthew 6:7). What He is offering is a pattern to be followed when we pray. We need to first of all acknowledge God and His relationship to every event that occurs on planet earth. His purposes and His plans must be honored in every request that we make. We cannot know what God's plans are and, therefore, we are likely to make requests that are in conflict with them. If this is the case, we acknowledge from the start that we submit our desires to His will.

Secondly, we are to acknowledge His authority over the physical world. He gives us our daily bread.

Third, we acknowledge His authority over the spiritual realm. He forgives sins, and when we receive forgiveness, we are obligated to then extend forgiveness—the one who receives grace is obligated to be gracious.

The final component is the recognition that God orchestrates the tests of life. We must always measure a test by the nature of the One who gives it. God has only our well-being in mind when He tests His servants. Tests are always intended to help, never to hurt.

Life stEP

On a very practical level in sanctification, grace will not work for those who are not gracious. If the flesh does not die with Christ at justification (by faith), it will reemerge in our post-justification experience and cause us to be like Martha, as opposed to Mary.

Luke 11:14-28

What is the writer saying?

How can I apply this to my life?

Two messages compete for the hearts and minds of a generation of Israelites. One of the messages is the same message that has been taught to them all of their lives. The other message is new, and the Preacher of that message is also performing a number of serious miracles. Miracles without message are meaningless, so Jesus ultimately brings the discussion back to correct message.

The old-school religious crowd hates the message, but they think they need to discredit the miracles in order to return order to the land. Therefore, they make one of the most contradictory claims ever made. They suggest that Satan is fighting himself and ask Jesus to prove that His miracles are from God. Christ ridicules their suggestion and then attacks their message.

Jesus shows the worthlessness of self-reformation, which is the incorrect message that has been leading the Israelites astray. He speaks of an unclean spirit that has left but then returns, making the situation worse than it initially was. What is needed is not reformation, but new life—not a house cleaned up, but a new heart. The religious crowd thought they could use the Law to clean up a person's life, but little did they know that in so doing they were breaking the greater commandment, of truly knowing God and living by faith in Him with a new life. The Law always denied that righteousness could be obtained through human effort; it taught that righteousness could only come from God. This is what Christ means when He proclaims, "Blessed are they that hear the word of God, and keep it" (Luke 11:28). This new message from Christ was the only way the people of Israel would find true life.

The Pharisees had convinced themselves that they were the true heirs of Abraham. They saw themselves as both keepers and protectors of the Law and loved it more than they loved the Law's God and His people.

sunday 23

Luke 11:29-41

What is the writer saying?

How can I apply this to my life?

pray New Zealand – The need for focused Youth Pastors and leaders.

Regardless of how many miracles Jesus performed, there were never enough to please the doubters because those who sought the signs were not seeking the truth but rather personal affirmation. Christ had already given sufficient signs to verify His words, but these people were not interested in listening; they only wanted the perks that came from the miracles, such as the fish and the bread. Therefore, Jesus offered them only one more sign: the prophet Jonah (v. 29). The sign was not the preaching of Jonah but rather the fact that he spent three days and three nights in the belly of the great fish. This sign corresponds to the message that both Jesus and John the Baptist had been preaching about Christ's role and fulfillment of prophecy.

Jesus also offers the example of the Queen of Sheba, which raises the question of what these two incidents have in common. The answer appears to be Gentile participation. Sheba was an ancient country in northern Africa, and Jonah went to Nineveh even though he despised the Assyrians, and the result was great revival. Israel had witnessed miracle after miracle throughout their history yet failed to grasp the real treasure: the message of the prophets. They were focused on the signs, but signs have no intrinsic value; they have one simple purpose: to be a sign. Israel wanted the signs without what these signs meant. If more signs would have helped these people, Jesus would have given them more, but He understood that any signs that He did from that point on would only cause them to think that this was their rightful reward on Earth. More signs would only fuel their growing rejection.

 The reason for and use of signs has not changed. Where there is no divine messenger, and a corresponding message, there is no need of signs. Signs were never a sign of salvation or spirituality, and when used that way, they always led to rejecting the message.

monday 23

Luke 11:42-54

What is the writer saying?

How can I apply this to my life?

pray Japan – For the believers to have a joyful heart in all circumstances.

Just as the signs were an external element of a much more spiritual concept, the external observation of the Law was also meant to show the righteous condition of one's heart. Thus Jesus had no problem with the Law of Moses, but He did have a serious problem with how the Pharisees and lawyers were using it to promote external obedience without internal change. Repentance has always been about the inside, about having God's worldview.

The religious leaders of Jesus day were using the Law to advance their own devious agenda. The more of the Law they obeyed, the more in awe of their own significance they became. But what Christ was most outraged by was that they were using this perverted version of the Law to enslave and destroy those whom they were entrusted to lead.

Jesus preached a message that empowered only the poor in spirit. He offered a righteousness that was there for those who asked, accepting the outcasts and sinners. He let a sinful woman wash his feet and ate with people that the religious crowd would cross the street to avoid. His was an inconvenient message.

The "woe" passages in the Old Testament are very helpful in understanding Jesus' words. When used in a list by the prophets, they are mostly reserved for those who have distorted the truth of God for personal gain (Isaiah 5:8-22; Habakkuk 2:6-19.). The leadership in Israel knew better than to behave that way, but they were willing to make sacrifices to keep their own personal position and prestige. They not only embraced a *graceless* system but also encouraged others to embrace it.

 Always present in the human heart is the temptation to use the grace of God for personal benefit, to turn the stones into bread (Matthew 4:3).The Pharisees and lawyers fell victim to that lust of the flesh (looking out for themselves above all else) and paid the price.

tuesday 23

Luke 12:1-15

What is the writer saying?

How can I apply this to my life?

pray Argentina – For godly, trained, Argentine leaders to become missionaries to lesser – reached, Spanish – speaking countries.

Jesus now shifts His focus and speaks to the disciples, warning them not to be intimidated by the religious establishment. The Pharisees had accumulated an incredible amount of power in the Jewish community. In many instances they held what amounted to a life-and-death control over the people. They answered to no one but Moses, but even then, it was a Moses that had been recreated in the image of themselves, not the Moses of Exodus who knew God.

Given that the Pharisees held so much power, it is not surprising that the Lord addresses the subject of fear. Note that He says, "Be not afraid" (v. 4) of any earthly power, but "fear him… who has the power to cast into hell" (v. 5). (Centuries later, Martin Luther said, "Fear God and you will have no one else to fear.") Jesus is saying that present power, present wealth, and present life—all of which the Pharisees had—are the enemies of a genuine relationship with God. They must be forsaken in search of the eternal. Eternal life is not an extension of present life; it is a gift from Almighty God for anyone who requests it.

Despite the emphasis on the eternal, though, God still looks after us right now. God orchestrates life's events for the benefit of His creation, not its demise. (Verse 6 says He even watches out for the sparrows.) As Paul said in Romans 8:28, "All things work together for good."

The blasphemy of the Spirit in this passage has to do with accepting human protection over divine protection, human wealth over divine wealth, human righteousness over divine righteousness and the Pharisees over Jesus.

We will always have days when we are frustrated over our weakness or lack of resources. But we need to think of Luke's primary message in those times: Our weakness allows the Holy Spirit to make us strong with an eternal strength, to soar with the wings of eagles.

Luke 12:16-34

What is the writer saying?

How can I apply this to my life?

pray Hungary – For God to call witnesses to the hard – to – reach groups: Gypsies, Yugoslavians, and Jews.

In today's passage the Lord continues to teach the disciples about the folly of present possessions and power. He offers a parable concerning the subject in verses 16-21. The individual here was a productive member of his community. He worked hard and was rewarded for his effort with his endeavors prospering. But he made one fatal mistake: he interpreted the eternal in light of the external, not the other way around. He strove for present significance and ignored his eternal soul, choosing the fruit of his labors over the fruit of the Spirit.

The Lord continues with some positive illustrations. Having already referred to the sparrows, He now adds the ravens, lilies, and grass of the field. As a general rule, people are not discontent because they do not have enough of this world's goods, but because they do not have as much as other people do. Even starvation, which does occur in some parts of the world, many times is due to human greed more than natural shortages. Jesus presents a higher calling than acquiring material possessions.

What you value the most will reveal the nature of your heart. Do not make the same mistake the rich man did. Value the things that Jesus valued, and you will live a life that is honoring to Him.

 Life stEP
Remember the warning that Jesus gave about the blaspheming the Spirit. The greatest danger that we face in this present world is substituting the external for the eternal. Don't go after the wrong kind of fruit.

thursday 23

Luke 12:35-48

What is the writer saying?

How can I apply this to my life?

pray   Thailand – For God to raise up honest leadership to establish a framework for a just government.

We live in a dangerous world, but not because of war, crime, and natural disasters. This world is dangerous because it lulls men into a false sense of security. Insignificant amounts of time are perceived to be extraordinary. What are the 2,000 years that have passed since the Lord walked on this earth? They are a mere pittance, an indiscernible speck on the dial of eternity. Still, we begin to wonder where the Lord is and why He has not returned. Some call His words legends and fairy tales. Rather than questioning why Christ is not here, people need to understand the incredible opportunity that is given to mankind as day after day is added to the time available to lead more souls to Him. Each day is an opportunity for those who have lived all of their lives in darkness to see the great light that lights the whole world.

But Jesus warns not to become complacent, because the day of His return really is coming. The weak will become strong, and the poor will become rich.

In this present world, the good die young and unappreciated. The wicked and rebellious are esteemed and rewarded. There is no justice. But Jesus' message is that justice is overrated—grace is to be desired. Those who demand justice will always find it, for justice always concludes at the Lake of Fire since there are none who are righteous (Romans 3:10). But those who love mercy will find the true point of life on earth as they walk with their God (Micah 6:8).

As believers, we stand before a great chasm. We call out to those who are about to perish, "Turn back. Repent!" Some do turn, but many don't. We need to stay on task. Don't cave in to the pressure and begin to think that we aren't making a difference. That's the big lie. The less we are concerned with our lives and the pressures around us, the more our lives will matter for others.

Luke 12:49-59

What is the writer saying?

How can I apply this to my life?

This passage makes it unequivocally clear that the world is not a friend of grace. Sometimes we are led to believe that the world is tolerant of all religions, and that in this *pluralistic* world we are accepted in the same way that other religions are. This is not the truth. In reality, to claim that Christ is the *only way* to Heaven brings immediate rebuke and ostracization. People consider declarations of absolute truth to be the worst of sins. In today's passage the Lord makes it clear that He is *the great divider.* True Christianity will always bring division because the goals and aspirations of the world are different than believers'.

The last part of our passage deals with the reason why Christ is rejected as the one way. Man is interested in man, not God. While intelligent in the ways of the world, such as discerning the weather (v. 54), he is unable to discern the essential truths necessary for life, such as the *signs of the times* (v. 56). What man needs is a new heart that is totally different from his current nature, not an improved heart. We need conversion, not reformation. It is not good enough to be all that we can be; we need to be all that Christ is. If we go before the Judge in our own strength, we will fail; yet Jesus can defeat our greatest enemy, death.

Many of us who have chosen Christ are going through rough times with relatives and friends, and some reading right now may be experiencing scorn from those they love about their new life and motives in following Christ. Let this passage be an encouragement to you. Verse 53 is an explanation of the condition. Remember your Lord who, in spite of His perfection as a person, was hated and despised.

Knowing that Christ is the one true way does not mean we should be deliberately disagreeable, nor does it give an excuse to react with a bad attitude. Instead, pray that you will react as the Lord did, with love in spite of mistreatment.

Luke 13:1-9

What is the writer saying?

How can I apply this to my life?

pray Philippines – Funding for the staff and supplies needed to continue Bible correspondence courses.

It would be nice to blame all the dangers we face in this world on some huge satanic plot. But there is so much suffering that is caused by natural phenomena that it is clear we are under the control of no one but God. Two events are mentioned here that must be considered. One is the act of a Gentile ruler, and the other is the result of human error and the forces of nature. How should believers assess such events? Did these people reap what they sowed? Do the righteous suffer and the guilty go free? How should we see this world from a faith perspective? Does every event have some hidden meaning and reflect some hidden justice? If God is in control, how do we account for the fickleness and uncertainties in life? Jesus' answer is as profound as it is simple. We must not judge. It is not our place in this world to determine guilt; judgment should be left to God.

But we should also not think that God is not actively at work in each one of our lives to mature and develop us (see Hebrews 12:6: "Whom the Lord loveth he chasteneth and scourgeth every son whom he receiveth"). The formula that Christ uses here is not all that definitive. It only gives us the broadest of outlines by which to function, asserting divine sovereignty and human responsibility with equal force. Rather than trying to answer these kinds of questions, however, we should instead place a priority on learning and never cross the line into judging.

Life stEP

Not all that feels good is good, and not all that feels bad is bad. Our hearts and minds are not good judges of these things. The solution that seems right to a man often leads to destruction. We must live and learn, keeping what we know about God's sovereignty and love at the forefront of our minds.

Luke 13:10-21

What is the writer saying?

How can I apply this to my life?

pray Hungary – For churches to mature in their giving and support of nationals involved in Christian work.

This section in Luke opened with a controversy about the Sabbath and this subject is where Luke now returns. Examining Jesus' treatment of the Sabbath is an important point in each of the gospels because Jesus was never guilty of breaking a single law. He only interpreted the Law differently than the leadership of Israel. They saw the Law as a way to earn favor with God; Jesus saw it a way to maximize the benefits of God's grace.

Left to his own resources, man would never figure out the best recipe for a meaningful life. But through the Law, God provided a skillful manual for living where He told man how to enjoy all the good He had built into this creation. Man chose, however, to use these guides as a means of death, letting these standards condemn him rather than tapping into them as a way to discover real life. Man chose to use it as a way to *get* life as opposed to a way to *live* life.

The contrast between these perspectives could not be more evident than in today's passage. The woman was so afflicted that she was unable to enjoy even the most routine pleasures of life. Without her even asking, Jesus intervenes and heals her, which results in her glorifying God (v. 13). Immediately the legalists become incensed, because this miracle was done on the Sabbath and once again show their hypocrisy (v. 15). In the context of this attitude, on the part of these leaders of Israel and the context of the barren fig tree (v. 6), the Lord gives two parables showing the future of the world to come. Both make the same point: no matter how gracious God is, there will always be those who crush all hope beneath a load of man-made righteousness.

Life stEP While the future may seem bleak, our confidence is that God will not leave us orphaned in this self-serving system. He will come to rescue us.

Luke 13:22-35

What is the writer saying?

How can I apply this to my life?

The sad truth in today's passage is not that there are so few who will find the right path, but that so many walk in the ways of darkness convinced that they are the true servants of the living God. They call out "Lord, Lord," but the Lord does not know them. They claim to be followers because they walked in the same streets and were born in the same communities as those who do know God, but Jesus quickly dismisses their claims. All Israel was betting its eternal future on an external relationship with the Messiah. They claimed to be a part of the same physical household and the same communities. But when judgment day comes, the external has no value whatsoever.

In Matthew 7:22-23 similar claims are made. There the same crowd claims to have done works and miracles worthy of reward, and again their claims are rejected. There is only one criterion by which men will be considered worthy to enter into that kingdom—whether or not they *know* Jesus.

The word here translated "know" has a much wider range of meaning in both Greek and Hebrew than it does in English. It speaks of an intimate relationship with another person. Unless we have a personal and intimate faith-relationship with Jesus Christ, nothing else matters. This passage also makes it clear that these people's failure to have this relationship was not because of some shortcoming on Jesus' part. In fact, He weeps because they will not come to Him. He longed to gather them together as a hen gathers her chicks, but they would not come.

Life stEP

What a sad day it will be when these people realize they never really knew Christ. It will be made even sadder because there will be no one to blame for the failure. No one will utter the words, "But Jesus, I didn't know." They did know, yet they chose their own righteousness over the righteousness of God.

Luke 14:1-14

What is the writer saying?

How can I apply this to my life?

In stark contrast to the way that the religious leadership treated Jesus, He was always willing to take the opportunity to sit and talk with them if invited. The passage seems to indicate that this particular event may have been some kind of trap since it was the Sabbath and all eyes were on Jesus. In the midst of the crowd was a man with the dropsy, a disease related to liver or kidney malfunction. Jesus discerns the situation immediately. He knew the religious leaders' hearts. They had placed the sick man in His presence to see what He would do on the Sabbath. After Jesus heals the man, He confronts these leaders about their motives. The situation really had nothing to do with Jesus or the Sabbath; it had everything to do with these men's status within the system. Jesus demanded that they become as little children, humbling themselves and fellowshipping with the unworthy. He demanded that they give up all they had acquired in order to attain what could not be bought. They needed to be poor in spirit, but they could not accept a kingdom in which they were not the center of attention. They would rather have no kingdom than to have a kingdom in which they were just as needy as the next person.

They needed to discredit Jesus in order to make themselves look good. But the more they tried, the worse they looked. They never considered that they might be wrong, and their hatred grew with each failed trap.

Life stEP   Christ knows the motives of our heart and whether we are truly seeking Him. Examine yourself today to see if you are being poor in spirit and looking for His heavenly kingdom, or whether your lifestyle is working toward a self-centered kingdom here on earth.

Luke 14:15-24

What is the writer saying?

How can I apply this to my life?

pray — Nigeria – For the Lord's guidance and direction in the training and follow-up of new converts that are won to Christ through evangelism.

One can only begin to imagine the heartache Jesus must have felt as He shared this particular parable. This is not a story about a simple banquet; it is an analogy about the people of Israel. These are people that Jesus had known for most of His life, people that filled the streets of His hometown, people He had played with as a child. What is most distressing about this parable is that almost everyone found some excuse to avoid the banquet. The excuses were not frivolous or silly. They were the kinds of situations that conscientious people face every day. But in the final analysis, they were still excuses.

We must always remember that Jesus is an inconvenient reality. There will never be a "good" time to be crucified with Christ or to be buried with Him by baptism. Our hearts will always see to it that there is something else that must be done first. The only right time to do God's will is now.

We always think there will be plenty of time to follow Christ, but the door of opportunity is not always visible. In the parable, after those invited were delayed, the servant began to comb the highways and byways for those who wanted to come. The Gospel marches forward with or without us. Ahaz thought that God needed him, but the Messiah was born of a virgin (Isaiah 7). The nation of Israel thought that God could not bless the Gentiles without them, but He did.

Step out for God today while you hear His call. Don't wait for tomorrow.

Life stEP — Life sometimes seems so long and filled with so many opportunities. But do not be fooled. As James 4:14 says, life is like a vapor that appears for a moment and is gone. Use every minute wisely.

Luke 14:25-35

What is the writer saying?

How can I apply this to my life?

pray Jamaica – For Jamaican believers to have greater access to and interest in Christian resource materials.

The first time we read this passage, it probably comes as a great shock to our preconceived ideas of biblical living. We have been taught to love our parents, siblings, and wives. Part of the shock we feel is cultural, though—in our postmodern world, love is almost totally an emotional response. In the ancient world (where marriages were arranged), love was a proactive choice. It was covenant loyalty. Jesus is not asking us to feel animosity toward any of these people; He is asking us to prioritize our commitments in such a way that He always comes first. Only when we do this can we truly love our families. Love built on any other foundation than the truth of Jesus' words will always fail.

Understand what Jesus is saying when He calls the crowd to count the cost. He is not asking for payment of any kind. Luke has already made it perfectly clear that salvation (justification and sanctification) cannot be earned or deserved. Jesus is saying that either we are "all in," or we are "all out." Half a building is no building at all.

This passage makes us wonder what God really wants from us. The answer is simple: faith, faith, and more faith. We may be tempted to think, "Why, that is no cost at all!", and we would be right because salvation is free. Its cost is really an un-cost. We must give up our failed righteousness and receive His divine righteousness and exchange our dying lives to accept His eternal life. We must lay down everything at the cross, for what we lay down is what has been killing us.

Life stEP The load we bear is very real and very deadly, and only getting rid of it can allow us to live. Yet we have grown attached to it. This is the cost: Lay down the old life in order to accept the new.

Luke 15:1-10

What is the writer saying?

How can I apply this to my life?

Some criticize the "faith alone" gospel as cheap grace. They think believers should somehow earn their status in the invisible world of spirituality. Never mind that grace, by definition, is free; there is always pressure from the human heart and mind to base spirituality on works. Fruit is a sign of spirituality, but it's not the cause—trees don't produce fruit for their own personal advancement; they produce fruit for reproduction and for the benefit of the eco-zone in which they live. Doing good is to benefit others, not to advance our own status within the community.

In today's passage, we encounter the first of three parables that Jesus uses to emphasize the true motivation for godly behavior. Notice that He seeks relentlessly until He finds the sheep. Once He does find the sheep, He takes the extra step and puts it on His shoulders—a place of safety and security, where that sheep is as strong and safe as the shepherd. The shepherd does all this while rejoicing; He finds His fulfillment not in what He had attained, but in the fact that the sheep is safe.

In each of these three parables, rejoicing is the end response. Jesus did not go to the cross because it made Him look good or because it was easy. Death was so alien and repulsive to Him that as He anticipated the cross, He was sweating drops of blood and asking the Father if there was another way (Luke 22:44). Our need was what motivated Christ, and He endured the cross for the joy it would bring as He found us, His lost sheep.

Life stEP Don't become self-absorbed in the Christian walk. We need to be concentrating on producing fruit that will bring more people to Christ.

Luke 15:11-32

What is the writer saying?

How can I apply this to my life?

The parables in this chapter have one main theme: the Lord is in the business of saving the lost. Our lives here on earth are primarily about finding those who are lost, although what Christ asks us to do as members of His family should also bring joy and benefit to the members of the family.

Yesterday, we saw the lost sheep and the lost coin. Today's parable is well-known and is generally called the parable of the prodigal son.

The prodigal is portrayed as an ungrateful and selfish child who squanders his inheritance without a second thought. Until he finds himself eating pig food, he doesn't realize how foolish he has been. At that point he returns home, where his father greets him with a lavish feast.

This is a parable about two sons, however. The older son who had stayed at home and had done all that his father requested is incensed by his father's reaction to the return of his younger brother. He resents that he had played by the rules and served his father many years while his younger brother was off squandering his portion of the inheritance. Now this younger, irresponsible brother is treated with all the glory he believes he himself is entitled to. He wanted fair treatment in a grace world, a world where God provides opportunity for those who are lost. The first son merely accepted that opportunity while the second son failed to understand God's great gift. Never complain when another sinner is welcomed in or resent the rejoicing that occurs. Life in the family is its own reward; it is the only real life that there is.

There is no joy like the joy of leading another to the Lord. Christ rejoices when He welcomes new believers and wants us to do the same.

Luke 16:1-18

What is the writer saying?

How can I apply this to my life?

Today's parable has raised many eyebrows. It appears Jesus is commending dishonesty when in fact He is commending a "principle" as opposed to a "practice." We may ask why Jesus would use a parable that could so easily be misinterpreted. The answer may be that He wanted to force the hearers to think through what they had just heard. What is happening here is that there is a man who became bankrupt and was fired. He decided to add sin to his sin by fixing the books and discounting the debts of his lord's debtors, and even this was done unfairly (the discounts being different). His logic was that by being a friend to the debtor now, when he was destitute, they would help him later.

His behavior was evil, but the principle is pure. Jesus is commending his astuteness, not his sin. The man realized that his present actions would have future consequences, and he would be unable to take care of his future needs if he did not do something in the present.

He knew his "now" decision was final. If he didn't do it when he did, then he would never be able to do it. This is the urgency of the present.

The principle of acting right now, while the opportunity is available, is what Jesus commends. We must decide now, or our forever will be decided for us. There are no second chances. If we do not choose Jesus in this life, we will never get the opportunity again.

God has entrusted us with the present. The past is gone and cannot be changed, and the future is not yet a reality. The incredible thing about this present is that we can make choices today that will have an effect on our eternal future.

Luke 16:19-31

What is the writer saying?

How can I apply this to my life?

pray Guatemala – Pray for missionaries to develop successful discipleship programs to train rural believers.

A lot of voices in the world today are convinced that everyone will get another opportunity to get things right with God. They suggest that we can change the future in the future. They say today is not the day of salvation; it is just one of many opportunities. This passage deals with the error of such beliefs. Two men who have lived very different lives are described for us. One is a rich man. Richness in that culture suggested more than just physical wealth; it was also perceived to imply divine approval and blessing. The other was a poor man who frequently found food in the rich man's garbage. His poverty supposedly marked him as rejected and cursed by God. The spiritual realities, however, were very different. As a result, the poor man went to Paradise, and the rich man to the place of torment in Hades. These are presented as real places where real people go once they die. Note also that there is no opportunity to trade places or cross over from one place to another. The key point here is that all opportunity for change evaporates after death; there are no second chances.

The rich man becomes intensely missionary-minded once he realizes his mistake. He is concerned for his five brothers who have not yet died because he now knows they only have one chance to repent. He suggests that if someone went back from the dead, his brothers would certainly believe that person. But the brothers already had messengers, and if they would not listen to the Scriptures, they would not listen to anything.

Man does not have an information deficit; he has a belief deficit.

Heaven and Hell are real. The decisions we make in this life cannot be changed in the next. Don't put off until tomorrow decisions that need to be made today. Choose wisely.

Luke 17:1-19

What is the writer saying?

How can I apply this to my life?

pray Germany – Churches to return to a dependence upon the teaching of the Word of God to change lives.

As the disciples watched Jesus' ministry, they were acutely aware that the people who were coming to Him were not the social and spiritual elite. In fact, in many cases these people were the outcasts and rejects of that society. They were people who often had serious sin problems. The disciples were wondering when it was appropriate to turn someone away because of their sin. They must have been thinking, "Surely, we cannot just go on forgiving these people." These new believers, who were so fragile and weak in their faith, are the ones that Jesus refers to as "little ones." The faith that brought them to Christ was often barely flickering and tentative. But Jesus welcomed them and surrounded them with love and acceptance. The disciples were not so sure.

When Jesus told the disciples they needed to keep on forgiving a brother who has sinned, they realized they needed a better, stronger kind of faith. They felt that somehow they needed to believe more ardently the things Jesus had taught them. Christ's answer must have been a shock. The mustard seed was the smallest agricultural seed used in that ancient world. But even that small amount of true faith could move mountains. The problem is never the size of our faith; it is the object of our faith. We must believe in God's promise, not His power. He always has the power, but we must put true belief in the promises He has given. The disciples weren't trusting His promises because they had a skewed view of forgiveness. They didn't need to believe more strongly in their own agenda; they needed to believe the new order Christ was living out before them—love one another as I have loved you.

Life stEP When God calls us to trust Him, we need to make sure we are placing our faith in *His* plans and promises. Look at your faith today—are you trusting in His forgiveness? Do you live this out by loving others as He loved you?

Luke 17:20-37

What is the writer saying?

How can I apply this to my life?

pray   Nicaragua – Praise the Lord that the church has doubled in the last 10 years!

Many have misunderstood today's passage. The request given by the Pharisees was, as usual, an attempt to trip Jesus up. They were trying to bring His claim of being the Messiah into question because there were no visible signs of the kingdom. Their question was half-right. The Old Testament did promise a very visible and physical kingdom in which the Messiah would deliver the nation of Israel and establish Himself as the ruler of the entire world. But the Old Testament also has many passages, such as Isaiah 53, that promised a suffering Savior who would bear the sins of His people. The common element to these different prophecies is the Messiah. That is what Jesus means when He says that the kingdom is "within you." The kingdom—the Messiah—was walking within the borders of their country in the person of Jesus Christ. Because they rejected the person, they also rejected the blessing.

Be careful that you don't "read the rapture" into these passages. Remember when Noah entered the ark, those taken were judged, but Noah survived. Two in one bed—one is taken (in judgment), the other left behind to enjoy the millennium. Two grinding together—one is taken in judgment, the other left behind to reign with the Lord. These verses are talking about Revelation, not the Rapture. The idea of being "left behind" can be confusing, but the context shows that those left behind are those (like Noah) who will be saved and blessed.

Let's not make the same mistake that these people did. They thought they could have the blessing without the blessing-giver. The same is true today. Life begins with Jesus.

Luke 18:1-14

What is the writer saying?

How can I apply this to my life?

As was mentioned earlier in this commentary, Luke focuses on the prayer life of Jesus more than any other gospel writer. Recent events have left the disciples with any number of questions about how the future was related to their plans and prayers. They did not want Jesus to die, and they wanted the kingdom to come as soon as possible. They must have wondered if there was any reason to pray since God's plan seemed to unfold in God's way even when they prayed differently. Jesus seems to understand their discouragement and offers two parables for their consideration.

The first parable concerns steadfastness in prayer. Jesus tells the story of a poor widow and a ruthless judge. The judge was not one to rule in favor of the victim in any given situation; he was more likely to rule based on what was in it for him. The widow, by interrupting his sleep on a regular basis, was able to get the judge to rule in her favor because that was in his self-interest. Effective prayer is shown as prayer that takes into consideration the nature and program of God. If we pray counter to God's character or God's expressed will, we should not expect to see our prayers answered. Prayer unleashes God's power to fulfill His will; it cannot change His will.

The second parable concerns the attitude that a person has when he prays. The Pharisee prayed as if God's response was guaranteed by his own righteousness. Such is never the case. God answers our prayers because He is faithful to His character and His promises. If a person understands these simple principles, that person will not be discouraged by the uncertainty of the future.

Don't let the sovereignty of God be used to devalue your prayer life. Pray according to His will, and you will see amazing answers.

Luke 18:15-27

What is the writer saying?

How can I apply this to my life?

pray Mexico – Believers to realize their responsibility to contribute to the support of ministers of the Gospel.

Today's passage is another well-known one. This incident is given in all three synoptic gospels, and it is always accompanied by the account of the children and followed by the reference to the rich man and a camel and the eye of a needle. The three are kept together because they can only be understood when viewed as a single unit. At issue is what a person must do to inherit eternal life.

The participants we see are the children. The disciples attempt to send them away, thinking they are incapable of benefiting from Jesus' teaching. Jesus rebukes the disciples and tells them that the opposite is true. Unless adults have child-like faith they will not be saved and enter the kingdom of God.

The second participant is the young ruler. He appears to be a perfect candidate for salvation. He has kept the Law from childhood and sees himself as a good person. Jesus picks up on this point when the young man calls Jesus good. Jesus remarks that only God is truly good. The young man continues to make his case. He is rich in both physical wealth and political opportunities. But Jesus wants him to become as a little child, one who comes with simple faith, not with self-proclaimed righteousness. The "rich man" Jesus refers to in verse 25 is not the one who is rich in material things but the one who is rich in self-righteousness. It is hard to leave behind all of that accumulated prestige and become like a little child.

Life stEP When Jesus asked the young man to sell all he had and give it to the poor, He was not saying that this was how a person was saved. He was showing the young ruler that he was not keeping the Law at all. He did not love his neighbor as himself.

Luke 18: 28-43

What is the writer saying?

How can I apply this to my life?

In verses 28-30 Luke wraps up the discussion that has been taking place over the last few chapters. The disciples still have a very limited grasp of what Jesus has been teaching since they are still focused on the physical and do not see the spiritual implication of Christ's teaching. Peter comments, "Lord, we have left all." Jesus answers that those who leave all, gain all, and those who cling to what they have, like the young ruler, forfeit all. What they lose is not just in the next world—they also lose the more abundant life on this earth that Christ came to give.

Beginning in verse 31, a new section in the book begins. Jesus' announcement that He is headed to Jerusalem to be put to death, as well as the disciples' failure to grasp the significance of the prophecy, is a literary divider that Luke uses to alert the reader that there is a shift in emphasis. The previous section ended with the young ruler. This section opens with a blind beggar and, as we will see tomorrow, a wealthy tax collector. Notice that the beggar receives sight from Jesus and a very special assessment: his faith has saved him. This puts him in the same category as the centurion, the sinful woman, and the unclean woman. This beggar believed that Jesus was the answer for all of his needs. His faith was simple and child-like, not from a life of keeping the Law. His faith came from a broken and contrite heart, which saw a hope for today as well as tomorrow in Jesus Christ.

One of the most difficult tasks we have as believers is to integrate our faith into our everyday lives. Salvation is not just a Heaven and Hell thing. It is about real life in the real world.

Luke 19:1-10

What is the writer saying?

How can I apply this to my life?

pray Peru – Apathy, doctrinal error, and cults are crippling churches. Pray for more trained Bible teachers.

Like many of the lives that Jesus touched, Zacchaeus was not on the "spiritual" radar in that society. He was a tax collector—the most hated of all people among the Jews. Apparently he was a rich man, having jurisdiction over Jericho, which was a major area of commerce. But with all his wealth and success, he was a very unhappy man. We read that "he sought to see Jesus" (v. 3) and that "he ran ahead" and climbed into a sycamore tree (v. 4). He was determined to see Christ. We do not know what Zacchaeus was expecting, but it seems clear that he was surprised and joyful when the Lord spoke to him and invited himself for dinner. The reaction of the others was not joy, but scorn, because Zacchaeus was not the kind of person with whom "spiritual people" associated.

At this point we need to compare Zacchaeus with the rich young ruler. One would think that a greedy sinner such as Zacchaeus would cling to his money. But Jesus did not have to ask Zacchaeus to give away anything. Zacchaeus brought the subject up himself. He understood what the rich young ruler failed to grasp—he understood that in comparison to eternal life, riches are meaningless. Zacchaeus chose to really live. He knew that Jesus could give him what no amount of money ever could. The rich young ruler was only looking for Jesus to affirm his righteousness; Zacchaeus was looking for Jesus to give him a new kind of righteousness.

Life stEP Many times we fear making a full commitment to Jesus because we think we are going to have to give up the things we love. We need to realize that Jesus only takes away the things that are neutralizing His blessing. An empty cup can hold a lot more than a full one.

Luke 19:11-27

What is the writer saying?

How can I apply this to my life?

pray India – Evangelization of children; 70 million child laborers, 13 million homeless, and two million orphaned.

Today's parable follows quickly on the heels of the two historical accounts regarding Zacchaeus and the blind beggar. The parable is designed to explain the two incidents more fully. Note the introduction to the parable, "Because they thought the kingdom of God should immediately appear" (v. 11). The crowd and probably the disciples thought Jesus was going to Jerusalem to receive something. Nothing could be further from the truth. He was going to Jerusalem to give everything. He was going to do as He had told the rich young man and sell all He had to give it to the poor. But Christ was not giving up material wealth—He was going to lay down His life so those who were poor in Spirit could receive life.

The parable depicts two types of servants: those who recognize and accept the opportunity placed before them and those who simply spin their wheels. Each servant is given the same opportunity. One reaches out by faith and experiences results. The other just yawns and sticks with the status quo. But the status quo is death; to reject this opportunity is to reject life itself. Some people we have met in the book of Luke accepted the salvation Jesus offered (Zacchaeus and the blind beggar), but some walked away convinced that they were all right just the way they were (the rich young ruler). This is perhaps the saddest of outcomes. These are people who have been given the greatest of opportunities, people who are striving to keep the Law itself, and yet they are people who are so convinced of their own worth that they wrap the treasure of God in a napkin and set it aside indefinitely.

Life stEP Opportunity ignored is opportunity squandered. Whether it is an opportunity to accept Christ or an opportunity to serve Christ, it is an opportunity lost. There is no guarantee that the opportunity will come again.

tuesday 26

Luke 19:28-44

What is the writer saying?

How can I apply this to my life?

pray   Korea – For seminary graduates to humbly commit themselves to less prominent, rural pastorates.

The wait is over. Jesus has been steadily heading toward Jerusalem and toward a final confrontation with Israel's leadership. Yet the initial incident appears quite harmless as Jesus rides into Jerusalem on a young donkey.

The events that are about to unfold were not unexpected; they were planned. The Lord gave specific instructions to His disciples (vv. 29-32). Christ was aware of every step. This is a fulfillment of Zechariah 9:9: "Thy King cometh unto thee: He is just, and having salvation; lowly and riding upon an ass, and upon a colt the foal of an ass." The crowd reinforced this image by quoting from the book of Psalms as they sang from a prominent praise psalm (118:26). There was excitement and tears of joy, but the crowd walked away from the opportunity uncommitted. This same crowd would later cry out to Pilate, "Crucify Him." There is a great difference between acknowledgement and commitment.

Many people in the land of Israel acknowledged that Jesus was Someone special. They cheered and applauded His healings, exorcisms, and raisings of the dead. They were vocal in their applause when He fed the 5,000. They came to Him for spiritual advice. But ultimately, the only interest was self-interest, and their only righteousness was self-righteousness. They were not interested in a salvation that involved giving up anything that they already had. When supporting Jesus became a liability, they switched sides immediately.

Life stEP   We sometimes wear our Christianity as a convenience. Jesus was never a leader of convenience. He always stands at a place of decision. The question is always, who will we choose, Him or ourselves?

Luke 19:45-20:8

What is the writer saying?

How can I apply this to my life?

In the midst of this huge celebration, the seeds of rejection begin to emerge. The episode in which Christ casts out the money-changers would be a message to the religious leaders that He was both a spiritual and political leader. As the legal "King of the Jews," His action here is the action that the temple authorities ought to have taken long ago. The response of the chief priests and the scribes indicates that they may have had a vested interest in these financial dealings. Every year Jews would come to Jerusalem and have to buy animals to offer. They had to buy from the Jewish vendors so the sacrifice would be "without blemish." Taking advantage of this, these vendors boosted the price. Also, foreign money was exchanged into the accepted currency at exorbitant rates. All this happened on Monday of the week Christ died.

On Tuesday, the Lord taught in the temple and preached the Gospel. The same chief priests and scribes attempted to demean Him by asking about His authority (credentials) to preach. Christ turned the tables on them by asking a question that they could not answer concerning where John the Baptist's baptism was from. If the answer had been "from Heaven," the religious leaders could not criticize Him since John spoke of the Messiah. If they opposed John, it would have caused trouble among the multitudes of people who still followed his teachings. The warning here is that by rejecting Christ, the Jewish leaders were painting themselves into a corner. The message of salvation is tied to the Savior. By rejecting His authority, they were rejecting all possibility for salvation.

 Life stEP If Christ has no authority in our lives, then we will struggle with our spiritual walk. Only by total surrender can we hope to experience present blessing.

Luke 20:9-26

What is the writer saying?

How can I apply this to my life?

After the leadership in Jerusalem rejected the clear and simple message Jesus preached in the Temple that Tuesday, Jesus returned to speaking to them in parables. This particular parable is a scathing rebuke of the religious crowd in Jerusalem. A man plants a vineyard and leased it, going into a far country. Servants were sent back but were rejected by the tenants. Finally, the man sends his son, who was rejected as well. The son, obviously, was the Lord Jesus—rejected by Israel. The word "so" is the pivotal point of the parable. Now that the oppressors have gone so far as to kill the son, what would happen to them? The answer is that they would be destroyed, and the vineyard would be given to others. This is precisely what happened to Jerusalem as those who rejected Christ faced eternal judgment, and other nations soon conquered Jerusalem. Jesus quotes from Isaiah 8:14-15: "The stone which the builders rejected, the same is become the head of the corner." Jesus is a "stone of stumbling" today to those who do not believe, and a "precious corner stone to those who believe" (1 Peter 2:3-8).

The reaction of the enemy was predictable. They sent spies in disguise to catch Jesus at His words. Then they openly attacked Him, asking whether or not one should give tribute to Caesar. If He said they should pay taxes, they would accuse Him of being a traitor to His people. If He said not to pay taxes, they would report Him to the Roman authorities. Christ's answer was devastating (v. 25). By telling them to give to God what is God's, Jesus is calling attention to that which bears His image: people. He is once again calling them to give Him their lives.

Life stEP When God created man, He created him in the image and likeness of God (Genesis 1:26). That image makes us different than any other part of the creation. God wants us, not our money.

Luke 20:27-38

What is the writer saying?

How can I apply this to my life?

pray Slovakia – For the church planting to be successful in bringing the Good News to many unbelievers.

By this time the chief priests and scribes were becoming frantic, and they ask a third question. This question came from the Sadducees, a group of people who did not believe in a resurrection and often used this question to mock the Pharisees. Their question was based on a commandment found in Law of Moses (Deuteronomy 25:5). The Law specified that if a man died, his brother was to marry and care for the wife. But what if there were seven brothers and each of them died, leaving the wife to the other—whose wife would she be? Christ's answer does not deny that we will know and recognize each other in Heaven, but it also does not suggest that we will not have a "special" relationship with the person to whom we are married in this life. What it does say is that marriage as we know it in this life does not exist in the next.

Much about that next life is unknown, and therefore we should avoid making arguments based on things about which we are unsure. But there is something we can know: Scripture. Again Jesus reverses the situation. This time He invokes one of the well-known passages from the Old Testament. At the burning bush God said to Moses, "I am the God of Abraham." In order for that statement to be true, Abraham would have to be alive. Otherwise, God would have to say, "I was the God of Abraham." This is not only a great argument for the conscious existence after death, but it is also a clear indication that Jesus thought that even the words of Scripture (and the grammatical features) were important. This argument can only work if we are willing to accept that the very words used in the Old Testament (and by extension the New Testament) were verbally inspired and are therefore inerrant.

 Life stEP

We all look forward to the new heavens and the new earth. What is probably most amazing about that place is how little we know about it. What an awesome adventure it will be to discover all of its joys.

Luke 20:39-21:4

What is the writer saying?

How can I apply this to my life?

pray Pray for the youth of your church to be godly testimonies at school and in their communities.

Jesus has so deftly silenced His critics that no one wants to ask another question. Jesus took this opportunity to ask a question of His own. Psalms is the most-quoted book in the New Testament, Psalm 110 is the most-quoted chapter, and Psalm 110:1 is the most-quoted verse. This is a very important passage that clearly establishes the priority of the Son over David, the father.

The leadership was plotting to kill Jesus because He claimed to be God. They considered this to be blasphemy. They thought that this proved that Jesus was not the Messiah because the Messiah would not make such a false claim. Jesus refutes this again by appealing to Scripture. He asks, "How could Christ be both the Lord over David and still be his son?" Of course, we know that the humanity of Christ is in view, in that He is from the line of David; and the deity of Christ is affirmed in that He is the eternal God, the Lord over David. If the religious leaders' theology was right, and they really knew who Jesus was, the question would have been unnecessary. As Jesus was talking before the crowd, He looked up and saw the self-righteous and wealthy leaders of Israel putting huge amounts of money into the temple treasury. Standing before one of the chests was a poor widow casting in all she possessed—two mites. A mite was worth about one-fifth of a cent. Jesus makes a very important spiritual observation at this point. God is not interested in how much the people were giving. The measure of a person's commitment is determined by how much we keep.

As humans we cannot help but measure things based on the size of the gift, but giving as a spiritual discipline is an all-or-nothing proposition. God wants us to put everything we have and everything we are into His hands. We are to be living sacrifices.

Luke 21:5-19

What is the writer saying?

How can I apply this to my life?

pray Nigeria – Pray for salvation among the more than 30 people groups that have no known believers.

As Jesus and His disciples are walking in the Temple complex, one of them comments on the magnificence of the stones used to build it. Jesus points out that this very temple would be totally destroyed, using the occasion to begin a discussion of the end times. The sermon is known as the Olivet Discourse and is also recorded in Matthew 24-25. Jesus draws on many portions of the Old Testament, but much of what He says is most directly related to Daniel's understanding of the seventieth week (Daniel 9:24-27). The final seven years prior to the setting up of the kingdom are divided into two parts, with the whole seven years commonly known as the Tribulation, and the last three and a half years designated as the Great Tribulation. Today's passage describes life in the first half of the Tribulation. Based on this passage and materials that would be written later (1 Thessalonians 5, 2 Thessalonians 2, and Revelation 4-19), we know that the first half of the Tribulation is a terrible time, but compared to the second half, it is comparatively mild. During this time the Antichrist, a political leader arises from in Europe, becomes the champion of the nation of Israel and defends them from the enemies who surround them. Many hail him as the Messiah. The period is filled with war and famine and death, but it is only a small taste of the horrors about to happen. The Antichrist has a much larger vision for himself. He wants to be king of the world.

Life stEP These words were written before the Church Age was introduced. Believers living today do not need to fear this horrible time of tribulation because they will be taken out before it begins. Paul described this event (the Rapture) in 1 Thessalonians 4:13-18.

Luke 21:20-38

What is the writer saying?

How can I apply this to my life?

This passage could be referring to one of two major destructions of Jerusalem. The first occurred in A.D. 70 with Titus. But Zechariah clearly prophesied a destruction of the city that will occur during Daniel's seventieth week. This is the destruction that seems to be prominent here. By comparing this passage with Matthew 24, it seems clear that this destruction occurs at the middle of the Tribulation.

The historical destruction of A.D. 70 was bad enough. According to the historian Josephus, when there were no more to plunder or slay after "incredible slaughter and miseries," Titus ordered the city to be "razed so completely as to look like a spot which had been never inhabited." In that first destruction of Jerusalem, an estimated 1.1 million Jews perished. Josephus tells us that 97,000 Jews were sent to various provinces and to the Egyptian mines. As horrible at that destruction was, it is only a foretaste of what will happen during the end times. The "times of the Gentiles" mentioned in verse 24 are prophetically significant. This period is the focus of the book of Daniel. Most of the empires Daniel speaks of in his prophecy have come and gone. Only the final version of the Roman Empire is yet to appear. The head of that empire will be the Antichrist.

Until these "times" have been completed, the kingdom of God will not be instituted on earth. The seventieth week ends with the return of the Lord from Heaven. This is not to be confused with the Rapture, which occurs seven years earlier. The reason the Rapture is not mentioned here is because the church has not yet officially started.

Life stEP Sometimes it seems that the world just keeps on spinning and that God's promises seem distant. Peter warned us that the Lord is not slack about these promises—He wants people to have an opportunity to be saved (2 Peter 3:9)

tuesday 27

Luke 22:1-20

What is the writer saying?

How can I apply this to my life?

pray Portugal – For biblically sound Christian musicians who will surrender their talent to God's use.

The final week of Jesus' earthly life is rapidly winding down. As chapter 22 opens, it is now Thursday. Hate is blinding the hearts and minds of the chief priests and scribes, and Satan enters into Judas. Luke briefly mentions these facts then quickly shifts his focus to Jesus and the disciples as they prepare for the Passover.

The Passover is and extremely important feast in the Jewish calendar. It looks back to the Exodus. But just as importantly it looks forward to the final salvation God had promised to His people. The lamb that was slain was a vivid picture of Jesus Christ: it was spotless, it was put to death in place of another, and no bones were broken. Amazingly, in the first century the lambs used in Jerusalem came from Bethlehem! The historical exodus was but a picture of a future time when God would bring His people into a permanent relationship with Him, a time when all of the promises made to Abraham and Isaac and Jacob would be fulfilled.

For the believer today this marks the institution of the Lord's Supper, or communion. Later in the New Testament the Apostle Paul refers back to this very incident when instituting the current church practice (see 1 Corinthians 11). Much like the Passover, the Lord's Supper also looks both forward and backward. It is a table of *retrospection,* looking back to Calvary and understanding that Christ is our *Passover.* It is also a table of *introspection* as we examine ourselves (1 Corinthians 11:28). Finally, it is a table of *anticipation*; we partake of the Lord's Table "till He come" (1 Corinthians 11:26).

 Jesus had offered the nation of Israel an opportunity to accept Him and His kingdom. They had refused. As He meets with His disciples this one last time, all of the loose ends are tied up. He is referring to His mission: to die as a substitute for His people.

Luke 22:21-38

What is the writer saying?

How can I apply this to my life?

The intricate beauty of the picture before the disciples seems to fall on blind eyes. They still don't understand that Jesus is about to die. In fact, they are more concerned with their own position than they are with what Christ is telling them in picture and in word. They are arguing about which one of them will be greatest in the kingdom of God. Luke focuses on this episode because it brings us back to his theme: The first shall be last, and the last shall be first. The disciples have seen with their own eyes that the rich and the powerful reject Jesus. They have also seen the weak and beggarly blessed. And yet they are still concerned with position. They still envision the kingdom in human terms, the way the "kings of the Gentiles" think of a kingdom.

Jesus has consistently taught and illustrated for His disciples that life in the kingdom is different than life in the world. In the kingdom of God, weakness is of greatest value. Jesus Himself became weak so that He could provide salvation for us by becoming a babe in swaddling clothes and placing Himself under the leadership of the Spirit. He was about to submit to the greatest injustice ever conceived: the Lord of Glory mocked and crucified by wicked men. What could be more humiliating? But that was the price of our salvation, and Jesus willingly paid it.

The disciples were still in the dark. They envision a kingdom similar to the Roman Empire, a kingdom built on power. But before Jesus shows Himself as the Lion of the tribe of Judah, He was the Lamb of God. He denied Himself just as we must deny ourselves. Jim Elliot put it this way, "He is no fool who gives what he cannot keep to gain what he cannot lose."

Life **stEP** Our natural instincts are to protect what we have and to try to add to it. Jesus said that the quality of our life is related to how much we give, not how much we get.

thursday 27

Luke 22:39-53

What is the writer saying?

How can I apply this to my life?

pray Japan – For an end to cult growth, which far exceeds the growth of Christianity.

There are numerous post-resurrection appearances by Jesus to His disciples. Luke chooses to report a rather unique and touching account of Jesus' encounter with two of the disciples as they walked along the road to Emmaus. This whole encounter (from here to the end of the book) is designed to wrap up the storyline concerning the disciples. At no point thus far in Luke have the disciples been presented in a consistently positive light. They were rebuked for having "little faith." They were constantly squabbling over who would be greatest in the kingdom. Their leader, Peter, had denied Jesus while He was on trial. One might be tempted to think that this band of fishermen and tax collectors were only fair-weather friends. This passage clears up a lot about how Jesus was preparing them for a greater responsibility.

As the incident opens, we are told that the eyes of the disciples were "held that they might not know him." This is not to say that they were not complicit in their blindness. It was not just Jesus' physical appearance that they did not see; it was His mission that they were blind to. They had read the Old Testament through selective eyes. They had seen the passages that spoke of the Messiah conquering the world, but they had missed the world of hurt that was to occur before the King would again reign from Jerusalem.

In keeping with Luke's focus on faith, Jesus did not start with Who He was. He started with the Scriptures and traced from them the importance and necessity of Messiah's humiliation. Finally, they understood.

 Life stEP It is no dishonor to be weak. Jesus embraced weakness because it is the only way. Only the weak survive.

Luke 22: 54-71

What is the writer saying?

How can I apply this to my life?

pRay Korea – For godly Chinese businessmen to use their easy access to North Korea to share the Gospel.

Jesus had clearly embraced weakness as essential to His mission, but the disciples were not so easy to convince. Peter was especially vocal. He had, in fact, cut the ear off of one of the High Priest's servants, and He wanted the others to follow his lead. In another gospel he vowed that even if the rest denied Jesus, he never would (Mark 14:31).

The disciples, who had just been arguing about who would be greatest in the kingdom, find themselves hiding from the temple police. Peter's denial is a very important element in the storyline. His self-sufficiency is exposed and proven ineffective. Peter needed a humble heart, and God delivered. Peter was a broken man. He would later write, "Humble yourselves therefore under the mighty hand of God, that he may exalt you in due time" (1 Peter 5:6).

The morning after Christ was mocked and beaten (vv. 63-65), the elders, chief priests and scribes came together. The assembly consisted of between seventy and seventy-two people. They could pass judgment on religious and civil issues, but they could not inflict capital punishment. They asked two questions to try to entrap Jesus. They were committed to using the technicalities of the Law in order to frustrate the true purpose of the Law. Just as they would not love their neighbors, now they would not love God.

We sometimes become frustrated that we do not have the power to change the world and make it into a better place. But power always corrupts. Faith is the only solution for the human heart. It may look wrong at times, but God does have a plan that will work. Trust Him.

Luke 23:1-12

What is the writer saying?

How can I apply this to my life?

pray Mexico – For discipleship programs that effectively teach how the Bible impacts family life.

In today's passage we find Christ before Pilate and Herod. The Sanhedrin found itself in a rather precarious position. They wanted Jesus put to death, but they did not have the authority to do so without Roman permission. They were willing to humble themselves before Pilate, who they hated, and ask him to grant them a favor, but they were not willing to humble themselves before God, Who they supposedly loved. Notice that the charges against Jesus have changed. The chief priests and scribes no longer accuse Him of blasphemy, but rather of trying to start an insurrection. Necessity often makes for strange companions.

Pilate is somewhat confused by the charges. He can tell that Jesus is no threat to Roman rule, and he does not like being manipulated by the Sanhedrin for selfish religious purposes. He tries to get out of the position he finds himself in by sending Jesus to Herod. This is the same Herod who had John the Baptist beheaded. He was also in charge of the region of Galilee. No doubt Pilate hoped that Herod would relieve him of all responsibility in this matter. Although it did not work out exactly as Pilate had hoped, he at least had someone to share the blame with if the matter got messy. The Sanhedrin was acting purely out of self-interest; Pilate was maneuvering to gain any political advantage that he could, but Herod clearly resented Jesus in the same way that he hated John. Herod's men treated the Lord with contempt and mocked him.

Only Jesus was acting out of love for others. It was not the power of the Sanhedrin, Pilate, or Herod that forced Jesus to submit to these atrocities. It was His trust in God and His love for us.

Life stEP A life lived for self is a life without meaning. A life lived for others is a life worth emulating.

Luke 23:13-25

What is the writer saying?

How can I apply this to my life?

Herod has been helpful, but he has not solved Pilate's problem. Pilate assumed that he was through with Christ when he sent Him to Herod. But Christ is sent back. Pilate does feel more confident in his assessment that Jesus is not guilty of any capital crime. So he now calls the chief priests and rulers as well as the people and makes it clear that neither he nor Herod can find a reason to condemn Jesus. But nothing could change the outcome—not the voice of reason (finding no fault), the voice of conscience, or the voice of his wife. The enemy insisted that Jesus be crucified. The overwhelming evidence that Jesus was innocent, and the political pressure that Pilate put on the Jewish leaders, only serves to demonstrate how much these people hated Jesus, and how they hated Him without cause. They still claimed to be protecting the Law, which they themselves primarily taught—that we should love God and love one another.

Pilate was not finished. The last tool he used was to bring Barabbas to the forefront. It was a custom at Passover to release a prisoner, usually one chosen by the people (Matthew 27:15). But Pilate tried to tip the scales heavily in Jesus' favor. He chose Barabbas, knowing his history. He had committed murder; he was *guilty as sin*, and they all knew it. But the issues that the Sanhedrin and the people had with Jesus had nothing to do with crime; it was always about hate: hating God and hating one another. They would rather murder an innocent man than accept that some miracle worker from Galilee was their Messiah. That would be uncivilized.

Life stEP — Don't miss the irony here. These were the people who claimed to keep the Law since childhood. But they would not believe because the Messiah was not Who they thought He should be.

Luke 23:26-43

What is the writer saying?

How can I apply this to my life?

pray Italy – Maturity in believers, as more churches have resulted from bitter splits than church growth.

Simon, a Cyrenian, is like so many of the people we meet in Luke's gospel. Like Zacchaeus or the centurion, he was not a person the Jewish population would respect. He was a foreigner. Suddenly, his life was changed. He was grabbed and told to bear Christ's cross as Jesus journeyed toward His death. But like a great many things in life, what seemed to be a sad situation turned out to be special. We are told in Mark 15:21 that Simon was the father of Alexander and Rufus. Luke would know these believers because of his relationship to Paul, who writes in Romans, "Greet Rufus, chosen in the Lord, and his mother and mine" (16:13). So once again, we see those with little or no value, according to the Jewish culture, contribute greatly in God's eyes.

A little later in the passage, Luke introduces us to two thieves. These two robbers are mentioned briefly in Matthew and Mark, but Luke allots a significant amount of time to the conversation that took place between them and Jesus. Like the other converts we meet in the book of Luke, these two are social outcasts. In fact, they are at the bottom of the social ladder. No respectable chief priest or lawyer would be caught dead talking to the likes of them. The cultured people had too much to lose. How sad! But the people who know they are "poor in spirit" have nothing to lose. Only the rich in spirit cling desperately to their false hope while at the same time denying everything they claim to hold dear by their selfish behavior.

Life stEP The thief on the cross had not been baptized or lived a good life, yet he was saved. The reason is simple. It was all of grace, not of works. And so it is with all of us.

Luke 23:44-56

What is the writer saying?

How can I apply this to my life?

pray — Nicaragua – Outreach to youth in a land where broken homes, poverty, and secularism are the norm.

The sixth hour was noon, according to the Jewish method of telling time. Yet there was darkness. We know from the other gospels that some very significant things were happening from the sixth hour to the ninth hour, but Luke mentions only two items that are in keeping with his unique emphasis. The first is the renting of the temple veil. This veil was a curtain separating the Most Holy Place from the Holy Place (2 Chronicles 3:14). Only the high priest was allowed to pass through the veil, and he was only allowed to do so on one day each year, the Day of Atonement (Leviticus 16:2). If there was anything in Jewish society that could be thought of as the ultimate status symbol, it was being allowed to enter the Holy of Holies. But now the veil was ripped from top to bottom (men would only be able to tear it from bottom to top), thereby abolishing the barrier between man and God (Hebrews 10:20).

After Jesus gives up His spirit to the Father, Luke recounts a number of different reactions to all that has just taken place. In keeping with his theme, the first two responses are from the weak and unnoticed parts of society. A centurion (remember that the first mention of faith in Luke is associated with a centurion), who would be despised by the Jews, cries out by faith that this was indeed the "Son of God." Women from Galilee, who were not allowed to serve in the temple or the synagogue, and other acquaintances from Galilee, stood afar off. And then it finally happens; a prominent person finally steps forward—not a resident of Jerusalem but a secret believer from Arimathea. He provides the tomb in which Jesus is buried.

Life stEP — God is the God of the broken-hearted. He longs to reach out and to save those who are desperate. Only the sick are looking for a doctor.

Luke 24:1-12

What is the writer saying?

How can I apply this to my life?

As we read along in chapter 24, we should begin to realize that the storyline has come full circle. Luke opened with great joy and angels proclaiming the birth of the Messiah. And so it ends. This is the resurrection chapter. The stone was rolled away, and angels stood in shining garments. Angels were there at Christ's birth, His temptation, His experience in the Garden of Gethsemane, and now at His resurrection. This time, however, they are not here to support Christ in His human frailty; they are here to proclaim His resurrection. New life has come, a new life that we as believers can share in. Paul sums this up so well in Romans 1:3-4: "Concerning his Son Jesus Christ our Lord, which was made of the seed of David according to the flesh; and declared to be the Son of God with power, according to the Spirit of holiness, by the resurrection from the dead."

Christ's resurrection was not revealed to the chief priest or the princes of this age; it was revealed first to the women in this passage, and they were ecstatic. They returned from the sepulcher and told "all these things unto the eleven, and to all the rest" (v. 9). What appeared to many to be the greatest travesty ever committed on planet earth had become an infinite and irreversible victory. Paul writes, "Which none of the princes of this world knew: for had they known it, they would not have crucified the Lord of glory" (1 Corinthians 2:8). Christ's weakness was necessary for our salvation. It is the same for those who wish to follow the same path. To be crucified with Christ by faith is to be resurrected with Christ into newness of life.

Life stEP If we were to drive a clunker into a car dealership and buy a new BMW, would we then hop into our clunker and drive away? That is the way it is with salvation. We cannot live two lives. Are you still driving the clunker even though you own the BMW?

Luke 24:13-27

What is the writer saying?

How can I apply this to my life?

There are numerous post-resurrection appearances by Jesus to His disciples. Luke chooses to report a rather unique and touching account of Jesus' encounter with two of the disciples as they walked along the road to Emmaus. This whole encounter (from here to the end of the book) is designed to wrap up the storyline concerning the disciples. At no point thus far in Luke have the disciples been presented in a consistently positive light. They were rebuked for having "little faith." They were constantly squabbling over who would be greatest in the kingdom. Their leader, Peter, had denied Jesus while He was on trial. One might be tempted to think that this band of fishermen and tax collectors were only fair-weather friends. This passage clears up a lot about how Jesus was preparing them for a greater responsibility.

As the incident opens, we are told that the eyes of the disciples were "held that they might not know him." This is not to say that they were not complicit in their blindness. It was not just Jesus' physical appearance that they did not see; it was His mission that they were blind to. They had read the Old Testament through selective eyes. They had seen the passages that spoke of the Messiah conquering the world, but they had missed the world of hurt that was to occur before the King would again reign from Jerusalem.

In keeping with Luke's focus on faith, Jesus did not start with Who He was. He started with the Scriptures and traced from them the importance and necessity of Messiah's humiliation. Finally, they understood.

Life stEP Sometimes we wish that we could talk to Jesus personally. But if we did, He would share with us the same way that He did with these disciples. If we will not believe the Scriptures, we will not believe.

Luke 24:28-40

What is the writer saying?

How can I apply this to my life?

pray Netherlands Antilles – Openness to the Gospel in a land where religious freedom has yielded little fruit.

The disciples still do not know they are with Jesus. They come to a village where they are planning to spend the night and ask Jesus to tarry with them. When He breaks the bread, they realize who He is, and immediately He vanishes from their sight. There was no question-and-answer time. What Jesus had shared from the Scriptures was sufficient and essential. Human nature always wants to know more—that was one of the issues with Eve in the Garden of Eden. These disciples had lots of questions, but Jesus left them with the greatest of all gifts, an understanding of God's Word.

To live by sight is a pathway to death. The "just shall live by his faith" (Habakkuk 2:4) and "without faith it is impossible to please him" (Hebrews 11:6).

You would think that the eleven had been afforded enough opportunity to assimilate the idea that Jesus was resurrected from the dead. Yet, with all of the eyewitness accounts they had heard, they still refused to accept the fact that Jesus had been resurrected from the dead. As they are listening to the two who were with Jesus on the road to Emmaus, Jesus appears in their midst. The text says that they are terrified, thinking He is a spirit (ghost). But Jesus once again calms their fears and allows them to touch His hands and feet. Even after this, the text says that they still "believed not for joy."

It is hard to imagine how, given all of the cold, hard evidence, these future leaders of the church still did not get it. But that is exactly what happened. Faith is not a reality-based activity; it is a Scripture-based activity.

Life stEP Many times we ask God for more proof that He exists. Proof is not what we need. We need to humble ourselves before the Word of God and believe.

Luke 24:41-53

What is the writer saying?

How can I apply this to my life?

Luke is about to lay down his pen. He had diligently searched the records and listened to the eyewitness accounts so that Theophilus would know the certainty of these events. Certainty is a precious commodity. The disciples were there, they saw Jesus, they spoke with Jesus, they touched Jesus, yet they still did not believe. Their eyes were not opened until Jesus opened the Word of God and explained to them all the things that must be fulfilled. Then He opened the eyes of their understanding.

Once the disciples were willing to listen to the Scriptures, Jesus was able to explain to them the prime directive of His mission. From the very beginning of Luke's gospel the message had been simple: "Repent for the remission of sins" (Luke 3:3). It was John's message as well as Jesus'. The disciples had heard this message repeatedly. But now, perhaps for the first time, they understand. They understand that Jesus had to humble Himself, even to dying on the cross in order to accomplish that which the Old Testament had predicted. They understand how they had read the Old Testament through the eyes of self-interest. They now understand how death was life, and last was first. They are now ready to go into the entire world and preach a new way of thinking that promotes death over life, weakness over strength, and last over first. As a sign that Christ was well-pleased with the disciples' new understanding, He was caught up into Heaven before their eyes. This is probably not the final ascension of Acts 1, but it is a clear indication that Jesus is now comfortable in turning the preaching of the Gospel over to the disciples.

Life stEP We can read this gospel as a historical account of a historical person who lived, died, and was resurrected 2,000 years ago. Or by faith we can understand the meaning of that person's life, death, and resurrection. Which is it for you?

Ezekiel's name means "God strengthens," a rather appropriate name for the ministry God called him to and the situation the people of Israel faced. He was a Zadokian priest, which was the priestly line of the high priest. The Babylonians took him into captivity in the second deportation in 597 B.C. He lived with the common Jewish captives about fifty miles from the capital city of Babylon, ministering to them for over twenty-two years. Daniel, by way of comparison, was taken in the first deportation in 605 B.C. and lived in the city of Babylon with a ministry to his captors. Jeremiah, the third influential prophet in this period, stayed in Jerusalem, ministering to the Jews left behind. All three prophets lived and ministered beyond the 586 B.C. destruction of the first temple (Solomon's Temple).

Ezekiel's wife died the year before Jerusalem was destroyed, and he was not allowed to mourn for her, just as God would not mourn the death of His wife, Jerusalem. Despite the horror of the deportation, once the Jewish people were established in Babylon, they eventually experienced a relatively pleasant life. They were free to build homes, write back to Judah, establish businesses, and enjoy their own Jewish culture. Their comfort in Babylon is illustrated in the fact that when they were allowed to return in 539 B.C., only 50,000 of the estimated 2.5 million Jews elected to go back to Jerusalem (see Ezra 2:64-65). Even though they were somewhat comfortable in Babylon, it was still a depressing thought to be uprooted from their homeland, as illustrated by the mournful words of Psalm 137:

"By the rivers of Babylon, there we sat down, yea, we wept, when we remembered Zion. We hanged our harps upon the willows in the midst thereof. For there they that carried us away captive required of us a song; and they that wasted us required of us mirth, saying, Sing us one of the songs of Zion. How shall we sing the LORD's song in a strange land? If I forget thee, O Jerusalem, let my right hand forget her cunning. If I do not remember thee, let my tongue cleave to the roof of my mouth; if I prefer not Jerusalem above my chief joy. Remember, O LORD, the children of Edom in the day of Jerusalem; who said, Rase it, rase it, even to the foundation thereof. O daughter of Babylon, who art to be destroyed; happy shall he be, that rewardeth thee as thou hast served us. Happy shall he be, that taketh and dasheth thy little ones against the stones."

The theme of Ezekiel is The Glory of the Lord. By way of comparison, the other three Major Prophets have similar themes: Isaiah, The Salvation of the Lord; Jeremiah, The Judgment of the Lord; and Daniel, The Sovereignty of the Lord.

The outline of Ezekiel is organized by topic and time:

<u>Before 586 B.C.</u>
Ezekiel's call
1-3

<u>Before 586 B.C.</u>
Ezekiel's condemnation of Judah
4-24

<u>In 586 B.C.</u>
Ezekiel's condemnation of the nations
25-32

<u>After 586 B.C.</u>
Ezekiel's country restored
33-48

There are a number of famous passages in the book:

<u>The wheel within the wheel vision:</u>
Chapter 1

<u>Messianic passages</u>
17:22-24; 21:26-27; 34:23-24

<u>The Battle of Gog and Magog</u>
Chapters 38-39

<u>The Millennial Temple</u>
Chapters 40-48

Finally, there are several key points of theology that the book addresses. Ezekiel tells the people that Jerusalem can fall (as opposed to the supernatural deliverance they experienced from Sennacherib in 701 B.C.). As the Jews are taken to Babylon, God promises and demonstrates that He is still with them and that He is not a local deity. In the book of Ezekiel, God is the source of spiritual life. Just as God breathed into Adam the breath of life, likewise He will give His people a new heart (chapter 35); He will resurrect their dead bodies from the Valley of Dry Bones (chapter 37); and He will cause a life-giving river to flow from the new temple in the New Jerusalem (chapter 47).

Ezekiel 1:1-14

What is the writer saying?

How can I apply this to my life?

pray South Africa – For believers within the government to apply biblical principles in solving problems.

In chapters 1-3 we see Ezekiel's call to his ministry. He is thirty years old, the typical age that priests would begin their priestly duties. He was from a priestly family—in fact, the family from which the high priests also came (the line of Zadok). Notice that Christ also waited until thirty years of age to begin His public ministry.

Ezekiel had been deported five years earlier with King Jehoiachin (also called Jeconiah or Coniah), which was the second Babylonian deportation in 597 B.C. This then dates the vision to 592 B.C.

The vision that follows is the famous "wheel within the wheel" vision that is popularized in the old folk song. While we can speculate on the exact appearance of this contraption, we do not have to guess at the purpose for it. By the time we get to the end of the chapter, it is clear that this is God's glorious chariot throne. Just as ancient kings had servants and special vehicles for transportation, so also does the great God of Israel. The characteristics of the throne underscore His attributes of omnipotence, omnipresence, and omniscience.

The servants are "cherubs," according to a later reference (Ezekiel 41:18). This name means "watchers," which implies that they are guardians of the holiness of God. This category of angel occurs ninety times in Scripture. They appear to be the same as the "seraph" (burning one) of Isaiah 6, but "seraph" only appears that one time in the Bible.

The vision left quite an impression on Ezekiel, as it is mentioned again in 3:23, 8:4, and 43:3. Each animal is the *best* in his or her category. They may have been the animals on the four tribal standards (flags) in the wilderness wanderings. Some see parallels to the four gospels of Christ's life.

Life stEP The Greek word for "fire" is *puros*, from which we get the word *pure*. The presence of God purifies us if we allow it; we must stay in His presence.

Ezekiel 1:15-28

What is the writer saying?

How can I apply this to my life?

The angelic creatures (called "beasts" in the parallel passage in Revelation 4) are blockheads—all four faces are on each of the four creatures. This apparently ensures that all four faces can be viewed from any angle. The lion parallels the gospel of Matthew, where Christ is presented as the king of Israel ("the lion of the tribe of Judah"). Mark, who was writing to Romans who appreciated servants, presents Christ as the obedient, diligent servant, which is pictured by the ox. Luke, writing to Greeks, presents Christ as the greatest man who ever lived (the face of the man). John presents Christ in His soaring majesty as God of very God (the eagle). Matthew gives Christ's genealogy back to Abraham through the kings of Judah. Luke gives Christ's genealogy all the way back to Adam. Mark gives no genealogy, for it doesn't matter for a servant. John gives no genealogy, for God has always existed.

The wheels appear to be designed to demonstrate mobility; God can go wherever He needs to. The angels and the throne do not need to turn in order to go in a particular direction. Perhaps there were four pairs of wheels, one pair under each angel, with the wheels at right angles for this multi-directional capability.

The multiple sets of wings on creatures are found elsewhere in Scripture (Isaiah 6:2). In addition to implying mobility, the wings are used to show respect by covering certain parts of the body.

Notice all the impressive colors. Fire is yellow. In Hebrew, amber refers to a bright metallic shine. Crystal is clear but sparkling. The rainbow has multiple colors. Beryl is golden brown, and sapphire is blue. The net effect: Ezekiel's God is an awesome God.

Life stEP — The ancients saw God and revered Him. We don't see God. How do we honor Him in our thoughts and prayers?

Ezekiel 2:1-3:7

What is the writer saying?

How can I apply this to my life?

Chapter two contains Ezekiel's charge to his ministry. In 2:1-2 he is indwelt for power. In 2:3-5 he is informed for confidence. In 2:6-7 he is encouraged for endurance, and in 2:8-10 he is programmed for success. Notice that God commands Ezekiel to stand on his feet to receive his charge, but the Spirit enters and lifts Ezekiel to his feet. Apparently our spiritual life is so empowered by God that we need to only assent to what He wants to do through us, not work up the courage, wisdom, and strength to do so.

As God gets Ezekiel ready, He does not hide the difficulties that Ezekiel will face. By this time, Jerusalem has already been attacked twice by the Babylonians. You would think that the Jews left behind would have been desperate to win God's favor. But one of the characteristics of sin is that it blinds the perpetrator to his or her faults. The majority of the Jewish people had centuries earlier abandoned pure Jehovah worship for a syncretism of Biblical and pagan theology. It was not that they rejected Jehovah outright—they just wanted Him plus all the other gods and goddesses. God steels Ezekiel for the negative reception and encourages him with the thought that it is not crucial that he be popular to successfully convince people to repent. He is merely required to deliver the message, and God will see to it that they recognize the message as having come from a prophet of God. (This should not be interpreted as the right of a preacher/witnesser to be rude to get a sinner's attention!)

The scroll represents the information that Ezekiel internalizes to then deliver. There is an abundance of it ("front and back," 2:10), and it is sweet since it is God's Word, but bitter because it is a word of judgment.

Life stEP Why do we believe, but so many others don't? How can we be more effective spokespersons for God? Why should we share when they reject?

Ezekiel 3:8-23

What is the writer saying?

How can I apply this to my life?

pray   Hungary – Pray that many Bible school students here from central Europe will become leaders at home.

If chapter one begins Ezekiel's call to the ministry, and chapter two contains his charge, then chapter three completes the process with his formal commissioning to the ministry. God again braces him for the rejection that he will experience. Psychologically, this prepares Ezekiel to avoid a martyr's complex. You would think that a prophet so commissioned and loaded with information would immediately begin a series of public meetings. Notice, however, that Ezekiel is clearly led by the Spirit of Jehovah— to keep quiet! *Seven days* was the length of time for the consecration of a priest to his duties. Ezekiel actually continued his silence for six years, only speaking when God directed him, until the final judgment on Jerusalem fell in 586 B.C. In this section we have the famous watchman scene, which is repeated in chapter 33.

We must note that in the Old Testament, the *righteous man* is not necessarily a *born-again man*, and conversely, an *unrighteous man* is not necessarily an *unsaved man. Righteous* and *unrighteous* refer to immediate obedience or disobedience, which results in temporal blessing or punishment. It does not automatically refer to eternal reward or punishment. Therefore you could have a *righteous man* ignore Ezekiel's warnings, die as a result, and still go to Heaven. It would not be a case of a *righteous man* losing his eternal salvation. "Blood on the hands" (v. 20) refers to murder. It underscores the seriousness of Ezekiel's call. If he failed to obey it, however, it would not lead to his eternal damnation (loss of salvation) but rather to immediate physical discipline from God.

Life **stEP** Being a prophet is more than blurting out passages of Scripture. It involves our total life, sharing the joy we have found in Christ.

Ezekiel 8:1-6, 16-18

What is the writer saying?

How can I apply this to my life?

pray Guatemala – For medical ministries to reach the 55,000 war orphans and 5,000 street children.

Chapters 1-3 constitute Ezekiel's call to the ministry. Chapters 4-24 describe the first part of his ministry, the condemnation of Judah. Since he was led to be quiet in chapter 3, much of his ministry involved role-play and recording visions he received. In chapters 8-11 Ezekiel sees four prophetic visions, the first of which details wicked pagan practices in the temple in Jerusalem. Time-wise, it is fourteen months into Ezekiel's ministry, the fall of 591 B.C.

Over ninety times in Ezekiel, the phrase "son of man" is used by God to address Ezekiel. The Hebrew idiom, "son of" means "characterized by." It emphasizes Ezekiel's humanity. More importantly, in the New Testament, Christ uses this phrase twice as many times as any other title to refer to Himself.

In the vision Ezekiel is transported to Jerusalem, where he beholds all the pagan idols and practices that have been brought into the temple of Jehovah. The idol was for Asherah, the goddess associated with Baal. Jezebel and Ahab promoted the religion in the northern kingdom and wicked king Manasseh promoted her in the southern kingdom (2 Kings 21). The gate mentioned indicates that the current king (Zedekiah) was actively involved in this travesty since it led from the palace to the temple. The twenty-five men would represent the twenty-four courses of priests plus the High Priest. With their backs to Jehovah, they were busy worshipping the rising sun.

Chapter 8 also mentions that seventy elders were involved (the precursor of the seventy men of the Sanhedrin), plus the son of the leader of godly Josiah's revival (2 Kings 22). "Branch to the nose" apparently refers to some sort of rude gesture, which would boomerang on them.

Life stEP Barely 30 years after Josiah's revival, abject apostasy controls Jerusalem. Every generation must be won afresh.

Ezekiel 10:1-5, 18-22

What is the writer saying?

How can I apply this to my life?

Details of the wheel within the wheel vision of chapter one are referred to in a number of these visions. Chapter 10 uses coals taken from the angelic creatures to burn Jerusalem. Likewise, in Revelation 8:5, coals from the altar in Heaven are used to burn the earth. The "house" mentioned is the temple in Jerusalem. In the Holy of Holies, the ark of the covenant had two golden cherubs. The Shekinah glory of God dwelt over the ark between these two cherubs. The curtain guarding the Holy of Holies had cherubs embroidered on it as well.

The angelic creatures lift Jehovah up and transport Him to the threshold of the temple. This is the beginning of God's departure from Jerusalem. He had been there since David brought the tabernacle up to his new capital (2 Samuel 6) around 1000 B.C., and Solomon built the first temple by 950 B.C. Here in 591 B.C, about 400 years later, God is leaving. It is a lingering, nostalgic departure. He will stop at the Eastern Gate (vv. 18-19) before proceeding across the Kidron Valley to the Mount of Olives. Jewish tradition states that the Shekinah glory remained for 3½ years on the Mount of Olives before continuing on to Heaven. This is amazing when compared to Christ's 3½-year public ministry, especially as Christ retraced this very route on Palm Sunday when He offered Himself as Israel's Messiah.

"Ichabod" ("the glory has departed," compare to 1 Samuel 4:21) is now written over Jerusalem in preparation for the 586 B.C. destruction of the temple by the Babylonians. Even when the 50,000 Jews return under Zerubbabel in 536 B.C., the Shekinah glory does not return to grace the second temple. Christ on Palm Sunday constitutes the first return of glory since Ezekiel 10-11.

Life stEP The Jewish people had so many advantages yet lost so much. Where are we missing opportunities?

Ezekiel 11:14-25

What is the writer saying?

How can I apply this to my life?

pray Ukraine – For God to give youth a passion to live for Him and reach their land.

In verses 14-21, the princes were justifying recent events through the self-serving theory of a *negative rapture* (they said that the wicked had been taken to Babylon and the righteous left in Jerusalem). God contradicts this theory and says their destruction is imminent. He then has gracious words for the exiles, saying He would bless them and bring them back to Jerusalem. All throughout the Old Testament, God talks about the *shear*, or "remnant." For instance, in Isaiah 7, when God predicts the 701 B.C. attack on Jerusalem by Assyria, He tells Ahaz that if he disobeys, "only a remnant shall return." This phrase is the name of Isaiah's son in that chapter: *Shear-jashub*. Usually the concept of the remnant is positive. In 1 Kings 19 God says that despite Elijah's complaint that he was the only one standing against Baal, God had 7,000 left who had not bowed a knee to Baal. The concept of "the remnant" is that no matter how bad things get, God in His sovereign plan has ensured that there are always a few who remain faithful and will eventually be blessed.

In verses 19-21 the new birth is described. This is the first of several descriptions of what we eventually refer to as the *new covenant*. The *old covenant* (the Law of Moses) was designed to protect Israel from the pagan religions. It proved that humans cannot obey the law in their own power, but it failed to empower them to live holy lives. Under the new covenant, the externals of the old covenant are internalized to provide the power to obey. In verses 22-25, the Shekinah glory of God goes to the Mount of Olives. In Ezekiel 43:1-4 it says that the Shekinah glory will come back through the Eastern Gate, just as Christ did on Palm Sunday.

Life stEP We enjoy the power of the new covenant due to the indwelling of the Holy Spirit. We further nourish our inner man as we feed on the Word.

Ezekiel 12:17-28

What is the writer saying?

How can I apply this to my life?

pray Brazil – For godly, seminary – trained men, willing to serve among the 139 unreached tribal groups.

In chapter 12 God directs Ezekiel to role-play two prophetic signs to the people of Israel. The first, in 12:1-16, is the sign of *exilic baggage* illustrating the coming third deportation in 586 B.C. The second sign, in verses 17-28, is the sign of *trembling.* Ezekiel was to eat his bread and drink his water with apprehension and trembling. This would illustrate the fear the people of Jerusalem and Israel would feel as the Babylonians attacked the third time. Notice that the people in Israel were comforting each other with the notion that despite the ongoing prophetic words, judgment was not imminent, God was not serious, and any judgment would not fall for years to come, if at all. God flatly contradicts that misconception and condemns them for the violence they brought to the land. It is not clear if this is referring to just idol worship, which would then refer to the spiritual violence done in Israel. Since human sacrifice was involved in some of the pagan religions, it could refer to that type of physical violence. It could also refer to interpersonal violence, as the Israelites' spiritual stupor led them to treat each other poorly (this was still a problem even after the Babylonian Captivity as Nehemiah rebuked the wealthy for abusing the poor in Nehemiah 5; violence is also condemned in Ezekiel 7:23 and 8:17). Another interesting feature of these symbolic acts is that Ezekiel is doing these pantomimes for the Jewish exiles in Babylon, but the lines of communication back to Jerusalem were such that the message could be expected to get back to the Jews in Israel as well.

Life stEP Humans have a perverse tendency to assume that the other guy is evil and deserving of his problems, but that we will be spared similar troubles. *But for the grace of God, there go I.* Every personal setback should elicit a heart cry, "Father, what are you saying to me?"

Ezekiel 13:1-9, 20-23

What is the writer saying?

How can I apply this to my life?

pray Japan – Holy Spirit to help these people see their sinfulness so that He can call them to repentance.

Chapter 13 condemns false prophets. There are two types of false prophets here. First are those who use Jehovah worship to feather their own nests (vv. 1-9). Second are those who worship other gods (vv. 20-23). In the Bible, the "fool" (v. 3) is not an intellectually deficient person but rather someone who is theologically or morally deficient (see Psalm 14:1 or Proverbs 10:23). Verse 4 says the false prophets of Jehovah are useless, like foxes that vaporize into hiding places when you need them most. They have seen the gaps in the defensive walls yet have done nothing to fill them (v. 5).

World-renowned evangelist D. L. Moody was famous for his humble origins. He did not attend seminary and his English grammar was unpolished, but he realized that the church needed more than just professional clergymen. With the lay worker in mind, he started Moody Bible Institute and called for *gap men*—laymen who could help the clergy after only a few years of Bible Institute training. Today there are many men who claim to be ministers of God, but as you watch their ministry, it is all about them and the money they can get from people—not about honoring the Lord. When we evaluate the ministry of current *men of God*, we should look at the man's message (theology), methods (ethics), motives (priorities), and fruit (both the spiritual quality of the man's life and also the spiritual quality of his converts).

Verses 20-23 picture female false prophets using various forms of magic to control people for their own purposes. They too will be destroyed by the truth of Jehovah.

Life stEP Competing truth claims will always be a part of this fallen world until the Prince of Truth arrives. We must be truth-seekers and truth merchants.

Ezekiel 14:1-11

What is the writer saying?

How can I apply this to my life?

Chapter 14 is a rebuke of the Jewish leadership. *Everything rises and falls on leadership.* Notice that the elders have gathered at Ezekiel's feet, which implies that God's rebuke is primarily against the leaders already in exile in this message (although with the good lines of communication, this message would get back to the leaders in Jerusalem as well). Apparently God knew that even though these men had already experienced the horrors of attack, capture, and deportation, they still harbored respect for the pagan gods and goddesses in their hearts. When you examine modern Judaism, with its disdain for the Christian concept of the Trinity (the worship of three gods in their estimation), it is hard to imagine a time when they were so quick to run to polytheism. Historically, the seventy-year Babylonian Captivity is identified as the defining event in Jewish history that solidified the current strict monotheism of Jewish theology.

Notice also how God repeats Himself in these verses. Repetition is often for the sake of emphasis. Certainly God's infinite mind does not need this repetition, but apparently knowing our finite minds, He decides to make His point crystal clear and emphatic by repeating His words and restating the concepts in various ways. He advances the thought to include the non-Jewish aliens living among the Jews (v. 7). In this verse, the word *stumbling block* in New Testament Greek is graphic, a word used for the *baited trigger* of a trap and is the source of our English word *scandal.* The Hebrew word here in Ezekiel refers to that which causes a person to fall down and thereby be severely hurt, which is what these prophets were doing. God judges the false prophet by making his prophecies fail.

Life **stEP** What traps have we harbored in our minds, thinking that no one knows or cares, but could cause our spiritual undoing?

wednesday 30

Ezekiel 14:12-23

What is the writer saying?

How can I apply this to my life?

pray — Uruguay – For God to save and call witnesses among the upper middle–class, which is estimated to be the largest group not evangelized.

By way of contrast with the wicked leadership and false prophets, God honors three champions of Jewish history: Noah, Daniel, and Job. All three are immortalized in the Bible for their integrity, righteousness, and perseverance in tough times. The mention of Noah and Job is understandable since by Ezekiel's day their exploits were over a thousand years in the past. Daniel's inclusion in the list is extraordinary because he was still living! This is so unusual that some liberal scholars claim that it must refer to another Daniel from an earlier time. There *was* a man with a name similar to Daniel, named "Dan'el" in the Ugaritic legends, but he was a non-Jewish idol worshiper, and it would make no sense for God to use him as an example of righteousness.

This passage introduces the concept of *Four Apocalyptic Evils*: sword, famine, wild beasts, and plague (v. 21). While earlier passages had warned the Jewish people of judgment for their disobedience (compare to Deuteronomy 28-30), this passage specifies four avenues of judgment, which are the basis for the first four judgments in the book of Revelation, the famous four horsemen of the Apocalypse. *Sword* refers to military attack. *Famine* can be nature-induced or the result of prolonged warfare. *Wild beasts* were a real issue in Israel's history; there were lions and bears in the region, and they could be a dangerous problem for the inhabitants of the land (compare 2 Kings 2:24, 17:25). This illustrates the deep connection between the Old and New Testaments and the idea that if we want to know anything in Scripture, we need to know everything in Scripture.

Life stEp — The Word of God is simple enough that even a child can read it and understand the basics. It is so complex, however, that even scholars can spend their whole life studying it and never exhaust the wonder of it all.

thursday 30

Ezekiel 18:1-18

What is the writer saying?

How can I apply this to my life?

Chapter 18 discusses individual responsibility, illustrated over three generations of family members. The quote in verse 2 apparently was a common pithy statement to excuse the behavior of the generation taken into captivity. They protested their innocence, claiming that they hadn't done anything wrong (they did not eat any sour grapes). It was their fathers who had eaten the sour grapes, and now they were experiencing the negative results (their teeth were being set on edge). Even though the text is not specific to any particular family, it is interesting that the pattern fits three of the recent kings of Judah at that time. Godly King Hezekiah can illustrate the just father. Ungodly King Manasseh, the most wicked king of Judah, can illustrate the unjust son. Godly King Josiah can illustrate the just third generation (he was actually the grandson of Manasseh and great-grandson of Hezekiah). This passage is very important theologically. In Exodus 20:5, it says that God visits the sins of the fathers onto the third and fourth generations. Some have argued from this that humans can inherit curses (or even demon infestation) due to the sins of ancestors. Ezekiel 18 contradicts this conclusion and requires that we re-examine what Exodus 20:5 means. In biblical times, it was not unusual for three and four generations to live together under one roof. Therefore the warning is the practical concept that a wicked great-grandfather can bring judgment upon all members of his household in that their failure to confront his sin makes them guilty by association or prone to follow his wicked example. This is illustrated in the way God judged the whole household of Achan (Joshua 7:19-26).

Life stEP Humans have a terrible tendency to shift blame. The first step toward victory over sin is taking personal responsibility for behavior.

Ezekiel 18:19-32

What is the writer saying?

How can I apply this to my life?

God pleads with the rebellious to repent. He clarifies that His dealings are always fair. Those being judged will not be punished for other people's sin. Therefore it is wise for them to repent because it will bring them blessing. Reading this passage in isolation from other Scriptures, it almost appears that salvation is by good works. We cannot, however, interpret Scripture in isolation from other passages. For instance, back in chapter two, God told Ezekiel to stand to his feet, but it was the Spirit of God who lifted him to his feet. Likewise, God commands us to be holy, knowing full well that we do not have the ability to live holy lives. When we ask Him for help by faith, He gives us the power to live lives that are pleasing to Him.

The word *repent* (v. 30) means different things to different people. For most of the religions of the world, it speaks of self-effort and striving to merit favor with God. Sometimes it implies strong emotions—some include expressions of grief, self-loathing, and even self-harm as part of repentance. There is a New Testament Greek word sometimes translated *repent* that has the root idea of *sorrow*. However, there are also statements that "godly sorrow produces repentance," which indicates that sorrow doesn't automatically mean that repentance has occurred (2 Corinthians 7:10). What then is the proper understanding of *repentance*? In verse 32 we have the root idea. It is the concept of *turning* due to a *change of mind*. In our sin, we are heading away from God and toward eternal destruction. As God convicts us of sin and His truth, and as we respond in faith, we also turn from our old way of life and turn to God, having changed our mind about Him and our lifestyle.

Ezekiel 20:1-16

What is the writer saying?

How can I apply this to my life?

pray Italy – For people to turn from the occult to Christ and for the city of Turin, a global center for Satanism, to be invaded by the power of the Gospel.

In Ezekiel 20, God reviews the rebellious heritage of the current generation. It is two years after the start of Ezekiel's ministry—590 B.C., which would be four years before the destruction of Jerusalem. In fact, it is four years to the very day that the temple would be destroyed, according to Jeremiah 52:12-13: "Now in the fifth month, in the tenth *day* of the month, which *was* the nineteenth year of Nebuchadnezzar king of Babylon, came Nebuzaradan, captain of the guard, which served the king of Babylon, into Jerusalem, and burned the house of the LORD...."

That God speaks of the sins of the fathers is not a contradiction of the teaching in chapter 18. This review will conclude with a condemnation of the sins of the current generation in the tradition of their fathers. The review begins with the Israelites in Egypt. Verse 8 indicates that even while in Egypt, some refused to give up the Egyptian gods, an act which would have enabled them to whole-heartedly worship the Lord.

God did not judge them in Egypt lest His name be defiled in the sight of the Egyptians. Then, despite their rebellion, He delivered them from Egypt (v. 9). At Mount Sinai He gave them the Law, but they disobeyed that as well, and the adults died in the wilderness (v. 13).

The land of Israel is referred to as a very desirable land, one rich in milk (from sheep and goats) and honey (bees' honey as well as sweet pastes made from grapes, figs, and dates). Although the territory is not very big, even today the land of Israel is one of the most amazing pieces of real estate on the planet. Nothing in the world compares to the Jordan Valley, with the fresh water Sea of Galilee and the salt water Dead Sea, the lowest spot on the face of the earth.

Life stEP This passage is another reminder to parents that children will imitate our behavior and must be given good examples to follow.

Ezekiel 20:17-32

What is the writer saying?

How can I apply this to my life?

pray Panama – Increased educational opportunities for those in or considering full-time ministry.

God continues His critique of the Israelites. Even though they disobeyed Him in the wilderness, He was gracious and did not destroy them. He challenged them to obey His law, keep His Sabbaths, and not worship other gods.

In the book of Genesis, when God called Abraham and his descendants out from among the Gentiles to be the *chosen people,* the sign of this special relationship was circumcision. Now with the Mosaic Code, which elevated the chosen people into a chosen nation, the sign was Sabbath observance. Not working on the Sabbath was just one of the Ten Commandments and just one of the total of 613 laws in the Law of Moses, but it is the one that epitomized Israel's obedience or lack of obedience to their God. As the Israelites continued to disobey once in the Promised Land, God gave them over to their reprobate minds (see Romans 1:28). They wanted to follow other gods, so He made them follow the laws of the other gods (v. 25),

including the human sacrifice of the first child born to each mother. Passing through the fire (v. 26) refers to the nature of this human sacrifice. Molech and Chemosh were two of the gods requiring human sacrifice. A bronze image of the god would be heated with fire, and the babies would be placed in the outstretched arms of the idol. It is hard to comprehend why the Israelites would follow a god who demanded that they kill their own children. But then, modern abortion practices are often the way our society worships the god of materialism and convenience.

Life stEP Christ fulfilled the Law of Moses on the cross, so circumcision and Sabbath observance are no longer significant. What is the sign of our covenant with God? Baptism, communion, and especially the indwelling Holy Spirit are good candidates.

Ezekiel 20:33-44

What is the writer saying?

How can I apply this to my life?

After thoroughly rebuking the elders who piously came to the prophet of Jehovah for a word of encouragement, God finally gives an encouraging word. But the encouragement is only for those who repent and forsake the sins of the forefathers.

God promises that He will eventually re-gather those scattered. The first scattering took place at the hands of the Assyrians in 722 B.C. when Sargon II finished the destruction of the ten northern tribes (whose capital was at Samaria) begun by his predecessor, Shalmaneser III. Ever since 722 B.C., there have always been more Jewish people living outside the land of Israel than within.

The second scattering was of taking place as Ezekiel was ministering. The promise in this chapter would look forward to the return from the seventy-year captivity under Zerubbabel (compare to Ezra). It would also encompass the final restoration under the Messiah. Some would argue that the Jewish people lost their *chosen people* status when they rejected Jesus of Nazareth and were scattered by the Roman destruction of the second temple in A.D. 70. This view fails to notice the constant statements in passages such as this one, which repeats the promise that God is longsuffering, gracious, and will not forsake His promises. Any person who wants to be blessed has to obey, but God will not use the disobedience of some—even the majority—to invalidate the ultimate fulfillment. The tribulation period is designed to see that the Jewish people either get saved and as obedient people are worthy of receiving their kingdom promises, or if they will be killed by the judgments of that period in order to purify the chosen people.

Life stEP   "God is not mocked: for whatsoever a man soweth, that shall he also reap." Galatians 6:7

Ezekiel 22:1-4, 23-31

What is the writer saying?

How can I apply this to my life?

 pray — South Korea – For seminary graduates to humbly commit themselves to less prominent, rural pastorates.

God rails against the wicked city of Jerusalem, the careless priests, the wicked princes, the false prophets, and the unthinking people. No one escapes God's critical evaluation. Because of the collapse of the entire Israelite society into spiritual adultery, they deserved the coming judgment. God's call upon Ezekiel to *judge* the wicked city means that Ezekiel is to announce the judgment that God will visit upon the city. Ultimately it will be the sword of the Babylonians, but already some of the judgments predicted in Deuteronomy 28-30 were falling upon them, such as drought. Attacks by wild beasts are another common judgment, but here it is the false prophets who tear the souls of their hapless victims (v. 25). Note that the false prophets are motivated by money. They are condemned for claiming to speak for Jehovah when He had not spoken to them (v. 28). This sounds suspiciously like some modern preachers who are known more for their outrageous claims and abuse of money than they are for godliness. The priests are also condemned for laxity. They don't even protect the sign of the Law of Moses, the Sabbath. They also go about the temple ceremonies carelessly, not maintaining ritual purity. They probably were not so crass as to offer pigs or eat pork, but the net effect would have been the same. The princes, like the prophets, were out to get all they could for themselves at the expense of others. *Untempered mortar* (v. 28) would not cure or set properly and therefore would be useless in repairing a wall. The false prophets claimed to have spiritual repairs, but they were defective and therefore ineffective. Even the common people afflicted whomever they could.

Life **stEP** — God notes the dangerous gaps in the wall of society. He looks for *gap men* and *gap women* to fill the voids.

Ezekiel 26:1-14

What is the writer saying?

How can I apply this to my life?

pray Mexico – For the discipleship in churches to continue their growth and impact on families.

The year was 587 B.C. Tyrus (v. 2) is another name for Tyre, one of two chief cities of Phoenicia. It might seem strange that while Babylon was the city that had been attacking Judah (605, 597, and 586 B.C.), Tyre received three chapters of condemnation (chapters 26-28). The answer is found in the fact that Tyre had exported Baal and Asherah worship, which had perverted the spiritual life of Israel and Judah. For instance, in 1 Kings 18-19, Elijah's big conflict with Ahab and Jezebel was over these false gods, and Jezebel was a Phoenician princess from Sidon. Phoenicia actually comes into the biblical story with Solomon as he married a daughter of the Phoenician king, Hiram. Solomon also bought cedar wood from Hiram for his palace and the temple and hired him to build a fleet of ships. (The Phoenicians were famous and wealthy due to their expertise in ship-building and trade. They also developed the alphabet that we use today). Phoenicia's might and influence is also seen in the fact that their colony, Carthage, in Northern Africa, almost conquered Rome under the Phoenician Hannibal (notice Baal's name in Hannibal). *Tyrus* means "rock." The city of Tyre had an island fortress one-half mile out in the Mediterranean with 150-foot high walls. Invaders could conquer the mainland city, but not the island fortress. The Assyrians tried for five years and Nebuchadnezzar for 13 years. Finally, Alexander was successful in just seven months. He defeated the island fortress by scraping the mainland city into the sea, forming a *mole* 200 feet wide out to the island. Today, you can visit Tyre in Lebanon and see the bedrock where fishermen spread their nets to dry (v. 14).

Life stEP It is a fearful thing to fall into the hands of an angry God, especially when you have touched the apple of His eye.

Ezekiel 28:11-17

What is the writer saying?

How can I apply this to my life?

 pray Italy – Pray for the more than 30,000 communities without an established gospel witness.

In chapters 26 through 28, Ezekiel shows an amazing knowledge of Tyre's international trade. Tyre was proud of the wealth and fame that her ships and seafaring skill brought her. In chapter 28, God condemns the pride of the leaders of Tyre.

In verse 2, God condemns the *prince* of Tyre (Hebrew: *nagid*). This apparently is a reference to the human king, who at that time was a man by the name of Ittobaal II. However, in verse 12 the word is against the *king* of Tyre (Hebrew: *melek*), which is apparently a reference to the power behind the throne, namely Satan. This becomes a perfect picture of what the Antichrist will be like. Apparently for the first 3½ years of the tribulation period, he will be a very successful human leader. At the mid-point of the tribulation period, he will be indwelt by Satan and will be *Satan in the flesh* (Revelation 17:8). In the ancient world, pagan kings did consider themselves to be divine (such as the Pharaohs of Egypt). They would also use oriental exaggeration to enhance their reputation among their subjects. However, the terminology here in Ezekiel 28:11-17 is more than just exaggeration. No human after Adam and Eve was "in Eden the garden of God" (v. 13) or "created" (v. 13) or could be called a "cherub" (v. 14) or "perfect" (v. 15) or visited the "mountain of God" (v. 14). All of these phrases look beyond the mere mortal to the malevolent spirit lurking behind the man. The man and his kingdom are still in view as verse 16 condemns the material wealth of his existence and predicts his humiliation before his peers. That both Satan and the man he uses are to be humbled is a fitting application to this prophecy.

Life **stEP** Sin is pleasurable for a season, but godliness is its own reward and blesses for eternity.

Ezekiel 33:1-9

What is the writer saying?

How can I apply this to my life?

pray Nigeria – For committed Christian leaders that will not just start strong but follow through with real preparation of Bible lessons and true discipleship.

Chapter 33 begins the final major section of Ezekiel, *Ezekiel's prophecies of Israel's restoration and kingdom blessing* (chapters 33-48). This section is so important that chapter 33 contains a renewal of Ezekiel's commission. God uses the same illustration of a *watchman* who has been hired by the king of a city to watch for the approach of the enemy and sound the alarm so the citizens would have time to flee. We know that even in modern times watch duty is very important, and in times of war the penalty for falling asleep at watch could be immediate execution. In chapter 3 the commissioning to the role of watchman was in preparation for the prophecies of judgment upon Judah (chapters 4-24) and the prophecies against the nations (chapters 25-32). In addition to the people of Tyre and Sidon being condemned in chapters 26-28, Ezekiel also predicts God's judgment on Ammon, Moab, Edom, and Philistia in chapter 25 (all nations immediately surrounding Judah). Then in chapters 29-32 he condemns Egypt, Assyria, Elam, Meshech, Tubal, and Edom. Even though Jerusalem had already fallen, Ezekiel does not receive the news until 33:21, about six months after the event. Ezekiel's commissioning this time is more for blessing than for judgment. His requirement to nevertheless treat the message seriously involves the same warnings as before. God would hold the watchman accountable for accurately and efficiently proclaiming the message. Failure would lead to capital punishment (v. 6 "his blood will I require at the watchman's hand"). This refers to immediate death (not eternal punishment). Perhaps Nadab and Abihu (Leviticus 10) and Ananias and Sapphira (Acts 5) are examples.

Life **stEP** Being a spokesperson for God is both an awesome privilege and an awesome responsibility.

Ezekiel 33:10-20

What is the writer saying?

How can I apply this to my life?

pray Poland – For God to protect missionaries and ministry equipment from criminal activity.

God explains that He does not delight in the death of the wicked (v. 11). His judgment is a moral imperative—not for retribution but for justice. If the unrighteous person repents, then God is delighted to withhold judgment and give blessing. This section can easily be confused as providing salvation by works, the loss of salvation by sin, and denying salvation by grace and grace alone. Since Scripture cannot contradict Scripture, we would insist that spiritual salvation is not under discussion in this passage. In Genesis 15:6, right at the beginning of the biblical record, God announces that Abram believed in the Lord and that "He counted it to him for righteousness." What then is this passage discussing? The answer is that God is referring to immediate blessing or judgment based on behavior. He is referring to *physical salvation*. Therefore, the eternal destiny of the individual is not under discussion in this passage, and an *unrighteous* individual who is not saved but does repent and obeys the letter of the law will be blessed in this life. Thus you could have a righteous man who also loves the Lord and is saved but gets confused, disobeys the Lord, and is killed (a classic example would be godly King Josiah in 2 Kings 23:30). He has lost his temporal life but not his eternal life. This is a good reminder for the messianic (millennial) reign of Christ. It says that He will rule the world with a rod of iron (Psalm 2:9 and Revelation 12:5) and that "the child shall die an hundred years old" (Isaiah 65:20). This implies that even saved people (not *glorified saints* but *flesh and blood* humans) in the millennium can be struck dead prematurely for temporal disobedience but still have eternal life (such as Ananias and Sapphira?).

Life stEP Our God is not a nasty being, but He is a serious being!

Ezekiel 33:21-33

What is the writer saying?

How can I apply this to my life?

pray New Zealand – For Bible schools and churches to convey a mission emphasis among their people.

The message of the fall of Jerusalem reached Ezekiel about six months after the event. It would have been December of the year. This would not be unusual due to the severity of the attack, the nature of the destruction, and the distances involved (about 900 miles by normal routes). God, of course, knew that the message was coming, and He was already working in Ezekiel's life. Ever since his call six years earlier, Ezekiel's ability to speak was limited to God's leading so that for everyday activities he was dumb. Now that Jerusalem's fall was public knowledge among the exiles, God lifts the symbolic dumbness, and Ezekiel can now speak freely. God then leads him to condemn the handful of Israelites that remained behind in Israel. They were reasoning that God had created the entire nation out of one man, Abraham, and they certainly could do it again with their relatively larger numbers. God cuts short that misconception by saying, in effect, "I knew Abraham. I've worked with Abraham, and you, my friend, are no Abraham." Whereas Abraham "believed God and it was counted to him for righteousness," these blighted souls reveled in their sin, mistakenly thinking that because they survived Nebuchadnezzer's third attack, God favored them. God condemns their eating meat with blood (a violation of Leviticus 17:10), idol worship, murder, and adultery. God then warns them of His four *apocalyptic evils*: sword, famine, wild beasts, and pestilence (compare to Ezekiel 14:21). These people will be destroyed, as will the people in exile who pretend to love Ezekiel's prophecies but criticize him behind his back and then refuse to obey his words.

Life stEP We can't make people obey the Word of God, but we can be sure that they know they have been in the presence of a person of God.

Ezekiel 34:1-16

What is the writer saying?

How can I apply this to my life?

Leaders in the ancient world, especially kings, were considered to be the shepherds of the people. In this section God condemns the bad shepherds who had abused the children of Israel while making sure that they themselves had plenty of food, shelter, and money. This would include the last three evil kings: Jehoiakim, Jehoiachin, and Zedekiah, who were also condemned by Jeremiah (see God's rebuke of the priests and prophets in Jeremiah 2:8).

The Israelite society had a tripartite system of *checks and balances* (similar to the United States system with the executive branch, legislative branch, and judicial branch). If the king was bad, then the priest or prophet should have stepped in to warn the king and the society. In the closing days of Judah's independence, only the one prophet, Jeremiah, seemed to function properly. The other prophets and the priests and kings were all evil. The good news is that one day the Messiah will come, and in His one person He will unite the offices of prophet, priest, and king. In this passage, after God rebukes the evil shepherds for their selfishness, He promises that He will send them a good shepherd. Historically, the Israelites returned from the Babylonian captivity, but at no point could it be said that they were prosperous and ruled by a good shepherd. In fact, Zechariah 11 uses this same analogy; the *evil shepherd* of Zechariah was probably foreshadowed by Herod the Great and will finally be fulfilled by the Antichrist during the tribulation period. It is Jesus Christ Who will finally gather the people together and will be their "good" (Psalm 22; John 10:11), "great" (Psalm 23; Hebrews 13:20) and "chief" (Psalm 24; 1 Peter 5:4) shepherd.

Life stEP People get the type of leaders they want and deserve.

tuesday 32

Ezekiel 34:17-31

What is the writer saying?

How can I apply this to my life?

God now turns His attention on the rich citizens. They had shouldered the weaker aside to be sure they themselves had plenty to eat and drink. Then they trampled on what they didn't eat or drink so it was spoiled for the weak when they got their chance. God will raise up a compassionate shepherd who will protect the sheep. In verse 23 this individual is called "my servant David."

We know from Genesis 3:15 that the Messiah would be a human. We know from Genesis 12:1-3 that the Messiah would come from Abraham. We know from Genesis 49:10 that the Messiah would come from the tribe of Judah. We know from 2 Samuel 7:11-17 that the Messiah would come from the line of David. In Christ's genealogies, this connection to David, Abraham, and humanity is underscored. Matthew, who presents Jesus's legal right to the throne, takes Jesus's genealogy back through the kings of Judah, including David, all the way to Father Abraham. Luke, who underscores Jesus's humanity, takes the genealogy from Mary's side (Jesus's biological genealogy). Mary's genealogy does not go through all the kings of Judah (thereby bypassing the curse on King Jeconiah's descendants given in Jeremiah 22:30) but does go through Nathan, a son of David and then back through David, Abraham, all the way to Adam, the first human.

Many think that in the messianic kingdom, Christ will rule from Jerusalem over the entire world (Psalm 2) while the resurrected David rules over Israel. To complete the picture of the millennial government, in the New Testament the twelve disciples were promised that they would sit on twelve thrones ruling the twelve tribes of Israel.

Life stEP   Our life now is the training ground and vestibule for eternity. What governmental position will I qualify for in Christ's kingdom?

Ezekiel 36:1-15

What is the writer saying?

How can I apply this to my life?

pray Netherlands Antilles – For the success of evangelistic outreaches presented through literacy classes.

God promises to bring the Jewish people back and bless them once again in their ancient homeland. When this takes place, they are told that never again will the nations harm them, nor will they ever be scattered again.

Within seventy years of the writing of this prophecy, 50,000 Jews had returned to Jerusalem, and the second temple had been built. Every step of the way was filled with opposition, however, by the local Gentiles. Besides this, only 50,000 of an estimated 2.5 million Jews had returned. From 516 B.C. to the time of Christ, conditions continued to be severe, and at no time could we say the Jews had been *re-gathered* and were under the watchful care of a *good shepherd*. When their *good, great and chief shepherd* appeared to them on Palm Sunday in A.D. 30, they did not recognize Him, and they rejected Him. In A.D. 70, the Romans destroyed the second temple, 1.2 million Jews were killed, and the rest were scattered once again.

In other words, the promises here in Ezekiel have never been fulfilled. There are evangelical Christians who are comfortable with the idea that God will not fulfill these promises to national Israel, saying they have forfeited the right to receive them because they have rejected Jesus Christ. This overlooks the fact that the promises God made to Abraham were unilateral—only God was making the pledge. If any one generation of the Jews wanted to be blessed, they had to obey to receive the blessing, but the ultimate fulfillment was always based on the sovereign plan of God. He will see to it that the terminal generation believes, obeys, and is worthy to receive the promises.

Trust and obey for there is no other way to be happy in Jesus, but to trust and obey.

Ezekiel 36:16-25

What is the writer saying?

How can I apply this to my life?

pray Paraguay – For Bible school students to earnestly seek God's guidance for future areas of ministry.

God affirms that He judged the nation of Israel for her gross sins—particularly the sins of murder and idolatry. When He scattered the people of Israel to the nations, it was like when a woman was declared "unclean" and separated from her people in Jewish society due to childbirth or the monthly menstrual period. Before a woman could return to worship in the temple she had to undergo a ceremonial bath (Hebrew: *mikveh*) in running water (the "baptisms" mentioned in Hebrews 6:2). The "sprinkling" of verse 25 refers to a similar process of ceremonial cleansing (compare to Leviticus 14:1-7). The important emphasis in this chapter is that God intends to return the Jewish people to their homeland, not because of their behavior but for His great name's sake. God has made promises, and He knew when He made those promises what the response of the people would be—their failures did not catch Him off-guard.

He predicted to Abraham, even as He was giving him the Promised Land, that Abraham's descendents would spend 400 years in Egypt (Genesis 15:13). When God affirmed His covenant with Abraham in Genesis 15, He alone walked between the pieces of the sacrificed animals, binding Himself, and not Abraham, to the ultimate fulfillment of the covenant. In Jeremiah 31, where the new covenant is announced, God concludes the chapter with a reminder that as long as the earth rotates on its axis, and as long as it revolves around the sun, His covenants with Israel still stand. In fact, even after the Jewish people had rejected Jesus and the Gospel had gone to the Gentiles (with the Church being defined and explained by Paul, the Apostle to the Gentiles), Paul still insists that God is not done with national Israel, and that one day all Israel will be saved (Romans 11:26).

Life stEP The gifts and calling of God are without repentance (Old English phraseology). Modern version: *God keeps His promises.*

Ezekiel 36:26-38

What is the writer saying?

How can I apply this to my life?

pray Nigeria – Protection for those working among the Fulani people and other Muslim groups.

Once again, God promises to bless Israel for His glory, so the heathen nations will know that He is the one true God. This passage is a repeat of the famous *new covenant*, which is first explained in Jeremiah 31. The Old Testament law was given to illustrate the sinfulness of man and to provide a fence to protect the chosen people of Israel from the perversion of the pagan nations. It was not a way to live to merit salvation (salvation is always a gracious gift from God appropriated by faith). Rather it was a guide to the people's spiritual development as they grew in their relationship with their God (sanctification). The weakness of the Mosaic Law was that it provided guidance, but it did not give the power for the sinful human nature to do what it requested. The *new covenant* is superior because the Holy Spirit of God takes up residence within the believer, and in the process, provides an inner sense of God's will while also empowering the believer to obey. This inner sense is directly connected to the believer's ongoing study of God's Word, which the Spirit helps us understand and apply. These features of the new covenant have been enjoyed by the Church ever since the Holy Spirit came in Acts 2, however, the nation of Israel must also receive this blessing in order for the new covenant to be fulfilled. This will take place during the tribulation period and millennial reign of Christ. This increased closeness to God and empowering from God may explain why King David fell so hard morally, while the New Testament heroes didn't.

Life **stEP** God justly desires that His greatness be published and acknowledged by His creatures. A *secret* of a successful prayer life is to figure out what would bring God glory in any situation and then ask Him to help you accomplish that.

saturday 32

Ezekiel 37:1-14

What is the writer saying?

How can I apply this to my life?

pray Argentina – Funding for students with a desire to study God's word at camps and Bible schools.

Chapter 37 pictures the resurrection of the nation of Israel. The bones in the valley have obviously been there for a while. The bodies have decayed, wild animals have separated the bones, and the bones are bleached white in the hot sun. Ezekiel and the Israelites had every reason to feel hopeless now that their capital city had been defeated, their temple destroyed, and their people uprooted from their homeland. Ezekiel had already recorded messages of renewed blessing, but when asked by God if these bones could live again, Ezekiel could not respond with confidence. God tells him to command the bones to come together. In a rather long process, including several commands and activities by the prophet and God, the skeletons are reassembled, the flesh comes back upon the bodies, and there are now corpses in the desert.

Since the late nineteenth century, Jewish people from around the world have moved back to Israel. Not only were they coming to renew an independent Jewish state that had not existed for over 2,000 years (Israel was annexed by Rome in 63 B.C.), but they also resurrected the Hebrew language that had not been used as a spoken language for over 2,000 years. Never in the history of the world has a dead language been resurrected to become the mother tongue of a nation.

Ezekiel 37:8 illustrates the current situation of Israel. She has come back to her homeland in unbelief. Israel is a complete but spiritually lifeless nation. The breath of God will come into them, and like Adam, they will become a spiritually alive nation. This evangelistic event will take place during the tribulation period.

Life stEP

With God there is always hope. Even when we are in the tomb, all is not lost. God has been in the tomb once before and knows the way out!

Ezekiel 37:15-28

What is the writer saying?

How can I apply this to my life?

pray   Korea – For the unblocking of Christian radio broadcasts that reach into North Korea with the gospel.

When Solomon was king, he violated the commands of the Lord not to multiply horses (for military purposes), wealth (for self-sufficiency and decadence), or wives (for international treaties, and lest they entice the king with their gods) (Deuteronomy 17:14-20). Unfortunately, despite Solomon's good start, he eventually violated all three of these principles. He especially allowed his wives to influence his spiritual life to the point that eventually he placed idols right next to the temple of Jehovah. For that reason, God decided to punish Solomon by dividing his kingdom in two. At his death, this happened, with ten tribes forming the Northern Kingdom of *Israel* with a capital at Samaria and two tribes forming the Southern Kingdom of *Judah* with a capital at Jerusalem. (The tribal designations are approximations, for actually the Hebrews had moved freely around the Promised Land. The *two tribes* were technically Judah and Benjamin, but Simeon also was represented in the Southern Kingdom, as were the Levites.) The Northern Kingdom never had a godly king, and its inhabitants were taken into captivity by the Assyrians in 722 B.C.

This passage looks forward to the day when members of all twelve tribes are returned and united in Israel. "Judah" and the "children of Israel" in verse 16 refer to the Southern Kingdom. "Joseph" and "Ephraim" (the son of Joseph and the largest tribe and home of the capital of the Northern Kingdom) refer to the Northern Kingdom. This passage promises eternal peace and blessing, which indicates that the prophecy still awaits fulfillment.

Life stEP   Oh, the unnecessary suffering of man due to rebellion. How great will be the blessedness of man when rebellion ceases and God can bless.

Ezekiel 38:1-12

What is the writer saying?

How can I apply this to my life?

This passage envisions a time when Jewish people have gathered back to Israel and are at peace, not needing walls for protection (v. 11). A number of nations join with *Gog and Magog* for this attack. Some are well-known today (*Persia* is modern Iran and Libya is modern *Libya*). Others are slightly changed (*Ethiopia* is modern Sudan). Others cannot be identified with a particular modern nation with certainty (*Meshech* may sound like Moscow and *Tubal* may be the root of Tobulsk, but language scholars conclude that there is no provable connection). In Genesis 10, Magog, Meshech, Tubal, and Gomer are all identified with nations to the north of Israel, in Turkey and southern Russia. Whoever these enemies may be when this prophecy is fulfilled, it is clear that they come—not just from the immediate north of Israel (such as modern Lebanon and Syria) but rather from the "far north" (Ezekiel 38:6,15; 39:2). As to the timing, the passage indicates (v. 8) that it will take place "after many days," in the "latter years," when the Jews have "gathered from many people (nations)." Ezekiel 38:16 adds that this will take place "in the latter days," a reference to the events leading up to the messianic kingdom.

From the time the prophecy was written until now, Israel has not dwelt securely in unwalled towns (v. 11). This must refer to the time during the tribulation period when Israel finally achieves security under the protection of the Antichrist. Perhaps he will even have a regional capital in Jerusalem. The Gog and Magog attack would then be against Israel and the Antichrist. After an initial defeat, the Antichrist recovers (Daniel 11:40-45) and God destroys Magog, leaving a power vacuum in which the Antichrist can then pursue world domination.

Life **stEP**   Israel had great promises, but the road to the Promised Land was difficult, as the path to future blessing will be.

Ezekiel 38:13-23

What is the writer saying?

How can I apply this to my life?

pray Peru – Funding for more scholarships that will make Bible training accessible to the poor.

"Sheba and Dedan" (v. 13) refer to Arab tribes that moved freely throughout the Middle East as caravan operators, traders, and herders. "Tarshish" is the city in Spain, not Asia Minor. It was also known for its accomplishments in the area of seafaring and trade (compare to 2 Chronicles 9:21). In verse 13, both of these groups of people would naturally be inquisitive about a traveling group looking for financial advantage. Some have argued that the *lion* refers to Great Britain and the *cubs* would be her colonies, including the United States of America. This is highly unlikely since Tarshish was a known entity in Ezekiel's day and Great Britain was not at that time known as a *lion*.

Gog is most likely the leader of Magog. In Ezekiel 38:2, in some translations he is referred to as the prince of *Rosh*. *Rosh* does not refer to Russia (although the country might actually turn out to be Russia). *Rosh* is the Hebrew word for "head" and is used metaphorically for *head of state*. Gog, therefore, is the *chief* prince of Magog.

God says that the prophets of old had talked about Magog. From Ezekiel's day, those prophets of old would be the prophet Isaiah and countries prior to the current Gentile enemy, Babylon. Assyria is a good candidate for this *enemy of old*. As the Bible looks forward to the tribulation period, it uses old enemies of Israel as metaphors for future enemies, such as the kingdom of the Antichrist being called "Babylon" in Revelation and Magog being "Assyria" here in Ezekiel. Since *Russia* is in the *remote parts of the north* in today's geo-political world, she and her Muslim allies would most naturally fulfill the role of Magog.

 Life stEP God's payday is coming someday. He will use nations to accomplish His will but still holds them responsible for their behavior.

Ezekiel 39:1-16

What is the writer saying?

How can I apply this to my life?

pray Nicaragua – Salvation among the Sandinista and Contra soldiers left disillusioned and angry from the war where they saw many atrocities meted out.

In chapters 38 and 39, the armies of Magog are pictured as unprecedented in size. Apparently this attack will be even greater in scope than the attacks by Assyria and Babylon. The horsemen and soldiers will cover the land of Israel. *Horses* seem strange in the modern context. Certainly modern military equivalents would not be excluded by the lack of mention, but due to the terrain from the Russian steppes down to Jerusalem, horses cannot be excluded.

Magog thinks she is acting under her own genius and power. God brought her to Israel (38:4). He uses her to upset the Antichrist and rattle Israel. Then He rains destruction upon her armies in Israel as well as her homeland. Certainly this could be literal fire and weather patterns sent by God. God can also use secondary means to accomplish His work, which could include man-made weapons. In Revelation 13, the Antichrist calls fire down from Heaven, imitating the powers of the two witnesses of Revelation 11 and perhaps implying that it was he who destroyed Magog on the mountains of Israel.

We are told that the people of Israel will burn the weapons left behind for seven years. Some have argued that this requires the battle to take place before or at the start of the seven-year tribulation period. While certainly possible, there is no obligation to fit the period of cleanup entirely in the tribulation period. As an event that sparks the rise of the Antichrist to international dominance, a mid-tribulation battle of Gog and Magog makes sense. Even today, the Israelis have specially trained inspectors to clean up all human remains after terrorist attacks. Likewise, God will have His people cleanse His land of these enemy bodies.

Life stEP The Bible and tomorrow's news—despite the horror, it is realistic, and we can imagine CNN reporting on site. Even so, come, Lord Jesus!

Ezekiel 39:17-29

What is the writer saying?

How can I apply this to my life?

pray Mexico – Effective ministry to youth through Christian camping, outreach activities, and social aid.

Revelation 19:9 announces the *marriage supper of the Lamb,* the great banquet that will inaugurate the millennial reign of Christ. Here we have the *marriage supper of Gog and Magog* as the birds of the air and the beasts of the field are invited to eat the bodies of the fallen on the hills of Israel. Since this same imagery is used of the Battle of Armageddon, some have argued that *Gog and Magog* refer to the Antichrist and his defeat at the Battle of Armageddon. Yet similar imagery does not prove identical events. Likewise, Revelation 19 refers to another *Gog and Magog* event, which will happen at the end of the millennial kingdom. Here again, we don't have to conclude that the events are one and the same but that the one event illustrates the other. For instance, when we say, "He met his Waterloo," we are not saying that person was in France with Napoleon and was defeated by the British, but rather *Waterloo* stands for any frustrating setback based on Napoleon's experience there. From Ezekiel's day until now, no enemy has come against Israel and been defeated in the way described in these chapters. Notice that in the aftermath of this episode, all the Jews will return to Israel, and "none" will be left in the nations (v. 28). This also specifies that the Jews have returned from multiple nations (in Ezra, the return under Zerubbabel was from one nation—Persia).

When all the Jews return from many nations, God will pour out His Spirit upon them (v. 29). This is one of the features of the day of the Lord in Joel 2:28-32. During the tribulation period, many Jews (and Gentiles) will be born again, and the Spirit of God will be evident in their lives and testimonies.

Life stEP Even in the world's darkest hours, God will be gracious, and many will come to Him for eternal safety.

Ezekiel 43:1-9; 44:1-4

What is the writer saying?

How can I apply this to my life?

pray Praise Him for giving us a living hope through the resurrection of Jesus Christ (1 Peter 1:13).

Ezekiel chapters 40-48 describe *kingdom blessings*—particularly, worship of the Messiah during that time. The year is 573 B.C., thirteen years after chapter 39. Israel was still languishing in captivity. God had already predicted her national resurrection (chap. 37). Now He shows them their new temple— the focus of Jewish nationl life. The temple described in Ezekiel 40-48 is significantly different from Solomon's Temple. There would be none of the following: ark of the covenant, table of shew bread, menorah, veil, high priest, feast of Pentecost, Day of Atonement or evening sacrifice. The temple complex will be located outside the walls of Jerusalem, about twenty miles to the north near ancient Shiloh (Hebrew for "he to whom it belongs"), one of the early sites of the tabernacle.

When the people returned in 536 B.C. and built a new temple, however, it was not patterned after Ezekiel's Temple.

Clearly the Jews considered Ezekiel's Temple to be a messianic temple. In Ezekiel 11, Ezekiel witnessed the Shekinah glory of God leaving the temple. He has never returned to this date other than temporarily on Palm Sunday in the person of Jesus Christ. Now, as the Messianic Age has dawned, Ezekiel views the return of the glory of God to His special city. The passage describes God's delight in Jerusalem and Israel. Once He has entered the temple by the Eastern Gate, the gate is shut and no human will use it, although the political leader will be privileged to eat and meet with the Lord at the Eastern Gate.

Life stEP For all of human history to date, God's creatures have defied Him. What a great day when all rational creatures join to honor their Creator and worship Him. Righteousness and knowledge of the Lord will cover the earth like the waters cover the seas.

Ezekiel 47:1-12

What is the writer saying?

How can I apply this to my life?

pray   Netherlands – For those crossing social and cultural barriers trying to spread the Gospel to the lesser reached people.

A river will flow from the temple to Jerusalem and then to the Mediterranean and Dead Seas, causing the northern half of the Dead Sea to come *alive* (v. 9). As strange as this may seem, the modern state of Israel has already contemplated building a *Med/Dead Canal* for the purpose of hydroelectric power and restoring the level of the Dead Sea.

The land of Israel will be distributed among the twelve tribes, from the Euphrates River in the north to the eastern branch of the Nile River in the south. Earthquake activity associated with the judgments of the tribulation period and the return of Christ will create a plateau on the former mountains of Judea, covering fifty square miles for a *holy precinct* for Jerusalem, the temple, and priests. The city is described to be about ten miles square.

Some would argue that the death of Christ abolished the need for animal sacrifices, but the book of Hebrews warns against applying Ezekiel to the Church

Age, not the millennium. The sacrifices in the millennium will be used to atone (apologize) for violations of messianic law, symbolize the substitutionary death of Messiah, and provide meat for the priests (Ezekiel 44:29). They will be a memorial looking back at the sacrifice of Christ just as our communion service is today. During a period in which death and suffering will be severely limited by the blessings of God, perhaps God wants a graphic reminder of the horror of sin and the price paid by His Son. Four other prophets also mention a millennial temple (Zechariah, Isaiah, Jeremiah, and Daniel). We actually have more details about this temple than Solomon's. Revelation 22 uses similar imagery for Heaven, but this does not require that Ezekiel is describing Heaven.

Life stEP   Ezekiel's final verse is the ultimate statement about the nature of the messianic era: "the name of the city (Jerusalem) ... shall be, *The Lord is there*" (48:35). Nothing could make any place or situation any better!

Philippians

Throughout this brief but exciting epistle, the Apostle Paul makes reference to the fact that he is in prison (1:7, 13-14). Only three of Paul's many imprisonments (Ephesus, Caesarea, and Rome) are of sufficient duration to allow the composition of an epistle such as this one. While there is a case to be made for Caesarea, a number of factors have led most biblical scholars to accept Rome as the location from which Paul writes. This imprisonment is referenced in Acts 28:16, 30-31, and the early church almost unanimously identified this epistle with Rome. The phrases "the palace" (1:13) and "Caesar's household" (4:22) would best fit the city of Rome. We may, therefore, deem this letter to have been written shortly after A.D. 60 from Rome.

The occasion for writing seems to be a most congenial one. Paul had recently received a gift from the Philippian believers. The gift was delivered by Epaphroditus who, shortly thereafter, became seriously ill. Upon Epaphroditus's recovery, Paul takes the opportunity to send a short thank you note to the Philippians and also include an update on his own circumstances.

The epistle itself is a celebration of the joy that is found in serving others. The key verse is Philippians 2:3. The following is a suggested outline:

Theme: Joy through others-mindedness

1. Joy through suffering
2. Joy through service
3. Joy through sacrifice
4. Joy through submission

As we progress in this study, we will clearly see the relationship between denying self and true joy. When we put ourselves first, we always diminish our ability to appreciate and enjoy life.

Philippians 1:1-7

What is the writer saying?

How can I apply this to my life?

pray Kenya – For the believers to live an exemplary life and speak out against what is wrong.

Paul is a prisoner, under house arrest. Timothy was able to visit with him, which is why Paul includes him in the salutation. This book is written to the "saints," a word only used for believers in the Lord Jesus Christ. All believers are saints—the word means "set apart." From the same Greek word we also get the word *holy*.

Notice the three groups of people that are mentioned in verse 1. The first group is the whole church, comprised of all of those who have trusted Christ. The second group is the bishops—a word used interchangeably in Scripture for pastors and elders. The third group is the deacons, servants who served the body. This shows that there are two offices in the church: pastors (elders/ bishops) and deacons.

In verse 2, Paul gives the common greeting of the day. If you were to say "hello" to a Greek, you would say "grace to you." If you were to say "hello" to a Jew, you would say "peace to you." Paul wants us to know that God is the source of both.

As we read this text, it is obvious the apostle is thankful for the faithfulness of these dear people. Every time he thought of them, he thanked God, doing so with a joyous spirit (v. 4). He was able to do so because these people were faithful to the Gospel. In verse 6, Paul gives a great statement of assurance for every Christian. He is confident that the One Who saved them would continue to work in their lives, not until the next time they sinned, but until the return of Jesus! The promise is that *He* "will perform" the work, not you!

Life stEP The God Who saved you is the One Who will continue to work in your life until Jesus returns. That should bring security to your life. Thank the Lord today for keeping you secure in Christ!

Philippians 1:8-14

What is the writer saying?

How can I apply this to my life?

pray Mexico – For the full implementation of religious freedom at the national and local levels.

Sometimes we may think of the Apostle Paul as kind of a superman, without natural feelings. Notice in today's section that Paul had deep feelings for the people at Philippi and missed them. But not being there physically did not mean he could not have a ministry in their lives—he could still have the ministry of prayer.

There are three major prayer requests here that can be a model for us in praying for one another. Paul's first request is that their "love may abound" (v. 9). Notice he says that he prays their love would grow, and that it also should be directed by knowledge and judgment. Love without knowledge will just lead to sentimentalism. And there are many who make terrible decisions based on love without judgment.

The second request is that the Philippians would make excellent decisions (v. 10). Paul knew that if they made good choices, they would be able to live the type of life that could be used by the Lord at any time.

The last request is that they would serve the Lord with all of their being ("being filled with the fruits of righteousness"). The motive of the prayer of Paul (that God would be glorified through the lives of the people) is seen at the end of verse 11. Paul was continually motivated by the glory of God.

In verse 12, Paul makes a shift in his thinking. He begins to let them know what is going on in his life. He knows that the people are discouraged because he is in prison, but he wants them to know that good things are still happening (see vv. 13-14).

These three prayer requests can guide our prayers for others. Write them as a guide in the prayer section of your quiet time, and pray these requests for your friends.

Philippians 1:15-21

What is the writer saying?

How can I apply this to my life?

During Paul's imprisonment, some men were "supposing to add affliction" by preaching the Gospel. How could that be? Apparently they claimed that Paul had failed the Lord and that God put him in prison as a punishment. They thought his troubles were a sign that the hand of God was no longer on his ministry, and now the mantle had passed on to them. They did this because of "envy" (v. 15)—they were jealous of Paul and the respect believers had for him. Others, however, did preach the Gospel with the correct motive of love. What is amazing here is the attitude of the apostle. Notice in verse 19 that he is willing to rejoice that the Gospel is being preached, even from people who were opposing him and seeking to hurt his testimony! This is a spirit of humility and a wonderful example to the church of Jesus Christ. The major issue to Paul is not that he receives credit, but that Jesus is being preached!

In verse 19, Paul shows he has confidence that all the things that had happened to him would work out in the end for his good. If he continued to live, he would preach the Gospel; if he died, it would be for the glory of God. The statement he makes in verse 21 is one of the most oft-quoted in the Bible. For the apostle, to live was to exalt Christ, to preach Christ, to honor Christ, and to emulate Christ. But what if he died in prison? That would be even better according to Paul, for he would be with the Lord, and that was great gain.

Differences with other believers in doctrine and practice are bound to occur, but we must *disagree agreeably* so the reputation of the Gospel is not hurt in the process.

Philippians 1:22-30

What is the writer saying?

How can I apply this to my life?

In verse 22, Paul says that if he continued to live, it would mean more ministry. We see here the struggle the apostle was having. He knew going to Heaven meant no more suffering, no more sorrow, and no more prisons! However, it also meant no more ministry with the people he dearly loved in Christ. This was a great conflict of passion for him (v. 23). He deeply desired to see the Lord face-to-face and to worship Him in glory. Yet he realized the people needed his ministry to be able to grow in Christ. He apparently believed that the Lord was going to keep him alive to be able to minister to them (v. 25). He was willing to stay and minister if it meant that God would be glorified in a deeper way. His heart's desire was to see them again, but in verse 27, he encourages them that even if he is not able to see them, he wants to hear that they are living lives that are honoring to Christ. Notice the emphasis on unity in the body. One of the continuing critiques of Christianity is that people do not get along. Jesus prayed for the unity of the church in John 17. One of the by-products of unity is that there will be no fear when others oppose you, for you have the godly on your side (v. 28). Paul closes this paragraph with a promise, but not one that you will hear many Christians claiming today! Just as we are given the gift of faith to believe in Christ, we are given the honor to suffer for His name, just as Paul did (vv. 29-30).

Life stEP When you suffer for Christ, it is a fulfillment of the promise of God! Let's thank God that we are worthy to suffer for His name's sake and maintain a positive attitude.

Philippians 2:1-8

What is the writer saying?

How can I apply this to my life?

Attitude. One of the most important decisions we make every day concerns our attitude. Paul knew our decisions are many times a result of our attitudes. In this text, we see the attitude Jesus had (v. 5), which should be the attitude all believers have who are in Christ Jesus. In verse 1, Paul lists three blessings the people had because of their relationship with Christ. They had the comfort of love, the fellowship of the Spirit, and tender compassion from God. In light of that, each of us should have the same love, the same mind, and the same purpose (v. 2). What is that purpose? Paul first shares what it is not. Our purpose is not to live for ourselves (v. 3) in any way at all. Our purpose is to live for others! As a matter of fact, Paul says that each person is to esteem others to be more important than himself.

The key to this is humility. Humility is *not* thinking poorly of one's self, as some assume. Humility is thinking of others as being *more important* than us. The result is that each person looks out for the interests of others (v. 4). This attitude was the attitude of Jesus. He saw the need of the human race, lost in sin. He esteemed our redemption to be more important than His comfort in Heaven! He "made himself of no reputation," or emptied Himself, laying aside the independent use of His attributes so He could become fully man. What a step of humility! Not only did He become a man, He then died on the cross for man.

Life stEP Some people don't see a reason to treat others well because they think they are better than others or more important. Jesus was surely *better than us* and yet He humbled Himself. Ask God for opportunities to imitate Christ today.

Philippians 2:9-16

What is the writer saying?

How can I apply this to my life?

There is a fear in many people that if they humble themselves, others will take advantage of them. That may indeed happen. However, if we humble ourselves, God will also exalt us in His time. Jesus illustrates that truth in this passage, where His humbling led to ultimate glorification. Notice in verses 9-11 that God the Father has given to the Son a name that is above every name. Some falsely assume that name is Jesus. But there have been many people with the name Jesus, so that cannot be it. In verse 9, the phrase literally means "the name which belongs to Jesus." This name is revealed in verse 11, where it says that every tongue will confess that Jesus is "Lord"! That name—"Lord" (Jehovah or Yahweh)—is the divine name for Jesus and is the same name used for God way back in Exodus 3.

Verse 12 is a point of transition—we see it with the use of the word *wherefore*. Paul is, in effect, saying, "In light of the humility of Jesus, which caused Him to pay the price for our sin, we are to 'work out' our own salvation!" What does that mean? We are to live our salvation out—to live like we are saved! But we are not to do it in our own power; God is the One Who works in us (v. 13), and He is the One Who gives us the power to do His will. We just need to live it out.

In verses 14-15, we see a number of ways we are to "work out" our salvation, while holding to the Word of life. The goal is to rejoice at the end, knowing we have done what God has asked.

saturday 34

Philippians 2:17-23

What is the writer saying?

How can I apply this to my life?

pray Portugal – Pray for more open doors with local churches and for more workers to help teaching and discipling students.

Earlier, Paul shared the principle of looking at others as more important than ourselves. He illustrated this with the life of Jesus, and now he is going to illustrate that truth with three more people: himself (vv. 17-18), Timothy (vv. 19-23), and Epaphroditus (vv. 25-30).

The Apostle Paul is an obvious illustration of putting others' needs above his own. He was willing to do that even to the point of death. In verse 17, the phrase "offered upon the sacrifice" literally means "to be poured out as a drink offering." A drink offering was made only of the purest wine. To purify the wine, you would pour the wine into a vessel and let it sit for a while. The dregs (impurities) would go to the bottom, and then the good wine would be carefully poured into yet another vessel, leaving the dregs behind. The process would be repeated until the wine was totally pure. Paul is saying that he had been poured from the vessel of one trial to another

and another, and now he was ready to be poured out before the Lord, for the trials the Lord takes us through are to purify us. What a beautiful picture this is!

The second illustration is that of Timothy. He was willing to come to them, putting their needs above his own comfort or his own desires. Notice the opposite in verse 21: "all seek their own." Seeking our own is the opposite of seeking Christ's desire for our lives, which is to serve Him by ministering to others. It is sad to think that of all the people Paul may have had around him, only two were willing to put others' needs before their own.

Life stEP Are you going through some trials right now? God is making you pure and helping you focus on others. Make a list of people you need to put above yourself.

Philippians 2:24-30

What is the writer saying?

How can I apply this to my life?

Paul had confidence that he was going to be able to visit the people at Philippi soon. We are not sure why he felt he would be getting out of prison, but it is obvious he sensed he was. He wanted to get this letter to them, so he said he would send Epaphroditus, who was originally from that area. Paul defines his dear friend in verse 25 as a brother, a companion in labor, and a fellow soldier of Christ. He had ministered to Paul's needs during his time in prison. His ministry to the apostle was so selfless, he got sick and was near death. The people at Philippi had heard he was sick and obviously were upset about it.

As a sign of what a completely selfless man he was, Epaphroditus was burdened because he had caused them to be upset. He is a tremendous illustration of the selfless servant that has been the topic of this chapter. In verse 27, Paul says that God had mercy on both Epaphroditus and himself.

Mercy is a misunderstood word. It means to withhold misery or to take it away, and in this case God took away the illness of His servant Epaphroditus. The Philippians would not know this until Epaphroditus showed up in Philippi with the letter from Paul in his hand.

We can only imagine what the reunion was like when Epaphroditus returned home. Paul knew all the people would rejoice and would love to see him again. This is a great mark of servants of God—they have a deep capacity to rejoice when others in the family of God rejoice. Paul was more concerned that they were ministered to rather than himself. In this way, Paul is illustrating the principle of verses 1-4 as well.

Do you rejoice when others experience blessings from God? There are times when we are better at sorrowing than we are at rejoicing. Find someone who is being blessed and celebrate with them this week!

Philippians 3:1-6

What is the writer saying?

How can I apply this to my life?

pray Papua New Guinea – Increased provision of aircraft and staff for missions reaching into remote areas.

When you see the word "finally" here, you expect that Paul is wrapping up his thoughts and is almost finished, and then he goes on for two more chapters. You may be thinking, "Typical preacher!" Actually, the phrase means "as for the rest of the matters," so he is winding down and still has a ways to go.

The warning (vv. 1-3) was concerning the Judaizers. These were people who believed in Jesus Christ but did not think one was saved by faith alone, but by faith *plus* becoming a Jew. The sign of that was circumcision. But Paul said circumcision has no saving benefit—it was simply cutting the flesh. There was no saving benefit in being circumcised. God does not look at the external ceremonies; He looks at the heart!

These people were telling those who believed in Christ that it was vital to believe, but you also had to keep the law and be a Jew—so, you were saved by faith *plus* works in their system. The circumcision the Lord is looking for is that of the heart being open to Christ (v. 3—"worship in the spirit").

In verse 3, we have a great description of a Christian. There are three marks: first, a Christian is someone who worships God in the spirit, or the inner man. Second, he rejoices in Christ, and third, he has no confidence in the flesh. These three marks should be seen in the life of each person who has put his or her faith in Jesus Christ, as opposed to the outward circumcision that was being called for by these converted Jews. Paul goes on to say that if being a good Jew got one into Heaven, he would have been first in line. The list Paul gives in verses 5-6 would be impressive to any Jew.

 The three characteristics Paul lists in verse 3 should mark your life. One way to keep these before you is to write them down on a card and rehearse them daily. Ask God to help you worship in the spirit, rejoice in Christ, and to have no confidence in the flesh.

Philippians 3:7-14

What is the writer saying?

How can I apply this to my life?

Paul possessed all the requirements of a fine, upstanding Jewish man in his culture. Did he lean on those as part of salvation? Absolutely not! He counted them as loss for Christ; that is, he left them all behind. He gave up trusting in his ability to keep the law, or in Judaism to save him, and put all his trust in Christ alone to save. The point is obvious: you cannot believe in Jesus alone for salvation and believe that somehow you have to do good works to be saved as well.

These two ways are mutually exclusive. A person is either saved by faith in Christ alone, or they are saved by faith in Christ *plus* keeping the law. Paul illustrates that we are saved by faith *alone*. Well, what about all the good things Paul did before he trusted Christ? Paul says that he counted them as *refuse*. The Greek word used here means *excrement,* which is the worst of all refuse. This reminds us of the words of Isaiah when he said that all our righteousness is as filthy rags. This does not mean these things are bad in themselves; it means they have no saving value at all. The righteousness we have now is the righteousness of Christ that was given to us when we trusted in Him (see v. 9). Instead of having zeal for the law, Paul now has zeal to know God with all of his heart, soul, and mind. Notice how driven the apostle was to follow Christ. In verses 12 and 14, he emphasizes that his passion in life was to press on to serve Christ. The word "press" in verse 14 means "to strain with all of one's might to reach the goal." It was used of a runner who stretched to reach the finish line.

Life stEP Think of sprinters at the end of the 100-meter dash. They strain and stretch to reach the goal. Are you straining to reach the goal of Christ-likeness?

Philippians 3:15-21

What is the writer saying?

How can I apply this to my life?

pray Japan – For more men to choose active church ministry over an obsession with career advancement.

In verses 15-16, the apostle is calling for unity of purpose in the body of Christ. The word *perfect* in verse 15 means "to be mature." Those who are mature in the faith should mimic Paul's desire of Christ-likeness. There will be some areas of differences, but we surely can agree on the need to be more like Christ. Since God has saved us and given us a great position in Christ, the apostle tells the readers to live up to this higher calling. In other words, if you are a Christian, you should act like one! What if someone who calls himself a Christian is not walking according to the Word and not seeking to be like Christ? In verses 17-18, Paul says they are enemies of the cross. This is an interesting assessment. In 1 John 2:3-4, we see the same principle. There are people all over the world who claim to be Christians, but they are not living according to His Word. They are liars and enemies of the cross, driven by their own passions and not by passion for God (v. 19). They put their minds on earthly things. Mature Christians, however, put their attention on Jesus.

Notice the emphasis on the return of Jesus in verses 20-21. There are trials and burdens in this world. Temptations seek to draw us away from the Lord. We must remember that our eternal home is in Heaven, and Jesus can come at any time to take us to that home.

If our citizenship is in Heaven, we should live according to Heaven's values. We should seek to "lay up for ourselves treasure in Heaven" (Matthew 6:20), not ones here on the earth. Do we live for things, or do we live for Jesus?

Philippians 4:1-7

What is the writer saying?

How can I apply this to my life?

Paul has great labels for his readers. They are "dearly beloved"; they are "longed for"; and they are his "joy and crown." Paul had a deep affection for the Philippians.

Think about what Paul has been emphasizing. We are not to live for ourselves, but for the Lord. As we live for the Lord, we are to esteem others more important than ourselves. I am sure that as this was being read, many people were saying, "Amen." Now he applies this to two women in the church who were obviously having a conflict (vv. 2-3). They are encouraged to apply this principle to their conflict and to rejoice in Christ instead of living in conflict (v. 4).

In verse 5, he tells them to let their moderation, or gentleness, be known to all. They were to stop the conflict and learn to be gentle so all would see. Paul addresses a by product of conflict—worry—in the next two verses.

In verse 6, he tells them to replace worry with believing prayer. Notice the progression here. When you worry, go to God in worship (prayer here is a worship word in the Greek), bring others' needs to God (supplication), and thank God for all He has done in your life. Then you bring your own request before God. When we worship, we focus on God, not the problem. As we do that, the problem shrinks in comparison to our great God. The result: the peace of God will keep your heart and mind.

Are you a worry-wart? Write verses 6-7 on a card, and carry it with you everywhere you go. When you worry, take it out, read, and pray!

Philippians 4:8-13

What is the writer saying?

How can I apply this to my life?

pray   Ukraine – For the failure of any doctrine that is contrary to biblical truth.

Doctors tell us that we are what we eat. The Bible teaches us that we are what we think (Proverbs 23:7)! Whatever you allow into your mind will affect you deeply. What kinds of things should you think about? Paul gives a representative list of the kinds of things we should think on as Christians. Not only should we think about biblical principles, but we should also obey them (v. 9). The result of thinking biblically is that the peace of God will be with you. The concept of peace is that of having a stable attitude in life, knowing God is in control. In Isaiah 26:3, we are told that peace is a result of thinking on God and trusting in Him.

Paul thanks the Philippians for the gift they sent to him. It meant much to him that these dear people sacrificed to help him. He was rejoicing over their love for him. You might be thinking, "It is easy to rejoice when you have just received a gift!" How true, yet in verses 11-12, Paul says that even when he was going without, he still was content in God. Notice that he had "learned" to be content; it did not come naturally. He learned that when he was in need, he was to trust in the Lord, and the Lord would give him all the strength he needed to make it through the trial (v. 13). It was part of Paul's life to enjoy plenty at one time, and to endure suffering at another. He had full confidence that God was in control.

Life stEP   Put verse 8 on your television and computer. Whenever you see something that does not match that list, *turn it off!* Also, ask God to help you be content with whatever you have. Don't live to get more things. Live to know God better.

Philippians 4:14-23

What is the writer saying?

How can I apply this to my life?

pray France – For American missionaries to overcome stereotypes and prejudices by reflecting Christ's love.

Paul expresses his deep appreciation for the generous gifts the Philippians sent. They were examples of Paul's principle that we should esteem others' needs to be more important than our own. Their poverty made their generosity even more impressive. Paul also mentions their selflessness in 2 Corinthians 8:1-6. They were so poor that when they gave him the gift, they had nothing left for themselves. Paul tried to give it back, but they would not let him do that. Paul called their gift a "sacrifice acceptable, well-pleasing to God" (v. 18).

Notice the context of verse 19. When you give to meet someone's need in such a way that you have little left over for yourself, you don't have to worry. God will supply all your needs in response to your sacrificial giving! How much does God have at His disposal? Only everything there is in the universe! Who deserves the glory when our needs are met? God and God alone (v. 20). The last three verses are a general closing, but if you read them quickly, you will miss a great blessing. Notice something in verse 22? There were saints in Caesar's household. How did they come to know the Lord? A good assumption is that they were fruit of Paul's imprisonment. Remember Philippians 1:21: for him to live was *Christ!*

Life stEP Pray that God will give you an opportunity to share Christ with someone today.

Isaiah has been called a miniature Bible. The book contains sixty-six chapters (as there are sixty-six books in the Bible) and divides at chapter 40. The first thirty-nine chapters (like the thirty-nine Old Testament books) are filled with judgment upon an idolatrous people. The last twenty-seven chapters (like the twenty-seven books of the New Testament) declare a message of hope.

The theme of the book is found in the meaning of Isaiah's name— "Yahweh is Salvation." The very word *salvation* appears some twenty-six times in the book, compared to only seven times in the remaining prophets combined.

Isaiah, who has been termed the "Saint Paul of the Old Testament," was evidently from a distinguished Jewish family. The grammar of the book leads us to believe that he was well educated. He was a man of political know-how, as he maintained close contact with the royal court. His messages, however, were not always well received.

His wife is named as a prophetess, and we know that they had at least two sons. Tradition says that his death came during the reign of Manasseh when his persecutors sawed Isaiah in two.

Isaiah's ministry spans the reigns of four kings, from about 740 to 680 B.C. He, along with contemporary prophets Hosea and Micah, prophesied during the last years of the Northern Kingdom but ministered to the Southern Kingdom. Isaiah is the one who warned Judah of judgment. The warning was not of the coming of the Assyrians, who had overthrown and taken Israel into captivity, but of the Babylonians, who had not yet even risen to power. Isaiah even predicted the return of Judah under Cyrus, which is especially interesting because Cyrus had not even been born yet. The prophecy came 150 years before the event.

Prophecies such as these have caused some Bible critics to challenge the unity of the book. Some argue that another man wrote chapters 40-66 at a much later date. But man always seems to be trying to discredit the sovereignty and omniscience of God. Let's remember that the New Testament writers clearly regarded the author of both sections to be the same person. Perhaps the greatest argument, however, is that Christ Himself quoted from both parts of Isaiah equally, ascribing the statements to the prophet Isaiah.

The book is a compilation of Isaiah's sermons preached over his long (50-plus year) ministry. These sermons are divided into eight volumes based on content:

Theme of Isaiah: The salvation from God—the coming Messiah.

Volume One
The Volume of Isaiah
Chapters 1-6

Volume Two
The Volume of Immanuel
Chapters 7-12

Volume Three
The Volume of the Nations
Chapters 13-23

Volume Four
The Volume of the Little Apocalypse
Chapters 24-27

Volume Five
The Volume of Israel
Chapters 28-33

Volume Six
The Volume of the Nations
Chapters 34-35

Volume Seven
The Volume of Hezekiah
Chapters 36-39

Volume Eight
The Volume of Comfort
Chapters 40-66

Isaiah has more about the person and work of Christ than any other book of the Old Testament. Parts of Isaiah 53 alone are quoted in Matthew 8, John 12, Acts 8, Romans 10 and 15, and 1 Peter 2.

Passages alluding to Christ:

His birth: 7:14; 9:6
His family: 11:1
His anointing: 11:2
His character: 11:3 4
His gentleness: 42:1 4
His death: 53
His resurrection: 25:8
His glorious reign: 11:3 16, 32

Isaiah 1:1-9, 16-20

What is the writer saying?

How can I apply this to my life?

Isaiah began his ministry the year Uzziah died (Isaiah 6:1, 739 B.C.). God condemns the people of Judah, especially since they had already been chastised for their sins and had not repented. Historically, we know that they were attacked by the Syrians and Israelites in 739-734 B.C. The motivation for the attack was to try to force Judah to join in a coalition against the Assyrians. In the process, horrible destruction came upon Judah: "For Pekah the son of Remaliah slew in Judah an hundred and twenty thousand in one day, *which were* all valiant men; because they had forsaken the LORD God of their fathers. ... And the children of Israel carried away captive of their brethren two hundred thousand, women, sons, and daughters, and took also away much spoil from them, and brought the spoil to Samaria" (2 Chronicles 28:6, 8). Unfortunately, the reason why Judah refused to join the coalition is because it had already made an agreement with the Assyrians. But even though the Assyrians did help Judah initially, they turned on Judah in the end, and by 701 B.C., every town in Judah had fallen to the Assyrians except Jerusalem. The Assyrian king, Sennacherib, made this boast at that time: "I have shut up Hezekiah in Jerusalem like a bird in a cage."

In verse 18, "reason" means "come to an agreement" as one would in a court of law. "Scarlet" was a dye-fast color made from crushing the "scarlet worm." Humanly speaking, this stain could not be removed. It would take God's divine power to remove it. In the first chapter, God introduces a very important Old Testament concept, the *remnant* (v. 9). Even when things are the worst, God always has His group of faithful, people "whose knees have not bowed to Baal" (compare to 1 Kings 19:18).

Life stEP God is not mocked: for whatsoever a man soweth, that shall he also reap. What seeds of disobedience can we avoid sowing today?

Isaiah 4:2-6

What is the writer saying?

How can I apply this to my life?

pray South Africa – For loving outreach by those in youth ministry to a very vulnerable generation.

In chapter 4, Isaiah looks beyond the period of judgment to the time of restoration. From our perspective in time—looking into the future fulfillment of prophecy—this would be the transition from the tribulation period into the millennial reign of Christ. The word *branch* (v. 2) is used by the prophets to refer to the humanity of the Messiah as one "from the earth" and specifically from the line of David. It also illustrates the Messiah's vulnerability and tenderness as a human. Just as the four gospels present different pictures of the person of Jesus, there are four variations on the concept of *branch* in the prophets. In Isaiah 4:2 Jesus is called the "branch of the Lord," which underscores His deity and is the emphasis of the Gospel of John. In Jeremiah 23:5 it is the Branch of David, which shows His kingship, like the Gospel of Matthew. Zechariah 3:8 calls Him "my servant the BRANCH," which underscores His servanthood, as does the Gospel of Mark. In Zechariah 6:12 He is called "The man, whose name is The BRANCH," which underscores His humanity and is the emphasis of the Gospel of Luke.

The *remnant* would be the Jewish people who survive the tribulation period, the Antichrist, and the Battle of Armageddon as born-again believers in Jesus. Those "written among the living" (v. 3) are the valued citizens of the kingdom (compare Revelation 3:5 and 22:19). The cleansing of Jerusalem in preparation for the righteous nature of the kingdom (v. 4) will be a negative rapture, like in Matthew 24:40: "Two men will be in the field; one will be taken and the other left." This will be the removal of the "tares" (Matthew 13:40) and the "goats" (Matthew 25:31-46). This apparently will be accomplished during the additional 75 days added to the tribulation period mentioned in Daniel 12:11-12.

Life stEP At this time, Christ will be the focus of all human attention and adoration, finally.

Isaiah 5:1-7

What is the writer saying?

How can I apply this to my life?

Chapter 5 is an imaginative parable likening Israel to a vineyard, with insights to how God feels and acts when what He cultivates turns out different than what He intended.

Isaiah addresses the parable to the "my well-beloved" (v. 1) Who is also the owner of the vineyard, namely God the Father. The vineyard is identified as the land of Israel. The "fruitful hill" is the Promised Land. The "stones" (v. 2) would be the Canaanites removed by Joshua. The "choicest vine" would be individual Jews, especially from Judah (v. 7). The "tower" is a watchtower provided for protection from thieves and animal destruction. The "winepress" might refer to the Law, which provides the standard and pressure to produce. The grapes represent the fruit of the lives of the Israelites. "Wild grapes" represent bad fruit, or the sins of the people. (*Wild* in Hebrew is the word for *stench*.) The last verse contains a play on words that is hard to reproduce in English: "and he looked for judgment (*mishpat*), but behold oppression (*mispach*); for righteousness (*tzedakah*), but behold a cry (*tzegah*)." Perhaps we could say, *He looked for equity but got iniquity; for right but received riot.* God is understandably puzzled as to why, after all His efforts, He did not receive the profit. He asks Judah what He should do. The people don't have an answer. God tells them that He will take away all the agricultural benefits that were designed to help them. The rest of chapter 5 contains "woes" upon specific types of sins. My personal favorite is verse 22, where God condemns men who are "mighty" men (Hebrew: *big men*) in drinking wine and mixing drinks!

God bends over backwards to give His sons and daughters every spiritual advantage to lead successful lives. Amazingly, we turn aside and miss the blessings, resulting in our own hurt. Don't shoot yourself in the foot!

Isaiah 6:1-13

What is the writer saying?

How can I apply this to my life?

pray North Korea – For opportunities to be given to godly Chinese businessmen so they may use their easy access to North Korea to share the Gospel.

This is Isaiah's first prophecy and message and his call to the ministry. Uzziah was the most prosperous of all the kings of Judah. He reigned for fifty years (790-739 B.C.). It would seem that Isaiah was enamored with him to the point that it wasn't until he died that Isaiah's attention was directed to the Lord.

In verses 1-4 we are introduced to the "thrice Holy God." The word for "Lord" in verse 1 is *Adonai,* the equivalent of *Master.* But in verse 3 it is changed to *Jehovah* (*Yahweh*). In John 12:41, John identifies this *Lord* as Jesus Himself. *Seraphim* (plural; singular is seraph) means "burning ones." This is the only time seraph/seraphim appear in the Bible. However, "cherub/cherubim," which occur many times, appear to be the same class of angels. *Cherubim* means "watchers." The meanings of both names are appropriate for those who spend time in the presence of the Holy God and are His body guards.

Verse 3 shows that the basic attribute of God is holiness, not love. This is repeated three times, not only for emphasis but also to illustrate the Trinity (like the use of "us" of verse 8). In verses 5-7 we have Isaiah's response. He experiences deep conviction of sin and pronounces a "woe" on himself before he ever pronounces a "woe" on Judah because of his sense of utter sinfulness in front of a holy God. To cleanse Isaiah, a coal is removed from the altar of sacrifice and laid on his mouth, the tool of a prophet, as the focal point of the cleansing ceremony. Pain is part of the cleansing process, too, and the mouth is especially sensitive. Finally, Isaiah was given a commission to a ministry of hardening, where the people would not listen because they had sealed their fate by their rebellion. Think of this, though: how many through the ages have responded to God by reading Isaiah's messages?

Life **stEP** The preacher must first be cleansed before speaking to others.

thursday 36

Isaiah 7:10-16

What is the writer saying?

How can I apply this to my life?

pray Paraguay – For pastors to actively model the disciplines of prayer, Bible study, and witnessing.

In chapter 7, ungodly King Ahaz chooses an alliance with Assyria over the will of God as Isaiah announces the sign of the coming Messiah, Immanuel.

Syria and Israel had been pressuring Judah to join with them against Assyria. When Judah refused, they attacked in an attempt to place a puppet king in Jerusalem. The first attack came in 734 B.C. (2 Chronicles 28:5-15), when 120,000 men were killed and 200,000 captured. Here Syria and Israel are planning a second attack. Instead of asking God for help, Ahaz makes an alliance with Assyria. Ahaz was out checking his defenses when God sends Isaiah, accompanied by his son, to rebuke him. Isaiah's son, Shear-jashub, was also a rebuke because his name means: "only a remnant shall return" (if you disobey!). In order to encourage Ahaz's faith, God offers to perform a miraculous sign for him. Ahaz refuses, but God gives a sign anyway. It is addressed not just to Ahaz, but also to the whole house of David. The great sign is the famous prediction of the virgin conception of the Messiah. "Immanuel" means "God with us."

The Hebrew word for *the virgin (ha-almah)* is never applied to a married woman in the Old Testament. Liberal theologians who want to deny the miracle of the virgin conception claim that the *proper* Hebrew term for "virgin" is *bethulah.* This is not correct as *bethulah* indicates an engaged woman or young woman whose virginity is assumed but not proven. The Jewish translators of the Greek copy of the Old Testament (LXX) used the Greek word *parthenos*, the same word used in Matthew 1:23, which only means "virgin."

Life **stEP** God takes on sinless flesh through the process of the virgin conception.

Isaiah 8:5-18

What is the writer saying?

How can I apply this to my life?

pray United Kingdom – For God to raise up a new generation of vibrant, doctrinally sound Bible teachers.

Chapter 8 provides another sign, and a third child with a symbolic name, Isaiah's second son, *Maher-shalal-hash-baz*. His name means "swift is the booty, speedy is the prey." Since godless King Ahaz rejected God's child *Immanuel* (God with us), this is what he would get instead. Within two years (i.e., by 732 B.C., v. 4) Assyria would move southward and kill the king of Syria (Rezin) and the king of Israel ("the son of Remaliah"—His name was actually *Pekah*, but because he had stolen the throne through murder, God wouldn't call him by name). Unfortunately for Judah, its ally would not honor the agreement and eventually took over Judea as well.

God's choice of words is precise. Notice in verse 6 that He refuses to call them "My" people. Specifically, verse 6 is referring to the people of the Northern Kingdom who did take delight in Rezin and the son of Remaliah. Even though Shiloah was in Jerusalem (and they were *enemies* of Judah), the people should have preferred the waters of Shiloah because that was their heritage, not the Euphrates in Assyria, and Shiloah was also near the temple of Jehovah. "Shiloah" refers to the Gihon Spring, which feeds the Pool of Siloam in the southern end of the City of Jerusalem. By 722 B.C., the Northern Kingdom of Israel had been exiled by Assyria. By 701 B.C., Judea was "up to the neck" with Assyrian soldiers. This was according to Immanuel's will, and He also intervened to protect Judah from drowning (vv. 8-10). In verse 10 "God is with us" in judgment, not blessing, because of the rebellion of the people.

Life stEP God has ample provisions for our spiritual and physical needs. He allows tests to come into our lives to see if we will look to Him for help or lean on our own understanding. In seeking help from the pagan nation of Assyria, Ahaz sowed in the wind and reaped the whirlwind.

Isaiah 8:19-9:7

What is the writer saying?

How can I apply this to my life?

At the crisis point, instead of turning to God, the people turned to the false religions with their supposed mystical knowledge. Their practice of ecstatic utterances is disturbingly similar to some modern mystical practices such as speaking in tongues, being slain in the spirit, laughing in the spirit and so forth. Any religious practice that revs the emotions and seeks an altered state of consciousness through chanting and mind-bending techniques is not biblical. In verse 20, instead of a mystical experience, God offers cognitive, objective, propositional, rational truth. This is what Abraham told the rich man in Luke 16 when he wanted Lazarus to return from Paradise to warn his brothers about Hades. "If they hear not Moses and the prophets, neither will they be persuaded, though one rose from the dead" (Luke 16:31). Chapter 8 ends in gloom, but chapter 9 announces the light brought by the Messiah. Christ brings light, and the Bible is light. This light is the final part of the progression shown in Isaiah so far. The Branch of Jehovah (4:2), *virgin*-born Immanuel (7:14) and Great Light of Galilee (9:2) is now seen in His full-blown glory as Jehovah!

The "way of the sea" is the coastal highway from Egypt to Damascus that travels through the Valley of Armageddon and past the Sea of Galilee. Zebulun and Naphtali were tribes by the Sea of Galilee. They were the first to experience Assyria, but they will also be the first to experience the Messiah (Christ spent most of His 3½ year ministry in the Galilee region). Verse 4 refers to Gideon's victory in Judges 7:25. In verse 6, "child" represents His humanity and "Son" His deity. He is the "Wonderful (*supernatural*) Counselor" as He leads, judges, and guides. He is "mighty God" as a powerful warrior. He is the Father of Eternity in that Messiah is eternally a Father to His people, guarding and supplying their needs.

The Prince of Peace offers us internal peace (with God and ourselves) and external peace (political).

sunday 37

Isaiah 10:16-27

What is the writer saying?

How can I apply this to my life?

The rest of chapter 9 and 10:1-15 condemns Israel and Judah for their sins. God announces that He will bring Assyria against them. In verse 6, two of the words in Maher-shalal-hash-baz's name occur (*shalal* which is "spoil," and *baz*, which is "prey"). Assyria is doing God's will, but she thinks she is the supreme one, so God then announces that He will also send punishment upon the Assyrians. In Isaiah 10:16-19 God says that He will send sickness and famine against the Assyrians so they waste away. He then likens the Assyrians to a forest. Israel will be ignited to devour the trees of Assyria. So few would be left that even a child with limited mathematical ability will be able to count them.

This chapter was fulfilled in 701 B.C., when Assyria conquered every town in Judah except Jerusalem. Hezekiah called out to God and in one night the death angel killed 185,000 Assyrian soldiers (Isaiah 37:36). As you would expect, King Sennacherib did not acknowledge this defeat, but he did not brag about conquering Jerusalem, either. The Greek historian Herodotus did refer to the massive death, but attributed it to mice eating the Assyrians' bowstrings and shoelaces.

The "standardbearer" (v. 18) is a military person who rallies the troops into battle carrying a flag. When he goes down (in this case due to a wasting disease), confusion reigns on the battlefield. God will destroy Assyria like he did the Midianites (v. 26 compare Judges 7:1-25) and Egypt. In Isaiah 10:33 Assyria is suddenly cut off. Who did it? The answer is given in Isaiah 11—the Messiah!

Temporary success cannot be interpreted as the blessing of God on our lives. Sometimes God uses us despite ourselves. We need to constantly evaluate our behavior and motivation based on the Word of God.

Isaiah 11:1-12

What is the writer saying?

How can I apply this to my life?

pray Finland – For creative, committed believers willing to invest their lives in this country's youth.

Israel and Judah would be chopped down by Assyria and Babylon. They would be like a dry stump, but nevertheless, the stump would sprout, with the sprout none other than the Messiah Himself coming specifically from the root of Jesse, the father of King David. This is a reaffirmation of the Davidic covenant (2 Samuel 7) as well as the Abrahamic (Genesis 12), Palestinian (Deuteronomy 29) and the New (Jeremiah 31) covenants. The behavior and character qualities of the Messiah will be the opposite of those shown by the Jewish leaders in 734 B.C. (vv. 2-5). The Messiah's superior behavior is based both on the fact that He is God in the flesh (Immanuel or "God with us") and that He moves with the anointing power of the Holy Spirit of God. This anointing was established at Christ's baptism. It started His public ministry, including His miraculous works. The ministry of the Holy Spirit in His life was also where He attributed His powers.

The Messiah's loins are girded for work (v. 5). When He takes charge, it will be a no-nonsense reign. Since He is all-knowing (omniscient), all-wise and fair, His ruling with a firm hand will not be oppressive. The animal kingdom will return to Edenic conditions (v. 6—compare to 35:9; 65:25). According to Genesis 1:30, animals were herbivores until after Noah's flood. Some commentators have noted that animals rebel against man to the same degree that man rebels against God. In the Garden of Eden, in Noah's Ark, and in Jesus's relationship with nature, we see animals at peace with the holy individuals.

Verses 11-12 show an exodus. The first Exodus was from Egypt. The final Exodus will bring Jews back from every part of the world for the Messianic Reign (compare to Matthew 24:31).

Life stEP Frustrated with current politics? Pray for the return of Jesus Christ!

tuesday 37

Isaiah 12:1-6

What is the writer saying?

How can I apply this to my life?

pray Pray for those who are parents in your church to have patience, wisdom, and discernment.

Chapters 10 and 11 view the destruction caused by Assyria and the blessings to follow. The portion of the nation of Israel that had received the greatest impact from Assyria (the Galilee region) would be the first to see the great light of the Messiah's ministry. The Old Testament only foresaw one coming of the Messiah. But that one coming had two aspects, a coming to reign and a coming to die for the sins of the people (compare Isaiah 53). This is so obvious that the Jewish commentators spoke of two Messiahs (not two comings of one Messiah as Christians would later interpret the situation). They spoke of a *Messiah ben Joseph* ("Messiah son of Joseph"), who would be the suffering Messiah like Joseph suffered at the hands of his brethren. They also talked of a *Messiah ben David*, who would be the victorious Messiah like King David. God knew that Christ would be rejected in His first coming. But when Christ left the disciples He promised to come back (Acts 1:11). Therefore, some of the events in Isaiah will relate to that second coming.

Isaiah 10-12 is anticipating all the trouble with "Assyria" (the "King of the North" of Daniel 11 and "Gog and Magog" of Ezekiel 38 and 39) that Israel will have during the tribulation period. When God moves to protect Israel, He will send Jesus Christ back as Israel's Messiah, and the blessings upon redeemed Israel and redeemed Gentiles will be great in that day. It is interesting to note that this chapter is considered to be a *hymn of praise* by the rabbis. In Jewish history this chapter was chanted at the Feast of Tabernacles as the High Priest drew water with a golden pitcher from the Pool of Siloam then poured it out on the altar in the temple, about a quarter-mile away. It was at this feast in John 7:37 that Jesus called out "If any man thirst, let him come unto me and drink."

Life stEP The Church will also enjoy God's blessings for Israel in the Kingdom.

Isaiah 13:9-20

What is the writer saying?

How can I apply this to my life?

pray Korea – For the salvation of North Korea's leadership.

Isaiah 13 and 14 predict and condemn the activities of the Babylonians. This is amazing because in Isaiah's day, Babylon was weak and Assyria was the dominant empire. It wasn't until 612 B.C. (over 100 years later) that Nineveh fell to General Nebuchadnezzar, who later became king of the Babylonian empire and attacked Judah. In Scripture and in ancient thought, Babylon is the source of political rebellion (Genesis 11, compare Revelation 18) and religious rebellion (Genesis 10:8-12, compare Revelation 17). The city of Babel was founded by Nimrod, who in Jewish tradition was the first idol worshipper. His name means "he rebelled," and a description of him in Genesis 10:9 can be read, "he was a mighty hunter against the Lord." The Greek historian Herodotus (c. 400 B.C.) taught that Babylon was the source of all pagan religions. In the pagan traditions, Nimrod's wife, Semiramis, miraculously conceived after Nimrod had died, and the male child Tammuz was a reincarnation of Nimrod. As a result, mother goddess worship spread throughout the cultures of the ancient world. The Temple of the mother goddess Diana in Ephesus was one of the seven wonders of the ancient world. Babylon also pioneered astronomy/astrology, as its people believed that the heavenly bodies were to be worshipped since they affected human lives.

That wise men from the East came to honor Christ at his birth is an amazing testimony to the grace of God. Apparently these men were the spiritual descendants of godly Daniel who had taught them of the eventual coming of a great Jewish King, the Messiah! Babylon lingered on until A.D. 500, and her final destruction will take place during the tribulation period.

Life stEP Even in the belly of the beast, faithful believers can have a lasting impact like Isaiah in Jerusalem and Daniel in Babylon.

Isaiah 14:12-17

What is the writer saying?

How can I apply this to my life?

Chapter 14 continues the condemnation of Babylon and concludes with judgment for Assyria and the Philistines. Verse 28 dates the message to 715 B.C. This chapter is very similar to Ezekiel 28, where God condemns a human king, but then shifts the focus to the malevolent spirit energizing the king, namely Satan. Verses 12-14 certainly look beyond a mere human to Satan. This is the only place in the Bible where he is referred to as "Lucifer," Which means means "morning star" or "Venus." It is interesting that Satan tries to steal Christ's title as the "bright and morning star" (Revelation 22:16). In these verses we have the famous five "I wills" of Satan. Clearly, Satan's fall into sin was caused by his pride. Each of these "I wills" underscores that pride. "I will ascend into heaven" indicates his desire to take over God's house. "I will exalt my throne above the stars of God" indicates the intent to dominate the angels of God (compare to Job 38:7 for angels called "stars"). "I will sit also upon the mount of the congregation, in the sides of the north" is based on the ancient idea that the gods held their councils in the north; Satan wants to stage a coup on God's government. "I will ascend above the heights of the clouds" speaks of Satan's desire to be more glorious than God. "I will be like the most High" clearly states Satan's intention of replacing God. How Satan thought he could accomplish any of this is not clear, unless we ponder the rational mind blinded by the smoke of its own pride. Verses 15-17 would apply to both Satan and the human he uses. Adolf Hitler and Saddam Hussein were modern examples. The Antichrist will be the ultimate fulfillment of this passage.

Life stEP Countless tragedies have resulted from Satan's and Adam's rebellion. How blessed will be the day when all free creatures freely obey their Creator!

Isaiah 24:21-25:9

What is the writer saying?

How can I apply this to my life?

pray New Zealand – For those helping immigrants with language training to be bold in sharing the Gospel.

In the ten chapters we have skipped, God condemns Moab, Syria, Ethiopia, Egypt, Babylon, Edom, Arabia, and Tyre. All of these nations had harmed Israel in some fashion and would pay the price for touching the apple of God's eye (Zechariah 2:8). These judgments were partially fulfilled in ancient battles, but they will find their final fulfillment in the tribulation period. In chapters 24-27 we come to a section known as the "Little Apocalypse" because it is similar to events predicted in the book of Revelation. Isaiah 24:17 talks about "fear," "pit" and "snare" which are similar words in Hebrew (*pachad!*, *pachat!*, *pach!*), making for a real attention-getter in street preaching!

Isaiah 24:19-21 sounds like atomic weapons. God could use man-made weapons or perform His own nuclear physics in that day of judgment. Isaiah 24:21-23 is very important because it clearly presents a premillennial time line sequence: a) Christ returns and punishes the kings, b) incarcerates them (for 1,000 years, according to Revelation 20), and c) then after "many days," punishes them (at the great white throne judgment of Revelation 20:11). Isaiah 25:1-5 foretells the destruction of Babylon (compare Revelation 17-19), which precedes the blessings of the millennial reign of Christ (Isaiah 25:6-12).

A shared meal (v. 6) was special because it often indicated close friendship and also marked covenants. "The Covenant of Salt" was a figure of speech for a covenant established with a meal. At the Last Supper, Christ left the fourth Passover cup on the table, the *cup of blessing*, which He will drink with us in the kingdom. Isaiah 25:8 is quoted in 1 Corinthians 15:54 and Revelation 21:4.

 Life stEP God's payday is coming someday. Righteousness will triumph. Unrighteousness will be judged. Christ and the saints will reign in luxury.

Isaiah 26:1-9, 19-21

What is the writer saying?

How can I apply this to my life?

pray Netherlands Antilles – For doctrinally sound literature to be printed in the Papiamento language.

Chapter 26 is a preview of the music we will sing in the messianic era. It will be a day of salvation, both spiritual and physical (v. 1). Only the righteous Jew and Gentile will be allowed into the capital city of Jerusalem (v. 2). "Jerusalem" (Hebrew: *Yerushalayim*) means "city of peace," and verse 3 says that the citizens of that city will be full of peace (literally *peace, peace* in Hebrew for *perfect peace*). One of the hymns of that blessed era will be an updated version of that old classic, "Rock of Ages" (v. 4) ("everlasting strength" is "rock of ages" in Hebrew). The arrogant nations that attacked Israel will be defeated, humiliated and abased (v. 5). Verse 7 is similar to the more famous Isaiah 40:3-4, which speaks of the forerunner making the way straight for the coming Messiah. It is built on the analogy of ancient cities carefully leveling and straightening the roads into their cities for royal visits. In Isaiah it takes on the added idea of moral and righteous alignment. (Our English word *wrong* comes from the Old English *wring*, as in "I will wring your neck!" It means "to twist." Unrighteousness is *wrong* or *twisted*. The *twisted* will be made straight or *right*). Isaiah speaks of his own longing for the Lord of that which is *right*. Even in his sleep, he dreams of that day when God's desire will be done on earth as it is in Heaven. The Old Testament does not talk much about resurrection and does not provide the details that we see in the New Testament. However, there are a number of passages that do teach bodily resurrection, such as here in verse 19 (compare to Daniel 12:2, Job 19:26, Ezekiel 37:1-14 and Psalm 17:15). A period of judgment during the tribulation period will quickly pass, and a time of blessing will follow (vv. 20-21).

Life **stEP** God's Word gives hope. Man's psyche needs hope. We can endure great trials as long as there is hope. Our hope is found in the Lord.

Isaiah 28:5-15

What is the writer saying?

How can I apply this to my life?

Isaiah 28:1-5 condemns Ephraim, who was one of the two sons of Joseph. Since Joseph was the favored son, he was given two tribal allotments (Ephraim and Manasseh), both in the Northern Kingdom. Ephraim was the most influential and contained the capital city of Samaria. Verse 1 condemns the "crown" of the drunkards in Ephraim, referring to the beautiful city of Samaria. It is the first of six "woes" pronounced in chapters 28-33 (similar to chapter 5 having six "woes"). Verse 5 continues the analogy and speaks of the glorious "crown" of their coming Messiah, Who will be better and more beautiful than any earthly city. In verse 6 we are reminded that only a remnant of the people will be true followers of the Lord and therefore worthy of enjoying His blessing. Those at the gate (v. 6) are the defenders of the city who Messiah will strengthen for their task. Verse 7 jumps back to the sinners of Ephraim that God will judge. The prophets and priests who should have been helping Israel (like the Messiah will) were ineffective because of their spiritual and physical drunkenness. Verses 9 and 10 are the mocking rejection of Isaiah's preaching by the people of Ephraim. They complain that Isaiah was talking to them like they were children. Verses 13-15 conclude that God will continue to methodically condemn both Ephraim and Jerusalem for their rebellion. Jerusalem thinks it has made a covenant with Assyria, but when Assyria is finished attacking Jerusalem's enemies, Assyria will turn on Jerusalem. (This was fulfilled in 701 B.C.) Verse 11 is quoted by Paul in 1 Corinthians 14:21 to prove that the gift of tongues was a sign to the Jews of the first century that God was getting ready to judge them for rejecting Jesus Christ.

Life stEP God is not impressed with human logic. It is better to just obey.

Isaiah 28:16-29

What is the writer saying?

How can I apply this to my life?

Judah's treaty with Assyria was sinful, both because it was not sanctioned by God and because the people used deceit and worship of the Assyrian gods to cement it (vv. 15-18). Verses 16 and 17 describe what Judah should have built on for security (its Messiah) by mentioning Zion, one of the original hills in Jerusalem that eventually became the name of endearment for the whole city. In Scripture, Christ is referred to as a *stone* in several ways. He is the "smitten stone" (by God, 1 Corinthians 10:4), the "rejected stone" (by Israel, Psalm 118:22), the "stumbling stone" (to the unsaved, 1 Peter 2:8), the "corner stone" (of the church, Ephesians 2:20), the "tested stone" (by Satan, Isaiah 28:16), and the "shattering stone" (to the nations, Daniel 2:34). In verse 16, "He that believeth shall not make haste" means those who believe "will not be moved from this firm foundation." Verse 20 is a pathetic illustration of insufficient provisions. Those who fail to trust in God likewise come up short. "Mount Perazim" and "Valley of Gibeon" (v. 21) are references to great victories God gave Israel in the past (David against the Philistines in 2 Samuel 5:17-25 and 1 Chronicles 14:16). Now God would turn against His people. This is a "strange" (v. 21) work (thankfully) as God delights in helping His people, not punishing them. Verses 23-29 are an extended agricultural analogy. Isaiah mentions several different kinds of products. "Fitches" (v. 25) is the herb *dill*. Both dill and cummin are delicate. Wheat, barley, and rye are more robust, but each of these items requires different types of implements to properly prepare them for the table. Different amounts of pressure can be safely administered to process the grain without hurting it. Likewise, God the master builder (v. 17) and the master farmer (v. 28) will use just the right punishment to make His people prosper once again.

Life **stEP** God spanks His own children for their ultimate good.

Isaiah 29:13-24

What is the writer saying?

How can I apply this to my life?

Despite their rebellion and worship of other gods and goddesses, the Jews were still going through the motions of worshipping Jehovah as well (vv. 1, 13). The "marvelous work" (v. 14) is again God's "strange work" of punishment. The word *marvelous* implies that it is something only God can do and that the humans who view it will be amazed, unable to comprehend that such a thing would happen. Verse 14 indicates that the men of Judah are convinced that by their wisdom and discernment they have created an infallible plan to protect themselves. Verse 15 mocks them for thinking that they could hide their schemes from God. Verse 16 says that they are mixed up. God can hide things from man, but man cannot hide things from God. Verses 17-24 describe the eventual blessings that God will bring to the land. For now, Lebanon to the north of Israel is afflicted with the presence of the enemy soldiers. When God removes the enemies, then Lebanon can go from "white mountains" (the meaning of "Lebanon") to a fertile farming field and finally to a thick, mature forest. Verses 9-12 use an illustration of people unable to read for a variety of reasons. Now in verse 18 there is a promise that the blind and deaf will be healed so they can read and hear the Word of God. Within thirty years of the writing of this material, the Assyrians had been removed from Lebanon, but the blind and deaf were not healed, nor was the land blessed, nor were "all that watch for iniquity are cut off" (v. 20). The healing prophesied here looks forward to the messianic era. That is why Christ did miracles in His public ministry, and it is also what He will do to redeemed humans in His Second Coming.

Life stEP Our old world staggers from one crisis to another. Even so, come, Lord Jesus.

Isaiah 30:8-18

What is the writer saying?

How can I apply this to my life?

In chapter 7, in 734 B.C., King Ahaz of Judah was condemned for trusting Assyria to protect him. Here in chapter 30, Isaiah now warns Hezekiah not to go to Egypt for help against the Assyrians. The Lord wants Judah's rebellion to be documented for posterity. Here we are 2,700-plus years later, and the documentation is still with us! The Lord condemns the people for rejecting the truth from the prophets and for asking them to preach entertaining messages instead. The name "Holy One of Israel" occurs thirty-one times in the King James Version (and about the same in other translations). It occurs most in Isaiah, with twenty-five appearances. "Holy" in both Hebrew (*kadosh*) and Greek (*hagios*) has the root idea of *set apart*. It is also the root idea of our words *saint* and *sanctify*. The primary idea is that God is separate from everything else in the universe, and therefore we owe Him honor and obedience. When we are *set apart* unto God as *saints*, we then become morally pure out of association with Him and are *holy* as He is *holy*.

This Holy God must deal with the sins of the people. Sudden destruction will come upon them like the sudden collapse of a heavy wall (v. 13). Their destruction will be complete, like a clay jar that is broken into such small pieces that none would be large enough to be used as a scoop (v. 14). Amazingly, they run the threat of utter ruin when all God wants of them is to be respectfully quiet in His presence, sense His guidance in their lives, and repent (v. 15 "returning") when convicted of their sins. The word for rest here is a synonym for *Sabbath* and is used in the same way *Sabbath* is used in the book of Hebrews to speak of salvation, as having entered into the Sabbath rest of God.

Life stEP — God's mercy and loving protection is there for the taking. All He wants us to do is ask for it and obey His leading in our lives.

Isaiah 32:1-4; 13-20

What is the writer saying?

How can I apply this to my life?

pray Paraguay – For new believers to sever all ties to former religious practices and superstitions.

The king in this passage is Messiah, Who will rule the whole world from Jerusalem (compare to Psalm 2). The "princes" could be the twelve disciples who were promised, "That ye which have followed me, in the regeneration when the Son of man shall sit in the throne of his glory, ye also shall sit upon twelve thrones, judging the twelve tribes of Israel" (Matthew 19:28). Unlike the wicked and self-centered kings, princes, and judges of Israel's history, these millennial governmental rulers will be refreshing, like a shelter from harsh weather or cool water on a hot day (v. 2). The blind will see, the deaf will hear, and the dumb will speak (v. 3-4). This will not only be literally true, but these words also contain the allegorical implication that those who are spiritually blind, deaf, and dumb will function perfectly in the spiritual realm as well. Verses 13-14 speak of judgment upon the people and their farmland. They will experience desolation until the Spirit of Jehovah is poured out upon them. Joel 2:28-32 envisions this taking place in the messianic era. Peter had reason to believe that this was starting as the Holy Spirit was poured out at Pentecost in Acts 2. In his sermon he quotes Joel 2; however, the Lord carefully protected what Peter said so that Acts 2 does not claim that this was the complete and final fulfillment of Joel 2. Ultimate fulfillment waits until the day of the Lord (tribulation period and the millennium). When man is in right relationship with God, nature is a blessing for man. The wilderness (one step away from a desert) will blossom like a fertile farmer's field, and the farmer's field will explode into a thick forest (v. 15). Verses 17-20 conclude that justice, righteousness, peace, and safety will mark this period for man and beast (v. 20).

Life stEP Hebrew society was basically agricultural. Greek society was urban. *Heaven* in the Old Testament is a farm, in the New Testament a city!

Isaiah 33:5-6, 15-22

What is the writer saying?

How can I apply this to my life?

 pray   Uruguay – For the spiritual awakening of a country that is disillusioned by secularism.

Isaiah 33:1-4 condemns Assyria. Even though it was God's will that the Assyrians attack Israel and Judah, He still holds them responsible for the sinful impulses that caused them to do so. As soon as God has used Assyria as a rod of chastisement, He will discard and destroy that instrument. Verses 5 and 6 honor the Lord for His glorious position so far above us mere mortals. From His lofty vantage point, both spatially (in Heaven) and morally (perfectly holy), He dispenses justice (that things might be done according to divine law) and righteousness (that things will be *straight* and not *crooked*). As a result, those societies that submit to His justice and righteousness will experience stability, knowledge, wisdom, and salvation (v. 6). *Knowledge* is accumulated facts. *Wisdom* is the effective application of those facts. *Salvation* elsewhere in Scripture is called "to come unto the knowledge of the truth" (1 Timothy 2:4). In the background of this chapter is the military threat of Assyria. Verses 15-22 use military terms to speak of the righteous person's safety in the watch-care of the Lord. There are no rivers in Jerusalem today, so verse 21 envisions the river of the millennial city (Ezekiel 47:1-5) and says that no Assyrian warship will sail up it to attack Jerusalem, and even the lame of Jerusalem will successfully defend the city (vv. 23-24). Verse 22 is the classic statement of the *tricameral* form of government (prophet, priest, and king) with the Messiah holding all three offices.

Life stEP
"Worship the Lord in the beauty of holiness." (I Chronicles 16:29). Unfortunately, we do not normally consider *holiness* to be *beautiful*. In God's *beauty pageant*, there are different standards than those in the current world system, but in the end, this *beauty* will be even more enviable than physical beauty is today.

Isaiah 35:1-10

What is the writer saying?

How can I apply this to my life?

Utopia has been the dream of humans from the dawn of history. The word *utopia* was invented by Sir Thomas More in a novel in 1516. It means "no place." In the early church, Christians sought relief from the world by withdrawing to the solitude of remote places for meditation in monasteries. Unfortunately, the world came right with them, because the world lives in the sin nature each individual inherits. Isaiah 35 is a gem. In ten short verses it nourishes the human heart with its fondest desires.

Much of Israel has a dry climate. There are vast sections of the country south of Jerusalem that are classified as *wilderness*, which is one step above *desert*. Very few trees and bushes grow. Only during the rainy season (November through March) is there any vegetation to speak of, and then only enough for grazing, not farming. During the messianic era, this will change. The desert will blossom like a flower in a protected and watered garden. The *rose* here is most likely our crocus or narcissus. "Lebanon" ("white mountains") was known for the beautiful cedars of Lebanon. "Carmel" ("garden land") was known for its olive trees. (The Christian oilman who read that "Asher would dip his feet in oil" and came to Carmel to drill for petroleum overlooked all the olive trees in the region!) The Plain of Sharon was a marshy area famous for the flowers that grew in that rich, damp soil; the desert will look like the lush fields of the wet Plain of Sharon in that great day! When John the Baptist was in jail and wondered if Jesus was really the Messiah, Jesus referred him to Isaiah 35:5. Jesus respected John's knowledge of the Bible and his faith and knew that this would answer his question.

When things get bad, remember that *this too will pass*, and before we know it, *Utopia* will be *Ourtopia (Our Place)*.

Isaiah 40:1-11

What is the writer saying?

How can I apply this to my life?

As we go from chapter 39 to 40, we will notice a change in the nature of the material. The first thirty-nine chapters of Isaiah parallel the thirty-nine books of the Old Testament containing the same themes, such as rebuke, prediction of judgment, an emphasis on repentance and the coming Messiah. In the last twenty-seven chapters, the themes are similar to those of the New Testament, such as the graciousness of God, His plan to redeem His people, the suffering servant, the offer of salvation, the blessedness of holiness and the greatness of the messianic kingdom.

George Frederick Handel used the first words of Isaiah 40 in his celebrated oratorio, "Messiah." The Jews of Isaiah's day, the Irish and English of Handel's day (A.D. 1742), and we in our day all long for the comfort of Jehovah. Chapter 40 predicts the coming forerunner of Messiah. In Malachi 4 the forerunner is identified as the prophet Elijah. John the Baptist operated in this role to the point that the Jewish leaders asked him if he was Elijah. God in His sovereignty knew that the people would reject Christ in His first coming, so God did not send Elijah, but allowed John to be there "in the spirit and power of Elijah" (Luke 1:17). During the tribulation period, Isaiah 40 and Malachi 4 will be fulfilled in the two witnesses of Revelation 11.

In ancient times, citizens would straighten and smooth the highway leading to their city for the visit of royalty (v. 4). Humanity longs for a visit from the Great King, but before He can come, the road must be ready. Spiritually, this requires repentance. Zechariah 6:15 indicates that the Jews will not receive their kingdom until they all obey. One of the purposes of the tribulation period is to see to it that all remaining Jews are true believers, worthy of the kingdom.

Isaiah 40:21-31

What is the writer saying?

How can I apply this to my life?

pray Papa New Guinea – For the leaders of this land to seek righteousness and guidance of God in the affairs of their nation.

The rest of chapter 40 (vv. 12-31) deals with the question of who the Lord really is. In a style reminiscent of the book of Job, God calls upon the greatness of creation to illustrate His exalted wisdom and power. In verse 21, when He asks, "Have ye not known?" the question comes in the context of what nature is screaming all around us. How could we have missed it—it is so obvious. The scientific anticipation of Scripture (v. 22) is impressive. During the Middle Ages many people thought that the world was flat. Christopher Columbus, a religious man both as a Roman Catholic and also as a man raised with sensitivity for his secret Jewish background, knew the Old Testament and the Hebrew language. He wrote a huge book on Old Testament prophecy and felt that his work was fulfilling prophecy. He knew that the world was round, not just because he could see ships sink over the horizon, but also because God told him that it was round in Isaiah 40:22.

God towers above mere mortals (v. 23). Even the greatest of humans are swept away by one move of His hand. We are like ants, both in size and significance. God could ignore us just as we carelessly tread on insects every time we walk outside. But He doesn't. He is mindful of our thoughts, feelings and concerns. Debt that has become a mountain in your life, sickness that sets you aside, friends who aren't true friends—God knows and cares about it all. He named all the starry hosts (v. 26), which number at least 100 billion times 100 billion stars. In Genesis, all He says about their creation is "and He made the stars also."

We do not have the strength to run with the horsemen, but we will fly if we let God supply the energy.

God is great; God is good. Because He is great and good, we live to see another day, not just with the bare necessities, but also with luxury.

Isaiah 41:8-20

What is the writer saying?

How can I apply this to my life?

In Isaiah 40-66 three different individuals are called the servant of Jehovah. Here, it is Israel (v. 8). In chapter 45 it is Cyrus, King of the Persians, who was predicted to allow the Jews to return and rebuild their temple. The third is the Messiah (52:13). There are four "servant songs" in this section as well, and all four speak of the ministry of the Messiah as the *Suffering Servant*.

Israel (v. 8) here refers to the entire nation—all twelve tribes. *Jacob* was the father of the twelve men who became the heads of the twelve tribes. His name was actually changed to "Israel" ("a prince of God"), after he wrestled with God (Genesis 32:24-30). Abraham was the start of the line of the chosen people. We mistakenly call him the first Jew. Actually, since the word *Jew* comes from the tribal name Judah, there were no Jews until Judah had his first child. Technically Abraham, Isaac and Jacob were Hebrews, which might come from Abraham's uncle's name, Eber, or more likely, is a geographic reference made by the locals describing Abraham as one who came from the "other side" of the Euphrates River. Amazingly, God refers to Abraham as "my friend" in verse 8. There has probably never been even forty years in human history when Israel and/or the Jewish people have experienced peace with their neighbors. For over 100 years in modern history, Jewish people from around the world have moved back to Israel and immediately put themselves in harm's way. Saddam Hussein lashed out against the Western world but rallied the troops by condemning the Zionist entity. A whole section of his armed forces were recruited and trained to help "liberate" Israel. Someday they will all bow and apologize for this affront to the God of Abraham, Isaac and Jacob (v. 11).

Life stEP Who is the most important person that might be willing to call you "my friend?" Would God be able to call you "my friend?"

Isaiah 42:1-9

What is the writer saying?

How can I apply this to my life?

Here, the King of the universe shows great deference to His servant. We will eventually learn that the servant is His own Son. For now, the cause for attention is the obedience of the servant. In order to accomplish the Great King's purpose, the Great King underscores ownership ("my servant"). He describes involvement ("I uphold") and He emphasizes destiny by calling him "mine elect." He also empowers the servant by placing His own Spirit upon Him. This occurred at Jesus's baptism, which marks the beginning of His public ministry (Matthew 3:16). Prior to the baptism and the descent of the Holy Spirit upon Him in the form of a dove, Jesus had not done any miracles. It could be argued that Jesus did not need the Holy Spirit to do the miracles since He was also God. However, even though Christ possessed the power to do miracles, He willingly submitted that power to the control of the Holy Spirit; the Holy Spirit in His life was therefore necessary in order to do the miraculous works.

Isaiah 42:1-4 presents Christ's meekness. He would be so sensitive that even a weak flame in His presence would not be extinguished. This is a general description of His ministry. He taught patiently, was not boisterous, and did not play to the grandstands. He even discouraged people from publicizing His miracles lest they detract from His message. However, when necessary, He could be firm, such as when He drove the moneychangers out of the temple.

Isaiah 42:5-9 underscores the obedient servant's deity. Verse 6 gives two reasons for the call of the Messiah: a) to fulfill the covenant and b) to be a light to the Gentiles.

When Jesus took on human flesh, He intended to show humans how to live a holy life using the tools that all believers have access to—Scripture reading and prayer. We should follow that example.

Isaiah 43:1-13

What is the writer saying?

How can I apply this to my life?

In this chapter, God demonstrates His ownership and control over Israel. He created them. He named them. He says they are His. He redeemed them. Ultimately, this redemption refers to their eternal salvation provided by the death of the obedient servant (Isaiah 53). However, here it refers to the price God would pay to the Persians so the Jews could return from the Babylonian Captivity and rebuild their temple in Jerusalem. The payment used for this redemption is the nations mentioned in verse 3, which eventually fell to the Persians under Cyrus's son Cambyses. "Fire" and "flood" (v. 2) are powerful illustrations of danger in general. By this time in Israel's history, God had already performed miracles with water (going through the Red Sea and Jordan River on dry ground). Later, Shadrach, Meshach, and Abednego would experience deliverance from fire (Daniel 3). Verses 5-7 envision the Jews returning from the four corners of the earth. This did not happen in 536 B.C. when the 50,000 came back to Jerusalem under Zerubbabel, with them all coming from one place. By the time of Christ, there were Jews from all twelve tribes living in Jerusalem, so the prophecy may have been somewhat fulfilled by Christ's day. In the last 100 years, however, there has been an undeniable migration of Jews from the whole world back to Jerusalem. Today over seventy languages are spoken in Israel, representing all the nations from which the Jews have returned. Verse 10 is where the Jehovah's Witnesses create their name. The amazing thing is that the very next verse proclaims that Jehovah is the only savior—there is none besides Him, which is contrary to the beliefs of the Jehovah's Witnesses and other false religions. In Luke 2:11 Jesus was announced as the Savior. He has to be Jehovah as well!

Life stEP Various cults deny the deity of Jesus. They think they are honoring God. They will be surprised to see His displeasure for insulting His Son!

Isaiah 43:14-25

What is the writer saying?

How can I apply this to my life?

"Thus saith the Lord" is repeated frequently in chapters 40-66. God's words are emphatic and to be taken seriously. He repeats His impressive titles to inspire awe in the listener. This great, powerful and doting God is going to destroy the Babylonians that God used to chastise Israel. During Isaiah's ministry, Assyria was the dominant power, so Babylon hadn't even risen yet, let alone done anything worthy of this punishment. But the Babylonians, who took pride in their horses, chariots, soldiers, and ships, would all be neutralized, even the ships (vv. 14, 17). "Tow" (v. 17) is the wick of a candle. Israel had already experienced some dramatic rescues by the Lord, such as the exodus from Egypt. God tells His people to forget these (v. 18) because God is getting ready to do even greater things. Their rescue from Babylon will be even more impressive than their rescue from Egypt. Ezra and Nehemiah both record God's blessings as they organized their trips from Babylon.

The ultimate fulfillment of this amazing return waits for the gathering of all Israel at the end of the tribulation period for the millennial reign of Christ (Matthew 24:31). God will do spectacular things to protect and return the Jews to their ancient homeland (Revelation 12:13-16). As Christ returns, the last unsaved Jews will be gloriously saved like Saul on the road to Damascus (Zechariah 12:10). Finally, for the first time in Jewish History, "all Israel shall be saved" (Romans 11:26). God concludes this section with another rebuke. Israel was not worshipping God properly. In verse 23 the "small cattle" refers to sheep. "Sweet cane" (v. 24) was used to make the anointing oil (Exodus 30:23). The people had not bothered with sacrifices, but they had loaded God down with their sins. Amazingly, He would forgive them for His name's sake.

We should not presume on the grace of God, but we can rely on it.

Isaiah 44:6-8, 21-24

What is the writer saying?

How can I apply this to my life?

In addition to some of the titles for God that we have seen recently, God adds "Lord of hosts" (v. 6), which has not been used since chapter 39. "Hosts" refers to armies of the angels of God. It is used to remind the people that God has adequate power to take care of them. He doesn't need to use angels, but since human kings have soldiers to do their bidding, God uses structures that we understand and appreciate. Verse 6 also addresses idol worship and polytheism, which was a constant problem for the children of Israel from the exodus out of Egypt (where they may have learned polytheism) until after the Babylonian Captivity, hence the warnings in Isaiah, Jeremiah, and Ezekiel against worshipping other gods and goddesses. The prophets get rather sarcastic. Not only is Jehovah superior to the other gods, the other gods have a major problem in that they don't even exist! It is a fact of religious history that the Babylonian Captivity permanently cured the Jewish people of the problem of polytheism. So thorough was their embrace of monotheism that 500 years later, when Jesus claimed to be God, many violently rejected His claim. Notice that Jehovah claims to be the "first" and the "last." God the Father also makes that claim in Revelation 1:8, as does God the Son in Revelation 1:11, 17 and 22:13. If there is no God besides Jehovah, then the New Testament writers had to consider Jesus to be Jehovah, not a lesser created being, as held by the Jehovah's Witnesses and Mormons. Verse 7 claims that God deserves His exclusive position as the only God because He can predict the future, which also means that He controls the future. Predictive prophecy is a mark of deity for God and a mark of inspiration for His Scripture.

Life stEP We do not know what the future holds, but we know Who holds the future. We also have read the back of the book, and the good guys win.

Isaiah 45:5-13

What is the writer saying?

How can I apply this to my life?

In Isaiah 45:1-4, God announces that He will raise up a man by the name of Cyrus who would do God's bidding. God refers to him as His "anointed" (Hebrew: *messiah*). It doesn't mean that Cyrus is *the* Messiah, but that he will be anointed by God for a specific task. The task is the return of the 50,000 from Babylonian captivity under the leadership of Zerubbabel, as described in Ezra 1-6. The "two leaved gates" (v. 1) and "gates of brass" (v. 2) were opened October 12, 539 B.C. as Babylon fell to Cyrus as he diverted the river that ran under the walls and snuck into the city in a surprise attack. The statement about "treasures of darkness" (v. 3) refers to the King of Lydia (Croesus), whom the Persians also defeated (in Asia Minor). He had the same reputation as Midas because of all the gold he possessed. Once again, God's exclusive infinite existence is verified by His sole ability to predict and control the future. This is the grand theme in verses 5-13. Verse 5 is still referring to God's choice and control over Cyrus (not Israel, although that is also true as seen in verse 11). Verse 6 would include the Gentiles living in the Western Hemisphere. God reaffirms His position as the Creator God (v. 7). The "evil" that God created (v. 7) is not sin but rather judgment upon sin and the dangers of nature which are also a result of man's sin. Verse 8 illustrates that God does not compartmentalize the physical and the spiritual, but rather desires that His creation experience both physical and spiritual blessing. This will be the situation during the messianic reign of Christ. Verse 11 has a three-fold description of God, one of the veiled references to the Trinity throughout the Old Testament. Verse 13 returns to Cyrus's job of returning the Jews home.

Life **stEP**   If God can control nations, He has the power to take care of us, too.

Isaiah 45:14-25

What is the writer saying?

How can I apply this to my life?

This section envisions the Gentile nations coming to Israel in peace and desiring to learn about Israel's God, Jehovah. Three nations are mentioned here. "Ethiopia" is a reference to ancient Cush, which included modern southern Egypt, the Sudan, and northern Ethiopia. The Sabeans were from southern Arabia, the home of the Queen of Sheba. Today that area would include southern Saudi Arabia and Yemen. All three areas in verse 14 are primarily Muslim today. In the history of Israel, there has never been a religion as violently opposed to Judaism as Islam has been. With this animosity in mind, it is amazing to consider such individuals coming to the Jews in peace and respect.

"Idols" are mentioned in verse 16. Certainly all the ancient enemies of Israel were idol worshippers, but it might be argued that Muslims today are not idol worshippers. We don't know what the religion of the nations who finally fulfill this passage will be, but Islam cannot be ruled out. In Mecca, the Black Stone in the Kabah certainly qualifies as an idol, despite Islamic denial. Verse 15 implies that God's salvation is not always readily apparent. Verse 17, however, says that delay is not denial; God's promises to Israel (here) and to believers (elsewhere) will always come to pass before the world goes out of existence. Certain theological systems argue that Israel's failure has altered God's plans for a physical kingdom on the planet. Verse 18 argues that God does nothing in vain. For Him, to allow human history to be ruined by Adam's fall and Israel's rebellion and for God to abandon it for a spiritual existence in Heaven would be a failure. God intends to *redeem* human history with a return to the Garden of Eden. Jesus will be victorious in the very arena where God seemed to have a defeat.

Life stEP God's timing is not our timing. We must patiently wait for His will to be done on earth as it is in Heaven.

Isaiah 46:3-13

What is the writer saying?

How can I apply this to my life?

The Babylonians had to carry their gods, while Jehovah carries Israel (vv. 1-3). Our God is the only God who provides cradle-to-grave service. In verses 5-7 Isaiah describes the foolishness of worshipping an inanimate object, made by human hands. In Isaiah 44:15 he mocks the man who cuts down a tree, uses half of the wood to build a fire and the other half to make a god to worship. The famous Scottish reformer, John Knox, made a similar observation about the idolatry of the Roman Catholic Mass: "With part of the flour you make bread to eat, with the residue you fashion a god to fall down to." In verses 8-10 God again establishes His authority on the fact that He can predict and control the future. The "ravenous bird from the east" (v.10) is a reference to King Cyrus of the Persians (compare to 45:1), who God would bring against the Babylonians. The gods of the Babylonians would be no help to them. In fact, they would be a burden for the Babylonians to place on animal backs in an attempt to save their idols from the Persians (vv. 1-2). Whereas the Babylonians had only judgment facing them, God would offer righteousness and salvation to His people, the children of Israel.

God punishes the Babylonians and in the process works it out that the tool of punishment (Persia) also becomes a tool of blessing to the Jews (vv. 12-13). The Assyrians and the Babylonians had a foreign policy of uprooting populations and placing them hundreds of miles away from their home to break their will to rebel. When Persia came to power, this tactic had lost its effectiveness. Cyrus used a different foreign policy known as "dollar diplomacy." The Persians did this with the Jews and with other nations. Ezra describes how Cyrus allowed the Jews to return and even paid them to rebuild the Temple of Jehovah. History records that the Jews felt kindly towards the Persians.

 Life stEP

When we are right with the Lord, the Lord makes even our enemies to be at peace with us.

Isaiah 48:1-11

What is the writer saying?

How can I apply this to my life?

In this section God once again rehearses His complaint with Israel's behavior. They gave lip service to Jehovah while busily worshipping other gods (vv. 1, 5). This is particularly ironic because He narrows down the line of the Jews to those from the tribe of Judah, the very tribal portion where Jerusalem and the temple were located – people who should have been utterly faithful to God. In verse 3, the "former things" are predictions of the Babylonian Captivity. All the way back at the exodus from Egypt, God warned His people that He would expel them from their Promised Land if they disobeyed (compare Deuteronomy 28:64). Because of this, we cannot say the Jews currently deserve to be in their land on the authority of the promises of Abraham, because peace in the land in any generation was contingent on their obedience when in the land—if they didn't obey, they were liable to be expelled. We can say that God has sovereignly brought the people of Israel back despite their unbelief, in possible preparation for the tribulation period. Someday in the future they will be obedient followers of Jesus and worthy to receive their ancient homeland as promised in the Abrahamic Covenant. Verse 6 speaks of "new things." The "new things" are the fact that they will return from the Babylonian Captivity. In fact, in Jeremiah God even specifies that the Captivity will only last for seventy years (Jeremiah 25:11-12). In Daniel 9, Daniel was reading Jeremiah and realized that they were almost at the end of the seventy years, and he asked God what would happen next. The answer was the prophecy of "The 70 Weeks of Daniel". That prophecy covered the 483 years leading up to the triumphal entry of the Messiah into Jerusalem around A.D. 30. Despite the rebellion of the hard human heart, God says that for His own glory, He will save the Jews from themselves (v. 11).

Life stEP Even "if we believe not, yet he abides faithful: he cannot deny himself" (2 Timothy 2:13).

Isaiah 48:12-22

What is the writer saying?

How can I apply this to my life?

pray Romania – For the lifting of government restrictions, which are hindering effective ministry growth.

God demands that His people listen to His predictions. They should listen because He is the all in all (*the first and the last*). He is the only God ("I am He"). He created everything the eye can see, but not with His whole being—it was *just* His hand that founded the earth and flung the stars into space. A "span" (v. 13) is the distance from the tip of the thumb to the tip of the little finger when the fingers are stretched to their maximum spread. Most carpenters and seamstresses know what that measure is so they can quickly get a rough measurement using their *span*. God's *span* can measure the light years between the various star systems!

Who are the "all ye" in verse 14? Is He commanding Israel and the stars to listen to His predictions? Perhaps He is including the gods, so-called, as He challenges once again, "Who can predict the future like I can?" The "him" of verses 14 and 15 refers to Cyrus, who the Lord will use to defeat Babylon.

Verse 16 looks beyond this messianic type to the messianic fulfillment in Jesus of Nazareth. The Messiah of verse 16 is clearly not just a human, but rather a member of the Trinity. The "Lord God" (v. 16) is God the Father. "His Spirit" is God the Holy Spirit. "Me" is the Messiah, Jesus Christ.

In the Book of Esther, Esther and Mordecai should have obeyed verse 20. They really had no business being in Persia. They illustrate God's dealings with Israel in her unbelief. Verse 21 promises Exodus-like protection as the Israelites return from the Babylonian Captivity. Verse 22 concludes with a warning that occurs three times in chapters 40-66 (48:22, 57:21, and 66:24), tipping us off to three subsections of nine chapters each in Isaiah 40-66.

Life **stEP** God's justice makes Him deal with sin. His love found a way to make the payment for our sin and redeem us. Love should lead us to forsake sin.

Isaiah 49:1-13

What is the writer saying?

How can I apply this to my life?

pray Uganda – For new missionaries to adapt quickly, live the Word, and persevere amidst opposition.

Chapters 49 through 57 constitute the middle nine chapters of the last twenty-seven chapters in Isaiah (the "New Testament"). The theme of these nine chapters is the faithful, suffering servant. The middle chapter of this section, the "Holy of Holies," is chapter 53. And the middle verse of chapter 53 is verse 6, "All we like sheep have gone astray"!

In verse 3 of today's chapter, this same individual is called "Israel." This is not a reference to the whole nation, as in verse 6 it says that this individual is going to restore "Israel." (The nation cannot restore itself). Rather, the one doing the restoring is the Messiah, called "Israel" in verse 3 in order to identify the Messiah with His people. This technique, called corporate solidarity, is seen in other Scriptures, such as when God had Jesus taken to Egypt so that just like Israel, He also was called out of Egypt (compare Hosea 11:1 quoted in Matthew 2:15). Just as Israel spent forty years in the wilderness, Jesus spent forty days there at the beginning of His public ministry.

The Messiah's humanity is clear in verse 5. Verse 6 indicates that the Messiah will not only be the Savior for the Jews, but also of the Gentiles. How strange that in the book of Acts the Jewish authorities were incensed that Paul was taking the Gospel to the Gentiles. Verse 7, which was not fulfilled in Christ's first coming, will be fulfilled at His second coming. It is reminiscent of the tradition for the audience to stand at the Hallelujah Chorus in Handel's "Messiah."

When the Messiah comes to be honored by the Gentile kings and nations, He will gather His Jews back to their land. The heat and the terrain will not hinder them (v. 10). They will come from the four corners of the earth (v. 12), and even remote places such as *Sinim* (in southern Egypt) will get the message for the Jews to return.

Why has the Lord waited so long for this glorious situation to take place on the earth? Peter's answer: *To give time for more to get saved.* (2 Peter 3:9).

Isaiah 49:14-26

What is the writer saying?

How can I apply this to my life?

pray   Jamaica – For churches to model compassion to the poor, who receive minimal exposure to the gospel.

In Isaiah's day, the people were so confused in their sin and rebellion that they felt like God had already abandoned them. They certainly would continue to feel that way in the Babylonian Captivity. God says, *Not so.* God could no more forget His children than a mother could forget her own baby—and even if a mother did forget her child, He won't forget His. In fact, He has their names etched into His hands; they are constantly on His mind, like the High Priest who wore the names of the twelve tribes of Israel on the two gemstone clasps on his shoulders and on the twelve gemstones on his breastplate. Verse 16 says Israel's presence to God is as though their pictures were on the walls of His bedroom as a constant reminder.

The enemies will be scared away as the contractors run to start rebuilding the city (v.17). As the builders finish the city, they will find out that they made it too small. So fruitful has God made the people that they spill outside of the walls of the city (v. 19). So startling will be the recovery of Jerusalem that the remnant will say, *I'm single, old and barren. Where did all these children come from? They can't be mine, can they?* (v. 21).God will now use the nations that had afflicted Israel to bless Israel. They will bring the Jews back to their land, kindly help them, and will even humble themselves and serve the Jews "in the dust." (The word for servant and deacon in the New Testament literally means "one who goes through the dust"!). God will do this so that the whole world, both Jews and Gentiles, will know that there is a God in Heaven who determines the affairs of men (v. 26).

Life **stEP**   Many believers live frustrating lives, year after year, decade after decade. One day the burden will be lifted, and we will never remember the former things again. In the meantime, take heart from this great hope.

Isaiah 50:1-11

What is the writer saying?

How can I apply this to my life?

pray Spain – Wisdom for pastors ministering in a society staggering under drug abuse, unemployment, and gambling addiction.

The Lord asks for proofs of His evil dealings with Israel—either a divorce document or bill of sale in a slave market that would expose His abandonment of them. But instead, it was actually Israel's own sins that had fractured her home and enslaved her to others. God proves His ability to redeem and His right to demand obedience based on His control of nature. He can move bodies of water at will. He can watch the fish he created die and rot, with no one able to question what He does. This same power has been there all the time, willing to heal and redeem Israel, if Israel would only repent. In verse 4 the suffering servant speaks. He talks of God's wisdom and direction in His life to make Him a good servant. "Opened mine ear" (v. 5) can refer to obedience, or perhaps the fuller example of surrender in the bondservant ritual. A Jewish person who voluntarily became a servant for life would pierce his ear lobe to signify this (Exodus 21:6 and Deuteronomy 15:17). This servant role is one Jesus would fulfill over 700 years after Isaiah wrote these words. Some have argued that the words apply only to Isaiah and the struggles he faced as he prophesied to his people. There are two problems with that view. First, even though tradition states that Isaiah was martyred, nowhere is it recorded that Isaiah was whipped or had his beard plucked. These things did happen to Jesus, however. Second, by the time we get to Isaiah 53, we are told that this suffering servant would bear the sins of the people as a guilt offering. A mere mortal cannot atone for the sins of a nation, but God in the flesh can as He becomes not only a perfect sacrifice but also an infinite sacrifice that can cover an infinite amount of guilt for an infinite amount of time (eternity in Heaven instead of in Hell for believers).

He who plays with fire gets burned (v. 11).

Life stEP Jesus's role as a bondservant is a pattern for us to follow.

Isaiah 51:1-16

What is the writer saying?

How can I apply this to my life?

God wants the righteous to know that He will revive Israel once again. God always has His *remnant*. The majority of humans may rebel, but God works it out that at least some are faithful and therefore worthy of receiving His blessings. They are encouraged to look to their humble roots. In a rock quarry (v. 51), once the valuable rock is taken, "negatives" are left in the ground as a reminder of the mining activity. God began the nation of Israel with two small pieces: an old man and woman. They were barren and past the childbearing years, but God was able to give them a son, and from that son, a whole nation. He did it once, and He could do it again. God could take the remnant from the rock, and these discouraged people could once again rise to great numbers and prosperity. John Milton wrote of man's tragic fall in *Paradise Lost* and his final restoration in *Paradise Regained*. The messianic age will be a return to the Garden of Eden. Verse 6 describes the Second Law of Thermodynamics: the observable universe is a closed system, and all the energy that has ever existed is still here, but it dissipates in the vastness of the universe, and as a result, *things wear out.* Since the universe is winding down, it must have been wound up. This verse is impressive because the people of Isaiah's day had no way of knowing that the earth was wearing out. While our bodies and even our planet cannot last forever in their current condition, God's Word and His plans are eternal (v. 8). "It" in verse 9 refers to the arm of the Lord. "Rahab" was a mythical sea monster, representing Egypt here. Just as God can *do it again* like He did with Abraham and Sarah, He can also *do it again* like He did with the Exodus.

A proud, rich man announced in church that all his success in life stemmed from a day long before when he put all he had, a quarter, in the offering plate. From the back, a voice said, "I dare you to do it again." How much do we trust the Lord to do as He has promised?

Isaiah 52:1-12

What is the writer saying?

How can I apply this to my life?

Circumcision was practiced by some Gentile societies, but not with the religious significance of Jewish circumcision. For Jews, circumcision was the sign of the Abrahamic Covenant. When God promised Abraham a land (Israel), a seed (son, descendants, and eventually Jesus Christ), and a blessing (physical and spiritual), Abraham was required to have all male members of his family circumcised. Since the promise involved reproduction, it is significant that the sign involved the reproductive organ. It also spoke of sexual purity and separation from the vile practices of the surrounding nations. Finally, it also involved pain and bloodshed, which speaks of sacrifice and dedication.

Verse 1 indicates that the profane and unclean nations who disdain the God of Israel will be abased. The marks of Israel's captivity will be removed (v. 2). The people of Israel were in Egypt for 430 years (1874-1444 B.C.) and were slaves for a good portion of that time, as predicted to Abraham in Genesis 15:13. Assyria had attacked Samaria and deported the ten northern tribes in 722 B.C. Assyria also attacked Jerusalem in 701 B.C. Verse 7, which is quoted by Paul in Romans 10:15, speaks here of the good news that Israel was free from Gentile oppression and could return safely to her ancient homeland.

In 538 B.C., when Zerubbabel and the 50,000 returned from Babylon, they rejoiced, but not as much as the Jewish people will when their Messiah brings this to pass in the messianic age. In 538 B.C., they were coming from only one nation, and only a few other nations noticed. In the messianic era, every nation on the planet will know, and the Jews from the whole world will come back to Jerusalem. *Rearward* (v. 12) means "rear guard."

Life **stEP** When in the midst of this life's warfare, we cry out, "Watch my back!" It is the Lord Who answers, "I've got you covered."

Isaiah 52:13-53:12

What is the writer saying?

How can I apply this to my life?

pray Slovakia – For salvation decisions resulting from the witness of Christians working in public schools.

Since the Eleventh Century A.D., Jewish commentators have attributed this passage to the sufferings of the Jewish people themselves, and not their Messiah. However, in 53:12, this entity dies for the sins of Israel, so it has to be someone other than Israel. The passage divides into five sections of three verses each. In 52:13-15, God the Father speaks, proclaiming the exaltation of the servant. Verse 13 gives the conclusion first, anticipating the resurrection, ascension, and enthronement of Christ. Verse 15 predicts that the Gentiles will believe, while the Jews will be confused. In 53:1-3, believing Jews speak, describing the background of the Servant. Verse 1 could have been said by the disciples on the Road to Emmaus. Other Jewish heroes were handsome (such as Joseph, David, and Daniel). The Jews of Christ's day wanted a King but they got a carpenter (v. 2). The Hebrew word for "despised" (v. 3) is used of Antiochus Epiphanes in Daniel 11:21, putting Jesus in the same class as a temple desecrator. In 53:4-6 the sufferings of the Servant are listed. Leprosy was called "the stroke" since it was often a judgment from God; the people thought God had judged Christ. He was "wounded" (physical) and "bruised" (emotional) (v. 5).

We were like sheep, wandering in the wilderness of sin while God, like an archer zeroing in for the kill, laid our sin on His back (v. 6). He became our scapegoat. Isaiah 53:7-9 describes the submission of the Servant. It was an unfair trial—a judicial murder. To die childless was a great disgrace. "Cut off" speaks of a premature and violent death. In Isaiah 53:10-12, God the Father speaks again announcing the reward of the Servant. The offering mentioned here, the guilt offering, was for a specific sin, requiring a bloody sacrifice and 120% restitution.

Life stEP He paid it all and then paid some more, so no debt remains for us.

Isaiah 54:4-17

What is the writer saying?

How can I apply this to my life?

Verses 1-3 promise that the remnant will be more fruitful than original Israel. In verse 5, the words "Maker" and "husband" are plural. Since they are referring to God, this is a hint at the plurality of the Godhead (the Trinity). Since Isaiah spoke these words around 700 B.C., Israel has never experienced the blessedness they describe. She has instead spent the vast majority of that time under Gentile rule. The only exceptions were the 100 years of freedom from 164-63 B.C. when the Maccabees, or Hasmonaeans, from the tribe of Levi ruled Judea and the current situation since A.D. 1948. Of course, despite the sophistication of modern Israel, she still is dependent on the good will of Gentile nations to stay independent. So great will be the time of blessing that the time of judgment will seem like a distant, brief sorrow. Just as God promised Noah that never again would He destroy the world with a flood, likewise, once He begins this time of blessing for Israel, never again will judgment come. God describes beautiful gemstones adorning the rebuilt city. In Revelation 21-22 John sees the heavenly city of Jerusalem constructed in a similar fashion. This has led some to conclude that these verses will not be fulfilled in time as we know it but in eternity. But God could also physically bless earthly Jerusalem and then use similar terms to describe the physical beauty of the heavenly city. In fact, the description of the heavenly city far exceeds the description here. Notice that even in physical blessing, there is a spiritual dimension. Faithfulness is a prerequisite for physical blessing. Likewise, during this time, spiritual instruction will continue (v. 13).

Life stEP When we arrive in the blessed time, life's frustrations will fade. Let's therefore determine to concentrate on things of eternal consequence.

Isaiah 55:1-13

What is the writer saying?

How can I apply this to my life?

Isaiah is the prince of the prophets. He controls an impressive vocabulary and eloquently presents *God's Invitation of the Ages*. In verses 1-3 we have the *Call to Salvation*. In verses 6-7 is the *Process of Salvation*, and in 12-13 are the *Blessings of Salvation*.

"Wine" and "milk" (v. 1) represent luxurious food items while "water" and "bread" were the staples of everyday life. In Christ's public ministry He referred to Himself as refreshing water (John 7:37) and nourishing bread (John 6:35). In Luke 14:16-24 Jesus uses a banquet in a parable saying that if Israel will repent and seek the Lord, He will reaffirm the Davidic Covenant with them. This covenant was first declared in 2 Samuel 7 when David was anxious to build a temple for the Lord. God told him that because he was a bloody man, he could not build that special house, but that God would make a house out of him. David was promised that his line would be the kingly line and that one of his descendants would sit upon the throne in Jerusalem forever. This will be fulfilled by Jesus Christ.

"Mercies" (v. 3) translates a Hebrew word that means *covenant loyalty*. It refers to the integrity of God, that when He makes a promise, He keeps it. Verses 4-5 envision the whole world giving allegiance to Messiah. Verse 6 argues that delay is foolish. Today is the time for this crucial decision; tomorrow may be too late. "Mercy" in verse 7 is a different Hebrew word than what is in verse 3. The root of this word is "womb," referring to the tender care a mother gives to her baby. Once the people respond in faith, the whole universe will rejoice (v. 12).

"Come unto me, all ye that labor and are heavy laden, and I will give you rest. Take my yoke upon you, and learn of me; for I am meek and lowly in heart: and ye shall find rest unto your souls. For my yoke is easy, and my burden is light" (Matthew 11:28-30).

Isaiah 57:15-21

What is the writer saying?

How can I apply this to my life?

Isaiah 57:1-13 condemns the wicked for abandoning their husband, the Lord, and going after other lovers. Verses 14-21 turn attention on the righteous and the blessings God has planned for them. This section is so potent that for centuries the Jews have read the passages of Isaiah 57:14-58:4 and Jonah on the holiest day in the Jewish calendar, the Day of Atonement.

In chapter 6, the Lord was "high and lifted up." Here He is high and exalted and lives in a different dimension—eternity. We struggle to comprehend a God who has always existed. We may reason, if He created the current universe about 6,000 years ago, then what was He doing 10,000 years before that? The problem is that we only comprehend time. We cannot imagine anything else. Scientists say that just as matter came into existence at a point of time, space and time also came into existence. We can't even guess what existed before space, matter, and time were created, but we know Who lived there. His name is "Holy" (v. 15), which means "set apart." As it relates to God, "holy" refers to the distance between Him and His creation and also His moral excellence. Notice that the passage does not say that we have to be holy to live with Him (for none of us would be able to do so on our own). It says that those with a humble and contrite heart are welcome. This speaks of a true estimation of our unworthiness and our complete reliance on God for salvation. Contrite means "to be crushed," as under a heavy weight. The load of our sin should bring us to our knees in repentance. "Froward" (v. 17) means "to turn away."

Life stEP Our eternity and destiny lie in the thoughts within our hearts. If we think right, we'll live right. If we live right, we'll die right and then have eternity to savor the reward of righteousness.

Isaiah 58:1-14

What is the writer saying?

How can I apply this to my life?

Here in chapter 58, Isaiah discusses true worship versus vain, hypocritical worship. Verses 2-7 say that the Jews were going through the motions of worship. They prayed to feel close to God and even fasted, hoping to attract His special attention. However, their fellow Jews were being abused by their unethical business practices. They had been released from the Babylonian Captivity only to be re-enslaved by their fellow countrymen. Therefore, God says their worship was useless. He says the type of fast He approves is one that includes fair social dealings. Social justice is one of the major themes of the prophets' writing just before and then after the Babylonian Captivity. Nehemiah contended with the wealthy Jewish landlords on this same issue (compare to Nehemiah 5:1-15). In Malachi God says He hates the sacrifices of half-hearted followers. This does not mean that they didn't have to do sacrifices or fast, but rather that they had to be done with pure motives and from a grateful, godly heart in order for them to be effective.

Verse 7 describes an appropriate and successful welfare state. Today, some Christians feel that passages such as this demand that we emphasize meeting the physical needs of our fellow earth dwellers before we share the Gospel with them. But Isaiah 58 is talking about helping *family members* (fellow Jews) and not every hungry person on the planet. We may use physical help as a vehicle to share the Gospel, but it cannot be an end in itself. The appropriate New Testament application is that members of the local church should help each other. If unsaved in the community want that kind of family help, they should join the church and become part of the family.

True religion is more than just words; it is also our deeds, as the fruit of our changed spiritual condition.

Isaiah 59:1-2, 12-21

What is the writer saying?

How can I apply this to my life?

Chapter 59 describes Israel's sinful condition in graphic terms. Fortunately, Israel confesses and God responds with the promise that He will blot out Israel's sins. Verse 1 indicates God's ample power to save. The fault lies not with God, but with man's rebellious heart (v. 2).

Verse 12 uses three words for *sin*. The word *transgression* means "revolt, rebellion, breakage of an agreement." The word *sin* means "to miss a mark." The word *iniquity* means "twisted." Because of man's behavior, all the qualities that God and even humans admire are damaged: "justice," "truth," "equity" and "righteousness" (vv. 14-16). Even the person who merely stops sinning opens himself up to attack from the more aggressive sinners (v. 15). Verse 16 explains how God looked down from Heaven to find one man who could be His mediator and bring salvation to sinful humanity. Since all humans are sinners, He found no one who was qualified to be the savior. Therefore, He had to do it Himself. "Arm" (v. 16) speaks of strength. God Himself became a man so that the strength of His perfection and infinity might provide eternal salvation for mankind.

While verse 16 speaks of the cross of Christ, verses 17-21 speak of His second coming to establish righteousness on the planet. The imagery is that of war coupled with God's holy standard. Those who rebel against the standard will be destroyed by the judgments of the tribulation period. Even remote places, such as the "islands"(coastlands) will feel the impact of His return. Verse 21 promises that the same Spirit which anoints the Messiah for His ruler will also be poured out on the Jews in that great day.

Life stEP For centuries believers have prayed, "Thy will be done on earth as it is in heaven." (Matthew 6:10). One day this will finally and eternally be so. Maranatha! (Aramaic for "our Lord comes").

Isaiah 60:1-6, 14-16

What is the writer saying?

How can I apply this to my life?

pray United Kingdom – For many teens to be saved through Christian camping and outreach events.

Chapter 60 announces the coming of light, something that was not always present in Israel's history. The Golden Era of Israel's history consisted of the forty years of Solomon's reign (971-931 B.C.). There were a few bright spots after Solomon, but basically it was all downhill after his reign. For most of Israel's history the kingdom dwelt in twilight, if not darkness. Christ's arrival and public ministry brought great light, but He was rejected. The Gospel message exploded from Jerusalem, but within a few centuries there were very few Christians in Israel. Finally, when Christ returns, light will once again bathe the nation of Israel. Gentiles from the farthest corners of the globe will stream to Jerusalem to worship the Lord in the beauty of holiness. The nations will carry the Jews back to Israel, bringing wealth with them to Israel.

Israel will be covered with the transport system (camels, v. 6). The nations mentioned in verse 6 are Arab desert areas known for camel caravans; the camels that the Arabs used to ride to attack Israel will now be used to bring her expensive gifts. When the wise men came from the east bearing gold, frankincense, and myrrh, they were anticipating the ultimate fulfillment of this passage in the messianic era. Looking back over the last 100 years of tension in the Middle East between the Jews and Arabs, it is difficult to imagine the Arabs coming and honoring the Jews. But, it is that type of peace that this passage envisions. In that great day, Jerusalem (the "city of peace") will be called the "city of the Lord." (Bringing this from Hebrew into English, it would be called *Jeruyahweh*.) It will be special because God will be there (likewise Heaven, compare to Revelation 21:3). "Redeemer" (v. 16) is the *Kinsman Redeemer*—that close blood relative who erases your debt (compare to the book of Ruth).

Life stEP It will be worth it all when we see Jesus. All the trials and struggles will be rewarded with His smile of approval and "well done." (Matthew 25:23).

Isaiah 60:19-61:3

What is the writer saying?

How can I apply this to my life?

 pray Bulgaria – Pray for the swift and accurate completion of the new translation of the Bulgarian Bible.

Verses 19-22 complete the description of millennial blessedness. The ancients worshiped nature, including the sun and moon (in Egypt, Amun-re was the sun god and in Babylon, Nebo was the moon god). The Jews frequently fell into such pagan worship. In the blessed age (and in Heaven—compare to Revelation 21:23) there will be no need for these heavenly bodies (nor any danger of worshipping them) as God will provide the light and be the center of attention. Israel in that era will be known for 100% obedience (v. 21). This fulfillment of God's sovereign plan will bring glory to His name.

Our Lord read Isaiah 61:1-2a when He visited the synagogue in his hometown of Nazareth in Luke 4. But He did not include 61:2b: "And the day of vengeance of our God," since this will be fulfilled during the tribulation period. When Jesus announced to the hometown crowd that this passage was being fulfilled in their presence, they were amazed. Then, when He chided them for their unbelief and implied that Gentiles were more receptive to the things of God than they were, they sought to kill him. The account in Luke 4 indicates that God performed a miracle and Jesus was able to disappear in broad daylight since it was not His time to die. (It was on this occasion that Jesus made the observation that a prophet is honored everywhere but His hometown.) Verses 2b and 3 will be fulfilled when "all Israel shall be saved" (Romans 11:26).

Zechariah 6:15 makes obedience the requirement for receiving the blessings of the kingdom. This will be the message of the two witnesses in Revelation 11. Those Jews (and Gentiles) who believe will enter the kingdom. The unbelievers will be killed and rejected by the events of the tribulation period.

Life **stEp** We are children of the Great King. We need to behave like our Father.

Isaiah 61:7-62:5

What is the writer saying?

How can I apply this to my life?

pray Portugal – Pray that saved teens will be encouraged to reach their unsaved friends through evangelistic outreach programs.

Isaiah 61 presents millennial peace, and Isaiah 62 speaks of millennial restitution. God promises to restore the former glory of Israel. He has destroyed in punishment, but He will restore double what He took, just like patient Job received double of all that he lost (compare Job 1 and Job 42:12).

The "double portion" (v. 7) was traditionally promised to the *firstborn* in Jewish culture. For instance, if there were four children in the family, the father's inheritance would be divided into five lots, with each child getting one lot, except for the *firstborn*, who would get two. The firstborn was not necessarily the *one born first* (although that was the normal idea). (Examples in Scripture of *firstborns* who were not born first: Isaac over Ishmael, Jacob over Esau, and Joseph over Reuben.) A father could designate who would receive the firstborn's blessing. In the secular cultures of the day, this practice was also illustrated in legal documents. This understanding of the firstborn is helpful when Christ is called the "firstborn" or "only begotten" in the New Testament. The emphasis is not on Him *being born* but rather on His exalted status.

Verses 10-11 seem to be the words that the Jews of that day will say as they experience the blessings of the Messianic Era. Their very existence will be consumed with God and His holiness. We've all seen pictures of grooms and brides in various cultures following different interesting customs, but they all stand out from the crowd by their wedding attire. In that day the Jews will wear their festive garments, and like a rich garden, they will put forth the fruits of righteousness (v. 11). Israel will no longer be called "forsaken" and "desolate" (v. 4). Her new names will be "Hephzibah" ("My delight is in her") and "Beulah" ("married").

Life stEP Every human longs to be accepted by others. In Christ, we are accepted by the greatest personality in the universe.

Isaiah 65:17-25

What is the writer saying?

How can I apply this to my life?

pray   Taiwan – For God to break this people's bondage to materialism and its devotion to Buddhism.

Isaiah 63-65 discusses millennial judgment. Isaiah 63:1-6 speaks of judgment on God's enemies. Isaiah 63:7-65:16 reveals judgment on God's people. Today's passage, Isaiah 65:17-25, predicts judgment on God's earth.

The Old Testament does not make a clear distinction between the blessings of the messianic era and the blessings of Heaven; similar terminology is used to describe both modes of existence. In Isaiah 65:17, "I create new heavens and a new earth" does not refer to the eternal state as described in Revelation 21 and 22. Rather, it describes the transformation created by the arrival of the Messiah. (Similar words do not require identical situations. The use of an earthly blessing to describe a heavenly blessing does not negate the actual occurrence of the earthly blessing.) In verse 20 God says that during the kingdom, a 100-year-old who dies will be considered just a child. With the curse lifted off the earth in this return to Eden, life expectancies will be extended to the originally intended human lifespan of 1,000 years. Remember, Adam was told that in the day he ate of the forbidden fruit he would die. He actually died at 930 years of age, but still within the *one day* of God's time (2 Peter 3:8: "One day is with the Lord as a thousand years, and a thousand years as one day"). Verse 21 teaches that free enterprise with be protected in the kingdom. Man's labor will not be futile with enemies or the IRS taking what he earns! Verse 22 predicts long life (like a tree) but not eternal life (that awaits in Heaven). Notice that in verse 25, not everything will revert to pre-Fall conditions. The serpent, still cursed, is going about on its legless belly.

God's payday is coming someday. He will not always tolerate the rebellion of mankind. Then utopia will be enjoyed by all the righteous.

Isaiah 66:10-24

What is the writer saying?

How can I apply this to my life?

Isaiah 66 is a millennial sermon. This passage, which wraps up the sermon, chapter, "New Testament" section of Isaiah, and the entire book, is about rejoicing (Isaiah 66:10-24). God envisions Israel being treated like a beloved baby, satisfied with her mother's provisions and loving care (vv. 11-12). Isaiah's expressive vocabulary is illustrated in this powerful message with lovely phrases, such as "peace…like a river" (v. 12), which resound in our hymns. Verse 15 is reminiscent of Elijah, who went up in a chariot of fire. The chariot was the battle tank of the day and speaks of God's military might. Verse 17 refers to pagan practices forbidden to the Jews such as worshipping other gods, eating pork (Leviticus 11:7), and eating mice (Leviticus 11:29). In verses 19-21 God explains that in the kingdom, Jewish citizens will be missionaries for Messiah. (Tarshish is in Spain, Pul is Libya, Lud and Tubal are in Turkey. Javan is Greece, and the distant isles certainly could include North America!) This is actually what God intended when He chose Israel. Exodus 19:6 says, "And ye shall be unto me a kingdom of priests, and an holy nation." A priest's job is to represent people to God, which the Levites did for the other eleven tribes. The nation of Israel was supposed to do that for the whole world. In Ezekiel 5:5, Israel is said to be the *navel* of the earth. This indicates that Israel was centrally located among the nations of the ancient world so the Jews could easily represent Jehovah among the nations.

Verses 22-24 describe the millennium and eternal state, including the destruction of unbelievers—no peace for the wicked.

We will have 1,000 years in the millennial kingdom and all of eternity thereafter to rest and relish our labors. Now is the time to work, for the fields are white unto harvest, and the night is coming. (John 9:4).

Psalm 114:1-8

What is the writer saying?

How can I apply this to my life?

pray   Italy – For missionaries working in a culture that is spiritually ritualistic, apathetic and cynical.

This psalm has the character of a *playful* nursery rhyme, with familiar poetic devices including rhythmic parallelism, imagination, and surprise. It highlights Israel's early history, touching on the crossing of the Red Sea (v. 3a; Exodus 14), the crossing of the Jordan River (v. 3; Joshua 3), the quaking of Mount Sinai (v. 4; Exodus 19:18), and God's provision of water in the wilderness (v. 8; Exodus 17:1-7; Numbers 20:11).

Using personification (giving the qualities of people to objects), the psalmist lightheartedly asks the Red Sea, the Jordan River, and Mount Sinai why they responded to the Lord as they did—that is, *fleeing away* in fear (v. 5a), *turning around* as if to get out of the Lord's way (v. 5b), and *skipping* as if full of joy due to the Lord's presence (v. 6). These playful images are intended to have us see that all Creation recognizes the Creator's presence and willingly obeys Him. These parts of Creation were all amazed and awestruck in the presence of the One who could set aside the natural laws that governed them. As a result, we are to consider how we ourselves respond to the Lord's presence in our lives!

On a more serious note, the psalmist closes with instructions before getting answers from these parts of nature. He tells the earth to tremble in His presence since He has the power to transform the earth's rocks into lakes and springs of pure, refreshing water so He can accommodate the needs of His people.

Life
stEP   What mighty obstacles or barriers stand before you? What sea or mountain of troubles is keeping you from doing what God wants you to do? Have you forgotten that such things are controlled by God? If all creation recognizes the Lord's presence and obeys Him, how can you find faith and courage in God's almighty strength to see you through your current difficulties?

Psalm 115:1-18

What is the writer saying?

How can I apply this to my life?

The first verse of this worship psalm is addressed to the Lord in the hearing of an assembled audience of Jewish worshippers. They are not gathered to glorify themselves, but to give glory to the true God. After denouncing the gods of the heathen people around them (vv. 2-8), the worship leader exhorts his listeners to trust the Lord (vv. 9-11), receive His blessings (vv. 12-16), and in return, praise Him (vv. 17-18).

In verse 2, the worship leader poses a question asked by the heathen nations, "Where is their God?", a question that appears six times in the Old Testament. To the heathen, Israel seemed to worship no one (consider the empty space between the two winged cherubim atop the mercy seat of the Ark of the Covenant). The audience confidently responds, "Our God is in Heaven" (v. 3)! This God, Who is above all that He created, does whatever He pleases because He is above and much greater than the men He created. In contrast, the idols of the heathen can do nothing (vv. 5-7). Anything made (v. 4) is inferior to its maker, and idols are therefore inferior to the men who made them.

The three-fold exhortation to all who fear the Lord—"trust in the Lord" (vv. 9-11)—is fortified by a three-fold assurance that He is trustworthy as "their help and their shield" (vv. 9-11). Just because God cannot be seen does not mean He is not active in bringing blessings into the lives of those who fear Him. The God of Heaven is "mindful" of His people (v. 12), which is the idea of remembering. This indicates that God continues to bring His people into His thoughts in order to pay attention to their needs and bring them help, protection, and preservation.

What a wonderful thought, that God always keeps us in mind! Since He is paying attention to your needs, how about taking a few minutes to list several areas of your life that need God's "help" and shielding? Trust Him to do something!

Psalm 116:1-14

What is the writer saying?

How can I apply this to my life?

pray Australia – For believers to reach out to the rapidly growing population of immigrants.

The use of the first-person singular shows that this psalm is a personal testimony. While this psalm is anonymous, it has a striking resemblance to the experience of King Hezekiah (Isaiah 38), whose life was threatened by sickness.

The writer starts by saying, "I love the Lord," a unique expression. Such a love is foundational for a believer's walk (Deuteronomy 6:5; Mark 12:30). This love is credited to God, Who delivered the psalmist as an answer to his prayers (v. 4) when he was hunted by death.

This psalm is also intended to be a means of instructing God's "people" (v. 18), so they would also consider their own love for the Lord.

In verse 5, the word used for "gracious" is one only applied to God throughout the Old Testament. He is the One Who is inclined to show acts of favor to His people, who have no real claim for such gracious treatment.

In verses 7-12, God also gives bountiful (v. 7) benefits to individuals! This is to say, God rewards faithfulness by dealing out acts of goodness. If King Hezekiah is writing, then he is referring to the fifteen years added to his life (Isaiah 38:5). The psalmist then says he will give self-dedication (v. 13a), worship (v. 13b), and payment of vows (vv. 14, 18) back to God.

In verse 8, God recovers (or rescues) us from our many troubles, whether it is death, tears, or falling (to be tripped by wickedness so as to bring about a downfall). "Delivered" also carries a subsequent idea of equipping, like making strong for battle.

Life stEP Why do you "love the Lord"? Because He is good, He protects, deals kindly, rescues, and even equips? Is there something in your life filling you with "tears" or threatening to cause you to fall into sin? How can you ask God for deliverance today?

wednesday 43

Psalms 116:15-117:2

What is the writer saying?

How can I apply this to my life?

pray Austria – Pray for churches to reach the younger generation who are increasingly turning to cults.

Verse 15 is of great comfort to those facing death because it says God does not take lightly the death of His own. "Precious" can refer to valuable jewels and is used here to say that a godly person is held by God as a great treasure. "In the sight of the LORD" refers to providential oversight of the Lord (Psalms 33:18) and promises that a godly person will not die except under circumstances that God oversees, and at a time and manner that will best accomplish His purposes. Death does not come as a surprise to God, for He has made full preparations beforehand for the transition of his saints ("holy ones") to their "life after death" (Psalm 49:15; John 14:2-3; Revelation 14:13). Psalm 117 is the shortest chapter of the Bible. It is also the Bible's middle chapter, with 594 chapters preceding it and 594 following it.

This little gem has a large call to praise. It is a simple reminder of four great truths:

Since the earliest time God has made known to the Jews that He intended to make His mercy and truth available to "all ye nations" through Abraham (Genesis 22:18). Romans 15:11 quotes from this psalm as part of Paul's proof that God's purpose all along has been for the Gentiles, along with the Jews, to partake in God's mercy through the death of Jesus Christ.

Two times "all people" are commanded to praise God.

With a look back through history, God's unfailing love (v. 2a, "merciful kindness") for His people has always been displayed.

With a look forward, God's "truth" (v. 2b) will continue to endure forever! We can place our faith in God's total dependability.

Life stEP Have you become one of God's holy ones through faith in the finished work of Christ? If so, how can you express your complete faith in His total dependability to care for you right now?

Psalm 118:1-14

What is the writer saying?

How can I apply this to my life?

pray Brazil – Pray that Christians in high profile positions would keep a moral and ethical testimony.

Psalm 118 completes a section of hymns (Psalms 113-118) that are recited during the Jewish Passover, or Seder Meal (Matthew 26:30). Originally this psalm was arranged to be sung in celebration of the laying of the foundation of the rebuilt Temple (Ezra 3:1-4, 11).

Subsequently, it was used by worshippers as a processional when ascending Mt. Zion for annual feasts at the Temple. Note that today's portion of Psalm 118 concerns the start (vv. 1-4) of the processional and then its journey (vv. 5-18). Tomorrow's passage considers its arrival at the Temple (vv. 19-29).

The psalm calls three times for an expression of thanks for God's enduring mercy. The basis for these calls are two great themes:

All Israel declares, as if the people were one, its personal experience of God's help (v. 7) in moving Israel from a narrow, confined place (the literal meaning of "distress" in verse 5 is "personal anguish from being 'bound up' on a constricting path") to a "large place."

Israel had known the fear of being compassed about by enemies and the disappointment of its people failing to measure up to the confidences placed in them. It had learned that trusting the Lord was the better way (vv. 8-14).

Verse 14 is from the song of Moses (Exodus 15:2), which was Israel's victory song to the Lord, Who saved them from Pharaoh's army at a narrow, confined place next to the Red Sea. It will be Israel's victory song in the coming Messianic Kingdom (Isaiah 12:2) and the victory song for the tribulation saints, and finally, all nations (Revelation 15:3-4).

Life stEP What great work of God in your life should be the subject of your victory song? How can you express thanks for His enduring mercy and help in your life? How can God be your strength as you face the next distressing situation that seems to be binding up your life?

friday 43

Psalm 118:15-29

What is the writer saying?

How can I apply this to my life?

pray Slovakia – For Slovakian and Hungarian believers to overcome cultural animosities and embrace unity in Christ.

Martin Luther said Psalm 118 was to him the dearest of all Scripture passages. Verse 22 is quoted six times in the New Testament, as is the first half of verse 26, which looks forward to the first (Matthew 21:9) and second comings (Matthew 23:39) of Christ.

As discussed yesterday, this psalm was sung as Jews made their way up to the Temple. In today's passage we see these worshippers arriving at the Temple's gates, here called the "gates of righteousness" (v. 19) and "gate of the LORD" (v. 20). These titles speak of the entrance's purpose of bringing sinful worshippers into a "righteous" (v. 20b) relationship with their holy God. The worshippers understood that the only *gate* to salvation from death was to be found here (vv. 14-17, 21b). Notice that they entered the *gate* with their sacrifice for the altar (v. 27), which is an Old Testament picture of the coming Lamb of God, Jesus Christ, who would become the Redeemer as He became God's perfect sacrifice for sin.

The word "stone" (v. 22) is used metaphorically throughout Scripture for Christ (Acts 4:11). To the Church, Christ is the "chief cornerstone" (see Ephesians 2:19-22 and 1 Peter 2:4-6). Christ was also a "stumbling stone" as the Jewish people rejected Him as the Messiah. Daniel prophesied of a "smiting stone" that would destroy the Gentile world powers at the end of this age (Daniel 2:34).

 Life stEP The concern that these Jewish worshippers had for their "righteous" standing before God reminds us that we too must be concerned about our standing before God today. Have you asked Jesus to become your sacrifice for sin? This is your only gate to God's salvation from sin and death! Do you keep the gate between you and your Lord open by regularly confessing your sin (1 John 1:9), so that Jesus will wash you of all unrighteousness?

Psalm 119:1-8

What is the writer saying?

How can I apply this to my life?

With 176 verses, Psalm 119 is by far the longest chapter in the Bible. It is also the most elaborate of the acrostic psalms. All eight verses in each of the twenty-two sections begins with the same Hebrew letter, with the sections working through each letter of the twenty-two-letter Hebrew alphabet.

In this context, the "law of the Lord" (v. 1) consists of all the instructions He has given to mankind. His testimonies (v. 2) are what bear witness to His person, purposes, and pronouncements. His ways (v. 3) speak of how He acts and how He wants His people to act. (Isaiah 55:8-9 says His ways are different than ours.)

The first three verses are addressed to the reader, then the psalm talks to the Lord. His precepts (v. 4) are authoritative principles by which to live. His statutes (v. 5) are written rules of conduct. His commandments (v. 6) are specific directives, and His judgments (v. 7) are judicial decisions.

In these eight verses the psalmist utilizes seven different Hebrew words to designate God's revelation to man. If our walk (v. 3, our hour-by-hour conduct) continues to be undefiled, we will be blessed. Seeking Him with a whole heart (v. 2), we will do no iniquity because we will be walking in His ways. We will not be ashamed (v. 6) but will praise Him with an upright heart and continue to learn from His law, testimonies, ways, precepts, statutes, commandments, and judgments.

Life **stEP** The key word in this first section of Psalm 119 is "keep" (vv. 2, 4, 5, 8). It means to continually observe. Look back at these verses and see what we are called to "keep" as we follow God.

Psalm 119:9-16

What is the writer saying?

How can I apply this to my life?

In this second section we find a new designation for God's Word, with the Hebrew word translated "word" pointing to the total revelation of God to man, which sums up the other ways "word" was used in yesterday's portion of Psalm 119. The exaltation of the Word of God is the theme of Psalm 119.

The psalmist recounts to the Lord four ways in which he has conducted his life in the past: (1) He has sought the Lord with his whole heart (in conformity to his observation in verse 2). (2) In obedience to the command in verse 4, he has memorized God's Word. (3) He has publicly declared God's message. (4) Rejoicing in God's ways has been more important to him than riches.

The psalmist tells the Lord how he intends to conduct himself in the future: (1) He will take time to meditate on God's Word, thereby showing due respect to the ways of the Lord. (2) He will keep God's words in constant remembrance by finding his delight in heeding God's Word.

In verse 15, the psalmist introduces a key theme that is developed in later verses—the benefits for those who meditate on God's Word. Think on the wondrous promises in Psalm 1:2-3 for those who meditate.

The psalmist has given us a pattern for a proper relationship with our God. We should ask Him questions and seek to find the answers in His Word. He is pleased when we make requests such as, "let me not wander" and "teach me thy statutes." It is good to evaluate our past conduct in respect to our relationship with Him and His Word. Then we need to declare our intentions and desires about the future of our relationship to Him.

Psalm 119:17-24

What is the writer saying?

How can I apply this to my life?

pray Venezuela – For missionaries to overcome the obstacles that make obtaining a visa a difficult process.

In each of the eight verses of this section, the psalmist employs one of the eight designations for God's Word. But he doesn't use all eight of the Hebrew nouns. "Ways" and "precepts" are omitted; "commandments" and "testimonies" are used twice.

By saying "deal bountifully" (v. 17), the psalmist is asking that he be classified among the blessed ones of verse 2. In verse 18, the psalmist is saying that except for the spiritual sight and insight given by the Lord, it is not possible for earth-dwellers to see the wondrous truths in God's Word (John 3:2; 1 Corinthians 2:9-12). Like Abraham, we must consider ourselves "strangers and pilgrims on the earth" if we are to see and embrace His promises and deep truths (Hebrews 11:13). We must at all times have a longing for His Word that can only be satisfied by a Spirit-supplied knowledge of His wonders.

Since God has rebuked people who err from His commandments (v. 21) and condemned them, the psalmist asks to be separated from them. Even though the leaders of society have verbally abused him, he continues to keep God's testimonies.

In verses 15-16 the psalmist announced his intent to meditate and delight in God's Word. In verses 23-24, meditation and delight have become the pattern for the lives of himself and his counselors.

As I hide God's Word in my heart (v. 11), He will open my eyes, that I may behold wondrous things (v. 18). As I meditate and take delight, I will become unconcerned about those who hold me in contempt and speak against me. They are blind leaders of the blind (Matthew 15:14), and they will all fall into the ditch of eternal damnation.

Psalm 119:25-32

What is the writer saying?

How can I apply this to my life?

In the first half of this section, the psalmist sends four petitions to the Lord: "Quicken (enliven) thou me," "teach me," "make me to understand," and "strengthen thou me." By adding the information in these four verses to that given in verses 22-23, we deduce the following: after suffering reproach and contempt from people in high office, he experienced severe bodily affliction. (He speaks more of his affliction later in the psalm.) He has spoken to the Lord about his deep despair, and he is confident God heard his plea. Although he has physical and emotional relapses (vv. 25, 28), he is growing spiritually by calling upon his Lord and trusting in His Word.

In verse 29, the psalmist asks to be separated from those who have chosen the path of lies, and to receive grace from God to live by His law. He has chosen the way of truth and follows that path by constantly keeping the Lord's judgments (ordinances) in his mind. During his time of trial, the psalmist has tenaciously clung to the Lord's testimonies and asks God for vindication because of this (v. 31). Verse 32 lets us know that he is on the road to victory and that he has regained his confidence.

Life stEP — What are your thoughts about what it means to have an enlarged heart? The psalmist believes that such a heart can only come from God. What does verse 32 say one will do when the Lord enlarges His heart?

Psalm 119:33-40

What is the writer saying?

How can I apply this to my life?

pray   Chile – For the Chilean church to overcome its spiritual isolation and develop a missionary zeal.

In these eight verses, the psalmist requests nine petitions of the Lord (two in verse 37). We have already heard the psalmist utter the plea "Teach me, O LORD" twice before (vv. 12, 26). This time he pledges to observe what he is taught for the rest of his life. In the previous section, he followed his plea to be taught with a request for understanding, so he would be effective in proclaiming the wondrous works of the Lord to others. Here he asks for understanding of the teaching so he can observe the law of God wholeheartedly. It is one thing to receive instructions but another to comprehend the teaching sufficiently to be able to use it. That comprehension comes through meditation (vv. 15, 23). The requests in verses 33-34 have to do with the activity of the mind. Verse 35 is a plea that the feet walk in the right pathway. The petition of verse 36 speaks of the heart—the innermost desires. The first petition of verse 37 seeks direction for the use of the eyes. The second asks for fervor of spirit in life's journey.

The psalmist wants the Word so established in his being that he will fear God rather than seek the approval of man. Since the judgments and precepts of the Lord are good, the psalmist longs for the life-giving righteousness they produce in one's life.

Life stEP

Notice the order in which the psalmist presents his petitions. That which enters our minds occupies our thinking, which in turn determines our walk. Our hearts' desires determine what we will covet. What we see with our eyes attracts us to the vanities of this world. The establishment of the Word produces the righteousness that may be offensive to man but is a delight to God (v. 11).

Psalm 119:41-48

What is the writer saying?

How can I apply this to my life?

In each of the forty verses already considered in Psalm 119, we have seen at least one of the eight synonyms used to designate the Word. Except for three or four verses later in the psalm, that pattern continues. In this section, verses 43 and 48 each have two, and the others one, for a total of ten.

Notice how the psalmist's experience (vv. 41-42) parallels our own salvation. It is from the Lord's mercy (Titus 3:5), by God's Word (1 Peter 1:23), and through faith in the Word (Ephesians 2:8) that we are saved. The psalmist trusts in the Word (v. 42), hopes in the Word (v. 43), and seeks the Word (v. 45) because he loves the Word (v. 47). He resolves to observe the Word always (v. 44). As a result, he will walk at liberty—that is, his path will be free from the stumbling stones of a sinful life. He will also have the boldness to proclaim God's Word and meditate in it.

Six times in this psalm, the writer speaks of his delight in God's Word. He is aware that the Word saved him. He is very grateful for the Word. He knows that he grows by the Word and needs to feed on it each day. He reveres the Word because of Whose Word it is. He is cognizant of the instruction and admonition he receives from the Word. He senses the comfort the Word brings into his life. He trusts and hopes in the promises of the Word.

Here is the question for us: Do we delight in the Word? One definition of delight is "enraptured attention."

Life stEP The Bible instructs us to hear the Word, read the Word, study the Word, memorize the Word, and meditate upon the Word. How pleased our Lord would be if we did all of this in an aura of enraptured attention!

friday 44

Psalm 119:49-56

What is the writer saying?

How can I apply this to my life?

pray Taiwan – For believers to accept a more active and committed role in their local church bodies.

The glad message of this section is that throughout God's Word, there is comfort in times of affliction. Romans 15:4 echoes this point: "For whatsoever things were written aforetime were written for our learning, that we through patience and comfort of the scriptures might have hope." Later, the psalmist says this again: "Thou hast caused me to hope" (v. 49) and "I have hoped in thy word" (v. 74). Hope is appropriated by trusting the promises of God in His Word (Titus 1:2: "In hope of eternal life, which God, that cannot lie, promised"). Hope in the Bible is not the type of hope that we talk about in everyday conversation: "My lawn is dying—I hope it rains today" or "I hope to pass this exam." Those are wishes that may or may not come to pass, but Scriptural hope is the present appropriation of a future, joyous certainty, such as Hebrews 6:19: "Which hope we have as an anchor of the soul, both *sure* and *stedfast.*"

Think of a seven-year old girl ten days before Christmas. She sees her name on a package from her grandmother. She doesn't wait until Christmas to become elated—she exults every day in anticipation. Hope is about the future, but it is expressed in the present. Right now, we are "looking for that blessed hope, and the glorious appearing of the great God and our Saviour, Jesus Christ" (Titus 2:13)—"wherefore comfort one another with these words" (1 Thessalonians 4:18). The apostle Paul called all of his afflictions "light" and "for a moment" (2 Corinthians 4:17). He was taking comfort in the trustworthiness of God's promises. His way of finding this hope is seen in Romans 15:13: "Now the God of hope fill you with all joy and peace in believing, that ye may abound in hope."

Life stEP Hope is not for enjoyment in Heaven, for there all hope will have become reality. There certainly is no hope in Hell. Hope is for now. If you are not, in this life, getting your share of hope by rejoicing in the certainty of God's promises, you are missing this great provision from God!

Psalm 119:57-64

What is the writer saying?

How can I apply this to my life?

pray Aruba – For outreach among those who have immigrated from Latin America, the Caribbean and Asia.

To begin this section, the psalmist repeats the first part of David's pronouncement in Psalm 16:5, which derives from Numbers 18:20. When the Promised Land was divided among the families of Israel, Aaron's descendants were to receive no portion. As the Lord's personal representatives on earth, they were to look directly to Him for present sustenance and future security.

In verses 57-61, the psalmist reflects on events that brought him to the point of proclaiming "Thou are my portion, O LORD." In effect, he was saying, "The Lord is all I need. My life is completely wrapped up in Him."

At a point in his life, he realized he was not walking according to God's Word. He made an about-face by resolving to keep God's Word, and he pled with his whole heart for God's mercy. Evidently he was recently robbed of earthly possessions (v. 61). But that would not deter him from his resolve to live by God's Word. Verses 62-63 tell how that resolve will govern his future. When he awakes in the night, he will take the opportunity to rise and thank his God for the righteousness the Word has produced in his life. He won't need sleeping pills! He'll sleep when the Lord provides sleep, and occupy himself with thanksgiving when he can't sleep. He will seek like-minded companions with whom he will praise the Lord, and he will be taught by God.

Life stEP

Like the prodigal son of Luke 15:17-20, the psalmist was received with open arms by a forgiving father when he "thought on his ways and turned his feet" to the Lord's way (v. 59). When we stray, hopefully we will think and turn before we fall into total degradation and bring reproach upon our Father, as did the prodigal son.

Psalm 119:65-72

What is the writer saying?

How can I apply this to my life?

This section advances two themes that we have been following in Psalm 119 – the desire of the psalmist to be taught, and of his affliction. The word *judgment* in verse 66 means *discernment*. It is not related to the word *judgments*, which was used eighteen times in Psalm 119 as one of the eight designations for God's Word. In vv. 25-40, the psalmist asked to be taught so he could understand God's ways. This would enable him to "talk of His wondrous works" and "go in the path of His commandments." His thirst for teaching was from a desire to use knowledge with discernment.

Affliction was what led the psalmist to his desire for learning (v. 71); therefore, it was good for him to be afflicted. What he received because of affliction was better "than thousands of gold and silver" (v. 72). The Bible has other examples of people who have benefited from affliction:

Because Joseph was afflicted, he preserved a posterity for a nation (Genesis 45:7; Acts 7:10).

Because Hannah was afflicted, she was exalted in the Lord and gave birth to Samuel, who became judge and prophet (1 Samuel 1).

Because Job was afflicted, the Lord gave him "twice as much as he had before" (Job 42:10).

Because Paul was afflicted, his "strength was made perfect in weakness" (2 Corinthians 12:7-10).

Because our Lord Jesus Christ was afflicted (Isaiah 53:4-7), we have life "purchased with his own blood" (Acts 20:28).

It is a great day when we truly learn that every affliction "worketh for us a far more exceeding and eternal weight of glory" (2 Corinthians 4:17). We will then say with the psalmist, "It is good for me that I have been afflicted." We will say with Paul, "I take pleasure in infirmities, in reproaches, in necessities, in persecutions, in distresses for Christ's sake" (2 Corinthians 12:10).

Psalm 119:73-80

What is the writer saying?

How can I apply this to my life?

In verse 63 and twice in today's section, the psalmist speaks of his relationship with those who fear the Lord. He wants their companionship, and they want his. The psalmist was severely afflicted. The affliction turned him to God's Word for comfort (v. 50). The Word showed him that he had gone astray (v. 67), and that the Lord, in righteous judgment, had brought the affliction upon him (v. 75). The psalmist realized that his chastisement was a manifestation of God's faithfulness to His own attributes of righteousness and justice. God was also showing His faithfulness as a loving Father (Hebrews 12:6-7).

In Deuteronomy 10:12, Moses instructed the Lord's people that they are required "to *fear* the LORD thy God, to *walk* in all his ways, and to *love* him, and to *serve* the LORD thy God with all thy heart and with all thy soul." This sequence is important; the affliction brought to the psalmist brought him the fear of the Lord. It also brought him a desire to be taught by God's Word. From the Word he learned that the God of righteousness is also a forgiving God of merciful kindness. He asked to be a recipient of God's tender mercies, with his reason being his delight in God's Word (as evidenced by his meditation in God's precepts). His further request was that the proud ones who dealt with him perversely, without cause, be brought to shame, like the shame they had brought to him. While they were punished, he wanted his heart to be made sound by the Lord's statutes.

Life stEP A dedicated Christian should fear and love the Lord. The two attitudes are essential and inseparable. Fear prevents love from degenerating into presumptuous familiarity. Without love, fear would result in cringing dread. Neither of these would be pleasing to God.

Psalm 119:81-88

What is the writer saying?

How can I apply this to my life?

pray Uganda – Pray for the continued and steady growth of the ministries in Uganda. For God to supply workers and open doors of opportunity.

"My soul faints." "My eyes fail." "They persecute me." "Help me!" The words are those of one who is deeply depressed by sore oppression. The psalmist appears to have reached a low point. "When will you comfort me?" He's saying, "I may not have many days left to serve You, so when will You execute judgment on my persecutors?" His faith is wavering because he sees no action from God against his oppressors.

Actually, the psalmist is on the way up. Although his reaction to oppression is pulling him down, he will be lifted up by his course of actins: His hope is founded on the Word. He is seeking comfort from "the Father of mercies, and the God of all comfort; Who comforteth us in all our tribulation" (2 Corinthians 1:3-4). He is calling to memory what he has read in God's Word. He is proclaiming God's faithfulness and His loving-kindness while still observing His precepts and testimonies.

The psalmist is in greater need of having his faith stabilized than he is of seeing judgment upon his persecutors. The Word in which he delights and upon which he meditates (vv. 77-78) will produce that faith for him (Romans 10:17). That faith will then permit him to see what is not visible. Then he will find rest for his soul (Psalm 37:7; Matthew 11:29). His prayers will be answered to his complete satisfaction, although not necessarily according to his thinking.

It is a work of the indwelling Holy Spirit to bring us to our knees when we have a pressing need. However, what the loving Father chooses to provide us with may not be what we asked for. There may be a more urgent need that we did not comprehend. He will supply according to that need.

Psalm 119:89-96

What is the writer saying?

How can I apply this to my life?

This section is the first where we don't find a verse employing one of the eight designations for God's Word; however, the word "faithfulness" in verse 90 has been translated "truth" in verse 30 and elsewhere. Verses 89-90 tell us our generation has equal opportunity for knowing God's perfect truth, as did the generation living when the original text was written (see also Psalms 100:5 and 117:2). Psalm 33:11 teaches the same principle.

God's Word is available to us only by God's direction. He used imperfect servants to translate His Word into the language we speak, and no translation is perfect in every detail. Verse 89 says that God's Word is settled (established, preserved, held firmly) in Heaven, not on earth. God sent the perfect author of His perfect Word to dwell within us as our teacher and guide (John 14:26, 16:13). If we trust Him, He will guide us to use His Word to the extent that we are yielded to Him and His direction for our lives. In John 7:17, Jesus gives a promise, preceded by a condition: that we must know God's doctrine (teaching) in order to do God's will. The problem is that we want the benefit of the promise without fully meeting the condition. We have our own preferences of translations and interpreters with little attempt to get the mind of the Spirit through ourselves totally yielding to Him for direction.

Here are some questions for self-examination: How much prayer do I put into the time I spend reading the Bible or others' interpretations of the Bible? How much Spirit direction do I seek in choosing speakers and writers who interpret God's Word? How much do I depend on the Holy Spirit's enlightenment of Scriptures?

Psalm 119:97-104

What is the writer saying?

How can I apply this to my life?

pray Portugal – For God to burden hearts with a passion to evangelize other Portuguese–speaking nations.

This is the first in which the psalmist asks nothing of God—there are no petitions. Also, he begins emphasizing the word *love* in describing his dedication to God's Word. Look again at Deuteronomy 10:12. Before this, the psalmist has been centering on fearing God in order to walk in His ways. The Word of God next teaches him to love God, and His Word, in order "to serve the LORD thy God with all thy heart and with all thy soul."

Love of the Word is evidenced by continually meditating it. Through meditation, the psalmist entered into the benefits of the Word as well as the obligations. He became more focused on the promises in the Word than on the afflictions by his enemies, because meditation made him wiser than his enemies (v. 98).

These verses focus on the importance of each individual personally seeking knowledge through God's Word.

Teachers of the Word are helpful, but one gains insight and understanding through meditation (v. 99). Experience brings a degree of understanding and wisdom, although it can sometimes be a hard teacher. Yet getting understanding and wisdom is sweet like honey when there is a love relationship with the Word. Jeremiah 15:16 says, "Thy words were found, and I did eat them, and thy Word was unto me the joy and rejoicing of mine heart." Psalm 19:10-11 adds, "More to be desired are they than gold, yea, than much fine gold: sweeter also than honey and the honeycomb. Moreover by them is thy servant warned: and in keeping of them there is great reward."

Is there a way to acquire spiritual understanding other than by meditation on God's Word? Can a cow chew its cud without first eating something? Is it possible to meditate without first hiding the Word in the heart?

Psalm 119:105-112

What is the writer saying?

How can I apply this to my life?

The psalmist confirms his vow to perform according to the Lord's righteous judgments and His statutes, always and to the end. Nothing will deter him—not the darkness of the way, not affliction, not dangers to his life, not the snares of the wicked. He will walk in darkness of night with the light of God's Word. With a rejoicing heart, he will offer praise and thanksgiving as his sacrifice to God (Psalm 50:14, 54:6, 107:22). He will not forget God's law or err from His precepts.

Jeremiah 10:23 recognizes that we cannot guide our own steps in this world of spiritual darkness: "O, LORD, I know that the way of man is not in himself: it is not in man that walketh to direct his steps." Without the light of God's Word we will surely join the sinning angels and the false prophets in chains of darkness forever (2 Peter 2:4, 17). God has given us prophecy as a "light that shineth in a dark place, until the day dawn; and the day star arise in your hearts" (2 Peter 1:19). As we walk on the pathway of life towards that light, it "shineth more and more unto the perfect day" (Proverbs 4:18). But we need lights along the way to guide us to that perfect light, and a lamp to show us where to place each footstep to avoid stumbling on the stones in the pathway. The Word is both of those lights.

Life stEP For Israel as a nation, the light of Bible prophecy is the promise of the dawning of the millennial day, when the Messiah appears on the eastern horizon as the "sun of righteousness" (Isaiah 60:1-3; Malachi 4:2). For the church, the Morning Star will appear before the dawning of that day (Revelation 22:16). His arrival, and our salvation, is the blessed hope already shining in our hearts (Titus 2:13).

Psalm 119:113-120

What is the writer saying?

How can I apply this to my life?

"I hate." "I love." "I hope." "I am afraid." In this section, the psalmist lets us know that he is a person of emotions. Twice in the eight verses, he describes his emotion towards God's Word as one of love. Does God have emotions? Of course. He loves (John 3:16), and love is an element of His essence (1 John 4:8). He is love and is able to bestow His ability to love (1 John 4:19). "The God of Love" is one of His names (2 Corinthians 13:11).

The psalmist expresses his hatred for every false way (v. 104), for wrong thinking (v. 113), and for lying (v. 163). Does God hate? The Bible tells of objects and behaviors that God hates (seven are listed in Proverbs 6:16-19), but never in Scriptures is He seen as the God of Hate.

Another name for God is "the God of Hope" (Romans 15:13). He does not need *to* hope but rather *is* hope, since hope is the *present* appropriation of a *future* joyous certainty (Hebrews 6:18-20). It is a gift from God for us "to lay hold upon" in this life while looking forward to a time with Him. There is no need for hope in Heaven—all that we hope for will be realized.

The psalmist also has the emotion of fear. When we are properly in awe of God and revere His Word, we don't need to fear anything else. When considering the emotion of fear, we should keep in mind the promise of 1 John 4:18. There is a fear that complements love in order to keep us in a right relationship with God, and there is a fear that torments.

Life **stEP**
We are creatures of emotion. Only the Holy Spirit, through the Word of God, can properly channel those emotions. The psalmist expresses emotions such as "delight" and "love" towards God's Word. We need to frequently take inventory of our emotions toward God and His Word and make sure we have the correct attitude.

Psalm 119:121-128

What is the writer saying?

How can I apply this to my life?

pray Philippines – For effective outreach to youth through evangelistic sporting events.

Some suggest that "judgment" in verses 84 and 121, as well as "faithfulness" in verse 90, does not designate the Word of God. Clearly, verses 122 and 132 contain no synonym for the Word. Otherwise, every verse in Psalm 119 names God's Word in some form.

A major portion of the psalm consists of petitions asking for the Lord's ministry on behalf of the psalmist. There are six such petitions in verses 121-125. Verse 122, however, is the only place in the psalm where he asks the Lord to be "surety" for him. A "surety" is one who assumes the obligation of someone else's failure (Proverbs 6:1). At the cross, Jesus did this by making full payment to God for our obligation to Him (the penalty of our sin). As our surety, He paid for what we owed but couldn't pay. If my true heart's desire is to please God, He will receive my imperfect service because Jesus Christ, my Mediator, makes up for my lack each day (Hebrews 7:22, 8:6).

The psalmist often submits reasons to God for why his petitions should be answered. He does this three times in verses 121-125. The Lord should grant his petitions because of his righteousness, because of God's mercy, and because, as a servant, he is entitled to be taught knowledge with understanding.

The psalmist knows the Lord will certainly deal with those who live as though there is no word from God. From observation, he believes the time has come for God to act.

Life stEP

From our present-day vantage point, we can conclude with the psalmist that world society has "made void Thy law," and it is time for God to act. Until He does, we should follow the example of the psalmist—loving God's commandments more than riches and esteeming His precepts while hating every false way.

Psalm 119:129-136

What is the writer saying?

How can I apply this to my life?

pray United Kingdom — Over 40% of evangelical churches have no one under the age of 20 in attendance. Pray for a harvest of souls amongst young people.

In the second half of the psalm, the psalmist has used the word "love" in expressing his regard for God's Word more and more. In verses 113, 119, and 127 he talked again about loving what God says. But it is not until today's section that we see the word "love" toward God Himself. The "name" of God (v. 132) includes all that He has revealed about Himself. God is zealous concerning His name; it is not to be used lightly or in vain (Exodus 20:7). The psalmist still appears to be hesitant in expressing his love for the Lord, but he wants to be identified with those who love His name.

In verse 133, the psalmist knows he is not capable of directing his own steps (Jeremiah 10:23). But he does know where the light comes from to keep iniquity from dominating him. The light of understanding enters his soul through his intense thirst for God's Word, which gives the direction he needs.

Verse 135's phrase "make Thy face to shine" derives from the Aaronic benediction of Numbers 6:24-26. These words are quoted several times in the Psalms, including three times in Psalm 80. The psalmist is saying, "Deal favorably with me concerning my request."

Compare verse 136 with Jeremiah 9:1, 13:17, and 14:17. Jeremiah wept over the plight of those who disregarded God's Word, as did the psalmist. So did Jesus (Luke 19:41). When was the last time you shed tears for the lost?

Life stEP Many Christians who would not think of deliberately using God's name in vain nevertheless fall into the habit of using exclamations that are obvious substitutes for His Holy name.

Psalm 119:137-144

What is the writer saying?

How can I apply this to my life?

The Hebrew word for righteous begins with the letter TSADHE, therefore, it is not surprising that this section begins with "righteous" and that the theme of the section is God's righteousness. The words "righteous," "upright," and "righteousness" appear six times in the eight verses.

Our God is a righteous God; therefore, His Word is righteous (v. 137). Our God is a faithful God; therefore, His Word is faithful (v. 138). Our God is a pure God; therefore, His Word is pure (v. 140). Our God is a God of truth; therefore, His Word is truth (v. 142). Our God is an eternal God; therefore, His Word is eternal (vv. 142-144). These are all sufficient causes for the psalmist to be consumed with zeal and love for the Word. The trouble and anguish that have taken hold of him are overridden by his delight in the Word and its promises.

Throughout the entire psalm, the psalmist continues to cry out for more learning, more knowledge, and more understanding. "Give me understanding that I may learn" (v. 73). "Give me understanding that I may know" (v. 125). "Give me understanding and I shall live" (v. 144). Instruction, knowledge, and understanding are pre-requisites for the psalmist if he is to live. Since he knows the Word is the source of understanding (v. 130), his zeal and love for the Word become more intense.

 As you read verse after verse about the psalmist's zeal and love for the Word, and his delight in it, something should be happening inside of you. Measure your zeal, love, and delight against his. What does God's Word mean to you?

Psalm 119:145-152

What is the writer saying?

How can I apply this to my life?

pray South Korea – Complete renewing of the mind for South Koreans saved out of Buddhism and Confucianism.

Today we again consider the subject of meditation. We've seen that meditating on God's Word is a major theme of Psalm 119. We've learned of the many benefits promised by God to those who take time for meditation. At this point we may ask, "When could I possibly find the time for such meditation?"

In modern English, verse 148 reads, "My eyes anticipate the night watches, that I might meditate in Your Word." The psalmist looks forward to the times he wakes up during the night so he can have the opportunity to meditate on the Word. Following this thought through the book of Psalms, we read: "Commune with your own heart upon your bed, and be still" (Psalm 4:4); "My reins (heart) also instruct me in the night seasons" (Psalm 16:7); "In the night his song shall be with me, and my prayer unto the God of my life" (Psalm 42:8); "My soul shall be satisfied as with marrow and fatness; and my mouth shall praise thee with joyful lips; when I remember thee upon my bed, and meditate on Thee in the night watches" (Psalm 63:5-6); and "I have remembered thy name, O LORD, in the night, and have kept thy law" (Psalm 119:55). Meditation is a blessed cure for insomnia! God will bless your meditation and transform it into restful sleep when needed.

Life stEP Let's remember that effectual meditation first requires commitment of God's Word to memory. Ask the God for verses that He wants you to specifically memorize for later meditation.

Psalm 119:153-160

What is the writer saying?

How can I apply this to my life?

Don Lough Jr., wisdom as he directs Word of Life Fellowship Inc.

There is a Hebrew word that is used three times in this section and sixteen times altogether in Psalm 119. Nine of those times the psalmist uses the word in petitioning the Lord. The King James Version renders the petition "quicken me." Some other English language Bibles translate it "revive me." Just what is the psalmist asking the Lord to do for him when he urgently cries "quicken me"? In verses 154 and 156, he adds, "according to Thy Word" (judgments). He expects to receive what for asks for because he is beseeching a God Who is merciful and kind to those who love His precepts. When the psalmist makes the same plea in verses 37 and 40, the context implies that he is asking for spiritual renewal and spiritual fervor. In verses 88 and 107 he seems to have his physical well-being in mind. His thought appears to be, "My enemies are after me—keep me alive so that I can praise You." Considering the use of the same word in verses 50 and 93 we can conclude that the psalmist is primarily concerned about his spiritual connection with the Lord. His heart's desire is for God to use His Word to do whatever is necessary to infuse and maintain vibrancy in his relationship with them.

The psalmist grieves for those who transgress because they don't observe the Word, while he is instead sustained by placing his confidence in that which is both true and everlasting.

Life stEP

Nothing in this world is everlasting except for the Word of God and the souls of human beings. In what should we invest our time and other resources in, then? Human society places much emphasis upon preparation for the future. For what future should we be preparing?

f r i d a y 46

Psalm 119:161-168

What is the writer saying?

How can I apply this to my life?

pray   Pray for those in your church who are seeking employment.

Although there are more than 100 petitions in Psalm 119, there are none in this section. These verses reveal that when a heart is filled with awe, rejoicing, and loving the Word, there is no room left for fear of persecutors. The liars are still there, but they do not rule the heart. The treasures found in the Word possess the thoughts instead.

"Seven times a day" (v. 164) is a poetic way of saying "all day long" or "constantly." In verse 165, inner peace overflowing into praise is the product of love for the Word. This love dispels all of the offenses that can cause stumbling stones in the pathway of life. Love for the Word brings love to all who regard the Word (1 John 2:10: "He that loveth his brother abideth in the light, and there is none occasion of stumbling in him").

The psalmist's occupation with the Word has brought him to a point of expressing his love for the Word three times in this eight-verse section. Not only that, he now expresses that love with superlatives like "exceedingly." It has brought him a hope of salvation "as an anchor of the soul, both sure and stedfast" (Hebrews 6:19). He has acquired "a strong consolation" because he has "fled for refuge to lay hold upon the hope set before" (Hebrews 6:18) him. He is "in hope of eternal life, which God, that cannot lie, promised before the world began" (Titus 1:2).

All the ways he should conduct himself in are before him because he determined to observe the precepts and testimonies of the Lord.

Life stEP   Oh, that we would reach the point in our relationship with God that His peace and our praise would override our concern for our circumstances! Then we could confidently say, "All my ways are before Thee."

Psalm 119:169-176

What is the writer saying?

How can I apply this to my life?

At first reading, this section appears to be a step backward from the lofty spiritual attainments of yesterday's verses. Actually, the psalmist is summarizing the spiritual journey he has taken. He has come from saying "my soul cleaveth unto the dust" (v. 25), "my soul melteth for heaviness" (v. 28), and "I went astray" (v. 67), to declaring "I rejoice at Thy word" (v. 162), "seven times a day do I praise Thee" (v. 164), "great peace have they which love thy law" (v. 165), and "I love them [Thy testimonies] exceedingly" (v. 167). In Psalm 119, the psalmist has reflected on the ups and downs of his spiritual growth, even if not in chronological order.

Here in the final section, he relates those reflections to his desires for a continued spiritual relationship with the Lord through His Word. The Word has affected his desires (vv. 169-170), his speech (vv. 171-172), his choices (v. 173), and his emotions (v. 174)—his entire life (v. 175).

Late in his ministry, after a life of dedicated service, the apostle Paul said that he still had not attained; he continued to press forward (Philippians 3:12-14). The psalmist acknowledges this same idea. In his desperate condition, having "gone astray like a lost sheep," he still needed a seeking shepherd, lest he forget the Lord's commandments.

"All we like sheep have gone astray; we have turned every one to his own way; and the LORD hath laid on Him the iniquity of us all" (Isaiah 53:6). We are included in the "all" at the beginning of this verse; therefore, how glad we are that we are also included in the "all" at the end of the verse. "For you *were* like sheep going astray" (1 Peter 2:25). The shepherd being sought in verse 176 is available to us, too.

The author of Romans is Paul, the apostle to the Gentiles. He writes to Gentile believers in the city of Rome, although he had not yet visited Rome, and the people he addresses by name are friends he met elsewhere. The book is dated A.D. 57 and would have been written from Corinth on Paul's third missionary journey.

In the book, we can see Paul's desire to•move his base to Rome for westward expansion (toward Spain). The end of the Book of Acts found Paul under house arrest in Rome. From a few statements in the New Testament and the consistent teachings of the early church fathers, Paul was apparently released from that house imprisonment. Tradition says Paul not only made it to Spain but also to the farthest reaches of the Roman Empire, such as Great Britain.

The Book of Romans has been called the "Foundation of Christian Theology," the "Cathedral of the Christian Faith," the "Constitution of Christianity," and the "Masterpiece of the Apostle Paul." It had a profound impact on Martin Luther and the Reformers. Historian Philip Schaff said, "It is the most remarkable production of the most remarkable man. It is his heart. It contains his theology, theoretical and practical, for which he lived and died. It gives the clearest and fullest exposition of the doctrines of sin and grace and the best possible solution of the universal dominion of sin and death in the universal redemption by the second Adam." John Calvin testified: "If man understands it, he has a sure road open for him to the understanding of the whole Scripture."

Romans and Colossians are the only letters written to churches Paul had not visited. In Romans, he quotes extensively from the Old Testament, referring to fifty-six passages, as opposed to forty-seven in his other twelve epistles total (excluding Hebrews, which has thirty-nine and whose authorship is disputed). There is a particular emphasis on Isaiah and the Psalms. Compared to other New Testament books, only Matthew uses more, with sixty-seven in one book, although Luke in his two works (Luke and Acts) quotes sixty-nine.

The book of Romans is powerful for its tightly reasoned presentation of salvation. The Greek language (as opposed to the picturesque Hebrew language) was ideally suited to this kind of theological discussion. Paul was also ideally suited, both because of his Jewish training (he would have held the equivalent of a doctorate degree in both religious studies and law and was certainly fluent in at least three languages) and also because he was the man chosen to bring "Jewish" salvation to the Gentile world. In the book, we find the atmosphere of the arena, forged in the heat of debate!

Theme of Romans: "The Righteousness of God"
Chapters 1-3: "The need for God's righteousness"
Chapter 4: "The provision of God's righteousness"
Chapters 5-8: "The results of God's righteousness"
Chapters 9-11: "The defense of God's righteousness"
Chapters 12-16: "The application of God's righteousness."

Romans 1:1-7

What is the writer saying?

How can I apply this to my life?

Romans 1:1-7 is Paul's greeting to the Romans. Notice that in verse 1, Paul refers to himself as a "servant" (*bond-servant*) of Christ Jesus. This refers to the Jewish practice, mentioned in both Exodus and Deuteronomy, of putting a fellow Jew into servitude for six years if he owed a debt. On the seventh year, he was to go free with his debt canceled. But if he wanted to stay with the wealthy land owner, he could become a bond-servant. Upon choosing this role, there was a ceremony in which his ear lobe would be pierced with an awl, marking the fact that he was now a bond-servant for life.

Also in verse 1, Paul says he was set apart for the Gospel. The Greek word for "separated" (*set apart*) means "from the horizon." The idea is that when you look at the horizon, there is a clear demarcation between the brighter sky and the darker land mass.

In verse 2, the word "promised" is a complicated Greek word made of three separate words: *before*, *upon*, and to *proclaim*. This speaks of something that was determined long ago, and with finality. The Greek word was also used to refer to a legal summons issued by a policeman or an officer of the court. Here it is emphasizing that Paul's position in Christ was no fluke.

Verse 4 says the Son of God demonstrates "power" in "the resurrection." This power is not just His own resurrection, but also in HIs making way for the resurrection of all righteous individuals. The Greek word for power is *dunamis*, from which we get our modern word *dynamite*. It refers to an explosive type of power.

Life stEP In verse 5, Paul's motivation is to bring glory to God. This is a good reminder to us: when we go to God in prayer for the things we think we need, our prayers should be motivated by the desire to bring glory to God, not just for our own personal needs and wants.

Romans 1:8-17

What is the writer saying?

How can I apply this to my life?

pray   Ecuador – Pray for God to call more laborers to reach the impoverished of Quito and Guayaquil.

In Romans 1:8-17, we have Paul's reason for writing the letter, which highlights how he felt toward the Romans and what some of his aims were for them. In verse 9, the amazing intensity of Paul's prayer life is recorded. The same Greek phrase is used in Romans 9:2 to refer to the incessant heart pain Paul had for his fellow Jews in his desire for their salvation.

In verse 11, the word *established* means "a prop." Paul wants to use his spiritual gift in the Romans' midst so he could be a prop, or support, to their spiritual life. In verse 12, the word *comforted* literally means "with comforters." In John 14-17, the Holy Spirit is referred to as a Comforter from the Greek word *paraclete*, which means "one called alongside to help" (*para* = "alongside," as in *parallel* lines). "Com" means *with* and "fort" refers to *strength*. This means the Holy Spirit is giving us strength before we go out into the battle.

In verse 14, Paul differentiates between Greeks and barbarians. By Greeks, he is referring to educated people such as Socrates, Aristotle, and Plato. The word *barbarian* was created from the unintelligible speech invaders of this culture spoke. The Greeks referred to anyone who could not speak Greek as barbarians, considering them uneducated.

Verses 16-17 are the theme of the letter. Verse 17 is quoting Habakkuk 2:4, a verse quoted three times in the New Testament, each time with a slightly different emphasis. In Romans, the emphasis is on the *righteous man*. (In Galatians 3:11, the emphasis is on "shall live," and in Hebrews 10:38, the emphasis is on "by faith.")

Life stEP   Paul knew where his power came from—the Holy Spirit. We may feel like children in our spiritual walk, but warriors for Christ *are* children—children empowered by an indwelling Holy Spirit.

Romans 1:18-32

What is the writer saying?

How can I apply this to my life?

In verse 18, we are reminded of Ecclesiastes 3:11, which says God has set eternity in their hearts. This means God has placed within man a natural sense of God's existence, God's authority, and man's responsibility, to obey the Creator God. It also means that man intuitively knows that life does not end with a hole in the ground. In verse 19, Paul argues that a knowledge of God is common sense. The word "manifest" means "to lay bare, open for every man to see and comprehend." This is what Psalm 19 is arguing. The physical universe—the sun, the moon, the stars, the mountains, lakes, the green valleys—all scream out that there is a Creator God. In fact, Psalm 19 says we feel the heat of the sun, implying that even a blind person who cannot see the sun can still know that it, and God, is there.

Paul describes the devolution of the Gentile world. In verse 22, the word "fools" is the Greek word *morons*. In the Bible, the word *moron* is not referring to a stupid person, but rather to someone who is morally or theologically deficient. For instance, the adulterer is called a fool. He is a moral moron. Or, "The fool has said in his heart, there is no God" (Psalm 14:1). He is a theological moron. In verse 23, Paul argues that in the devolution of the Gentile, he confusingly worshiped the creature instead of the Creator. As a result, in verses 24-32, Paul concludes that God has abandoned these men to their sinful ways. God is like a rider who gives the horse his head and lets him go wherever he wants. In verses 26-27, Paul condemns lesbian and homosexual sexual activity, arguing that it is not natural, not inborn, and not a normal physical activity.

Life stEP

Man has a sense that there's life after death. We can use this to our advantage when we witness, knowing that even when a person proudly says he is an atheist or agnostic, deep down inside he knows differently.

Romans 2:1-16

What is the writer saying?

How can I apply this to my life?

pray Papua New Guinea – Effectiveness of literacy ministries that enable nationals to study God's Word.

In Romans 1:18-32, the Gentile needs God's righteousness. Now here in verses 1-16, Paul explains how the moralist needs God's righteousness. The moralist in Paul's thought is that *noble savage*, the Gentile who escapes the vulgarities of pagan religion for a personal philosophy of life that promotes a high moral code. Since the moralist has not received the Law of Moses like the Jews did, he thinks he can escape any legal punishment. Paul argues that ignorance of the law is no excuse, and that even without the Law of Moses, the moralist stands condemned by his own words. At the final judgment, all God would have to do is play back all the comments the moralist had ever made about other people's behavior and attitudes, and then judge the moralist by his own man-made laws.

In verse 1, "inexcusable" means you have *no apology*—you can't worm your way out of this logical trap. In verse 5, "impenitent" means "no change of mind" (no repentance). The smugly self-righteous barely hide their contempt for God's authority in their life as they pull the cloak of *socially accepted behavior* around them. "Render" (v. 6) means *to give back*. The saints will receive "immortality" (v. 7; no corruption), while those who reject God's gracious offer of life-transformation will devolve into a worse condition than any horror show could imagine. Paul talks about man's "conscience" (v. 15), which refers to joint knowledge ("to know with"). This is a knowledge of our behavior in comparison to a known standard. Every man has a natural sense of right and wrong, but that small voice can be ignored, damaged, or programmed with wrong standards, making it ineffective as a guide.

Life stEP We can safely let our conscience be our guide only when it is programmed with the Word of God, and we allow the Holy Spirit to control it.

Romans 2:17-29

What is the writer saying?

How can I apply this to my life?

pray Serbia – For genuine forgiveness between ethnic groups that have been at war for so long. Pray that people would rebuild trust and cooperation.

In Romans 2:17-3:8, Paul's attention turns to his fellow Jews, who also need God's righteousness. He argues that the Jews have sinned by not keeping the Law. Most Jews of Paul's day would have argued vehemently that they were keeping the Law, but Paul knows the difference between obeying the Law out of respect for Jehovah and obeying the Jewish re-interpretation of the Law of Moses for social acceptance and self-righteousness. For instance, Exodus 20 tells us we are to honor our father and mother, but the Jews reworked their understanding of the Law to allow them to not follow the core principle. Jesus condemned the practice of religious Jews claiming that their personal possessions had been given as a "gift" (*corban*) to the Lord and therefore could not be used to support their elderly parents while they themselves continued to enjoy these possessions (Mark 7:11). As hard as it is to imagine, it appears that some of the Jews of Paul's day were known for even worse offenses, such as adultery. Perhaps this explains the strange event in John 8 where it appears that none of the men who brought accusations against the woman taken in adultery felt guiltless (of the same offense?) to throw the first stone! "Blasphemed" (v. 24) means "to injure with speech." By the religious authorities' poor example, Judaism had become odious to even the pagan Gentiles. As twenty-first century Gentile Christians, we have to be careful with our use of this material, in that coming from our lips, it can easily be interpreted as anti-Semitic—a real problem in the history of the church and in church-synagogue relations. Paul, on the other hand, was an insider (Pharisee) with firsthand knowledge of the hypocrisy of the human heart, whether Gentile, moralist, or Jew!

Life **stEP** Does the watching world have reason to accuse the Church—or you—of hypocrisy today?

Romans 3:1-8

What is the writer saying?

How can I apply this to my life?

Paul explains that his fellow Jews have sinned by not believing the promise of God. They had the responsibility of obeying the 613 rules in the Mosaic Law and were expected to be circumcised (a Jewish rite given to Abraham in Genesis 12). These burdens and the failure of most Jews to obey leads to the suggestion that perhaps it wasn't a benefit to be one of the chosen people. (As some modern Jewish comedians have said, "God, could you please choose someone else?")

The word "oracles" (v. 2) means "little words" (referring to their preciousness, as we might refer to a child as "little one") and is used of the high priest's breastplate in Exodus 28:15. It was there in the breastplate that the Urim and Thummim ("lights" and "perfections") were kept. We don't know exactly how they functioned, but they represented the high priest's right to ask God questions for leading the Israelites, which He would answer. The simplest idea is that they provided "yes" or "no" answers. Some rabbis argue that the letters spelling out the names of the tribes of Israel on the gemstones of the breastplate would light up to spell out specific responses. Paul's idea is that it was a tremendous advantage and great privilege to have received the Word of God. It is from statements like this that we suggest that every book of the Old and New Testaments was penned by Jewish individuals. The only possible exception among the known authors of the Bible is Luke, the doctor. He clearly was raised in a Gentile culture, but there are good reasons for thinking that even he was Jewish.

In verse 4, we have the first of many occurrences of an emphatic phrase that Paul uses to express an illogical and unacceptable conclusion. It is translated "God forbid" and means "let it not be."

Like the people Paul mentions, man will do almost anything to justify his sinful lifestyle. Avoid blame-shifting and self-justification!

Romans 3:9-20

What is the writer saying?

How can I apply this to my life?

After dealing with three categories of humans—the Gentiles (pagans), the moralists, and the Jews—Paul now concludes that all are the same in that they all need God's righteousness. The Jews, while having a great historic advantage, don't have a personal advantage over the Gentiles, because the sin nature of each man blinds him to spiritual truth; no man seeks the true God on his own. Man has a natural sense of the divine, which leads him to seek answers and to claim that he wants to pursue *ultimate truth*, but the sin nature re-directs that pursuit into selfish avenues. That is why so many of the gods and goddesses of the ancient world behave like humans—they were made in man's image!

The sad story of humanity is that, left to our own devices, not one of us would ever reach out to the true God. This is the theological concept of "total depravity"—not that every man is as bad as he could be, but that every man is as helpless as he possibly could be. Paul says that as a result, we are all useless (v. 12, "unprofitable"). Our immediate response is to say, "Not me! Not my friends!" But all we have to do is pay attention to our attitudes and realize that, but for the grace of God, "there go I" into the worst activities known to man. Our newspapers serve up daily reminders of this in every society in the world.

"Guilty" in verse 19 means "under judgment" (brought before a judge in a court of law for a trial). Paul then explains the purpose of the Law of Moses. It was not given as a guide to merit salvation, but rather as a proof that man stands condemned before a Holy God.

Life **stEP**

For those who never have believed to the point of salvation, the law becomes their judge at the final judgment. (Ignorance of the law is no excuse, as the primary laws—"thou shalt not steal," etc.—are very logical and self-evident.) Those who become saved do so once they are convinced of their lost condition by the power of the Word of God.

sunday 48

Romans 3:21-31

What is the writer saying?

How can I apply this to my life?

pray Slovakia – God to mobilize broadcasters committed to producing programming in the Roma language.

If man cannot merit salvation by *law righteousness*, then what hope do we have? Paul points to *faith righteousness*, which has nothing to do with our behavior but everything to do with Christ's character and behavior. (Christ is both righteous by nature and by His lifestyle.) The English word "righteousness" comes from the Old English word *rightwiseness*. "Wise" here is the idea of *way*. Together, it means "the right or straight way." The opposite term is *wrongwise*, with "wrong" coming from "wrung," which we still use in phrases such as, "Keep it up and I'll wring your neck!" Wring or wrung means "twist." The opposite of righteousness is twistedness. "Sinned" means to "miss the mark"—in this case, the mark of God's holiness. "Short" means "to come late, be last, be inferior." Every man falls short of God's perfect standard and His *manifest excellence* ("glory").

"Justified" (v. 24) describes the legal act of being "declared righteous" in a court of law—in this case, the ultimate court in the universe! The word "redemption" is an economic term used in the slave trade to refer to a slave who is "purchased, loosed, and set free." "Propitiation" (v. 25) refers to the "satisfaction of God's anger at sin." Christ is called the "sacrifice that propitiates."

"Remission" (v. 25) means that as we accept God's offer of salvation, God passes over our debt. In the process of this financial and legal transaction, God publicly announces ("declare") that He has done this for us, and therefore, we can be considered righteous. This righteousness is not our good works. Actually, when Christ forgives our sins, at that point we are only neutral. It is when He gives us His own righteousness that we then have positive holiness.

Life stEP

In reality, "paid in full" is stamped on our account in Heaven. The requirements of the law have been met with the blood of Christ!

Romans 4:1-12

What is the writer saying?

How can I apply this to my life?

pray Eritrea – For Christians to be fervent for Jesus and make a significant impact on their nation and beyond.

In verses 1-8, Paul re-emphasizes the fact that we have a problem, not just because we are born with a bend toward sin, or because we do sin, but also because we cannot work to reverse that. "Reckoned" (v. 4) comes from same root word as the word for logic. It means that we should *calculate* or *count* something as being true. Paul uses it nine times in chapter 4. He wants us to be like a sharp accountant who keeps track of every last penny. Unfortunately, translators don't always translate the same Greek word the same way in every occurrence. The word for "reckoned" actually appears in verse 5 as "counted" and in verse 8 as "impute" ("to take into account").

In verses 9-12, Paul shifts from *good works* to *good ceremonies*. Neither have saving grace. The Jews were proud of their ceremony of circumcision, but Paul says it does not save. It was the "sign" (distinguishing mark or autograph) that God gave to the Jews (v. 11). It was also a "seal" (referring to rabbis calling circumcision "the seal of Abraham"), which in Biblical times was a mark of ownership and security. This distinguishing mark would be pressed, such as with a signet ring, into clay or a wax ball in order to represent the particular individual. The Jews weren't the only ancient society to practice circumcision, but it was the covenantal sign for the Jews. Every Jewish boy is welcomed into the Jewish family in a circumcision ceremony (*Brit Milah*) on the eighth day of his life. Circumcision may be a reminder of Isaac's supernatural conception (pre-figuring Christ's); the importance of sexual sanctity; or the need for the shedding of blood and self-sacrifice in a right relationship with God. Paul points out that God had already declared Abraham righteous by his faith *before* he was circumcised.

Life stEP Even Gentiles can follow Abraham in his example of having faith in God and thereby being declared a righteous individual.

Romans 4:13-25

What is the writer saying?

How can I apply this to my life?

pray Croatia – Evangelical Christians have cared for the ethnic communities during war. Pray that this testimony of love and compassion will have a lasting impact.

Good works don't save. (For instance, Abel was saved by the faith he displayed when he brought his animal sacrifice, not by any good things he did. Likewise, it was Cain's attitude—not his sacrifice—that condemned him.) Circumcision doesn't save, nor does the Law of Moses (vv. 13-15), because only faith in God saves (vv. 16-25).

A "transgression" (v. 15) occurs when someone *goes aside or oversteps a boundary*. This is trespassing, implying a violation of a known law. The law does not make men sinners, but it makes them transgressors; their sin then becomes exceedingly sinful (Romans 7:7).

"Hope" in the English of yesteryear meant "favorable and confident expectation," not the wishfulness that we associate with it today. Abraham was told he would have a son. He believed this would happen, even when it was humanly impossible due to his advanced age and the age of his wife, Sarah. Paul says he "staggered [wavered] not" (v. 20). This does not speak of a little faith that gets weaker and stronger in turn, but rather comes from a word that means *not argumentative*. If Abraham had argued or wavered, it would have meant no faith at all. But Abraham was "fully persuaded," or able to carry the full load of what was promised, showing no doubt or uncertainty (v. 21). As a result, this faith of Abraham was "imputed" or considered righteousness.

Jesus Christ was "delivered up" (v. 25) by God on the cross for our sins. The word is used to describe molten metal being poured into a mold to give it a purposeful shape. Christ was raised by God to prove that our justification was acceptable to Him.

Doing things to impress God and merit His favor flatters the human ego but falls short of what God wants. We have nothing to be proud of and can only cast ourselves on the mercy and grace of God for our salvation.

Romans 5:1-11

What is the writer saying?

How can I apply this to my life?

pray Papua New Guinea – For Christian youth camps to see significant salvation and consecration decisions.

Having described man's need for God's righteousness in chapters 1-3 and the provision of this righteousness in chapter 4, Paul explains the results of God's righteousness in chapters 5-8. In verses 1-11, he talks about the benefits of this righteousness. In verse 1, "peace" is the root of the English word *irenic*. This word occurs in every New Testament book except 1 John. It is used to describe peace between men and nations, and also between man and God. It speaks of freedom from war, crime, contention, and strife. The Hebrew equivalent is *shalom*, which has the root meaning of "wholeness." In Joshua 8:31, it is used of uncut stones, and in Nehemiah 6:15, of the finished wall. It is the heart of the name Jerusalem ("city of peace").

The "peace offering" in the Old Testament is translated "salvation offering" by the Greek translators of the Old Testament, a good translation because Christ's death has brought salvation and peace to mankind.

In verse 2, "have access" means "to lead to someone for a formal introduction." The phrase only occurs three times in the New Testament, and all three times, it is because we are "in Christ." Likewise in verse 8, "commendeth" means "to place together so as to introduce one person to another favorably." Finally, in verse 10 the word "reconciled" means "to put an end to hostilities." What a picture of the ultimate Peace Negotiator and Peace Keeper in the universe.

Life stEP

Sin is horrifically destructive. It tears humans within and also apart from each other. There is only one remedy: salvation through the blood of Christ, Who not only makes us to be at peace with His Father but also with ourselves and others. Even persecution for our faith can't rob us of that peace!

Romans 5:12-21

What is the writer saying?

How can I apply this to my life?

Now Paul addresses the availability of God's righteousness for mankind. Adam, the first man, plunged the human race into sin. Eve was the first to disobey, but God implies that she was tricked by the serpent, whereas when Adam was tempted to eat, he knew exactly what he was doing (1 Timothy 2:13-15). Since Adam is also the biological head of the race, his sin is passed on to us. We were there, in him, when he did this, and the implication is that we would have done the same thing. Theologically, we say that Adam was our *seminal head* (seed representative) and that the sin nature is passed on from him, affecting the development of our soul or spirit in the womb just like our physical ancestors affect our genetic development. Christ was preserved from the sin nature by only being biologically connected to His mother Mary via the virgin conception, which by-passed His legal father, Joseph.

Death began with Adam's rebellion. Sin also started with Adam, but it was not revealed as such until the law defined what constituted a violation of God's will. Once the Law was given to Moses, it was as though a spotlight was turned on. The extreme sinfulness of mankind was exposed and magnified. In fact, just having a standard written down now induced the sin nature of man to rebel even more. But just as one man's disobedience started all the problems, one Man's obedience made forgiveness of sin, grace, and eternal life abundantly available to mankind. In verse 16, a "gift" is *something given*, while the "free gift" is actually a *charisma* (grace) gift.

Life stEP It is tempting to resent what Adam did until we humbly consider that we would have done no better. Fortunately, Christ, "the second Adam from above," has come to "reinstate us in His love."

Romans 6:1-12

What is the writer saying?

How can I apply this to my life?

pray Romania – For building materials and skilled laborers to meet the demand for new church construction.

In a long section, Romans 6:1-8:39, Paul discusses our growth in holiness once we have received God's righteousness in salvation. In verses 1-12 of today's passage, Paul answers the absurd suggestion that perhaps we should continue to sin in order for God to show even more grace. While believers will have times of defeat and spiritual decline, the general trend should be upward toward perfection (theologians refer to this as "progressive sanctification"). Perfection cannot be achieved in this life, as the sin nature (the "old man" or the "flesh") is still with the believer. But at the resurrection, the believer will receive his new body with no sin nature. This end of the sanctification process is known as glorification.

Baptism speaks of *identification*. It is a picture of our death, burial, and resurrection with Christ. In baptism we proclaim that when Christ died on the cross, we were legally there (since He was dying for us), and we legally died too. For this reason, the law (and the sin stimulated by the law) has no more power over us. We have the God-empowered capability to say "no" to the world, the flesh, and the devil—we don't have to sin. Sinning is illogical (just as you would not expect a corpse to speak at its own funeral). In fact, sin is an embarrassment to our new status as adult sons in the family of God.

Life stEP

We are in alien territory; this place is not our home, and we are just pilgrims passing through. Satan wants to poison our spiritual life. For our spiritual protection, God has provided a *space suit*. Reading the Bible is like breathing in the right atmosphere to sustain spiritual health. Praying is exhaling. When we fall into sin, it is like pebbles clogging up the pipeline. We begin to choke. At that point, we need to have a 1 John 1:9 experience of crawling up on our Daddy's lap and agreeing with Him that we have done wrong. This restores the broken fellowship.

Romans 6:13-23

What is the writer saying?

How can I apply this to my life?

pray   Ghana – Pray for God to send laborers to the 15,000 villages with no bodies of believers.

Paul continues his argument for personal holiness. "Yield" in verse 13 refers to a self-introduction (*self-promotion*) as opposed to an honorable introduction by someone else. We don't have the power to control sin, but we have the right to give our bodies over to Christ's mastery so He can give us the victory. Similarly, in verse 14, "dominion" means "to be lord over."

"Members" (v. 13) refers to all aspects of our bodies, thoughts, and lives—anything that can be misused for sinful purposes. Rather than being a tool of Satan, Paul wants us to be tools of God. Notice that in Paul's thinking, the law gives power to the sinful impulse whereas God's grace gives us power to say "no" to sin. This is not a sacrifice on our part because, by choosing God's way, we choose life and avoid death. This includes not only eternal life in Heaven but also a happy abundant life now.

The term "world" in Greek is *cosmos*, which refers to *order* (for instance: the orderly orbits of the planets around the sun; the opposite is *chaos*, which means that in the morning, as we do our *cosmetics*, we are turning chaos into cosmos!) In Scripture, cosmos refers to the mindset that Satan has placed in this world to achieve his nefarious ends. He wants to use the philosophies of this world to strangle our spiritual life. That is why in Romans 12:1-2, we are told not to be conformed (*pressed into the mold*) of this cosmos.

Life stEP

Once saved, we belong to Christ and are under *new management*. We do not have to allow sin to be king over us. We can escape it by acknowledging Christ's lordship over our life.

Romans 7:1-13

What is the writer saying?

How can I apply this to my life?

As Paul struggles with those who want to keep the Law of Moses, he asks two questions: "Is it better to be under the law?" (vv. 1-6) and "Is the law evil?" (vv. 7-14). It is clear from verse 1 that he is addressing Jewish believers at this point (those who know the law inside and out). He uses legal logic to dislodge their mistaken thought—that it is to their benefit to remain under the Law. He uses the analogy of how marriage vows work. As long as a husband is alive, the wife is accountable to the marriage vows. In verse 2, "bound" means "tied up." In the same verse, the word *loosed* is made up of three Greek words: *down*, *not*, and *to work*, meaning "to reduce to inactivity." ("Not" and "to work" make our word *argon*, an inert gas that does not work to affect any other substance.) Paul's point: death negates the Law. Since we are dead with Christ, the law has been negated in our lives.

Paul then counteracts the potential accusation that his assessment has made the law itself sinful. His reply is emphatic ("God forbid," or "may it never be"). He points out that there is a difference between a requirement and the power to meet the requirement. The law showed the requirement (and was thereby considered "holy" and "good"), but it didn't have the power to fulfill it (and therefore was ineffectual).

"Concupiscence" (v. 8) is a *passionate desire* for something.

In verse 9, Paul may be referring to his life from birth to age thirteen before the Jewish rite of passage into adulthood (the *Bar Mitzvah* or "son of the commandment"). Once he was a Jewish adult, he was obligated to obey the Law—the spotlight came on; it revealed his sinful heart; it became his death sentence.

Life **stEP** We are liberated from the Law of Moses, yet the lessons taught by the Law live on. Here, we are indirectly warned that marriage is serious business. Only death severs the marital bond in God's eyes!

Romans 7:14-25

What is the writer saying?

How can I apply this to my life?

Like a fish caught on a sharp hook, in pain and desperately fearful of being pulled from the water, Paul expresses the titanic struggle he feels between his old man and new man. The verbs are in the present tense in this section, so the verses refer to his struggle as a saved individual, not just prior to salvation. The law is spiritual in that it represents God's ideal, but Paul is not entirely spiritual; he is also "carnal" or *subject to the weaknesses of the human flesh*. His spiritual part sides with the law, but his carnal part runs in the opposite direction. The word *dwelleth* is actually *indwelling*—the same term used of the Holy Spirit's residence within us.

In verse 21, Paul uses the word "law" to refer not to the Mosaic code but to a *principle*. In fact, Paul makes various uses of the word *law* in Romans: the Law of Moses (3:19); principles of faith (3:27); the law of sin (v. 23); the law of the mind (v. 23); and the law of the Spirit (8:2). Here the principle he notices is that he can't escape sin under his own power. He is *captivated* by sin, literally a prisoner—"one taken at spear point." He calls himself "wretched," a word that means *miserable*. Is there an answer? Yes, the power is in Christ, not the Law of Moses, nor the human flesh.

Life **stEP** In the past, before we met Christ, we were not able not to sin. In the present, with Christ, we are able not to sin. In the future, with Christ and our glorified bodies, we will be not able to sin!

tuesday 49

Romans 8:1-11

What is the writer saying?

How can I apply this to my life?

pray Jamaica – For quality staff and increased enrollment among Jamaica's Bible schools and seminaries.

In chapter 8, Paul describes the process of trusting God for salvation and sanctification. In verses 1-11, he talks about emancipated living. "Therefore" is a transitional term. It means that Paul is drawing conclusions based on the previous discussion. Because of what Christ has done for us and God's grace in making it available, there is no condemnation to those trusting in Him. "Condemnation" means "to pass down a judgment in a court of law." "Who walk not after the flesh" does *not* mean "those who do not sin." Rather, it is referring back to the law discussion and means "those who are not trying to merit salvation by obeying the law." Instead of trusting the power of the flesh, they are resting in the power supplied by the Spirit of God as they respond in faith to God's offer of salvation and sanctification.

Christ became flesh, was holy in the flesh, obeyed the law perfectly in the flesh, and then died in the flesh to deliver us from the flesh. "Carnal" in verse 6 is a synonym for *flesh*. In verse 9, Paul says the alternative to living in the flesh—having the Spirit—is a sign of salvation. In verse 11, "quicken" means "to make alive." It is the Greek word *zoe*, which we use as a female name and also is the same root as the word *zoo*—the place where we go to see living things. We are talking about issues of eternal life and death. The death Christ raises us from is not a death that produces eternal unconsciousness or non-existence, but a death that is devoid of anything positive—eternal ruin and destruction.

Life stEP "You only go around once in life!" "Go for all the gusto!" "Eat, drink, and be merry for tomorrow you die!" These are the feeble encouragements the world has to offer. If you really want to live, then you need to go to the eternal energy source—the Lord Jesus Christ.

Romans 8:12-25

What is the writer saying?

How can I apply this to my life?

pray   Germany – For new and effective ways of reaching the youth for Christ.

In verses 12-17, Paul talks about the exalted lifestyle Christ offers us. In verses 18-25, he adds the concept of expectant living. Fleshly existence, both in the Epicurean style of "if it feels good, do it" and the opposite Stoic style of "control every bodily desire" leads to frustration, defeat, despair, and death. In today's society, many prefer the unhindered, sensual, decadent approach. There are others who self-righteously promote rigid discipline. Both are fleshly. We successfully control the flesh only once empowered by the Spirit.

In verse 15, "adoption" literally means "son placing." It is not referring to babies, but to adult sons. We become "children of God" by the new birth, and only then are we placed into the position of adult sons in the family of God. This is different from how adoption works in our legal system, where parents adopt someone else's children, not their own.

God never adopts any but His own children!

Abba is the Greek word for Daddy (not just "dad," which would be *Ab*). The Holy Spirit not only empowers and energizes, but He also awakens our mind to the new relationships we have with God the Father and God the Son. But verses 17-25 explain that this new relationship does not guarantee absence of conflict. In fact, if the sinful world mistreated the perfect Lord, it certainly will mistreat His associates.

In verse 22, the word "groaneth" is made of two Greek words which mean "with" and "to grieve." Ever since the fall of man brought sin into the universe, all creation has been uttering distress signals!

Life stEP   It is easy to become frustrated with our less-than-perfect world and our less-than-satisfying life. But all this will change permanently when Christ returns and lifts the curse from us and creation. In the meantime, we can enjoy previews of that joy when we walk close to the source—Jesus Christ.

Romans 8:26-39

What is the writer saying?

How can I apply this to my life?

pray Netherlands – For those crossing social and cultural barriers trying to spread the Gospel to the lesser reached people.

In Romans Paul demonstrates that the law is powerless to help us obey God. Since we are also powerless, the result is that instead the law acting as a balloon lifting us to God, the law becomes an anchor sinking us deeper into sin. Once we acknowledge our helpless condition and call out to God for saving grace, the Holy Spirit empowers us, even praying for us when our own prayers fail. "Intercession" in verse 27 means "falls in with while walking for the sake of making a request."

Paul continues with the emphasis that the power of salvation is totally of God. Our responsibility is just to believe that He can and will save us. After that, our daily relationship is one of continuing to believe, and act, that He is the source of our power to overcome sin.

Paul logically traces the steps from our unsaved state all the way into the glorification of eternity. In verse 29, the Greek word *foreknow* is made of two parts: *fore* means "ahead of time" and *know* refers to "intimate knowledge," such as "Adam knew his wife, and she bore Cain." In the Greek language foreknow does not mean "know ahead of time" like it could in English, but rather "to set love upon ahead of time." It is only used of people in the Bible. Acts 2:23 shows God's decision to love us even when He knew men would crucify His Son. In verse 29, "predestined" means "to mark out boundaries ahead of time." The goal of this process is that we be "conformed" (the words *with* and to *morph* [shape]) into the image of God's perfect Son.

Life *stEP* Paul is convinced that we are not only conquerors but "hyper conquerors." In Latin, that is "super" conquerors. Super men and women in, through, and for Jesus Christ!

Romans 9:1-16

What is the writer saying?

How can I apply this to my life?

Chapters 9-11 are a unit comprising the defense of God's righteousness. Paul argues that God has not forgotten His promises to the Jews. In fact, in the Old Testament, the younger son was frequently (and surprisingly) chosen over the elder (as the Gentiles in the church have been over the Jews). But God's final surprise will be to restore the elder son, Israel, in the end of days.

In chapter 9, he reviews Israel's past and her election as the chosen people. In verses 1-5, Paul expresses his sorrow over his fellow Jews. By "accursed" (*anathema*), Paul means he was willing to take eternal punishment in Hell in place of his fellow Jews. In verses 4-5, Paul lists eight advantages Jewish people have over Gentiles. The wording of verse 5 indicates that Christ was not just blessed of God, but that He was and is God in the flesh. In verses 6-13, Paul discusses the difficult issue of election. "Love" and "hate" is another way of saying *chosen* and *rejected*. Since we immediately think this must be unfair, Paul argues in verses 14-16 that God by nature cannot be unfair. Here's a theologically accurate argument for man's free will and responsibility:

1. By definition, whatever God does is just.

2. By definition, "responsible" means that man can be justly rewarded or punished.

3. In Scripture, God is said to punish human sinners.

4. By definition of Who God is, this punishment is just.

5. Conclusion: Those so punished are responsible; therefore their choice must have been freely made (if God says that sin is the sinner's fault, then the sinner must have been free to make the decision).

God has chosen to lead us not just to salvation but also to a holy walk with Him. Our responsibility is to continue to listen for His leading and submit to it.

Romans 9:17-33

What is the writer saying?

How can I apply this to my life?

pray Cuba – Fruitfulness and a greater area of outreach for the Christian radio feeds out of Latin America.

God's election does not force an individual to behave in a certain way. In Exodus, before God hardened his heart, Pharaoh had already hardened his own heart, as 1 Samuel 6:6 explains. Therefore in verses 19-22, Paul argues that man is still fully responsible. In verse 23, he argues that those of us who are elect have been prepared *by God* for salvation, a positive action. On the other hand, in verse 22, those who demonstrate they are not elect by never getting saved are fitted for destruction, but the verses don't say this negative action is by God. The verb is in the middle and passive form. If translated as a middle voice, then "they fitted themselves." If taken as a passive, then "they were fitted." Thus, it does not specify who did soothe fitting for destruction.

In verse 25, Paul refers to the prophet Hosea (*Osee*), who had a child named *lo-ammi*, which is Hebrew for "not my people." In Hosea, it referred to God's rejection of unfaithful Israel. However, the "not my people" period will one day become the *ammi* ("my people") period. Likewise in Isaiah (*Esias*) 62:4, Israel was *lo-hephzibah* in her rebellious state but through God's saving grace would one day become *hephzibah* ("beloved"). The concept of the "remnant" (v. 27) occurs frequently in the Old Testament prophets. In Isaiah 7:3, Isaiah had a son symbolically named *Shear-jashub*—"only a remnant shall return." Left to themselves, Old Testament Israel (and all men as well) would constantly rebel and end up utterly destroyed by God's judgment, as were Sodom and Gomorrah. Election, then, is a positive doctrine (unto salvation) not negative (rejected to damnation).

Theology is fun to discuss, but there comes a point when we have to fall silent and let God be God. Notice Paul's warning: "Nay but, O man, who art thou that repliest against God?" We may not understand or see God's way as fair, but we must honor God and His Word.

sund@y 50

Romans 10:1-13

What is the writer saying?

How can I apply this to my life?

pray Romania – For the lifting of government restrictions, which are hindering effective ministry growth.

In verses 4-13, Paul says Israel missed the concept of righteousness by faith despite having a "zeal for God" (v. 2). Paul knew about this. He himself had been very proud of his heritage (see Galatians and Philippians). His conscience did not bother him as he felt he was blameless in his attempts to obey the 613 commandments in the Mosaic Code. He even thought he was doing God a service by assenting to the stoning of Stephen and traveling to Damascus to imprison and possibly kill more Christians. Zealous actions such as Paul's have been echoed by other Jews in modern times. In 1948, when the Arabs had cut off the Jewish community in Jerusalem, the taxi drivers would weld chains onto their bumpers and drive around the hills leading up to Jerusalem to make the Arabs think tanks were coming. In the confusion, convoys could slip through to smuggle life-preserving food to the trapped Jews. Yet some ultra-orthodox Jews protested and stoned those who did so on the Sabbath because they were violating the holy day! In verse 6, Paul quotes Deuteronomy 30:12-14, where Moses is trying to convince his fellow Israelites that obeying the Mosaic Code is not difficult if they trust God for strength to do so. In the four phrases of verses 9-10, the first and fourth build on the key word "mouth," and the second and third build on the key word "heart." Paul repeats his words backwards for emphasis. The "Lord" of verse 9 certainly refers to Christ's deity. This word, *Jehovah*, occurs 6,000 times in the Old Testament.

Since no work can be added to saving faith, we would argue that *confession* is the natural result (*fruit*) of a true conversion experience and is synonymous with *believing* in these verses. Verse 13 is a quote from Joel 2:32. Peter also preached this passage in Acts 2:21.

Open the heart and God will fill it. Open the mouth and God will use it.

Romans 10:14-21

What is the writer saying?

How can I apply this to my life?

After explaining where salvation comes from, Paul concludes by saying that despite the advantages the Jews had, they needed to hear the Gospel message again before they could call on Christ. His logical progression in verses 13-15, given in reverse order, is: (a) send preachers, (b) preach the Gospel, (c) listen, and (d) call upon the name of the Lord. The "beautiful feet" quote is from Isaiah 52:7 (right before the famous "Suffering Servant" passage in Isaiah 53!). In verses 16-21, Paul argues that Israel has no excuse for not believing, for even their prophets foretold of this future Savior Who they would initially reject. Paul quotes a number of Old Testament passages to demonstrate this, the first being Isaiah 53:1. In context, this verse is the words of believing Jews lamenting that their fellow Jews did not believe their reports about Jesus. While general in nature, we could imagine these words coming from the surprised disciples on the road to Emmaus (Luke 24:13), or the disciples preaching in Acts, or even the two witnesses and 144,000 Jewish evangelists in the tribulation period (Revelation 11 and 14).

In verse 17, the "word of God" refers to messages about Christ (through preaching and witnessing), with these messages coming from the Word of God (the written Scriptures). Verse 18 says the message has gone to the ends of the earth. Some ways this has happened are non-verbal testimony (Psalm 19:1-4—the heavens declaring) and also the many Jews around the world. Ever since 722 B.C., there have been more Jews living outside Israel than within. Paul may be thinking of the Jewish Scriptures being carried to the ends of the earth by the dispersion (*diaspora*). Moses's quote (v. 19) is found in Deuteronomy 32:21. Isaiah's bold statement (vv. 20-21) is in Isaiah 65:1-2.

People cannot call until they hear. Will you have an opportunity to spread the "word of God" today?

Romans 11:1-12

What is the writer saying?

How can I apply this to my life?

Chapter 11 talks about Israel's future. In verses 1-10, Paul explains that Israel's rejection is national, not personal. Some have suggested a *replacement theology* in which the church has replaced Israel in God's program. Paul says "no way!" ("God forbid" = "not logical"; used 10 times in Romans). God has not given up on the hard-hearted, stiff-necked, rebellious Jewish people.

In verse 2, we have another example of how *foreknowledge* is used in the New Testament (clearly God is the mover, not man). "Remnant" (v. 5) is that rich Old Testament concept that, despite the apparent failure of God's program, He always has His small band of the faithful few. This word is *shear* in Hebrew, as in Isaiah's son, Shear-Jashub, which meant in Isaiah 7 that only a remnant would return if King Ahaz continued to trust himself and the Assyrians instead of God for his deliverance from Israel and Syria.

Romans 11:9-10 is a quote from Psalm 69:22-23. The psalm was written by David when he fled from his enemies and also clearly refers to Messiah and His death on the cross (Psalm 69:21). In verses 11-15, Paul argues that while tragic, the Jewish rejection of Jesus has led to the Gospel going to the Gentiles, which is a great result. Seeing Gentiles getting saved and finding satisfaction with God will make the Jews jealous and may motivate them to reconsider the claims of Jesus Christ. Finally, if something great came from their rejection of Christ (Gentile salvation), imagine what will happen to this planet when the bulk of the Jews accept Christ and are born again!

Life **stEP** We sometimes think that Jewish Christians would be better witnesses to fellow Jews, but Paul says Gentiles are effective, too, because eventually the Jewish individual will be envious of their relationship with God.

Romans 11:13-24

What is the writer saying?

How can I apply this to my life?

pray China – For the failure of all government attempts to impose false doctrine on registered churches.

Paul identifies himself as the "apostle of the Gentiles." This is significant, not just for his argument in chapter 11, but also for God's whole plan for human history. Why did God choose Paul to write thirteen books of the New Testament and explain "the mystery of the church"? Didn't Christ pray all night before choosing the twelve disciples? Didn't He spend three and a half years training them? Why would He then choose an outsider and spend another three years training him (as Paul explains in his testimony in Galatians)? Answer: The twelve disciples were trained to offer the Messianic Kingdom. Their message in the Gospels was: "Repent, the kingdom of heaven is at hand."

Paul, on the other hand, was chosen when the Jews rejected the spiritual requirements of the kingdom. He explains and leads a new entity—the church. In verse 15, "life from the dead" implies that although it seems impossible now, eventually the Jews *will* come to Christ. In verse 16, the "firstfruit" and "root" refer to the start of the Chosen People with the patriarchs (Abraham, Isaac, and Jacob). Paul then develops the image of an expert orchard farmer who selects hardy root stock for his fruit trees and then grafts in a different kind of branch to produce sweeter, more prolific, or better fruit. The church, with its Gentiles, is like a "wild" olive tree that has been grafted onto the *fat [rich] root* of the Jews. We benefit for now, but someday God will remove the church (in the Rapture and then in the ensuing apostasy of the remaining professing church) and will graft back into the rich root the branches He had originally designed for His olive tree.

The centuries seem to roll by lazily, but here we are 2,000 years after Christ, and Israel is still a nation. God is poised to bring them to Himself despite centuries of rejecting Jesus of Nazareth.

Romans 11:25-36

What is the writer saying?

How can I apply this to my life?

pray Guatemala – For the growth and maturity of the churches in the nation.

In verses 25-32, Paul explains that Israel's rejection is temporary. The church does not replace God's plan for Israel but is in addition to that plan. Jews now can be part of the church. When the church is removed at the Rapture, God will ignite His program with Israel in the ministry of the two witnesses (Revelation 11) and the 144,000 Jews who are saved (Revelation 7 and 14). Those rejecting the Gospel will be killed by the judgments of that period. Zechariah 12:10 talks of a few remaining Jews accepting Christ even as He descends at the Second Coming. At that glorious point, Paul's saying will come true: "And so all Israel shall be saved" (v. 26). Israel and the church will dovetail nicely in the kingdom, where the church is the bride of Christ, the queen of the kingdom. In eternity, both the land promises for Israel and the heavenly promises for the church will be merged as the heavenly city of Jerusalem descends upon the New Earth (Revelation 21-22).

In verse 25, the "mystery" (something not revealed in the Old Testament) is that God would set aside His chosen people for the time being and would graft in the Gentiles until the "fullness of the Gentiles" is complete (the complete number of Gentiles God intends to save and make part of the church). Verse 29 means that God's promise to Abraham still stands. We are confident that God won't break His promises with the Church, so we should also be confident that He will fulfill His promises to national Israel, He could also break His promise with us. In verse 32, Paul is not saying that everyone is "concluded [shut up] in unbelief" at once, but rather, *in turn*. In other words, when the Gentiles were *shut up*, the Jews were blessed. When the Jews were *shut up*, the Gentiles were blessed. In verse 36, the Father is the source ("of Him"); the Son is the guide ("through Him"); the Spirit of Holiness is the goal ("to Him").

Life stEP It is a great priviledge to share the gospel with both Jews and Gentiles. Ask the Lord to send such an opportunity your way today.

Romans 12:1-8

What is the writer saying?

How can I apply this to my life?

pray Venezuela – For the despair caused by poverty, crime, and violence to cause people to seek Christ.

We come now to the final major section of Romans, chapters 12-16: the application of God's righteousness. Verses 1-2 hold an application to us and in verses 3-8, an application to the church as a whole.

In verse 1, the popular view is that "therefore" is based on the glorious benediction of Romans 8:35-39: "Who shall separate us from the love of Christ?" Others argue that it refers to the equally passionate conclusion in Romans 11:33-36: "Oh, the depth of the riches both of the wisdom and knowledge of God!" Actually, it is best to see verses 1-2 as a call to consider everything Paul has said to this point about God's righteousness and how we can obtain it despite our sinful condition.

"Conformed" (v. 2) comes from the Greek word *schema*, from which we get our word *scheme*. "World" is *cosmos*, a Greek word referring to order, as opposed to *chaos*, the Greek word for disorder. It refers to the philosophies

and mindset of this world order as masterminded by Satan, the god of this age and the prince of the power of the air. A good translation of the first phrase would be: do not let this world system press you into its mold! "Transformed" (v. 2) is the Greek word *metamorphosis*. It is only used three times in Scripture— two times when referring to Christ's transfiguration before Peter, James, and John, and the third time talking about us believers. The best example of metamorphosis in our world today is the transformation of the lowly caterpillar as it goes into a cocoon and emerges as a beautiful butterfly.

"Renewing" (v. 2) means "to make new again." Verses 4-8 are a discussion of spiritual gifts, emphasizing that not everyone has the same gift, and therefore, we need each other. We all can't be eyeballs because each function is needed for the whole to succeed.

Life stEP The reason we need to evaluate our dedication to the Lord daily is because "living sacrifices" have a tendency to crawl off the altar!

Romans 12:9-21

What is the writer saying?

How can I apply this to my life?

pray Korea – Protection and perseverance of nearly 100,000 believers confined in North Korean camps.

In this section, Paul applies God's righteousness to how we should be living in society. He chooses specific words to show how important certain actions are. In verse 9, the word "dissimulation" is the word for *hypocrisy*. It comes from the ancient Greek theatrical practice of having actors wear masks for various speaking parts in a play, thereby hiding their true identity. It means "not speaking from under a mask in order to deceive." The word "abhor" is made from two Greek words, *away from* and *styx*. The River Styx was the border of Hades in Greek mythology and the damned would be taken across it by boat at death. Therefore "abhor" is a strong term of fear and repulsion: "to shudder away from a hated object." "Cleave" (v. 10), on the other hand, refers to a strong attachment. It means "to glue."

"Brotherly love" (v. 10) speaks of family-like love, using the word *phileo*, such as Philadelphia, the "City of Brotherly Love." "Slothful" (v. 11) means "lagging behind." "Fervent," on the other hand, means "to be hot, to boil," an intense action. "Hospitality" (v. 13) is literally "lovers of strangers." Paul is presenting a Christian lifestyle that is others-centered instead of self-centered. Verse 12 develops the idea of being others-centered. It is easy to weep with those who weep; the hard job is to rejoice with those who rejoice. ("Praise the Lord—I just got a raise!") When we weep, can we say, "Praise the Lord anyway"? The theologically correct response is, "Praise the Lord because of it!"

Verse 20 quotes Proverbs 25:21-22. The "coals" are not necessarily a symbol of burning shame but perhaps the nice gesture of giving someone in need coals for their fire pot, which was carried on the head.

Life **stEP** God is not surprised by what happens; therefore, we should never feel "Fine—under the circumstances." We are *on top* of the circumstances!

Romans 13:1-14

What is the writer saying?

How can I apply this to my life?

In this chapter, Paul applies God's righteousness to human government (vv. 1-7), neighbors (vv. 8-10), and personal purity (vv. 11-14). In verse 1, "be subject" comes from the concept of *putting soldiers in proper rank*. "Ordained" comes from same root word. Paul lived and wrote under the Roman Empire, which had a reputation for brutality and an uncaring attitude towards human life. Nevertheless, he commanded Christians to obey the government officials. He argues that those in power are ordained by God, and God has given human government the right to enforce law and order in society by force, if necessary (v. 4, "the sword"). This would require the concept of deadly force and capital punishment in extreme cases. Paul even argues that the tax collector is a "minister" of God (v. 6) when he does his work. "Minister" is the same word used for the activities of the priests in the temple worship system!

Verse 8 is a challenge to be equitable in our dealings with fellow Christians. Some have the gift of hospitality, but we should not take advantage of their generosity. If you are always taking but never giving, then you are not participating fairly in the family of God.

In verses 12-14, Paul gives insight into the question of how to "put on" the whole armor of God, as commanded in Ephesians. This passage indicates that we put on each piece of armor by "putting on" Jesus Christ. If we are living our life with the consciousness that He lives and that we live for Him, then we will have the armor on for the battle against our external foe (the world), our internal foe (the flesh), and our infernal foe (the devil). Making "provision" (to think before acting), both positively and negatively (v. 14), is vital to the success of the Christian soldier.

Life stEP How do we "put on Christ"? This is accomplished in our daily prayer time and Bible study. Learning the mind of Christ is how we put on Christ which is how we put on the armor of God.

Romans 14:1-12

What is the writer saying?

How can I apply this to my life?

In Romans 14:1-15:13, Paul addresses the issue of Christian liberty in the gray areas of life. He starts by saying in verses 1-12 that we should not punish one another. He acknowledges that certain practices are not sinful for the average believer, but if the activity offends a *weaker* brother, then we shouldn't participate and run the risk of driving him away from Christianity and back into the fleshly living of the world. The particular issue here, and in a parallel discussion in 1 Corinthians 8, is whether a Christian can eat meat that was sold by a pagan temple since the animal would have been offered to the gods in an idolatrous sacrifice. Paul's answer is that, on the one hand, there is nothing wrong with the meat because the gods don't really exist, and no magic properties have passed over onto the sacrificed meat. On the other hand, some believers had so recently left the pagan temple with its sensuous worship that the very act of eating the dedicated meat would cause them to stumble, either feeling they had offended God or worse yet, drawing them back to those practices.

Paul concludes that should we be given meat to eat, we shouldn't ask where it came from and just enjoy it. But, if we are told that it came from the pagan temple, then we shouldn't eat it out of respect for the Christians who might stumble because of our poor example. "Judge" in this passage does *not* mean evaluate or discern. We are called to be discerning. It means "to pronounce judgment in a court of law" and refers to some people's tendency to be a judge, jury, and executioner, committing character assassination on the target of their resentment.

Life stEP   As the English poet and preacher John Donne said, "No man is an island." Our behavior affects all who behold us. We should live not for ourselves but for the welfare of others.

Romans 14:13-23

What is the writer saying?

How can I apply this to my life?

pray United Kingdom – Wisdom for those ministering among the 900,000 college and university students.

The Christian liberty discussion continues with Paul saying that we should not be a stumbling block. A "stumbling block" refers to the baited trigger of a trap. It is the Greek word *skandalon*, from which we get the English word *scandal*. The *bait* may be neutral, just as cheese is nutritious for a mouse but deadly if attached to a trap. Therefore, we have to evaluate not just if an activity is morally neutral, but whether it is also *safe* for all to participate in that activity without slipping into a morally negative situation. For instance, using games of chance as a fundraiser may be innocent fun for those who were never trapped by gambling, but for those who have known that addiction, it is a horrible *baited trigger* to place before them.

Some commentators have lifted verse 17 out of its context and tried to make it a proof text for their idea that the kingdom of God is not a physical, earthly kingdom (the millennium) but rather is a spiritual kingdom in existence right now. This ignores the point of the passage (not causing a weak believer to stumble) and tries to apply the verse to a different situation than what Paul was addressing. When Paul says, "The kingdom of God is not eating," he does not mean that we will not eat in the kingdom, but that the primary emphasis in kingdom living is our righteous behavior towards one another and God in all that we do, including eating. In verse 19, the word "edify" means "to build up." We are to be strengthening fellow believers, not weakening them.

Jesus, Others, and You—what a wonderful way to spell JOY. Unfortunately, in our selfish society, many Christians have a priority system of Me (number one), Others (at least the ones I think are worthy), and Jesus (a distant last) spelling "MOJ," which means *nothing* before the judgment seat of Christ.

Romans 15:1-13

What is the writer saying?

How can I apply this to my life?

Paul encourages believers to follow Christ's example in considering the welfare of others before their own. The "ought" of verse 1 is a moral imperative; we are duty-bound and honor-bound to do this as children of the king, for the "edification" or *house-building* of fellow believers. Christ should be our example of self-sacrifice for the benefit of others (v. 3).

The word "learning" in verse 4 refers to *formal learning*. "Patience" comes from a compound Greek word that combines *under* with to *abide*. Proper edification allows us to hold up under stress. The word for "comfort" (v. 4) is the famous word *parakaleo*, from which we get a title for the Holy Spirit, Paraclete. "Para" means "alongside of," as in *parallel*. "Clete" comes from *kaleo* which means "to call." The Holy Spirit and the Scriptures are both *one called alongside of another to help*.

In verses 9-12, Paul reminds us that he is the apostle to the Gentiles and that he is writing to Gentiles. He quotes four Old Testament passages (2 Samuel 22:50 and Psalm 18:49; Deuteronomy 32:43; Psalm 117:1; Isaiah 11:10). All four are quoted word-for-word from the Greek copy of the Old Testament (as opposed to Paul freely translating the Hebrew into Greek), as these Greek readers would be more familiar with the Greek copy of the Old Testament (this also is a practical illustration that "inspiration" extends to the translations of the original text as well). It is important to Paul for these Gentile Romans to know that God envisioned them coming to Christ even as He chose and worked through the Jews in the Old Testament. In fact, God always intended the Jews to be a missionary force to bring the Gentiles to God (Ex. 19:6).

Life **stEP** It is easy to become a Christian. It is hard to become Christ-like! How can you "build up" other Christians today?

Romans 15:14-33

What is the writer saying?

How can I apply this to my life?

Paul had already been faithful to present the Gospel to the Gentiles of the Mediterranean world. He could justly be proud of what God had accomplished through him, not by his own might but as he allowed Christ to work through him. Likewise, as we allow the power of God to turn us into His masterpiece (Ephesians 2:10), we will be happy and rewarded for the results. In verse 19, "signs and wonders" are the marks of the apostle's authenticity, as stated in 2 Corinthians 12:12 (see also 1 Corinthians 1:22; Hebrews 2:3-4). These signs are the equivalent of a valid signature—the autograph of God (the word is so used in 2 Thessalonians 3:17, where it is translated "token").

Following the pattern of Acts 1:8, Paul says that his ministry went from Jerusalem all the way to central Europe ("Illyricum" is the area of modern Albania and Croatia). Early church legends say that eventually Paul took the Gospel all the way to Great Britain (which was included in the Roman Empire of the first century). Verse 21 is a quote from Isaiah 52:15, which is the introduction to the "Suffering Servant" passage in Isaiah 53. "Hindered" in verse 22 is a military term meaning "to break up the road" (so the opposing soldiers can't use it). We cannot begin to imagine the effort it would have taken Paul to cover the thousands of miles he did for the sake of the ministry. "Strive together" in verse 30 is an athletic term for the sport of wrestling, which can be translated "agonize with" (the Greek root is *agonizomai*).

The modern motto in our pleasure-oriented society is "no pain, no pain" (as opposed to "no pain, no gain"). Paul put his all into his work. Do you think, as he faced his final moments, that he said, "I shouldn't have worked so hard to bring the Gospel to the Gentiles"?

Friday 51

Romans 16:1-16

What is the writer saying?

How can I apply this to my life?

pray Taiwan – For revival in the one Han Chinese nation that remains resistant to the Gospel.

In chapter 16, Paul greets twenty-eight people by name and sends greetings from eight of his co-workers. Not all the meanings of the names are necessarily significant, but the definitions which are known are given here for interest sake. Phoebe ("moon") was from Cenchrea, one of the two ports of Corinth in Greece. She is called a "servant," which is *deaconess* in Greek, but this does not necessarily require a church office (unlike the word used for the office of deacon in 1 Timothy 3). The word could simply mean that she had a servant's heart. "succourer" is Old English for *helper*. Priscilla ("ancient") and Aquila ("eagle") were wife and husband and also tentmakers by trade (Acts 18:2-3). Epaenetus means "praise-worthy." He was Paul's first convert in Asia (not Achaia, which is a scribal misprint). Mary comes from Miriam which means "rebellion." Andronicus ("man-conqueror") and Junia were Jews, probably from Paul's tribe of Benjamin. The phrase in verse 7 means they were *well-known by the apostles*. Many of the names were common slave names. Amplias means "enlarged"; Urbane, "pleasant"; and Stachys, "ear of corn." Aristobulus ("best counselor") may have been the grandson of Herod the Great and brother of Herod Agrippa I (Acts 12). Narcissus ("unfeeling") might have been a famous wealthy friend of Emperor Tiberius. Tryphena and Tryphosa (both mean "delicate") were probably sisters and perhaps twins. Persis is a female "Persian." Rufus is "red." Asyncritus is "out of sync." Phlegon is "burning zeal." Hermes is "mercury." Philologus is "talkative." Julia is "downy." Nereus is "liquid." Olympas is "bright."

A modern equivalent of verse 16 would be, "Greet one another with a holy handshake."

Life stEP Paul's ministry was supported by his many friends. What does Proverbs 18:24 say about creating friendships?

Romans 16:17-27

What is the writer saying?

How can I apply this to my life?

In verse 17, "mark them" means both to mark and to watch. In Ezekiel 3:17, Ezekiel is called a watchman in a watchtower (*scopus* in Hebrew, from which the famous Mt. Scopus in Jerusalem gets its name). "Avoid" means "to bend out of the way" in order to keep away from something undesirable. Verse 20 is jarring in the juxtaposition of the "God of peace" with "shall bruise [crush] Satan"! This is a reminder of the first promise of the Gospel in Genesis 3:15, where the seed of the woman would crush the head of the serpent.

Timotheus means "God-honorer." Lucius (see also Acts 13:1) means "nobleman." Jason is "Joshua," which means "Jehovah is salvation." He may have been the Jason in Thessalonica who had to post a bond to guarantee that Paul would leave Thessalonica (Acts 17). Sosipater (Acts 20:4) is "saving a father." "Kinsman" (v. 21) means "fellow Jew," not necessarily a family member.

Tertius is "third." He was Paul's secretary (Paul apparently had poor eyesight—see also Galatians 6:11).

Gaius (v. 23) may be the man baptized by Paul in 1 Corinthians 1:14. Erastus was an important government official. A paving stone attributing the road to him was found in Corinth. Quartus is "fourth."

In verse 25, Paul emphasizes "my gospel." He is differentiating his Gospel (see 1 Corinthians 15:3-5) from the gospel of the kingdom, namely, "Repent! The kingdom of heaven is at hand!" He refers to this new Gospel as a "mystery." (See Romans 11:25-36, and the day's commentary for it, for a complete explanation on the "mystery" of the Gentiles being able to come to Christ on equal footing as the Jews.)

Life stEP — Matthew Simpson's *The Preacher*: "His throne is the pulpit; he stands in Christ's stead; his message is the Word of God; around him are immortal souls; the Savior, unseen, is beside him; the Holy Spirit broods over the congregation; angels gaze upon the scene, and Heaven and Hell await the issue."

The Lord called Hosea to prophesy to the ten Northern Tribes of Israel about thirty years before the Assyrians took that kingdom captive around 722 B.C. His prophecy, lasting about fifty years, paralleled that of Amos and extended into the time of Isaiah. He brought a message of judgment and doom to a generation that had forsaken God and turned to idolatry. At the same time, he preached hope to those who turned to the Lord and prophesied about when the nation would be under the future rule of Messiah.

Hosea talked about the kingdom Ephraim thirty-seven times and Samaria six times. Ephraim was the predominant tribe, and Samaria was the capital. The name Israel is used forty-four times, sometimes referring to the Northern Kingdom and sometimes for the combined twelve tribes, depending on the context.

At the time of his commission, the Lord told Hosea to marry Gomer, even though she would be unfaithful to her marriage covenant. The marriage illustrates unfaithful Israel, the *wife* of the Lord (Isaiah 54:5; Jeremiah 31:32), who rejected His love for idolatry (Hosea 4:17, 11:2, 13:2). Gomer bore Hosea a son, Jezreel. Then she gave birth to two children who were "children of whoredoms (adultery)" (Hosea 1:2). Hosea cared for his adulterous wife and her children until she became brazenly promiscuous, and he cast her out of his house. After years of harlotry, she became a slave. The Lord told Hosea to buy her at the slave market, administer a process of cleansing, take her back, and love her.

The book of Hosea depicts the relationship between a faithful, caring God and His chosen people, as shown by the relationship between Hosea and Gomer. God chose and loved Israel even though He knew she would be unfaithful. The book presents Israel's past before the people were taken captive; the present, while Israel as a nation is estranged from God; and the glorious future of Israel, with her God.

Hosea 3:4-4:11

What is the writer saying?

How can I apply this to my life?

pray Aruba – Pray that the gospel radio broadcasts going out in the Papiamento language will yield fruit.

Hosea 1:1-3:3, a prologue to the rest of the book, was summarized in yesterday's introduction. Verse 3 connects the prologue to the prophecy of verse 4, which was fulfilled in the captivities of Israel in 722 B.C. and Judah in 586 B.C. The Lord removed the people of Israel from their own evil governments and their corrupted form of worship. Verse 5 looks forward to a time still in the future, when the "greater David" will reign as the Messiah (Ezekiel 37:21-28).

Chapter 4 begins an indictment against Israel that extends through chapter 8. The prophet presents the reasons why the Lord must cast the people of Israel from the Promised Land. The sins listed in verse 2 prevailed because there was "no truth, nor mercy, nor knowledge of God in the land" (v. 1). Hosea places the first responsibility for the woes of verse 3 upon the priests (vv. 4-8). They rejected their responsibility of bringing the knowledge of God's laws to the attention of the people. Therefore, sin was destroying the people. The priests were sinning against the Lord by using their office to increase their own material welfare rather than the spiritual welfare of the Lord's people. Therefore, the priests and the people had "set their heart on their iniquity."

In verses 9-14, Hosea makes it clear that the people must bear the responsibility for their own conduct (Jeremiah 5:30-31). They knew that their harlotry, drunkenness, and idolatry were against God's laws.

Life stEP

Our Lord graciously provides leaders for our spiritual welfare (Ephesians 4:11-13). Their privileged position brings greater accountability, "for unto whomsoever much is given, of him shall be much required" (Luke 12:48). However, "every one of us shall give account of himself to God" (Romans 14:12). There will be no "blaming the preacher" on that day.

Hosea 4:16-5:10

What is the writer saying?

How can I apply this to my life?

pray Ukraine – For believers willing to translate biblical resource material into the Ukrainian language.

The Lord is the Good Shepherd Who wanted to lead His flock, Israel, into green pastures, but the people of Israel were stuck in the mire of idolatry. They were like an untrained, half-grown cow that stiffens her front legs and will not be led out of the mud into the good grass. Resisting the tug to safety, she'll slip backwards, deeper into the mire. Her obstinacy seals her doom.

The prophet has indicted the priesthood (4:6-8), the people (4:9-17) and the rulers (4:18). They are all guilty of rejecting knowledge by forgetting the law (4:6). They asked counsel of their idols, departing from their God (4:12). They will not change their ways in order to turn to the Lord (5:4).

When their idols failed to meet even their basic needs (4:10), they drove flocks of animals to sacrifice to the Lord. But they sacrificed them on Mizpah (East of Jordan) and Tabor (West of Jordan), and on other high places where they worshipped idols. The Lord had decreed that sacrifices would be acceptable only at the place of His choosing (Deuteronomy 12:10-14). Like Cain, they wanted to worship on their terms, not the Lord's. Changing God's rules (5:10) is like removing the ancient landmarks (Deuteronomy 27:17; Proverbs 22:28).

The blowing of the trumpet (5:8) is a call for assembly for judgment (5:8; 8:1; Joel 2:1). That is the only remaining remedy for continuous, willful sin (Numbers 15:30-31).

We may not habitually sacrifice to idols, but 1 Samuel 15:23 says, "For rebellion is as the sin of witchcraft, and stubbornness is as iniquity and idolatry." The remedy is found in Romans 6:13: "Yield yourselves unto God, as those that are alive from the dead, and your members as instruments of righteousness unto God" (Romans 6:13).

Hosea 5:14-6:6

What is the writer saying?

How can I apply this to my life?

pray Spain – For missionaries to be humble, loving, and culturally sensitive as they seek to minister.

Hosea prophesies concerning Ephraim's (Israel's) near future (5:5-14). The nation's people will "fall in their iniquity" (v. 5), "be desolate in the day of rebuke" (v. 9), be "oppressed and broken in judgment" (v. 11), and be torn, like by a lion (v. 14).

The prophet transports us into a time still future (5:15-6:3). As a nation, the people will yet "acknowledge their offense" (5:15, see also Zechariah 12:10). They will call upon the Lord with a true heart and be received by Him (Zechariah 13:9). This same idea is seen in the New Testament in Matthew 23:39.

The words of Hosea 6:1-3 are not the words of Israel living in Hosea's day, but of those brought before us in 5:15. (Remember, there were no chapter divisions in the original text.) If 2 Peter 3:8-9 were applied literally to the "two days" of Hosea 6:2, then we are now living in the "third day," since the Lord said, "I will go and return to my place." We deduce that He is speaking of the departure of His presence from the temple (Ezekiel 9:3, Hosea 11:23). He *turned His face* from His people and permitted them to be taken captive. The "glory of the God of Israel" (Ezekiel 43:2) will return to His people, and they "shall live in His sight" (6:2).

The prophet returns us to the thoughts of the Lord toward the Israel of Hosea's day (6:4-7:16). He explains the reasons why He must administer corrective chastisement upon His people.

Six verses of Hosea are cited a total of nine times in the New Testament: 1:10, 2:23, 6:6, 10:8, 11:1 and 13:14. Most Bibles have a cross-reference in the margin showing the New Testament passage. You will better understand and appreciate how this book relates to the first and second comings of Christ if you shine the light of the New Testament context on this Old Testament book (Luke 24:27).

Hosea 10:9-15

What is the writer saying?

How can I apply this to my life?

Chapters 8-9 pronounce that judgment is coming swiftly because of Israel's awful sins, which are exposed in chapters 4-7. "For they have sown to the wind, and they shall reap the whirlwind" (8:7). "The days of visitation are come; the days of recompense are come" (9:7).

In 10:9, Hosea compares Israel's present sins to the most repugnant and reprehensible sins recorded in Scriptures. This happened in Gibeah of the tribe of Benjamin, as recorded in Judges 19-20. It resulted in civil war and the near annihilation of Benjamin.

Verse 11 contrasts the productive, pleasurable tasks God planned for Israel with the arduous toil the people will experience in captivity. Treading grain without yoke or muzzle was light work for a trained heifer. In captivity, she would be yoked and muzzled under the prod and lash of a cruel master, pulling a plow through resistant soil.

Although their doom has been pronounced, the prophet still has a heart for his people. In verse 12 he pleads with them to sow righteousness and thereby reap God's mercy. "Break up your fallow ground" means to give evidence of a softened heart that is prepared to receive the seed of righteousness that God wants to rain down. The hour is late; the time is now or never. The chapter concludes with the prophet warning of the consequences of the people continuing in wickedness and relying on their own resources instead of God's mercy.

Life stEP Sin causes the sinner to run from God, trying to hide from His wrath against sin (Genesis 3:10). In mercy, God sends His servants to proclaim God's love for the sinner, manifested by His provision for reconciliation. The sinner may heed or reject the call to repentance unto salvation. But he will face his Creator, either in confession or judgment.

Hosea 11:1-9

What is the writer saying?

How can I apply this to my life?

pray   Columbia – For an end to violence and widespread corruption within the government.

"And Abram went up out of Egypt…unto the place of the altar" (Genesis13:1, 4). "Say unto Pharaoh, Thus saith the LORD, Israel is my son…Let my son go, that he may serve me" (Exodus 4:22-23). "Out of Egypt have I called my Son" (Matthew 2:15). When God calls His sons to worship Him and serve Him, He calls them out of Egypt. Spiritually, Egypt represents Satan's world system, which first allures, then captivates.

"I loved him" (v. 1). "I drew them… with bands of love" (v. 4). Instead of worshipping and serving the loving Father who led them and fed them, the people worshipped and served false gods. Therefore, "The sword shall abide on his cities" (v. 6).

"How shall I give thee up, Ephraim?… Mine heart is turned within me" (v. 8). When Isaiah (Hosea's contemporary) pronounced judgment on Ephraim, he called God's act of judging His own people God's a "strange work" (Isaiah 28:21). As a Father, God's desire was to shower love and goodness. The people's actions brought about the necessity for chastening instead.

Admah and Zeboim were cities destroyed, along with Sodom and Gomorrah, for the same sins that were being committed by Ephraim. In verse 9, God promises not to utterly destroy Ephraim. Ephraim is a prodigal son of God, not a sinning son of Satan.

Before we were saved, we were *dwelling in Egypt*. We "walked according to the course of this world, according to the prince of the power of the air, the spirit that now worketh in the children of disobedience" (Ephesians 2:2). God called us out of Egypt to "walk in newness of life" (Romans 6:4) as God's dear children.

Hosea 13:4-14

What is the writer saying?

How can I apply this to my life?

pray South Africa – Boldness for pastors in a society that no longer holds to moral absolutes, and where abortion, pornography, prostitution, and gambling are pushed.

The prophet's message continues to be, "Turn thou to thy God" (12:6). But Ephraim provokes the Lord "to anger most bitterly" (12:14) as the people "sin more and more" (13:2).

In verses 4-6 of today's passage, the Lord reminds His people that He is the only God Who could save them out of Egypt and sustain them in the wilderness. They have forgotten Him and given their allegiance to the gods of the heathen.

Verse 7-8 are further described by Daniel 7:3-7, where Daniel saw a vision of four predatory animals, representing the four successive world powers that would oppress Israel until it returned to its God. First was Babylon (a lion). Next came Medio-Persia (a bear), and then Greece (a leopard). The fourth beast is an end-time oppressor of the future. Although they all rule over Satan's world system, ultimately it is God who "removeth kings, and setteth up kings" (Daniel 2:21). This is "to the intent that the living may know that the most High ruleth in the kingdom of men, and giveth it to whomsoever he will, and setteth up over it the basest of men" (Daniel 4:17). Satan's devices become God's means of accomplishing His purposes.

Israel demanded a king (1 Samuel 8:19-20). But those kings led the people of Israel astray. God took away their kings and they became captive to heathen kings who have since subjected them to troubles. God has now paid the ransom price by sending His dear Son Who, as the Messiah, will redeem them from destruction.

The Apostle Paul cites Hosea 13:14 to proclaim our glorious victory over death in the resurrection, provided through our Lord Jesus Christ, in 1 Corinthians 15:54-55: "Death is swallowed up in victory. O death, where is thy sting? O grave, where is thy victory?"

Hosea 14:1-9

What is the writer saying?

How can I apply this to my life?

pray Praise God that He supplies all our needs according to His riches in glory by Christ Jesus (Philippians 4:19).

To the end, Hosea's main message is, "Return unto the LORD thy God" (v. 1). So did Israel heed that message? Yes and no—from Hosea's day until now, there has always been a remnant of Israelites faithful to God's program on earth. Daniel and his friends were among that remnant during the captivities. A faithful remnant returned to rebuild the temple and the walls of Jerusalem in the days of Ezra and Nehemiah. Zacharias and Elisabeth (Luke 1:5), along with Simeon and Anna (Luke 2:25, 36), were some of the faithful when Jesus was born. The 120 praying and waiting in the upper room (Acts 1:13-15) were the nucleus of faithful Israelites upon whom the church was founded. In our day, thousands of Jews are receiving Jesus Christ as Savior and are being used to bring about His purposes. But the nation as a whole continues to resist the Lord's way and to travel its own course.

The time will surely come, however, when as a nation, Israel will "render the calves of our lips" (v. 2) unto the Lord. The phrase is figurative language for offering praise and thanksgiving (Psalm 69:30-31; Hebrews 13:15). In continued use of metaphors, verses 4-8 tell of the glorious relationship between the Lord and Israel when the nation says the words of verses 2-3.

Life stEP

Hosea closes his book by offering advice to every one of every age who reads, and desires to heed, the words he received from the Lord (v. 9). The prophet speaks of the wisdom and understanding that comes only by following God's Word. That is the only doorway to prudent living in this sinful world system. The choice is between knowing and following the Lord's ways, which are right, or falling with the transgressors of God's rules of conduct.

The following chart is provided to enable everyone using Word of Life Quiet Times to stay on the same passages. This list also aligns with the daily radio broadcasts.

Week 1	Aug 29 – Sep 4	Psalms 104:1-105:45
Week 2	Sep 5 – Sep 11	Psalms 106:1-108:13
Week 3	Sep 12 – Sep 18	Psalms 109:1-113:9
Week 4	Sep 19 – Sep 25	2 Corinthians 1:1-4:18
Week 5	Sep 26 – Oct 2	2 Corinthians 5:1-8:24
Week 6	Oct 3 – Oct 9	2 Corinthians 9:1-13:14
Week 7	Oct 10 – Oct 16	1 Samuel 1:1-9:27
Week 8	Oct 17 – Oct 23	1 Samuel 10:1-17:16
Week 9	Oct 24 – Oct 30	1 Samuel 17:17-20:42
Week 10	Oct 31 – Nov 6	2 Samuel 5:1-23:7
Week 11	Nov 7 – Nov 13	James 1:1-3:10
Week 12	Nov 14 – Nov 20	James 3:11-5:20
Week 13	Nov 21 – Nov 27	Proverbs 21:1-23:25
Week 14	Nov 28 – Dec 4	Proverbs 23:26-25:28
Week 15	Dec 5 – Dec 11	1 Peter 1:1-3:7
Week 16	Dec 12 – Dec 18	1 Peter 3:8-5:14
Week 17	Dec 19 – Dec 25	Luke 1:1-2:14
Week 18	Dec 26 – Jan 1	Luke 2:15-4:15
Week 19	Jan 2 – Jan 8	Luke 4:16-6:26
Week 20	Jan 9 – Jan 15	Luke 6:27-8:15
Week 21	Jan 16 – Jan 22	Luke 8:16-9:50
Week 22	Jan 23 – Jan 29	Luke 9:51-11:28
Week 23	Jan 30 – Feb 5	Luke 11:29-13:9
Week 24	Feb 6 – Feb 12	Luke 13:10-15:32
Week 25	Feb 13 – Feb 19	Luke 16:1-18:43
Week 26	Feb 20 – Feb 26	Luke 19:1-21:4

Week 27	Feb 27 – Mar 5	Luke 21:5-23:12
Week 28	Mar 6 – Mar 12	Luke 23:13-24:53
Week 29	Mar 13 – Mar 19	Ezekiel 1:1-11:25
Week 30	Mar 20 – Mar 26	Ezekiel 12:17-20:16
Week 31	Mar 27 – Apr 2	Ezekiel 20:17-33:20
Week 32	Apr 3 – Apr 9	Ezekiel 33:21-37:14
Week 33	Apr 10 – Apr 16	Ezekiel 37:15-47:12
Week 34	Apr 17 – Apr 23	Philippians 1:1-2:23
Week 35	Apr 24 – Apr 30	Philippians 2:24-4:23
Week 36	May 1 – May 7	Isaiah 1:1-9:7
Week 37	May 8 – May 14	Isaiah 10:16-26:21
Week 38	May 15 – May 21	Isaiah 28:5-35:10
Week 39	May 22 – May 28	Isaiah 40:1-44:24
Week 40	May 29 – June 4	Isaiah 45:5-49:26
Week 41	Jun 5 – Jun 11	Isaiah 50:1-57:21
Week 42	Jun 12 – Jun 18	Isaiah 58:1-66:24
Week 43	Jun 19 – Jun 25	Psalms 114:1-119:8
Week 44	Jun 26 – Jul 2	Psalms 119:9-119:64
Week 45	Jul 3 – Jul 9	Psalms 119:65-119:120
Week 46	Jul 10 – Jul 16	Psalms 119:121-119:176
Week 47	Jul 17 – Jul 23	Romans 1:1-3:20
Week 48	Jul 24 – Jul 30	Romans 3:21-6:23
Week 49	Jul 31- Aug 6	Romans 7:1-9:33
Week 50	Aug 7 – Aug 13	Romans 10:1-12:21
Week 51	Aug 14 – Aug 20	Romans 13:1-16:27
Week 52	Aug 21 – Aug 27	Hosea 3:4-14:19